Shakespeare's Sonnets

Shakespeare's Sonnets

With a New Commentary by

David West

Duckworth Overlook

London • New York • Woodstock

First published in 2007 by
Duckworth Overlook

LONDON
90-93 Cowcross Street, London EC1M 6BF
Tel: 020 7490 7300
Fax: 020 7490 0080
inquiries@duckworth-publishers.co.uk
www.ducknet.co.uk

WOODSTOCK
The Overlook Press
One Overlook Drive
Woodstock, NY 12498
www.overlookpress.com
[for individual orders and bulk sales in the United States,
please contact our Woodstock office]

NEW YORK
The Overlook Press
141 Wooster Street
New York, NY 10012

A catalogue record for this book is available
from the British Library

ISBN-10: 0-7156-3661-8 (UK)
ISBN-13: 978-0-7156-3661-9 (UK)
ISBN-10: 1-58567-921-6 (US)
ISBN-13: 978-1-58567-921-8 (US)

Typeset by Ray Davies
Printed and bound in the USA

Contents

to Philip Howard

iucundo amico

Introduction

The poems are more properly regarded as a collection than as a sequence. They do not hang together on the thread of a single narrative or by virtue of a single addressee.

(Edmonson & Wells 2004, 28)

Shakespeare was born in 1564, and from *The Taming of the Shrew* in 1590–1 to *The Two Noble Kinsmen* in 1614, the year of his death, he wrote nearly 40 plays. In 1593–4 the London theatres were frequently closed because of plague, and it is in those years that he wrote his two long narrative poems, *Venus and Adonis* and *Lucrece*. Perhaps he took to print publication in order to attract a wealthy patron. The Sonnets were being written about this same time, and the first surviving mention of them is in Francis Mere's *Palladis Tamia* (1598), referring to 'Shakespeare's sugared sonnets among his private friends', and versions of Sonnets 138 and 144 were printed in 1598 or 1599 among the 20 poems in W. Jaggard's *The Passionate Pilgrim*, but the first complete publication was the Quarto edition of 1609.

I knew from the anthologies that some of Shakespeare's Sonnets are magnificent love poems, and occasionally tried to read them through, but never got very far. This may be because 154 love poems in sonnet form are too rich a diet, but another deterrent is the subject matter of the first seventeen, all of them pleading with a young man to marry and have children in order to preserve his beauty for posterity.

Shakespeare had a reason for this arrangement. Sonnets 18–126 chart the course of the speaker's love for a young man from ecstasy through suspicion and infidelity to its bitter end. In 127–52 a black lady is now his mistress, but it soon becomes clear that this is not love but lust, and it ends in loathing. That is the arc of the plot, and the Sonnets of Shakespeare are a drama with three main characters, only one of whom speaks. The first 17 poems, the procreation sonnets, are the prologue to that drama.

There are many commentaries. What is unusual about this one is that it treats the poems as a sequence, not a collection. They form a plot, and therefore cannot be understood unless each one is read in the light of its neighbours. The general point is argued at the end of this Introduction, and details are mentioned in the notes to the individual poems. (Sonnets 153–4 are not part of the plot.)

This Edition

The purpose of this book is not to solve 'the Problem of the Sonnets', but to explain *words* where necessary, to clarify *arguments*, and to suggest how *the poetry* works.

Most other commentaries go line by line from difficulty to difficulty, but these notes attempt to understand each poem by interpreting the words in their context. The thought is often complex, but it makes a mare's nest of the poems when commentators simply list irrelevant definitions from the *Oxford English Dictionary* (*OED*). A vivid example is given in the note on 'cast' in 49.3. These poems are intensely, sometimes fiercely, argued, and this commentary pays particular attention to the argument, as will be mentioned at the end of the note on the sonnet form below. Poetry is a personal matter, and every person who reads a poem is bringing a different past to it, so the attempt in this book to suggest how the poetry works is only an attempt to suggest some of the ways it works for me.

The Quarto edition of 1609, the only version that appeared in Shakespeare's lifetime, is a shabby piece of work. He was busy in Stratford in 1609, and that 'would help to account for the mediocre printing of the text and the apparent absence of authorial correction' (Duncan-Jones 1997, 12). The printing is full of mistakes and the punctuation is lazy. In order to present a text which will be comprehensible to readers who are not familiar with Elizabethan English, this edition is punctuated according to the sense, and the spelling is modernised. Another interference is that final -ed is printed with a grave accent if the verse demands it and it is not sounded in modern English; so 'Cheerèd and checked' in 15.6. It also adds an acute on syllables which would not be stressed in modern English, like 'accéptáble' in 4.12, and 'áccessáry' in 35.13.

The Sonnet Form

The Shakespearean sonnet consists of 14 lines. Each line has 10 syllables and the metre is iambic, te-tum, five times, occasionally varied by the inversion of the stress at the beginning of the line. Sonnet 65 begins with the usual iambic 'Since bráss, nor stone, nor earth, nor boundless sea', but 66 starts on the beat, 'Tíred with all these, for restful death I cry'. The other occasional variation is the 'feminine ending', the addition of an extra syllable at the end of the line, as in 'A woman's face with Nature's own hand painted' (20.1).

The sonnet began in Italy in the thirteenth century and came to its

Italian perfection, mostly in love poems, in the works of Petrarch (1304–74). It consisted of 14 lines rhyming ABBAABBA followed by CDECDE or CDCDCD or any such combination except a rhyming couplet. This is the form in which Sir Thomas Wyatt and the Earl of Surrey brought the sonnet to England at the beginning of the 16th century. English is more difficult to rhyme than Italian, and Surrey established an easier pattern – ABAB CDCD EFEF GG – and this is the rhyme scheme adopted by Shakespeare.

The sense often falls into these divisions, three quatrains and a final couplet, but sometimes the structure of the argument is different, and the logic is such an important and neglected part of the poetry that this edition divides each poem accordingly, and adds a brutally brief summary similarly divided. The hope is that this will bring out the pace and tone and drama of the argument. This way of printing the Sonnets has no authority, and different readers will see the logic differently. In that case the device will have fulfilled its purpose – to draw attention to the argument.

The first sonnet cycle was Sir Philip Sidney's *Astrophil and Stella* (printed in 1592). It came with a spate of others, drawing to a close in Spenser's *Amoretti* in 1595. The vogue was dying even as Shakespeare was bringing it to new life.

The Sound

Almost all these poems are presented as words spoken to one or other of two lovers, and Shakespeare was the master of the music of speech. To help realise this music, this edition makes free use of apostrophes, distinguishing for example 'e'en' in 15.6 from 'even' in 35.5, and 'Heav'n' from 'Heaven' in 29.3 and 12. It even prints 'melanch'ly' to show that it sounds as three syllables in 45.8. Such apostrophes do not suggest that a vowel is lost in pronunciation but rather that two vowels are slurred into one. The need for apostrophes is acute in 59.11–12.

Vital to the sound is the syncopation of verse beat with word accent. This poetry should not be read or heard as doggerel. 'Let mé not tó the márriage óf true mínds' is unspeakable. Antony Hecht argues the case in his introduction to Evans's commentary: 'Deviations of stress supply the rhythmical variety that is essential in a long poem … They make possible a flexibility of syntax and a directness of colloquial speech that a strictly regular metre would distort. They serve as a sort of counterpoint or syncopation, if the "ideal" pattern of the regular iambic line is kept in mind' (Evans 1996, 13). The importance of this syncopation may be gauged from a few examples. The word accent is marked where it does not coincide with the expected iambic beat, as in

When lofty trees I see bárren of leaves	12.5
Nativity, ónce in the main of light	60.5
Gentle thou art, and therefore to be won,	
Beauteous thou art, thérefore to be assailed.	41.5–6

This last example of syncopation demonstrates also a variation which conveys the vital accent of the spoken voice. This occurs when the same syllable is used once with the metrical beat and once without, as in

Suff'ring my friend for mý sake to approve her	42.8
Doth teach that ease and thát repose to say	50.3
Yoursélf to pardon of sèlf-doing crime	58.12
Love is too young to know what conscience is,	
Yet who knows not cónscience is born of love?	151.1–2

A similar variation occurs also with

Was it his sp'rit, by spirits taught to write	86.5
Weeds among weeds, or flow'rs with flowers gathered	124.4

Monosyllabic lines are used to great effect in these poems, particularly at dramatic moments, often in lines 1, 8, 9, 13 and 14. This distribution shows that Shakespeare felt the power of short words, mainly Anglo-Saxon. As Gascoyne observed, 'The more you use the monosyllable, the less you smell of the inkhorn.'

Rhetoric

Roman education concentrated on rhetoric, the art of public speaking, and Latin poets were practitioners, none more so than Ovid. Ovid would have been staple fare in the grammar school at Stratford, which Shakespeare attended, and these sonnets are saturated in Ovidian rhetoric. Invention and argument are technical terms of rhetoric and they occur together four times in Shakespeare's Sonnets (38.1–4, 76.6–9, 103.3–7, 105.9–11). The first 17 poems might serve as a display of invention, the finding of 17 different arguments urging a young man to marry and have children.

Rhetorical teaching required technical terms, and three of these are

4

essential equipment for readers of the Sonnets – chiasmus, polyptoton and similation, vile words, but there are worse. See Booth (1977), cited at the end of the note on Sonnet 43.

Chiasmus

This is the ABBA arrangement:

Featured like him, like him with friends *possessed*	29.6
With what I *most enjoy contented least*	29.8
My *thoughts* and my *discóurse* as madmen's are,	
At random from the truth vainly expressed,	
For I have *sworn* thee fair, and *thought* thee bright	147.11–13

There are virtuosic displays as in 96.1–3, 'fault', 'grace', 'grace' and 'faults' overlapping with 'grace', 'faults', 'faults' and 'graces' in 3–4:

Some say thy fault is youth, some wantonness,
Some say thy grace is youth and gentle sport.
Both grace and faults are loved of more and less.
Thou mak'st faults graces that to thee resort.

There are four examples in the catalogue 129.2, 9, 11 and 13, interlaced with antitheses, ABAB. In 43.4, 6, 10–11 and 13–14 there are four examples of chiasmus or feints at it.

Polyptoton

In Latin and Greek, nouns and adjectives came in different cases: nominative, accusative, genitive and dative. The nominative was visualised as vertical, other cases as oblique, a falling, in Latin *casus*, in Greek *ptosis*, giving the adjective *ptotikos*, connected with cases. Polyptoton is therefore the use of different forms of the same word in close contexts, and Shakespeare frequently uses it to great effect:

And in fresh numbers number all your graces	17.6
Then happy I that love and am beloved	25.13
Had, having, and in quest to have, extreme	129.10
For as you were when first your eye I eyed	104.2

This last example has been derided. Friends went to Ovid one day and begged him to remove three disastrous lines from his vast *oeuvre*. 'Certainly,' he said, 'but there are three that I will not remove.' The selections were of course identical. My guess is that in Ovid's position Shakespeare would have refused to alter 104.2. Ovid was accused of being excessively in love with his own genius, but those who love him change 'excessively' to 'justifiably'. Shakespeare and Ovid each had a prodigious love of language.

Similation

This is very common in Shakespeare, but I have never seen it named or discussed. When he wishes to put two things together he often highlights the resemblance or the difference by words which sound similar. The first four of these examples will be resemblances, the others differences:

And being *frank*, she lends to those are *free*	4.4
My *life* hath in this *line* some interest	74.3
That heavy Saturn *laught* and *leapt* with him	98.4
Take all my comfort of thy *worth* and *truth*.	
For whether *beauty*, *birth*, or *wealth*, or *wit*	37.4–5
Be scorned, like old men of less *truth* than *tongue*	17.10
Thy *adverse* party is thy *advocate*	35.10
Making their *tomb* the *womb* in which they grew	86.4
O in what *sweets* dost thou thy *sins* enclose	95.4
Not by our *feeling* but by others' *seeing*	121.4
The wiry *concord* that mine ear *confounds*	128.4
On whom *frown'st* thou that I do *fawn* upon	149.6

The Plot

The procreation sonnets

The first 17 sonnets use 17 different arguments to persuade the young man to marry and beget children in order to preserve his beauty for posterity. Sonnet 18 is a passionate declaration of love, 'Shall I compare thee to a summer's day?' This is a shock, but read in sequence it is seen to be skilfully stage-managed by a drip-feed of information. In urging the young man, (B), to preserve his beauty, the Speaker, S, finds himself praising him, and the praise drifts gradually towards love. The first hint comes at the beginning of Sonnet 8, where B is sweet:

> Music to hear, why hear'st thou music sadly?
> Sweets with sweet war not.

In Sonnet 10 S protests:

> Shall hate be fairer lodged than gentle love? ...
> Make thee another self for love of me

Sonnet 13 begins by addressing B as 'love' and ends:

> Dear my love, you know
> You had a father. Let your son say so.

And at the end of Sonnet 15 S is at war with Time 'for love of you'. The stage is set for the *coup de théâtre* of Sonnet 18.

The immediate sequel is also carefully managed. When a man falls in love, what more natural than that he should wish to offer gifts to the beloved, but what can an actor/poet give an aristocrat? Only immortality, and it is promptly offered in 18 and 19, 'My love shall in my verse ever live young.' In 20 S takes stock. He loves a man, 'the master-mistress of my passion', and finds him truer than any woman. But the poem ends with the first premonition:

> Since [Nature] pricked thee out for women's pleasure,
> Mine be thy love, and thy love's use their treasure.

At the beginning of this love drama, Shakespeare now places a programme poem. Sonnet 21 satirises the trite figures and feeble sentiments of contemporary love poets, and distances himself:

> O let me, true in love, but truly write ...
> I will not praise, that purpose not to sell.

Similarly, soon after the first poem addressed to the Black Lady, in 130, again he mocks pretentious love poetry and claims to tell the truth.

Sonnets 1–17 are a carefully crafted introduction to the plot of the Sonnets.

Pairs

An indication that the Sonnets are to be read together is the fact that so many of them are paired. Sonnets 5 and 6 urge procreation as a device for preserving beauty by distillation. Sonnet 15 suggests one tactic for the 'war with Time', and 16 immediately recommends another:

> But wherefore do not you a mightier way
> Make war upon this bloody tyrant Time ...?

Painting follows acting in 23–4; the stars that guide S's moving are sighted in 25 and 26; in 27 a journey, in 28 the journey back; in 29 and 30 (according to Evans 1996, 'the first of the great sonnets ... followed immediately by the second)' misery is lightened by the thought of the beloved, 'I think on thee' being the pivot in each; the survival of S's past lovers in 31 is followed immediately by the survival of S himself in 32; the glorious morning of love in 33 is followed by the beautiful day in 34, each followed by an ugly rack of base clouds, yet in each last couplet S forgives. Sonnets 44 and 45 play with the four-element theory – earth, water, air and fire. In 50 he is riding away from B, and in 51 he is riding back. Sonnets 64 and 65 both start with the perishing of stone and brass and sea and land. To look for just one pair in every ten sonnets, see 67–8, 71–2, 83–4, 97–8, 100–1, 113–14, 123–4, 135–6, 139–40, and 151–2.

Drip-feed again

But what was there to forgive in Sonnets 33 and 34? In 33 the sun did 'permit the basest clouds to ride ... on his celestial face' and 'was but one hour mine' – a veiled suggestion that the young man had fallen among evil companions. In 34 'the strong offence' leads to S's wound and grief and loss. In 35 the truth is plain: 'thy trespass', 'thy amiss', 'thy sensual fault' is clearly infidelity. In the last two lines of 33 and 34, S forgave, but now at the end of 35 he admits 'civil war is in my love and hate', and in 36 he proposes a form of separation:

> Let me confess that we two must be twain,
> Although our undivided loves are one.

This is a tactic for continuance which permits him to glory in the abundance of B's qualities in 37, 'And by a part of all thy glory live.' In 38 he celebrates B's excellence and his own humility, 'The pain be mine, but thine shall be the praise.' In 39 he is still searching desperately for an argument to establish that separation is a good thing, but the outburst of 40 contains the vital information, the next step in the plot, 'Take all my loves, my love, yea, take them all.' B has taken S's mistress. In 41 S tries to excuse him on the grounds of his youth and beauty:

> And when a woman woos what woman's son
> Will sourly leave her till he have prevailed?

In 42 he reveals that the loss of his lover grieves him more than the loss of his mistress, but excuses them both by telling them that they love each other because they love him. He knows this is self-deception, 'Sweet flattery' (42.14).

Free-standing sonnets?

Four great sonnets, 66, 87, 94 and 116, have often been thought, wrongly, to be disconnected from their neighbours:

Sonnet 66: 'Tired with all these, for restful death I cry'

Sonnets 63–5 lead up to 66. In 63 and 64 S is contemplating the end of his lover's life, ruminating in 64 'That Time will come and take my love away.' In 65 he rages against Time, 'Or who his spoil of beauty can forbid?' Now in 66 he lists his own reasons for being tired of life, such things as

> Art made tongue-tied by Authority,
> And Folly, doctor-like, controlling Skill
> ...
> from these would I be gone,
> Save that to die, I leave my love alone.

This last word is surprising. It certainly does not mean that S is afraid that poor B would be left alone in the world. S is only too aware that B has many friends. The explanation is given immediately in 67. Why should B go on living in a world where faces are painted, and there is no true beauty except his own, 'now Nature bankrupt is' and 'hath no exchequer now but his'? This is confirmed in 68. After cosmetics, wigs. Nowadays false hair is all the fashion, and Nature stores B 'To show false art what beauty was of yore.' Why should he live on as the only true beauty in this false world? The apparently detached social satire of 66 is a platform for this new praise which follows in 67 and 68.

Sonnet 87: 'Farewell, thou art too dear for my possessing'

A collection of 152 love sonnets, each of 14 iambic pentameters, might cloy, but Shakespeare insures against nausea by the variety of tones he uses. In 71–4, S plays the pity card. He is old, he will soon die, and his verse is worthless. This sentimental gambit is followed by satire in 76–86, a scornful assault on rival poets who are also rival lovers, supported by continued protestations of his own incompetence in 86.13–14,

> But when your countenance filled up his line,
> Then lacked I matter. That enfeebled mine.

It is an easy glide from this to the farewell in 87, but the farewell is not a farewell. A long crawl back begins in 88 and 89, where he takes all the blame upon himself, playing for pity again in 90 and 91 – your love is everything to me, and I am

> Wretched in this alone, that thou mayst take
> All this away, and me most wretched make.

He contradicts this immediately in 92 by calculating that the loss of love could not make him wretched because he would die the moment it happened, but he destroys his own argument in the last two lines:

> But what's so blessed fair that fears no blot?
> Thou mayst be false, and yet I know it not.

The false farewell of 87 is an amorous stratagem. S is not the only lover who has stormed out into the night and come back next morning.

Sonnet 94: 'They that have power to hurt and will do none'

According to Kerrigan (1986), 'This elusive poem is perhaps the most discussed in the collection', the crucial difficulty being the clash between the negative tone of lines 3–4:

> Who moving others are themselves as stone,
> Unmovèd, cold, and to temptation slow,

– and the apparent approval of 5–7:

> They rightly do inherit Heaven's graces
> And husband Nature's riches from expense.
> They are the lords and owners of their faces.

Line 7 points to the simple solution: 'faces' refers back. If S were betrayed, argued Sonnet 93, he would not know it because 'love's face | May still seem love to me', 'Thy looks with me, thy heart in other place', 'in thy face sweet love should ever dwell', and Heaven decreed that

> Whate'er thy thoughts or thy heart's workings be,
> Thy looks should nothing thence but sweetness tell.   93.11–12

The reason for the positive tone of 94.5–7 is that the betrayed lover is skating on thin ice, and trying to soften the harshness of his protests. He wants to tell the truth, but is afraid of the consequences, so lards it with compliments as in 93, 13–14:

> How like Eve's apple doth thy beauty grow
> If thy sweet virtue answer not thy show.

'Show' is the last word in 93 and in 94.2. Sonnet 93 ends with a rotten apple and 94 with festering lilies.

After eight poems hinting that B is false, in Sonnet 95 S will speak the truth, 'How sweet and lovely dost thou make '*the shame* ... thy *sins*':

> O what a mansion have those *vices* got,
> Which for their habitation chose out thee,
> Where beauty's veil doth cover every *blot*.   95.9–11

Sonnet 116: 'Let me not to the marriage of true minds'

'Shakespeare's best sonnet' has traditionally been seen as the noblest expression of the constancy and strength of human love and is therefore frequently read at marriages and funerals. This view of the poem has been challenged. Kerrigan (1986), for example, the shrewdest of commentators, finds it boastful and sentimental.

Sonnets 109–21 form a group in which S is at last forced to admit his own infidelities and begs to be forgiven, flattering, pleading for pity, and

11

constructing outrageous sophistries in an attempt to win his way back into favour. The whole of 109, for example, is a virtuoso display of hypocrisy, and in 115 he poses as an honest man by admitting to a lie, a harmless one of course – he lied at the beginning of their love when he said that he could never be more in love. The most outrageous excuse comes at 117.12–14, where S begs B not to hate him,

> Since my appeal says I did strive to prove
> The constancy and virtue of your love.

So then the praise of unalterable love in 116 is embedded in admissions of infidelity cushioned in evasions, excuses and flattery. Read in context, this noble expression of the constancy and strength of human love is a diplomatic manoeuvre, calculated praise by an inconstant lover of the constancy and virtue of love, addressed to a lover whose inconstancy he has often railed against. In the light of this, 'Let me not to the marriage of true *minds*' chimes with 109.1, 'O never say that I was false of *heart*' –admittedly our bodies have not been true but we do truly love each other, and surely our love can never alter:

> Love is not love,
> Which alters when it alteration finds,
> Or bends with the remover to remove.

This eulogy of love in 116 is S's appeal to the young man to honour it, and his own promise to do the same himself from now on.

Conclusion

Sonnets 1–152 have a continuous plot, carried forward by connections between the poems, as observed throughout this commentary. If the case is made, it is a loss to read them one by one. The sonnets which appear in anthologies are glorious poetry, but to read only these is to read every eleventh scene in Shakespeare's plays – great stuff, but not understood.

Apart from a few soliloquies, they are addressed to one or other of the two lovers, not letters, but utterances, full of arguments, exclamations, questions, colloquial tones and sudden turns characteristic of living speech. A text conveying a plot in the form of utterances is the text of a drama. The Sonnets are a drama with one speaker and two silent characters. As far as I know, drama in sonnet form was a new genre. It has succeeded remarkably well.

The Sonnets invent episodes that might arise in love, and arguments that a lover might deploy. They tell us no more about Shakespeare's own life than do *Hamlet, Lear* or the adventures of Falstaff. No more and no less. London theatres were often closed in the years before the publication of the Sonnets in 1609. In pouring his exhaustless creativity into these poems this playwright, the supreme master of spoken English, has written a play in 152 scenes, but he enjoys some release from the dramatist's bondage of continuity of cause and effect, of motive and action, and finds a form of drama, with surprises, inconsistencies and mysteries which have intrigued readers for four centuries. Two mysteries which have been heavily debated are the identity of W.S., to whom the Sonnets are dedicated, and the identity of the 'Dark Lady'. A sane treatment of such problems will be found in 'Shakespeare's Autobiographical Poems', the second chapter of Jonathan Bate, *The Genius of Shakespeare* (Picador, 1997).

Books Used

The Sonnets are a battleground, littered with conflicting interpretations. I am not an English scholar, and do not pretend to do justice to printed scholarship in the field, working only with the sources listed below, but at the end of some of the notes I have cited other views, usually without comment, sometimes to demonstrate that they are possible, sometimes to demonstrate that they are not, but I have tried to avoid polemics.

The Compact Oxford English Dictionary (Oxford, 1991).

Bartlett, J., *A Complete Concordance of Shakespeare* (Macmillan, 1894).

Rollins, H. E., *Shakespeare's* Sonnets *and Interpretative History* (Lippincott, 1944). A priceless compilation of three centuries of comments.

Booth, S., *Shakespeare's Sonnets* (Yale University Press, 1977). Quarto text with modern version on opposite page. Enormously learned.

Ingram, W. G., and Redpath, T., *Shakespeare's Sonnets* (Hodder and Stoughton, 1978).

Kerrigan, J., *The Sonnets and A Lover's Complaint* (Penguin, 1986). With shrewd and stimulating commentary.

Evans, G. B., *Shakespeare's Sonnets* (Cambridge University Press, 1996). With detailed commentary.

Duncan-Jones, K., *Shakespeare's Sonnets* (Arden, 1997). Good on the history of the publication of the Sonnets.

Vendler, H., *The Art of Shakespeare's Sonnets* (Harvard University Press,

1997). Prints Quarto text above her own version. Each sonnet is followed by an essay.

Burrow, C., *The Complete Sonnets and Poems* (Oxford University Press, 2002). With an up-to-date but selective commentary.

Honan, P., *Shakespeare: A Life* (Oxford University Press, 1999). A golden book.

Standard modern commentaries on the plays.

References to the plays are based on the Folio Society edition by S. Wells and G. Taylor (1997). The poems are cited from Burrow's edition listed above. For the Bible I have used the Authorised King James Version, although it was not licensed until 1611, two years after the Sonnets were published.

Having spent my working life on Lucretius, Horace and Virgil, I took to the Sonnets in retirement, stimulated by the rush of three commentaries in 1996–7. Finding that they did not give me the help I needed, particularly with the argument of the poems, I began working on them knowing nothing about Elizabethan history, and nothing about Shakespearean criticism. The commentaries and Park Honan's book helped with the history, but I had no time for the criticism.

Author's Note

The Sonnets are great and glorious poems, but readers new to them would be well advised not to try to read them straight through. They might begin with the rapture in 29 and 30 (noting the self-mockery), and move through the early fears in 34 and 35 to such as 55, 60 and 66, then perhaps through satire in 76 to fun in 100 and 101, and so on to the self-loathing and despair of 151 and 152. These are poems addressed to a young man (1–126) and a lady (127–152), and they form a continuous drama, almost every poem being linked to its neighbours. It follows that they should be read in sequence. In the early days I would take two per day, Sonnets 1 and 2 followed by 2 and 3, followed by 3 and 4, all read slowly – an unimaginably rich experience of love and life.

D.W.

Abbreviations of Works
by Shakespeare

AC	Antony and Cleopatra	MND	A Midsummer Night's Dream
AW	All's Well That Ends Well		
AYL	As You Like It	MV	The Merchant of Venice
CE	The Comedy of Errors	MW	The Merry Wives of Windsor
Cor	Coriolanus		
Cym	Cymbeline	Oth	Othello
Ham	Hamlet	Per	Pericles
1H4	King Henry IV, Part 1	PP	The Passionate Pilgrim
2H4	King Henry IV, Part 2	PT	The Phoenix and Turtle
H5	King Henry V	R2	King Richard II
1H6	King Henry VI, Part 1	R3	King Richard III
2H6	King Henry VI, Part 2	RJ	Romeo and Juliet
3H6	King Henry VI, Part 3	TC	Troilus and Cressida
H8	King Henry VIII	Tem	The Tempest
JC	Julius Caesar	TGV	The Two Gentlemen of Verona
KJ	King John		
KL	King Lear	Tim	Timon of Athens
LC	A Lover's Complaint	TA	Titus Andronicus
LLL	Love's Labour's Lost	TN	Twelfth Night
Luc	The Rape of Lucrece	TNK	The Two Noble Kinsmen
MA	Much Ado about Nothing	TS	The Taming of the Shrew
Mac	Macbeth	VA	Venus and Adonis
MM	Measure for Measure	WT	The Winter's Tale

ॐ 1 ॐ

From fairest creatures we desire increase,
That thereby beauty's rose might never die,
But as the riper should by time decease,
His tender heir might bear his memory.   4

But thou, contracted to thine own bright eyes,
Feed'st thy light's flame with self-substantial fuel,
Making a famine where abundance lies,
Thyself thy foe, to thy sweet self too cruel.   8

Thou, that art now the world's fresh ornament
And only herald to the gaudy spring,
Within thine own bud buriest thy content,
And, tender churl, mak'st waste in niggarding.   12

Pity the world, or else this glutton be
To eat the world's due, by the grave and thee.

We expect beautiful creatures to reproduce to preserve the stock.
But you are consuming your own body,
burying your beauty in the bud, and wasting by hoarding.
Give the world what you owe. Don't keep it for yourself and the grave.

1–4 The first 17 sonnets plead with a young man to marry and have children. From the beginning they stress his beauty. He is clearly one of the fairest creatures, a very rose of beauty. Men and roses age and die. Their beauty is preserved in their descendants.

Shakespeare is in love with language. Typical is the play between 'creatures' and 'increase', 'From fairest créatures we desire incréase.' The words sound alike, and this helps to make the argument persuasive. He also heard the rhyme in 4, 'his tender *heir* might *bear*', and a good reading would bring it out. But the play is not only with the sound. Typical too is the jolt of thought. It is clear enough that the heir *bears* the memory of his parent,

17

he carries his father's likeness around with him. But is there a glimpse of a paradox – an heir giving birth to, *bearing* the memory of, his own father?

In Elizabethan English 'his' is often used where modern English writes 'its'. The word 'its' occurs only ten times in the plays and never in the poems. This is a valuable poetic resource which Shakespeare repeatedly exploits. Here 'riper' and 'tender' point back to the rose, so 'his' could be read as impersonal. The rose bears the memory of *its* forebear. But the line also refers to the young man, whose son would bear the memory of *his* father.

5–8 'But you will have no heir because you are contracted to your own bright eyes', implying that there is a contract between the young man and his own eyes, he is betrothed not to a woman but to himself, and also that his arc of vision is narrowed, 'contracted', as when the death of Hamlet's father caused the whole kingdom 'To be contracted in one brow of woe' (*Hamlet* 1.2.4). The flame of his light is visible in the brightness of his eyes, and he is feeding it with the substance of his own body (6), as if he were a candle. Even large candles consume their own substance, and end as next to nothing. So the young man is making famine where there is now abundance [of beauty]. A similar idea occurs in Paroles's magniloquent indictment of virginity in *AW* 1.1.140–2, 'Virginity breeds mites, much like a cheese; consumes itself to the very paring, and so dies with feeding his own stomach.' This last phrase, like line 4 above, contains an example of the personal/impersonal use of 'his'. 'His' makes both virginity and cheese into persons.

9–12 Now the young man is a new ornament suddenly appearing in the world, proclaiming the arrival of the gaudy spring. Heralds wore tabards emblazoned with heraldic arms. In line 11 buds are waiting to burst into life, but the young man's bud buries its contents as though in the grave. There will be no flower and no fruit. In line 8 the young man was sweet and also cruel. Line 12 contains two such paradoxes. A 'tender churl' is a 'gentle miser'. To make waste in being niggardly is to be extravagant *and* thrifty. A paradox packed into two words is an oxymoron, and Shakespeare enjoyed them, and enjoyed making fun of them, as in *RJ* 1.1.173–80:

> O brawling love, O loving hate,
> O anything of nothing first create;
> O heavy lightness, serious vanity,
> Misshapen chaos of well-seeming forms,

Feather of lead, bright smoke, cold fire, sick health,
Still-waking sleep that is not what it is!
This love feel I that feel no love in this.
Dost thou not laugh?

13–14 'By the grave and thee' is puzzling. How could the young man eat the world's due by the grave and himself? Commentators explain as though the verb were passive and the world's due, his beauty, was to *be eaten* by the young man now, and eventually by the [worms in his] grave.

This first sonnet illustrates an important principle of construction. I have printed it with gaps between steps in the argument, because all these poems argue a case. It would be easy to paraphrase in a short sentence: 'The youth here addressed is urged to obviate the idle waste of Nature's treasure by marrying and perpetuating himself [i.e. giving himself a kind of immortality] through his offspring.' This would be to annihilate it. The above division of the lines may help to show that the first quatrain is a general statement of what the world expects. The second refers to the present behaviour of the young man. The third refers to his blighted future, and the final couplet is an appeal. These poems do not consist of saying the same thing a dozen times. The argument is shaped to a point. This is important. The first 17 sonnets do say the same thing but they are all totally different. The difference lies in the argument, and also in the images. Here they glide from one to another and back, and are not always connected or consistent – the birth and ripening of the rose, betrothal, beauty as a flame, the feeding of that flame leading to famine where there was abundance, a cruel foe, a herald, spring as a monarch in gaudy robes of state, the young man as a bud which is a tomb, the miser and the waster, and feeding again in line 14.

❧ 2 ❧

When forty winters shall besiege thy brow
And dig deep trenches in thy beauty's field,
Thy youth's proud livery, so gazed on now,
Will be a tatter'd weed of small worth held.   4

Then, being asked where all thy beauty lies,
Where all the treasure of thy lusty days,
To say, within thine own deep-sunken eyes,
Were an all-eating shame and thriftless praise.   8

How much more praise deserved thy beauty's use,
If thou could'st answer, 'This fair child of mine
Shall sum my count, and make my old excuse',
Proving his beauty by succession thine.   12

This were to be new made when thou art old,
And see thy blood warm when thou feel'st it cold.

When you are forty you will be wrinkled and no one will look at you.
If they ask where your beauty is, it will be a poor answer
*   to say it is in your old eyes.*
Better to point to a beautiful son and say, 'There's my account, he'll show you.'
That will make you new when you are old. Your blood will feel cold,
*   but you will see it warm.*

1–4 Forty winters are an army in forty units besieging a fortress, and
digging deep trenches round its walls. The fortress is the young man's
brow, and the trenches are wrinkles. The 'proud livery' may then be a
military uniform, once splendid, but now torn and shabby after a forty-
year siege. In this context 'weed' is clothing as at *MND* 2.1.256, where
Oberon says that the slough of a snake is 'weed wide enough to wrap a fairy
in'. But another meaning is in play. After the field in line 2, 'a tatter'd weed
of small worth held' is a wild plant, withered and unvalued.

20

5–8 When the young man is old he will be asked where his beauty lies, the treasure of his lusty days (when he was vigorous and full of sexual desire). His answer may be that it is still there in his 'own deep-sunken eyes', a strange answer for an old man to make. The explanation is to be found in 1.5–6, where he was contracted to his own eyes and feeding his light's flame on his own substance. Now that they are deep-sunken, to praise them is thriftless, they ought to be ashamed of their gluttony, after consuming all the treasure of that beauty, 'Making a famine where abundance lies' (1.7).

9–12 Lines 10–11 are a vivid little scene in which the old man is challenged about his accounts, and proudly points to his handsome son, who will act as his accountant not by totting up figures but by existing, and as his advocate not by presenting his case but by being beautiful, making his 'old excuse'. This does not mean that the son will be trotting out an excuse his father has been making for a long time. It is not the excuse that is old but what is excused, his father's age. This application of an adjective to a noun to which it does not strictly belong does not make for ease of understanding, but it does add force. 'Proving his beauty by succession thine' means that the son will establish the father's beauty by succession. He has obviously inherited it.

13–14 The old father will *feel* cold blood and *see* warm, in both cases his own. The bite of this ending is sharpened by the metre. First, each of the last two lines consists of ten monosyllabic words. Second, a lesser poet might have written 'Thís were to bé made néw when thóu art óld', but Shakespeare avoids the jogging rhythm. Sense demands an emphasis on 'new' where there would be no stress in the metre, perhaps 'Thís were to be néw máde when thou art óld.' The tiny variation may affect the meaning. For an old man to be new made is to be new born, even more of a miracle than being made new, being repaired. Third, in the last line, 'warm' would not bear the metrical beat, but calls out to be read with emphasis, 'To sée thy blóod wárm when thou féel'st it cóld', thus adding ice to the last word.

ஐ 3 ைஐ

Look in thy glass and tell the face thou viewest
Now is the time that face should form another,
Whose fresh repair if now thou not renewest,
Thou dost beguile the world, unbless some mother.   4

For where is she so fair whose uneared womb
Disdains the tillage of thy husbandry?
Or who is he so fond will be the tomb
Of his self-love, to stop posterity?   8

Thou art thy mother's glass, and she in thee
Calls back the lovely April of her prime.
So thou through windows of thine age shalt see,
Despite of wrinkles, this thy golden time.   12

But if thou live remembered not to be,
Die single, and thine image dies with thee.

Look in your mirror and tell your face to propagate. Otherwise
you are cheating the world, and some possible mother.
What woman will refuse you? What man will kill himself with self-love,
to make sure he has no descendants?
You are your mother's mirror. In you she sees her own spring.
When you are old you too will see your youth in your children.
But if you wish to be forgotten, die unwed, and your image dies with you.

1–4 An amusing dramatic scene. The young man is told to look in his mirror
and talk severely to his own face. 'Lóok in thy glass ... Nów is the time'. Each
of the first two lines starts with inversion of stress. This is common, but not
twice in succession in the first two lines (I hear it in the music of 8.1–2, more
faintly in 21.1–2, and then not again till the waves roll in on the pebbles in
60.1–2). This rhythm gives emphasis to the command, and the urgency is
maintained, 'if now thou not ... thou dost', but the humour begins when 'that

face' is told so sternly to form another. Men look in the mirror every morning, but do not often ask their faces to breed. If he does not renew his by having a child, he will be cheating the world as in 1.14. There is a woman who could be blest with his child but will remain unblest.

5–8 Now a compliment, 'Does any woman refuse you?'. An uneared womb is a shock. 'To ear' at this date could still mean to plough as in *OED* 1a (1603), 'When you ere it (the ground) up with the plough', in *AC* 1.4.49, where pirates 'ear and wound' the sea with their keels, and in Shakespeare's Dedication to *Venus and Adonis*, when he promises the Earl of Southampton that he would 'neuer after eare so barren a land, for feere it yeeld me still so bad a harvest'. So the uneared womb is a womb unploughed. The metaphor is forceful here, but not bawdy, as it is in *AC* 2.2.234, 'He plough'd her and she cropp'd', or in Sophocles, *Antigone* 569, where Creon points out that if he executes Antigone there will be many other fields for his son to plough. 'The tillage of thy husbandry' ends the agricultural metaphor with a pun.

The argument now proceeds from the rhetorical question about the mother to a rhetorical question about the father. 'Fond' implies foolish affection. 'Who dotes upon himself so much that he will turn himself into his own tomb, and block the possibility of descendants?'

9–12 The argument here is not profound, 'Your mother looks at her son and sees her own youthful beauty', but what about the words?

> Thou art thy mother's glass, and she in thee
> Calls back the lovely April of her prime.

Since 'call back' is not cited in *OED* until 1850 to mean 'remember', this means that she can summon her *primavera*, her springtime, and it will come in the person of her son. If the young man has a child, he will in his old age be able to look at it, and despite his wrinkled face he will see his own golden time, the time of his youth. The mirrors of lines 1 and 9 have become windows. In 12 he will look at his son through the windows of his age, and will see himself as he once was, as in a garden, in the golden time of spring and in the golden time of his life.

13–14 If on the other hand he is living in order to be forgotten – here the speaker loses patience. The plain assertion would be 'If you die single, your image will die with you.' 'Die single', is much more forcible, and the present tense of 'dies' is brutal. The dying is already happening.

ᔰ 4 ᔯ

Unthrifty loveliness, why dost thou spend
Upon thyself thy beauty's legacy?

Nature's bequest gives nothing, but doth lend,
And being frank, she lends to those are free.   4
Then, beauteous niggard, why dost thou abuse
Thy bounteous largesse given thee to give?

Profitless usurer, why dost thou use
So great a sum of sums, yet canst not live?   8
For, having traffic with thyself alone,
Thou of thyself thy sweet self dost deceive.

Then how, when Nature calls thee to be gone,
What ácceptáble audit canst thou leave?   12
   Thy unused beauty must be tombed with thee,
   Which usèd, lives th'executor to be.

Lovely spendthrift, why squander Nature's legacy of beauty?
She does not give, she lends. She gave for you to give to others.
You are a non-profit-making moneylender, spending your capital
   on yourself, and cheating yourself.
What accounts will you leave behind? What is not used will be buried
   with you. If you use your beauty, it will live and be your executor.

1–2 'Unthrifty … spend … legacy' – there is a score of financial terms in
this sonnet (if 'use' can be counted as five in lines 5, 7 twice, 13 and 14).
Shakespeare himself was a man of property, and took to the law courts on
occasion. He exploited the poetic possibilities in the language of finance in
several other sonnets, notably in 67, 74, 87, 134 and 146.

   The beautiful young man is addressed as 'Unthrifty loveliness', as a
spendthrift who squanders his wealth of beauty on himself. Lines 3–6
consider the role of his benefactress Nature. Lines 7–10 mock him as a
moneylender who does not lend, and the last four lines point out the
consequences of this folly.

3–6 In line 4 frank lending to free is a favourite Shakespearean trick. When he compares or contrasts two things, he likes to make them sound similar, as though to reinforce the comparison or stress the contrast. Compare 'beauteous' and 'bounteous' in 5–6 and see Introduction, p. 6, on similation. The fourth line means 'Being generous, she lends to those who are generous', and a generous testator would clearly be displeased if her heir hoarded her bequest. 'Unthrifty loveliness' is now inverted as 'beauteous niggard'. AB is followed by BA. The beloved is a spendthrift wasting his beauty on himself; he is also a miser, hoarding it instead of using it. He is like the servant in the parable in Matthew 25:14–30, who hid his talent in the earth, although he knew that his master reaped where he sowed not, and wanted his capital back with interest. In the last verse of the parable the master gave his orders, 'cast ye the unprofitable servant into outer darkness.'

7–10 The third address is to the 'Profitless usurer', the moneylender with capital to invest, who makes no profit and cannot even have a life, because he will not put that capital out to work. He does use it (7) but only on himself. The financial metaphor continues with the largesse '*given* thee to *give*' (6) and in lines 7–8, when the one who ab*uses* becomes a *u*surer and *uses* a *sum* of *sums*. This close repetition of the same word in different forms is known as polyptoton, a vital weapon in Shakespeare's rhetorical armoury. '*Thou* of *thyself thy* sweet *self* dost deceive' is another example. See too lines 3–4, 6 and 13–14; and 3.14.

The 'sum of sums' has been said to be a Latinism, but it is not a native Latin construction, It seems rather to be imported from other languages, as in *The Song of Songs* and in 'The King of Kings, and Lord of Lords' in Revelation 19:16. The most famous occurrence of the phrase *summa summarum* is in Lucretius 3.816, in a passage strangely like this sonnet at other points.

11–14 At Lucretius 3.933, Nature takes voice to scold the old man who grumbles about having to die, 'You are mortal, why are you giving way to all this grief? Why do you moan and weep at death? Why don't you leave like a guest who has had enough?' S too fires off derisive questions, 'why dost thou' in lines 1, 5 and 7, coming to a climax in the double question in lines 11–12:

> Then *how*, when Nature calls thee to be gone,
> *What* acceptáble audit canst thou leave?

At 'how … What' Nature's mounting exasperation has eloquently overcome her command of syntax. In Shakespeare there are five questions in 12 lines, whereas Nature in Lucretius in the same scolding tone of voice poses four questions in 11 lines. The third line of the sonnet is nearly a translation of Lucretius 3.971, *vitaque mancipio nulli datur, omnibus usu*, 'and life is given to none as a possession, to all for use', and the last word, *usu*, is the core of this poem.

In 7–12 the young man is an incompetent moneylender. When his estate is wound up, it will be clear that he has not left an ácceptáble account of his management of what he inherited. The *usurer* of 7 makes a fleeting reappearance in the condemnation of beauty *unused* for procreation, which, if it had been so '*usèd*', would live on to represent the deceased. A son would inherit it and act as executor for the property, just as a son would have been his father's accountant and defending counsel at the end of Sonnet 2.

Five aggressive rhetorical questions set the tone of Sonnet 4, and it is sharpened by 'why dost thou' three times, in 1, 5 and 7, leading to the exasperated climax of 'Then how ... what ... canst thou' in 12. Before each of the first three questions there comes an abusive vocative, 'Unthrifty loveliness', 'beauteous niggard' and 'Profitless usurer', suggesting three different kinds of financial management, extravagance, miserliness, and the lunacy of the moneylender who lends no money. This poet is a dramatist, and one of his gifts lies in characterisation. The argument so telegraphed is part of the characterisation of the speaker called S in these comments, a character not to be confused with William Shakespeare. Here he is a pleader reaching for an argument to carry his point. It may be illogical, over-ingenious, incredible. But he will deploy it.

Nowottny (1977)
Thus this sonnet, which in its absence of visual imagery has little attraction for the hasty reader, reveals itself to analysis as having an intricate beauty of form to which it would be hard to find a parallel in the work of any other poet.

Duncan-Jones (1997)
1–2 **spend/Upon thyself** The primary image is of self-contemplation and a failure to turn to women as the 'other' as in 3.1–6; but there is subsidiary allusion to masturbation. That Shakespeare, like Pepys, used 'spend' for 'discharge semen' is shown in *All's Well that Ends Well* 2.3.277–8. [Here the man who declines to go to war is the man 'That hugs his kicky-wicky here at home | Spending his manly marrow in her arms.']

❦ 5 ❧

Those hours that with gentle work did frame
The lovely gaze where every eye doth dwell,
Will play the tyrants to the very same,
And that unfair which fairly doth excel.   4

For never-resting Time leads Summer on
To hideous Winter and confounds him there,
Sap checked with frost and lusty leaves quite gone,
Beauty o'er-snowed and bareness everywhere.   8

Then, were not Summer's distillation left,
A liquid prisoner pent in walls of glass,
Beauty's effect, with beauty, were bereft,
Nor it nor no remembrance what it was.   12

But flowers distilled, though they with winter meet,
Lose but their show, their substance still lives sweet.

Time made your gaze beautiful, and will unmake its beauty.
For he leads Summer on to Winter, and destroys him.
If summer flowers were not preserved by distillation,
   their beauty and its effect would be lost.
But flowers distilled lose only their show, not their sweet substance.

1–4 The word 'hour(s)' occurs 36 times in Shakespeare's poems, but here alone it is pronounced as two syllables. This could be a meaningless statistic, or it could be that the poet was happy to slow down 'hours' because of the gentle work they were engaged in. The line reads better read slowly.

   It would not be unusual to say that every eye dwelt on a young man's face. But Shakespeare, who was sensitive to eyes (see on 1.5), says not 'face' but 'gaze', suggesting a steadiness in the young man's eyes. The hours were gentle when they were making that lovely gaze, but they will play the part of the tyrant Time, whose will is to make unbeautiful that which excels in beauty, 'to unfair that which fairly doth excel'. 'Unfair' as a verb is used only here in Shakespeare and attested only here in the *OED*. Shakespeare thinks nothing of coining a word for the sake of his rhetoric, here the contrast sharpened by the polyptoton 'unfair ... fairly'.

5–8   Time is never still and it leads Summer on to hideous Winter. Capital letters are used here and sometimes elsewhere in this edition to help readers to see the personifications. It is put beyond doubt by referring to Summer as 'him'. Time lures Summer to a wintry wood and murders him, 'confounds him there'. In the next two lines the landscape is human as well as vegetable. Sap is both, as in 15.5–7 'men as plants increase' and 'Vaunt in their youthful sap'. 'Lusty' refers to the vigorous growth of leaves, but it often includes sexual vigour, as at 2.6. It is not difficult to make the same transfer from a snow-covered landscape to the white hair of an old man, but what in human life corresponds to 'bareness everywhere'? Old men do not go around naked. There is some reason to think that in its human application the bareness could refer to baldness. In lines 233–5 of Arthur Golding's translation of Ovid's *Metamorphoses* 15.212–13, 'Then ugly winter last | Like age steales on with trembling steppes, all bald, or overcast | With shirle thinne heare as whyght as snow' ('shirle' means 'rough'). This is too close to the Shakespeare to be a coincidence. 'Beauty o'er-snowed' is like 'overcast with ... snow', and 'bareness everywhere' is like 'all bald'. It seems that Shakespeare had read the passage and used it, but blurred the undignified or satirical reference to baldness. The satirical tone is there in the Ovid, where old Winter has lost her hair, or what she has is white, *aut spoliata suos aut quos habet alba capillos*. Bareness might also be a vivid glimpse of the emotional condition of some old people. The bleakness of the thought is supported by a bleakness in the syntax of lines 7–8. 'Sap checked', not attached to any word in the context, is an 'absolute' construction.

9–12   In the distillation of flowers, for example to make rose oil, attar of roses, water is boiled off to isolate an aromatic essence which could be preserved in glass phials. This essence is personified as a prisoner in a glass-walled cell. This rose oil and also rose-water, the fragrant water boiled off in distillation, were used in cookery, perfumery and medicine. 'Bereft' means lost, taken away, as *3H6* 2.6.60, 'his understanding is bereft.' If flowers were not distilled, in winter their beauty would be lost, and so would its effect (of taste, fragrance and cure): 'Beauty's effect, with beauty, were bereft.' There is poetry in this precision, and great intelligence.

This loss is conveyed in 12, a line heavy with negatives, and with the same bleak syntax as noted in 7–8. ' Nor it nor no remembrance what it was' also stands free from the structure of its sentence, and both are laconic.

The distillation metaphor occurs in Sidney's *New Arcadia* 333 on 'crystalline marriage': 'Have you ever seen a pure rose-water kept in a crystal glass, how fine it looks, how sweet it smells while that beautiful glass imprisons it?' Shakespeare applies the metaphor not to marriage but to the begetting of children, another distillation which preserves the original in miniature, but there is no room here for this human application of the argument. The sonnet form is too short. That comes in Sonnet 6.

13–14   For 'lose' the Quarto reads 'leese', meaning 'set free', 'release'. The word never occurs in Shakespeare and makes poor sense here. Flowers do not set free their show.

Vendler (1997)
One may choose to regard Sonnets 5 and 6 as a single, logically complete, poem; but since it is true that 5 is certainly a complete poem in itself, I prefer to see it as a poem requiring from its reader a silent extrapolation of its syllogistic warning logic into completion-by-exhortation, thereby generating Sonnet 6.

Then let not winter's ragged hand deface
In thee thy summer ere thou be distilled.
Make sweet some vial. Treasure thou some place
With beauty's treasure ere it be self-killed.   4

That use is not forbidden usury
Which happies those that pay the willing loan
(That's for thyself to breed another thee),
Or ten times happier, be it ten for one.   8
Ten times thyself were happier than thou art
If ten of thine ten times refigured thee.

Then what could death do if thou should'st depart,
Leaving thee living in posterity?   12
    Be not self-willed, for thou art much too fair
    To be death's conquest and make worms thine heir.

Do not let your beauty die, but preserve it by distillation.
Usury is permitted if it makes the borrower happy, as it would you,
    or even ten times happier, if you bred ten replicas of yourself.
Death would be thwarted if you survived in your offspring.
    You are too beautiful to be worm food.

1–4 According to Sonnet 5, *hideous winter unfairs summer*, but *distilled flowers* and their *sweetness live* on 'in walls of glass', glass *vials*. The argument is not complete. Summer's beauty lives on, but how does that apply to the young man? The answer comes in the first four lines of Sonnet 6, with many corresponding terms as italicised – 'Then let not *winter's ragged* hand *deface* | In thee thy *summer* ere thou be *distilled.* | Make *sweet* some *vial.*' 'Ragged' corresponds to 'hideous' in 5.6, and often means 'rough', but here there may be just a suggestion of the jagged work of frost, the bony hand of a ragged old man, with chapped, arthritic, icicle fingers. Winter has 'icy fingers' in *KJ* 5.7.37. Unlike the hands of the hours which did gentle

30

work in 5.1, winter has a *ragged hand*, and it does not beautify but *unfairs, defaces*.

In 'Make sweet *some* vial. Treasure thou *some* place' the choice of a woman seems to be unimportant (3.5–6), a strikingly functional view of the role of the wife in this transaction. Such undervaluing of heterosexual love perhaps anticipates the misogyny of Sonnet 20.

When the young man is told to treasure some place with beauty's treasure, that place is the womb of the woman he should marry, and he is to treasure it not with gold or jewels, but with his own precious beauty. This must be done before he kills it.

5–10 'Forbidden usury' touches upon a contemporary problem of conscience, the Shylock problem raised in *The Merchant of Venice*. A statute of Henry VIII, revived by Elizabeth in 1571 as 13 Eliz. Cap. 8, gave legal permission for usury, but condemned it as sinful: 'all usury, being forbidden by the law of God, is sin and detestable.' But 39 Eliz. Cap. 18 ruled in 1597 that usury was 'very necessary and profitable'. 'Forbidden usury' would be lending at an exorbitant rate of interest. Line 6 is difficult. One solution might be to suppose that in 3–4 the young man would be borrowing the womb of a wife as a place to store his treasure. He would willingly pay for the loan in order to breed a replica of himself (7). His wife would not be guilty of forbidden usury because he would be a happy borrower, in fact it would happy him 'ten' times over, if he were given ten children instead of one (8).

'Ten' occurs five times in three lines, a parody of a moneylender muttering his percentages. The same metaphor occurs when tears will be 'Advantaging their loan with interest | Of ten times double gain of happiness' in lines 36–7 of the additional passage of *R3* to go after 4.4.273 in the Folio Society text as printed by Wells and Taylor, page 454, (in Hammond's Arden edition 4.4.323–4). There is a teasing variation of stress on 'ten' in line 10, 'If tén of thíne ten tímes refígured thée.' This calculation envisages ten children reproducing their father's image ten times in all, but it has led some readers to saddle the young man with a hundred grandchildren. Pooler, as reported in Rollins (1944), provided the above evidence from the statutes, and also notes that the highest permissible rate of interest was 10 per cent. If the young man multiplied his treasure 'ten' times, this would be a superb investment.

11–14 'Death' carries the metrical accent in 'Then whát could déath do if thou shóuld'st depárt?' where the repetition of -d- drills home the message, and 'Leaving thee living' continues the ridicule. 'If thou should'st depart', death would be 'Leaving thee living' in your descendants, and making a mockery of him. These descendants are the heirs the young man should be acquiring, rather than the heirs in the brutal last line of the poem.

The tone of Sonnet 6 is brusque throughout. The first four lines offer three imperatives, with a mid-line break in 3. Such punctuation is not very common, and when it does occur it often has a vigorous effect, as at 6.3, 13.14, and 104.3. This is talking seriously, and the poem ends by leaving the young man to imagine what worms would do to him when they inherit.

This is the only sonnet in the collection whose opening completes the argument of its predecessor. This ends at line 4, leaving the poet with 10 more lines to write for a full sonnet. To knit the poem together, the financial metaphor in 5–10 picks up 'treasure' from 3 and 4; 'breed' in 7 and 'posterity' in 12 link the last four lines to 3 and 4; and 'death' in 10–14 looks back to 'self-killed' in 4.

෨ 7 ෫

Lo, in the Orient when the gracious light
Lifts up his burning head, each under eye
Doth homage to his new appearing sight,
Serving with looks his sacred majesty,   4

And having climbed the steep-up heav'nly hill,
Resembling strong youth in his middle age,
Yet mortal looks adore his beauty still,
Attending on his golden pilgrimage;   8

But when, from highmost pitch, with weary car
Like feeble age he reeleth from the day,
The eyes, fore duteous, now converted are
From his low tract and look another way.   12

So thou thyself outgoing in thy noon
Unlook'd on diest, unless thou get a son.

The sun is adored like a king as he rises,
and in his splendour at noon,
but as he sets, eyes look away.
So you decline at your noon, and die neglected unless you get a son.

1–4   A normal simile might say, 'Like the sun you rise in glory and set neglected.' By devoting 12 lines to the sun, Shakespeare builds up suspense. Readers wait to learn the point, until all is resolved in the final couplet. 'So thou thyself ...' turns description into simile.

     The sun king appears as early as the first line with the word 'gracious' suggesting his gracious majesty, and majesty itself is mentioned in 4, where 'sacred' glances at the contemporary doctrine of the Divine Right of Kings. But before that 'each under eye' is each subject lifting up his eyes to adore the new king, and 'homage' and 'serving' contribute to the metaphor. 'His' is used as in 1.4 where we would write 'its'. 'His burning head' is a dazzling way to advance the description both of the literal sun as 'its' and also of the metaphorical king as 'his'. In 'each under eye' 'under' is an adverb describing a noun, a vivid resource of Shakespearean syntax, like 'By *oft* predict' meaning 'by frequent predictions' in 14.8, 'the fine point of *seldom* pleasure' in 52.4, and 'my *often* rumination' in *AYL* 4.1.18.

5–8 In line 6 the metre supports the bold picture of a middle-aged man with youthful powers. If the line is read according to the iambic rhythm, it is reduced to doggerel, 'Resémbling stróng yóuth ín his míddle áge'. Given a natural reading, 'Resémbling stróng yóuth in his míddle áge', it highlights the robustness of youth. In line 7 the mortal subjects of the divine king adore him as he climbs the 'steep-up heav'nly hill', presumably to a shrine or palace, in formal robes of gold surrounded by his courtiers. The irony soon strikes.

9–12 The king is mortal. In such a cluster of royal elements the car of the sun brings to mind a gilded royal coach, but now it is weary and reeling out of control with an aged monarch too feeble to manage it, while none of his subjects, so dutiful before, 'fore duteous', pays any attention to him. In 9–10 the very rhythm is regular, and the lines are a picture of weariness:

> But when, from highmost pitch, with weary car,
> Like feeble age he reeleth from the day ...

Charles Cotton's 'Pastorale' also has fun with decrepitude of the sun:

> The Day's grown old, the fainting Sun
> Has but a little way to run,
> And yet his Steeds, with all his skill,
> Scarce lug the Chariot down the Hill.

In Benjamin Britten's *Serenade for Tenor, Horn and Strings* the orchestra drops dead a quarter of the way through the final line, and the listener is left to pity the horses having to lug the chariot *down* the hill.

Vendler (1997) has an interesting interpretation of lines 11–12:

There are some odd words in the poem – among them *fore duteous* and *tract* – which beg for explanation.... . Nothing in the requirements of meaning or sound alone would have prevented Shakespeare from writing
> The eyes [**once**] duteous now converted are
> From his low [**path**] and look another way.

... At the risk of seeming overingenious, I can only suggest that the golden sun generates, throughout the sonnet, French puns on **or**, **or**ient, a**dor**e, **mor**tal, and – our point of origin – **fore**: and that the central image of the sun's **car** generates anagrammatically scrambled cars elsewhere in g**rac**ious, sa**cr**ed, and – our point of origin – t**rac**t.

A simpler approach would be to ask what the words mean. 'Once' is just wrong. That would suggest that the sun king's subjects had been dutiful at some time in the past. But 'fore' is an older form of 'before'. They had been dutiful that very morning as he rose, and before noon, and that is the cutting edge of the argument and of the poetry. Neglect comes suddenly to the great. Similarly the literal sense of the Latin *tractus* is 'drawing out, dragging', and some of that survives in 'tracts of time', glossed in the *OED* as 'the course of time'. The sun's low tract is the low course on which his evening chariot drags him. 'And don't you see the torches of the sky trailing long *tractus*, draggings, of flames?' asks Lucretius 2.207, '*nocturnasque faces caeli ... nonne vides longos flammarum ducere tractus?*' Shakespeare and his educated readers had enough Latin to know that *tractus* was part of the verb *trahere*, to drag, just as they would have sensed the Latin *orient(em)*, rising, when the sun lifted up his head 'in the Orient'. Vendler's 'once' and 'path' are wrong in meaning, and to this ear are weak in sound.

13–14   The last two lines contain two shocks. The first is the present tense of 'diest' (one sharp syllable). Here, and at 3.14, even at his peak the young man is dying. The second is the pun in the last word of the poem. He is dying unless he gets him a son. The sun has coped with this difficulty. His successor, another sun, will arrive next morning. The young man should make a similar arrangement.

It is no longer true that men gaze on the sun in the morning and at noon, but not as it sets. It might seem as though Shakespeare is bending the facts to fit his case. But, whatever men now do or did then, there was an ancient proverb, cited by Booth (1977), 'the rising, not the setting, sun is worshipped by most men.' Booth also cites *TA* 1.2.141, 'Men shut their doors against a setting sun.' Shakespeare may be false to modern observation, but he was true to folk wisdom, and this glorious metaphor might stir anyone who has ever watched the sun rise or set.

Vendler (1997)
Sonnet 7 has little to recommend it, imaginatively.

ဆ 8 ca

Music to hear, why hear'st thou music sadly?
Sweets with sweets war not, joy delights in joy.
Why lov'st thou that which thou receiv'st not gladly,
Or else receiv'st with pleasure thine annoy?   4

If the true concord of well-tunèd sounds
By unions married do offend thine ear,
They do but sweetly chide thee, who confounds
In singleness the parts that thou should'st bear.   8

Mark how one string, sweet husband to another,
Strikes each in each by mutual ordering,
Resembling sire and child and happy mother,
Who all in one, one pleasing note do sing,   12
    Whose speechless song being many, seeming one,
    Sings this to thee, 'Thou single wilt prove none.'

Your voice is music to my ears. Why does music make you unhappy?
    Why do you love what makes you sad?
Harmony offends you because you are single.
Lute strings sound in sympathy with one another, a harmonious family.
    Their many voices seem as one. Being one, you will be none.

1–4 'Music to hear' is a bold address. To hear the young man speak is to
hear music. Sonnet 128 begins in the same way, 'How oft when thou, my
music, music play'st'. S has seen the young man listening to music with
sadness in his face, like Jessica in *MV* 5.1.69, 'I am never merry when I hear
sweet music.'

These first four lines almost turn language into algebra. 'Music-hear-
hear'st-music' is ABBA, a chiasmus. If 'war not' is taken to correspond to
'delight', the second line is something like AABCBC. Lines 3–4 look like
another chiasmus, 'lov'st - receiv'st - receiv'st - pleasure', but there is a

deception. Despite 'or else', line 4 simply repeats line 3 without inverting the order, 'Why do you love what makes you sad? Or else, why do you take pleasure in what causes you pain?' The words look like ABBA, but the sense is ABAB. Shakespeare loves to play with language.

5–8   The answer to these questions is that harmony saddens the young man by scolding him for being single. To bolster this implausible case S expresses musical harmony in matrimonial terms. It is 'a true concord of well-tunèd sounds | By *unions married*' which 'doth sweetly chide' the young man, just as happily married couples tend sweetly to advise their single friends to marry. The music has been described in human terms; now in 7–8 the human is expressed in musical terms. The young man who was music in the first word of the poem is now scolded for being unison instead of harmony. In playing in an instrumental ensemble or singing in consort, performers had to bear their parts. The young man should bear his parts, not just sing in unison. In human terms instead of being himself, husband and father, he fulfils only the first of the three functions, and confounds in singleness the parts he ought to bear.

9–14   For this section I have received priceless advice from Linda Sayce, who plays ravishing music of the period with the Charivari Consort. The verb 'strike' in line 10 is a technical term, 'to play upon (a harp, lyre etc)', as in *OED* 29b (1587), 'a passion that fadeth away like the sound of a Lute when the player ceaseth to strike'. In the double-strung lute, strings in the middle courses are tuned in pairs in unison. The pairs are close together and are played as one string. So one string is husband to the other. Line 10 is usually explained in terms of the sympathetic resonance of one of a pair when the other is struck, but 'It's actually quite difficult to pluck one string of a course and leave the other free to resonate. Usually this sort of mis-strike results in the plucking finger damping the unplucked string in the course of the stroke. So I'm afraid you won't get any sympathetic resonance from a string's neighbour, though you may get some from elsewhere on the lute.'
    In line 11 it seems that a lute is being tuned, and that an important part of the operation is to tune the bass and treble and middle courses so that they resemble 'sire and child and happy mother, | Who all in one, one pleasing note do sing.' A difficulty about this explanation is that not all three notes could be struck at the same time. Shakespeare and other contemporary poets use technical terms of music as analogies for human experience, but, as Sonnet 128 demonstrates, they do not always use them correctly.

The fusion of music and family is completed by the picture of family life as a pleasing song without words. He now gives the familiar paradox another twist, by including the words of this speechless song, 'Thou single wilt prove none', which is, like 136.8, a variant of the old proverb 'One is no number' (cited by Burrow 2002). It was exploited by Marlowe in his *Hero and Leander* 1.255–6, as printed by Orgel in his Penguin edition ('then' means 'therefore'):

> *One is no number*; maids are *nothing*, then,
> Without the *sweet* society of men.

Marlowe is playing with arithmetic, 'One is not a number, therefore a single woman is nothing.' Shakespeare offers a different calculation: 'Since many equals one, you, being one, by a similar reduction are equal to nothing.' Shakespeare is pointedly producing a mathematical variation.

Marlowe was murdered in 1593, and his poem must have been ringing in Shakespeare's mind when he was beginning to write the Sonnets:

> Then *treasure* is *abused*
> When *misers* keep it; being put to *loan*
> In time it will return as two for one.   236
> (See 1.12, 2.6, 4.7–8, 6.4 and 6.6.)
> [The miser's] golden earth remains,
> Which, after his *decease, some other gains*;
> But this fair gem, *sweet* in the loss alone,
> *When you fleet hence*, can be *bequeathed* to none.   248
> (See 1.3, 4.3 and 11, and 9.10.)
> Base bullion for the *stamp's* sake we allow,
> Even so for men's *impression* do we you.   265
> (See 11.14.)

Booth (1977) on lines 5–8
One can almost always make a general paraphrase of a Shakespearean sonnet and give a satisfactory gloss for any particular word in it, but if one puts together a new sentence replacing Shakespeare's words with their glosses, one will often get a sentence that makes no sense at all. Sometimes Shakespeare's own sentences can be demonstrated to mean nothing at all – even when readers actually understand them perfectly. This second quatrain of Sonnet 8 is an excellent example.

℘ 9 ℃

Is it for fear to wet a widow's eye
That thou consum'st thyself in single life?

Ah, if thou issueless shalt hap to die,
The world will wail thee like a makeless wife.   4
The world will be thy widow and still weep
That thou no form of thee hast left behind,
When every private widow well may keep,
By children's eyes, her husband's shape in mind.   8

Look what an unthrift in the world doth spend
Shifts but his place, for still the world enjoys it;
But beauty's waste hath in the world an end,
And kept unus'd, the user so destroys it.   12

No love toward others in that bosom sits
That on himself such murd'rous shame commits.

Are you staying single in case you die and make a widow weep?
If you do, the world will be your widow, and unlike a widow
*   it will have no likeness to recall your beauty.*
Money wasted is redistributed, but beauty wasted is lost.
There is no love for others in the heart that commits self-murder.

1–2   A possible tactic for an orator is to propose a feeble case for his opponent, destroy it, and claim that he has won the argument. So here Shakespeare
advances an implausible excuse for the young man's single state, and expresses
it in terms which make it sound ridiculous –'wet a widow's eye' indeed.

3–8   'Ah' has a part to play in making this imagined conversation vivid,
'No, no! If you happen to die without a son the world will mourn for you
as though it were a makeless wife, a wife without a mate, a wife whose
husband has died.' The world will lament that he has not left behind him

a living replica of his beauty. In 5 'still' is best taken as a peg on which to hang lines 7–8. The world will still be weeping when an individual, 'private', widow would have ceased to weep. The sarcasm sensed in the first line intensifies in lines 4 and 5, each beginning 'The world' and each with four soundings of the initial letter 'w', to guy the weeping and wailing. To bring this out, readers might stress 'the wórld will wáil thee ... The wórld will be thy wídow.' The polyptoton in line 6, '*Thou* no form of *thee*', weirdly imitates the sense, since 'thee' is another form of 'thou'. Line 8 suggests that any one widow has only to look into the eyes of her child to see her dead husband. Shakespeare looked at eyes (1.5, 2.7, 5.2 and 104.2).

9–12 'Look what' means 'whatever', as at 11.11, 37.13 and 77.9. Money squandered by a spendthrift is recycled; it continues to exist in the world, having just changed 'his' (that is, 'its') place. On the other hand, beauty not used for creating children is lost to the world. The vital involvement of the whole world is stressed by being mentioned in the same place in each of lines 9–11, just as it is in lines 4–5.

Line 12 has another striking polyptoton, 'unus'd ... user'. If beauty is kept unused [for procreation], the man who so uses it destroys it. The spending metaphor of lines 9–10 is not exhausted. Sonnets 4.7 and 6.5 lurk behind this polyptoton, and activate 'unused' and 'user' in the sense of money-lending.

13–14 The first couplet implicates the young man in a foolish proposition. The middle of the poem refutes it. The last couplet looks back to the first. The reason for the young man's refusal to marry has nothing to do with love for a possible wife or with the grief his death might cause her. There is no love in a bosom which commits this shameful murder of beauty. The condemnation is made the more severe by placing the responsibility in the bosom. The crime is in the heart. Self-murder is a sin of the heart.

Vendler (1997)
This 'Fantasy on the letter W' (as it could be entitled) arises, I believe, from Shakespeare's fascinated observation of the shape of the word widdow (the Quarto spelling):

w i d d o w

[Vendler counts three dozen instances of the letters -u-, -v- and -w- in these fourteen lines in the Elizabethan spelling of the Quarto. There are more than that in Sonnet 8, for example, if 'one' is included in the count, and here in 9 there are more than forty occurrences of the letter –s-.]

❧ 10 ☙

For shame! Deny that thou bear'st love to any
Who for thyself art so unprovident.
Grant if thou wilt thou art belov'd of many,
But that thou none lov'st is most evident,　　　　　　4

For thou art so possessed with murd'rous hate
That 'gainst thyself thou stick'st not to conspire,
Seeking that beauteous roof to ruinate
Which to repair should be thy chief desire.　　　　　8

O change thy thought, that I may change my mind.
Shall hate be fairer lodged than gentle love?
Be as thy presence is, gracious and kind,
Or to thyself at least, kind-hearted prove　　　　　12
　　Make thee another self for love of me,
　　That beauty still may live in thine or thee.

Others love you, but you don't love anyone, certainly not yourself,
　　and so you murder the beauty you ought to preserve.
Change your thinking, and my mind will change. Be kind to yourself,
　　so that beauty can live on either in a son or in yourself.

1–8 In 9.13 S accuses the young man of having no love towards others.
(Between sonnets the young man has denied it.) In 10.1 S repeats the
charge, and embarks on an argument which ends by appealing to the young
man to beget a son 'for love of me'. The plot of the Sonnets moves on.

　　The above text adds an exclamation mark after 'For shame', where the
Quarto has no punctuation: 'Shame on you! Admit you love no one, you
who have so little thought for your own future.' Shakespeare begins a score
of sonnets with exclamations. Most of these poems are not internal mus-
ings, but are presented as though they were spoken to the young man or
the Black Lady. They are dramatic. A sonnet or part of a sonnet which
begins with an exclamation is immediately a vivid representation of living

speech, and here it is enforced by six commands in the poem, and by the rattle of monosyllables in line 9.

In line 3 the tone of 'if thou wilt' is difficult to catch – perhaps 'Do please agree, don't pretend to be modest, many love you'. In line 5 the 'murd'rous hate' recalls the 'murd'rous shame' of the last line of the previous sonnet. He is so bent on self-murder that he does not hold back from conspiring against himself by this refusal to marry and have children. 'Unprovident' harks back to 'unthrift' and 'waste' in 9.9 and 9.11.

In line 6 'thou stick'st not to conspire' the violence of the language is like the aggrieved tones of the First Citizen in *Cor* 2.3.16: 'He himself stuck not to call us the many-headed multitude.' In line 7 another poet might have accused the young man of 'seeking that beauteous house to ruinate'. Why does Shakespeare say 'roof', not 'house'? Because it is a cogent detail. What the youth is destroying is beauty, the surface of the body, as the roof is the top of the house. It is also vivid. When a roof leaks the whole house rots. Besides, the repeated sounds of the lines (as in 64.11) contrast what the youth is doing with what he ought to be doing:

> Seeking that beaúteous róof to rúinate
> Which to repáir should'st be thy chief desíre.

There is no need to suggest that 'roof' means 'family', thus asking the young man to do his duty to preserve the lineage. That reasoning is not used in the Sonnets. Shakespeare's avoidance of the obvious word 'house' is perhaps a deliberate strategy to avoid bringing in that extraneous argument.

9–14　In line 9 the modern reader has to purge his mind of the cliché, 'I'll change my mind and have X instead of Y'. S will change the analysis offered in lines 1–8 if the young man changes his way of thinking about marriage. Having just accused him of self-hate, he now preserves the housing metaphor of 7–8 by protesting against the lodging of such hate in such a beautiful body. In 10–11 'gentle', 'presence' and 'gracious' are all words associated with aristocracy, and have been cited to support the deduction that the young man is of a higher social class than S. His 'presence', his outward appearance, has all these qualities, so his thought, which lodges in his heart, should be more worthy of its lodgings and should also be kind, at least to himself.

In 13 'thee' is important in the argument. It means 'for yourself', as in common parlance 'Make yourself a cup of tea.' Nobody in their right mind hearing this thinks that he is being invited to change into a cup of tea, but Kerrigan (1986) repeats Booth's absurd suggestion that the phrase suggests 'make yourself into another self', that the young man should undergo some moral reform – an idea irrelevant to the characterisation and the context. He is making for himself another self, having a son, not making himself into another person.

In this same line comes a shock, where the young man is asked to marry and have children 'for love of me'. The first nine poems are all devoted to pleading with the youth to marry. They praise his beauty as part of the argument for procreation. Now, for the first time, comes clear mention of love between poet and addressee, a sudden change of course in the argument of the Sonnets. This shock is not a clear statement of S's love for the young man, but just a passing cliché suggesting that the young man could possibly love him in some sense. By itself, it could mean very little, but, in the light of the poems that follow, it has to be given more weight. The young man allows S to speak like this, while S is writing a cycle of 17 poems urging him to marry. It is the first appearance of a love that will be roundly declared in Sonnet 18, and will provide the basic subject matter of the whole collection.

This revelation calls for a rereading of the previous sonnets, and this shows that the sudden intrusion may not be so sudden. The first line of Sonnet 8 may be the stirrings of this emotion, and it may even be lurking in 9.13. 'For love of me' demands also a re-reading of this whole Sonnet 10. Lines 1 and 4 have said that the young man loves nobody. Line 9 asks him to change his thought, and turn to love. Now in 10.13 'for love of me' is an appeal to the young man to marry a woman and beget children to oblige the man he loves. This is a glimpse of the astonishing dramatic situation which has burst into the narrative of the Sonnets. The full realisation is yet to come in Sonnet 20.

Vendler has a valuable comment: 'Sonnet 10 is the first poem to use the first-person singular, *I* and *me*. Such a moment in lyric is the equivalent of the entry of a new *dramatis persona* on the stage ... In what asks to be taken as a startling moment of personal sentiment, the speaker cries ... *O change thy thought, that I may change my mind.*' She also calls this a 'rather uninteresting sonnet'.

The last two lines plead with the young man to have a son so that beauty should live on in himself while he lives, or after his death in his children 'in thee or thine.' This is plain sailing, but it is not what is written: 'That beauty still might live in thine or thee.' The order 'in thine or thee' is tantalising. Perhaps 'in thee or thine' would have come too close to contemplating the death of the beautiful youth. Or perhaps, more simply, the cliché is abandoned for the sake of the rhyme.

℘ 11 ℃

As fast as thou shalt wane, so fast thou grow'st
In one of thine, from that which thou departest,
And that fresh blood which youngly thou bestow'st,
Thou mayst call thine, when thou from youth convertest.   4

Herein lives wisdom, beauty, and increase;
Without this, folly, age, and cold decay.
If all were minded so, the times should cease
And threescore year would make the world away.   8

Let those whom Nature hath not made for store,
Harsh, featureless, and rude, barrenly perish.
Look whom she best endow'd, she gave thee more,
Which bounteous gift thou should'st in bounty cherish.   12

    She carv'd thee for her seal, and meant thereby
    Thou should'st print more, not let that copy die.

As quickly as you decline, so quickly will you grow in a son,
   and the blood you give when young you can call yours when you are old.
In this lies wisdom; outside it mankind would soon cease.
Those who are not good breeding stock can die out, but Nature
   has endowed you, and your duty is to take care of her riches.
She made you to be her seal, and meant you to print more,
   not let the original die.

1–4   The crude paraphrase above says 'will you grow', but Shakespeare is
bolder, 'thou grow'st'. It is already happening, although his point is that it
isn't. The steady pace of the monosyllables in the first two lines mimics the
pace of the waning and growing. To say a man wanes as fast as he grows is
a paradox, heightened by the fact that waning is usually a matter for the
moon, which does not wax and wane at the same time. The young man
grows from that [point] which he departs [from], and 'depart a place' is the

same usage as our 'depart this life'. That point is the birth of his child. From that moment he waxes in the person of his son, though in himself he wanes as he ages. In 3–4 he will be able to say that when he was young he gave fresh blood to his child, and, although he is converting to being old, he will be able to claim that young blood as his own. The rhyme is better than it looks. 'Convertest' was pronounced 'convartest' (see also 14.12).

5–8 To have children is three things, and not to have children is three others. This could easily be a turning of the rhetorical handle to produce three neat contrasting pairs – wisdom is the opposite of folly, and increase is opposed to decay. But the triple balance is disturbed to shake the reader into sensing that age brings the opposite of beauty. Emphasis may be given to 'increase', the point of the argument, if line 5 is read in strict iambic rhythm with an accent on 'and', 'Hereín lives wísdom, beáuty, ánd incréase'.

At the centre of the poem the focus moves out to a world-view. Without procreation, 'the times', the generations of men, would cease, and 60 years would make man's world decay. This is vividly put, but not an exaggeration. The broad thought is common enough. Evans (1996) quotes Thomas Wilson (1553), 'Take awaie mariage, and howe many shall remain after a hundreth yeres.' Shakespeare is sharper. In Elizabethan times very few survived into their sixties (Picard 2003, 89). If there were no births from 1600 to 1660, the few survivors would be geriatric, and that would dispose of life on the planet, 'would make the world away'.

9–12 The argument moves on. Breeding is essential but not everyone should breed. The young man, however, has a duty to do so. 'Store' was regularly used of livestock (*OED* 4), so in 9 'those whom Nature hath not made for store' has an agricultural tinge, those she does not intend to keep for breeding, not her 'store cattle'. These ill-favoured specimens are described in the harsh rhythms of 12, 'Hársh, féatureless, and rúde, bárrenly pérish.' The first two syllables jolt metrical expectations, and so does the key word 'bárrenly', where the expected iambic beat would come on the second syllable, 'barrénly pérish'. The extra syllable of the feminine ending, 'perish', adds to the effect.

In line 11 'Look whom' is a dramatic way of saying 'whoever', a turn of phrase met also at 9.9 ('Look what'). 'Whoever Nature best endowed [with beauty], she gave more to you, and you ought to cherish this generous gift by generously passing it to succeeding generations' (11–12). The thought has already occurred in 4.4–6. In the Quarto this line ends 'she gave the more', but 'the' makes poor sense in the argument. It would be fatuous to say, 'Whoever she best endowed she gave the more to'. 'The' was a common spelling of 'thee', as in *The Marriage of Wit and Wisdom* (before 1590), 'Didest the nere se man before?' (*OED* thee 1c).

13–14 In Elizabethan English a copy could be a pattern which is copied (*OED* 8c), as in *H5* 3.1.24, 'Be copy now to men of grosser blood.' Nature has 'carved' the youth [with her own hands, as though he were a woodcut] as a seal with which to stamp future copies. It is his duty not to allow that original to perish.

Duncan-Jones (1997), on 'youngly thou bestow'st' in line 3
You give your blood (semen) to a wife while you are young, and, perhaps, in a youthful manner.

When I do count the clock that tells the time
And see the brave day sunk in hideous night,
When I behold the violet past prime
And sable curls all silver'd o'er with white,   4
When lofty trees I see bárren of leaves,
Which erst from heat did canopy the herd,
And summer's green all girded up in sheaves
Borne on the bier with white and bristly beard –   8

Then, of thy beauty do I question make
That thou among the wastes of time must go,
Since sweets and beauties do themselves forsake,
And die as fast as they see others grow,   12
   And nothing 'gainst Time's scythe can make defence
   Save breed, to brave him when he takes thee hence.

*When I count the ticking of the clock, see day become night, and seasons pass,
then I realise your beauty too must die. The only defence is to breed.*

1–8 The monosyllables of the first line demand to be read at a measured
pace, to make the ticking of the clock audible, not only in the alliteration
of the stressed syllables in 'count the clock' and 'tell the time', but also in
what comes between the ticks, 'the … that … the', a wearisome sound in
a [sleepless] night. This leads to a catalogue of decay, to day submerged in
hideous night, to violets past their prime, bare winter trees, summer's
green dead in the harvest, and then to thoughts of the end of the young
man's beauty and his life, articulated in this one great arch of a sentence,
'When I do count and see', 'When I behold', 'When I see', all gathered in
by 'Then, … do I question make'.

   The key to the working of the poetry is line 4. The sable curls clearly
refer to human beings, and so invite the reader to see references to human
life in other items in the catalogue. In line 2 'brave' is often applied to
splendid apparel, as in 15.8. The line is about day and night, but it also
about the swagger of youth and the hideousness of age. The violet is past

47

its prime, its spring, but a human being also has a prime, like the mother's prime at 3.10 or the beloved's 'pure unstainèd prime' at 70.8. Lines 5–6 may picture powerful men who have lived in state and protected their people, but are now old, all the more vividly suggested by the jolt in the iambic rhythm at 'bárren', 'When lófty trées I sée bárren of léaves', recalling an effect already found in 11.10. The grain which had been green in the summer is now white like the old man's hair in line 4, tied up in sheaves and carried in carts (a bier is defined as a hand-barrow in OED 1). But corpses also are carried on biers, 'movable stands' (OED 2). Elizabethan men often had beards, and barley has a beard, its awn, or 'spinous process that terminates its grain-sheath'. The girded (bound) sheaves carried on carts are seen as old men's bearded corpses strapped on biers as they were borne to their graves. Sound patterns add to the gloom:

> *And* summer's *green* all *girded* up in *sheaves*
> *Borne* on the *bier* with white and *bristly beard.*

Line 8 is the climax of these indirect allusions to human life, and it is marked by metre. It is the first line in the poem which begins with inversion of the initial stress, 'Bórne on the bier'.

9–14 This inversion could occur again, as audible punctuation, in line 9, and only there, 'Thén, of thy beauty do I question make', but the question is answered without being asked. He must go among the wastes of time. Before him, in Marvell's words in *To his Coy Mistress*, 'lie deserts of vast eternity'. Beauties and sweets, like the young man (13.4 and 8), cease to be what once they were, 'themselves forsake', and move towards death as fast as their successors grow. Of course, if he had sons he would grow as fast as he declines (11.1).

The harvest analogy resurfaces in the final couplet, where Time is the reaper with his irresistible scythe, and it is felt again in the final words, as they speak of the death of the beautiful young man as his removal hence, 'taken away', no doubt as described in line 8, cut down and carried away on a bier. There is only one defence against Time, and that message of hope is not advanced until the last line of the poem, where 'breed' is sometimes taken as a noun meaning 'offspring', 'nothing can make defence | Save offspring to brave him, when he takes thee hence.' The word 'breed' occurs some ninety times in Shakespeare, and except for half a dozen of these it is always a verb, and it makes much more vigorous sense if read as an imperative verb here, 'nothing can make defence unless [go] breed.' Besides, if the word is understood as a verb, it is the dead father that will brave Time, even as Time takes him away. It is easy for a young heir to brave death, but much more spirited if the deceased testator shows defiance. The comma here supplied after 'breed' makes this clear and dramatic. On this explanation the twist in the language when 'breed' is an imperative is colloquial and effective, as in lines 9–10 above, where a question becomes a statement even as it is asked, 'Then of thy beauty do I question make *that* thou must go'.

Duncan-Jones (1997) on line 13
Sexual innuendo furnishes a more positive reading. The *nothing* which lies between women's legs (cf. *Ham* 3.2.115–17) can *save*, or preserve, the *breed*, or offspring, which will counteract the destructive force of *time's scythe*.

O that you were your self, but, love, you are
No longer yours than you yourself here live.
Against this coming end you should prepare,
And your sweet semblance to some other give.   4
So should that beauty which you hold in lease
Find no determination. Then you were
Your self again after yourself's decease,
When your sweet issue your sweet form should bear.   8

Who lets so fair a house fall to decay,
Which husbandry in honour might uphold
Against the stormy gusts of winter's day
And barren rage of death's eternal cold?   12
    O none but unthrifts. Dear my love, you know
    You had a father. Let your son say so.

If only you were the owner of yourself, but, since you are not,
    you ought to hand on the pattern, so that your beauty may survive.
    Then your sweet self would live on in your son after your death.
The tenant has to maintain a house and keep out the deathly cold.
    You had a father. Let your son say the same.

1–8 Sonnet 10 ended with a passing mention of love for the young man.
Sonnet 13 begins and ends addressing him as 'love' and 'Dear my love'.
More subtly, Kerrigan (1986) explains that 'the poet takes a further step
towards intimacy … by shifting from "thou" to "you".' He argues that
'thou' has a more formal ring, and that in using 'you' Shakespeare is
seeking a less conventional idiom. This may be confirmed by the pleading
tone of the opening and praise of the young man's sweetness (three times),
his beauty, and the fair body he inhabits. It is as though Shakespeare's
feeling has been gradually deepening, or as though he were becoming ever
more aware of it, building up dramatically to the rapture of Sonnet 18 and
the realisation in Sonnet 20.

Sonnet 13 plays prodigiously with two senses of 'yourself': emphatic, 'You know it yourself'; and philosophical, 'You have a self, but is it yours, or do you have only a temporary lease of it?' In each of the four occurrences in the poem the Quarto follows the normal Renaissance practice of writing as two words, 'your self'. To help the reader through this thorny argument, this edition prints 'your self' when the philosophical sense is uppermost, in lines 1 and 7. In reading the first line it may be useful to stress 'your' against the metre, 'O that you were yóur self'. It is only *his* self while he lives. It will not be his when he is dead. 'Against this coming end' (Shakespeare makes no bones about it) 'you should give a likeness of yourself to a child.' Then (6–8), 'If you do that, you would be yourself again, your self would still exist in the person of your offspring, although you yourself would no longer be alive. Your lovely children would then have your loveliness.' Those who find this explanation too simple may be helped by Booth's analysis reprinted at the end of this note.

In line 5, the beloved's beauty is his only on leasehold, but, if he marries and has a son, it will be held on a lease which has no expiry date. 'Determination' is a legal technical term for the 'cessation of an estate or interest of any kind' (*OED* 1).

9–14 At 10.7 the young man's beauty was a roof, with some poetic effect. Now his sweet form is a house, its whole structure in danger of collapse by the action of wind and rain, but it could be saved by 'husbandry in honour'. 'Husbandry' refers to the management of a household or a farm (*OED* 2) and also, as here, to other functions of a husband. The same pun works in 3.6. 'Husbandry in honour' is a direct allusion to the first prayer in the Solemnization of Matrimony in the Book of Common Prayer, 'to join together this man and this woman in holy Matrimony; which is an honourable estate'. The youth is being urged to marry, to have children and to maintain a house. But the house is also his beauty, and who could neglect 'so fair a house?' Without husbandry the house is exposed to cold and to gusts of winter winds on stormy days; without a wife the young man's beauty will suffer the barren cold of death for all eternity.

13–14 After the long and eloquent question, the short answer, 'O none but unthrifts.' The drama, as in so many of these sonnets, is in the speaking voice, and here the bite is in the brevity. A strong break in sense in mid-line is not common in these poems, and when it does occur it tends to be at dramatic moments. Perhaps line 6 above is one of these after 'determination'. This tone is lost by those who follow the Quarto and punctuate at the end of line 13. With the punctuation given above, what he knows is more to the point, and it is stated in a smiling, wheedling tone –

> Dear my love, you know
> You had a father. Let your son say so.

– which teasingly wrongfoots the young man by appealing to his common-sense: of course he knows he had a father.

Booth (1977) on lines 1–2
These lines present four different sentences; each succeeding phrase changes the nature of what precedes it. *O that you were yourself* is a standard idiomatic expression meaning 'I wish you were in good health' or 'I wish you were as you usually are'; the completed line presents a simple contradiction, an apparent paradox: 'I wish you were yourself (i.e. in good health), but you *are* yourself'; the next potential sentence demands that a reader take conscious note of the posses-sive element, 'your', in *yourself* (Which Q prints as two words – see Preface p. xvii): *O that you were yourself, but love you are | No longer yours*, 'O that you were your own (i.e. were free, were owner of yourself [with a play on the idea of being self-possessed – cf. 94.7]), but, my love, you are not in possession anymore'; the final phrase of line 2 reveals the 'no longer than' construction and again changes the meaning of the whole by making the reader's understanding of *no longer* obsolete: 'you own yourself only as long as you remain alive.' See 141.13–14, note; and compare 133.5.

Vendler (1997)
As I understand this poem, it is the first of many 'reply-sonnets', poems which respond to an implied anterior utterance from the young man. We are to imagine that the young man has said, in response to earlier reproaches, 'I am myself, sufficient to myself.' The speaker replies, as the sonnet opens, 'Oh that that were true! *O that you were your self* [*in some permanent fashion*]; *but, love, you are No longer yours than you yourself here live.*' Such 'replies' to implied remarks by the young man reach their apogee in sonnets 76, 110, 116, and 117.

Not from the stars do I my judgement pluck,
And yet methinks I have astronomy,
But not to tell of good or evil luck,
Of plagues, or dearths, or seasons' quality.   4
Nor can I fortune to brief minutes tell,
Pointing to each his thunder, rain, and wind,
Or say with princes if it shall go well,
By oft predict that I in heaven find.   8

But from thine eyes my knowledge I derive,
And, constant stars, in them I read such art
As truth and beauty shall together thrive
If from thyself to store thou would'st convert.   12

Or else of thee this I prognosticate—
Thy end is truth's and beauty's doom and date.

I have astronomy, not to predict plagues or famines or the weather,
and not to advise princes.
I derive my knowledge from those constant stars, your eyes,
where I read that truth and beauty will live on if you breed,
and, if not, that truth and beauty die with you.

1–8 'Astronomy' is here used in its archaic sense of 'astrology', and astrology is the target of Shakespeare's ridicule throughout, although he never uses the word. It is the astrologer who plucks (note the effortless ease) knowledge from the stars. 'Methinks' is gently ironic as always in the Sonnets. At 62.5, 104.11 and 112.14 it occurs where he does not seriously mean what he is saying. In 'I have astronomy' he is pretending to boast about his proficiency ('have' as in 'he hath neither Latin, French nor Italian' in *MV* 1.2.66–7). But S's area of expertise is not predictions of plagues, or famines, the stock in trade of contemporary prophets, nor is it long-range weather forecasting, 'seasons' quality' ('It will be a bad winter and a late spring'), nor will he be able to point at every minute of the day and point to his thunder, rain or wind ('his' in the sense of 'its', as usual with a touch of personification). The astrologer points at the sky and tells the minutes who are his customers, 'You will have thunder, you will have rain, and you wind'. The 'brief minutes' in line 5 add to the contempt, since the minute was the minutest unit of time usually measured by the Elizabethans. The first recorded use of 'second' in a chronological sense was in 1588. This degree of precision would be true virtuosity in an astrologer. The implication is that astrologers, like contemporary weather forecasters, cannot predict the weather, and the satire is intensified by 'Pointing' in line 6. Ancient astronomers, and no doubt astrologers too, used a rod – Greek *rabdos*, Latin *radius* – to measure distances and angles in the heavens. An astrologer might well use his rod with a flourish. Anchises, with a curl of the lip, leaves that sort of work to Greeks in Virgil, *Aeneid* 6.849–50, '*caelique meatus describent radio*', 'Others will measure the courses of the heavens with a rod.' S here leaves it to astrologers. The more frequent their favourable predictions, the greater would be their rewards. The phrase 'by oft predict' is doubly odd, first in that 'predict' never occurs elsewhere as a noun in Shakespeare or in *OED*, second in that 'oft' is an adverb used to qualify a noun (7.2). All this pomposity smells of gobbledegook.

9–12 S has mocked astrologers, yet claimed in the second line that he is one. Line 9 echoes line 1, minus the sneer in 'pluck'. But he is no ordinary astrologer. They base their prophecies on *wandering* planets (in Greek the planets are *planetai*, wanderers). He derives his knowledge from *fixed* stars, his beloved's eyes. The young man's eyes will not wander to infidelity. For the first time in the sonnets the young man's truth is an object of praise.

In line 7 he insisted that he could not predict whether 'it *shall go well*' with princes. Now he claims that he reads in the stars 'such art | As [can show that] truth and beauty *shall* together *thrive*' if the beloved would beget a son, if he would transfer from himself to put into store for future generations. 'Store' has just been used in 11.9 to mean 'breeding stock'.

13–14 The wit continues to the end with the portentous polysyllabic verb 'prognosticate' (only here in Shakespeare) and no doubt with the alliteration of 'doom and date', the very stock in trade of astrologers. This is his grand prognostication, delivered with a smile. The message might be pointed by an emphasis against the metre on 'this', 'Or élse of thée thís I prognósticáte'.

℘ 15 ℃

When I consider everything that grows
Holds in perfection but a little moment,
That this huge stage presenteth nought but shows
Whereon the stars in secret influence comment;   4
When I perceive that men as plants increase,
Cheerèd and checked ev'n by the selfsame sky,
Vaunt in their youthful sap, at height decrease,
And wear their brave state out of memory,   8

Then the conceit of this inconstant stay
Sets you most rich in youth before my sight,
Where wasteful Time debateth with Decay
To change your day of youth to sullied night,   12
   And all in war with Time for love of you
   As he takes from you, I engraft you new.

When I think how short is the prime of life for everything that grows;
  when I see that men increase and decrease like plants –
then I visualise your decay, and engraft you on to a new stock.

1–8 The sun in Sonnet 7, music in 8, growth and harvest in 12, house maintenance in 13, astrology in 14 – many of these sonnets have a dominant metaphor. Here in 15 there are three minor motifs, the theatre, astrology, and war, all of them ignored in the above summary to highlight the overarching metaphor from plants.

   The theatrical scene appears in lines 3–4, where perfection lasts a little moment on the world's huge stage. The metaphor continues in 5–6, when men and plants are 'cheerèd and checked'. Actors are sometimes applauded, and sometimes rebuked, as they certainly were by the robust audiences in the Elizabethan theatre. They were 'checked' in the sense that Prince Hal was rebuked by Falstaff for boxing the ear of the Lord Chief Justice: 'I have checked him for it, and the young lion repents' (*2H4* 1.2.196). 'Cheerèd and checked' is an example of the delight Shakespeare takes in making two different things sound similar, called simulation (4.4).

After its role in Sonnet 14, astrology re-enters in line 4, where shows are put on for an audience of stars. 'Influence' is a technical term, 'the supposed *flowing* from the stars of an etherial *fluid* acting upon the character and destiny of man, and affecting sublunary things generally' (*OED*). Shakespeare refers to this as 'skyey influences' in *MM* 3.1.9, and 'planetary influence' in *KL* 1.2.123. 'Comment' often suggests adverse criticism, as in 95.6, so the stars are influential critics – a return to the theatrical metaphor. 'Secret' points to astrology as one of the occult sciences. It also hints at a paradox. How could a theatrical performance be affected by secret criticism? Astrology lingers in line 6, where men and plants are affected by that same 'skyey influence', and in 7, where men and plants 'at height decrease' (see also 7.9–10). 'Influence' is pronounced as two syllables with a slurring of -ue-. Booth (1977) reads the word with three syllables and so produces a twelve-syllable line, 'Whereón the stárs with sécret ínfluénce commént'. This has disadvantages. No other line in the Sonnets has twelve syllables, and this pronunciation of 'commént' weakens the rhyme with 'móment', which was never perfect.

These are minor motifs, but in 5 the plant metaphor takes over, 'men as plants increase', both cheered [by sun and rain], and their 'Sap checked with frost' as at 5.7. Both glory in that youthful sap and at their peak they both decline, and even decrease in size. 'Brave state' implies rich colouring in flowers and in the robes of men. In *PP* 12.4, Shakespeare has 'Youth like summer brave', and *OED* offers: 'One man is ragged, and another brave' (1612). But bravery soon departs. The bright colours of flowers and the gorgeous robes of the wealthy and powerful fade, but old petals hang on and shabby old robes and uniforms are still worn when the splendour of their wearers is forgotten and their bodies shrunken. They 'at height decrease | And wear their brave state out of memory'.

9–14 In rhetoric a conceit is a fanciful or ingenious expression or thought, here the notion that plants and men have a short life, 'this inconstant stay'. But all is not simple. The phrase is also an oxymoron, defined in the commentary on 1.12. A *stay* should not be incon*stant*, but should *stand* a while. In 9 enter the young man in all the richness, the brave state, of youth, its flamboyant costume. In an inveterate punster like Shakespeare we might hear a pun in line 10. 'You-th is you-ness in this adoring pun,' writes Vendler (1997), and there are six echoes of it in the last three lines, which Vendler dares to call 'a hymn to the human love- syllable *you*'.

There he stands (on the stage?), where a debate is going on between Time and Decay as they plot to see this youth's 'brave day sunk in hideous night' (12.2). Against these forces S declares total war. He loves the young man, and sees Time stripping his shoots, no doubt with his sickle, scythe or crooked knife (100.14, 116.10), so 'As he takes from you, I engraft you new', picking up the cuttings and grafting them on to a new root-stock, namely his own poetry. He will defeat Time and Decay by giving immortality in his verse. After the war metaphor in which two irresistible enemies plot against defenceless Beauty and the poet takes arms against them, the poem now returns to the plant metaphor.

Careful writers avoid mixed metaphors. Shakespeare glories in them and intertwines. It is as though he cannot bear to leave number one when he is embarked on number two. If this note is near the truth, the imagery here is complicated and important. Given 14 lines and 4 metaphors, it could be charted as follows, where P = plant, T = theatre, A = astrology, W = war:

1	2	3	4	5	6	7	8	9	10	11	12	13	14
P	T	AT	P	APT	AP	P			T	TW	W	TW	APW

This is perhaps an over-simplification. Some see King Lear in 8 and the sky in 12.

It is difficult to write usefully about the sound of poetry, but the sound must be heard. A standard variant is inversion of the iambic te-tum beat in the first two syllables, 'Hólds in perféction' (line 2). Another, less common, is the addition of an eleventh syllable, as in lines 2 and 4, known as the feminine ending, discussed in the commentary on Sonnet 20. These are common variants, but it sometimes pays to heed them. Here, for instance, 'Hólds in perféction' has emphasis and space, and the duration of perfection becomes pitifully short as the verse dribbles to its trivial close, 'Hólds in perféction but a líttle móment'. Here, 'but' would be expected to carry the verse accent, but if it is not accented 'perfection' is snuffed out and the line is more expressive. The monosyllables which begin line 3 demand a broad delivery. 'That thís húge stáge' overwhelms our iambic expectations. In line 4, 'Whereon the stars in sécret ínfluence cómment', the four sibilants in 'stars in secret influence comment' might be spoken in relief to mimic the whispering of the silent stars, the critics. This suggestion is so tentative that it would not have been made but for similar sounds from the audience in line 6, 'cheerèd ... checked ... selfsame ... sky'.

In line 5, 'When I perceive' keys into the first words of the poem, 'When I consider', and the two are caught up by the voice at the beginning of line 9, 'Then'. This poem is one sentence, and these constructive words articulate the syntax and the rhetoric. In line 6 plants are 'cheerèd' in the full and generous form of the verb, but 'checked' in a sharper, scanter sound. In line 8 a measured delivery of 'and wéar their bráve státe out of mémory' would use the three stressed monosyllables to inflate what is about to be punctured, 'out of mémory'. As discussed at the end of the note on Sonnet 12, monosyllables are common weapons in Shakespeare's armoury. They perform again in 15.10, 'Sets you most rich in youth', and in all of the last three lines. This device of Anglo-Saxon eloquence is particularly to be caught by the voice where it occurs most conspicuously, in the first lines or final couplets, often too in lines 8 and 9, the end of the octet and the opening of the sestet.

Alliteration is another mighty weapon. It is not easy to interpret alliterations like 'Cheerèd and checked' or 'conceit of this inconstant stay', but it is important to hear them. Assonance, repetition of vowel sounds, as in 'trúth's and beáuty's dóom (14.14), is subtler but no less vital. It is easy to make such suggestions about the delivery of verse, and easier still to overact the sounds. But the poetry takes on new life if we hear it well read in our heads or, better still, read it aloud slowly in private.

Pooler (1918) in Rollins (1944), on line 6
What is marvelous is that Shakespeare by means of these inexplicable hints and glimpses succeeds in turning the solid earth into a scene of illusions and change.

ʂ 16 ೞ

But wherefore do not you a mightier way
Make war upon this bloody tyrant Time,
And fortify yourself in your decay
With means more blessèd than my barren rhyme?   4

Now stand you on the top of happy hours,
And many maiden gardens yet unset,
With virtuous wish would bear your living flowers,
Much liker than your painted counterfeit.   8

So should the lines of life that life repair
Which this time's pencil or my pupil pen,
Neither in inward worth nor outward fair,
Can make you live yourself in eyes of men.   12
    To give away yourself keeps yourself still,
    And you must live drawn by your own sweet skill.

In the war against time you have a more effective weapon than my verse.
Many maidens wish to bear your son, a likeness closer than your portrait.
Neither painting nor my poetry can give you life.
   To keep yourself you must give yourself away.

In Sonnet 15, S proposes to keep the young man alive by his verse, but now
in Sonnet 16 he urges a more effective method. The two poems are closely
related. The first word of 16 attaches it to the end of 15, 'I engraft you new',
but there is 'a mightier way'. Other links are the war against the enemies
Time and Decay in 15.13, a war which continues in 16.1–3 with 'mightier',
'bloody' and 'fortify'. In 15.7 men 'at height decrease', and in 16.5 the
beloved is standing 'on the top of happy hours'; the plant metaphor of 15
fills 16.5–8; S's claim for his poetry at 15.14 is undermined not only in 16.1,
but also in 10–12, and particularly in line 4, where the rhyme is barren. The
graft of 15.14 has not taken.

1–4   The obvious advice would be to 'fortify yourself *against* decay', but the young man is a sadder case: he is already *in* decay, since men begin to decay the moment they reach maturity, 'at height decrease' (15.7). Decay has ceased to be a combatant by 16.3, and so loses his capital letter. The Quarto has no authority for its use of initial capitals. For no imaginable reason it capitalises Time in 15.13 and 16.10, but not in 15.11 or 16.2.

The gist of the argument is that the young man should marry and have children. In view of that, 'blessèd' before 'barren' suggests 'blessed with children' (as in 3.4). Shakespeare thinks in opposites (see 'living' and 'painted' in 7–8, and also the examples in lines 10, 11 and 13). Not only that, when he is looking at a pair, he often uses words similar in sound, 'blessèd' and 'barren', 'pencil' and 'pen', 'inward' and 'outward'. (See Introduction, p. 6, on simulation.)

5–8   The primary meaning of line 5 is that the beloved is at the peak of his life (and therefore has to act soon), but there may be an extra picture. In an Elizabethan garden sundials were sometimes mounted vertically on a south-facing wall with a projecting pointer which cast its shadow on the hours numbered in an arc beneath it. The 'happy hours' would be the bright hours in the middle of the day, and what stands above them would be the sun, casting the shadow of the pointer down to the number XII at noon. If this conceit was in Shakespeare's mind, the young man is standing above the hours. In Sonnets 7 and 33 he is as the sun; here he is as the sun at noon.

In horticulture, to set often means to plant, usually a seedling (*OED* 12). So here 'unset' gardens are virtuous maidens who would wish to bear the young man's children within the bonds of holy matrimony. These children would be flowers grown from his seed, and they would be living likenesses and therefore more like him, 'Much liker than' his painted portrait could be. This 'painted counterfeit' has been used to support the guess that the beloved was from a family of substance which would be likely to commission a portrait of their young son.

9–14   The young man is in decay in line 3, and the 'lines of life' in 9 should repair that life, renew it. In 10 a pencil is a fine paintbrush (Latin *penis* = tail, *peniculum* = little tail, brush), and neither contemporary painting, 'this time's pencil', nor S's pen can repair his life. 'Lines of life' has exercised commentators. Ingram and Redpath (1978) list ten different interpretations, culminating in one of Empson's mischievous suggestions, that 'line' here is 'the line fixed in the continuum with which space-time theorists describe such reality as they allow to a particle'. It is his blood lines that will renew his life, not lines drawn in a portrait, and not the lines of S's poetry. Painter and poet are both gently mocked. The painter's pencil would try to show the 'outward fair', that is the visible beauty; the poet is just a learner and his pupil pen might hope rather to catch the 'inward worth'. But neither would succeed in making him live for men to see.

On the other hand, he keeps himself if he gives himself away in marriage and is seen in the person of his son. No artist or poet has the skill for this. He has to draw himself by his own skill, and that is sweet because it is deployed in love. If he is going to live, he must live by means of that. Readers will hear, and use, the variation in the iambic beat, perhaps

To gíve awáy yoursélf kéeps yourself stíll
And you must líve dráwn by your ówn swéet skíll.

ဆ 17 ଔ

Who will believe my verse in time to come
If it were filled with your most high deserts,
Though yet heav'n knows it is but as a tomb
Which hides your life, and shows not half your parts?   4

If I could write the beauty of your eyes
And in fresh numbers number all your graces,
The age to come would say, 'This poet lies.
Such heav'nly touches ne'er touched earthly faces.'   8
So should my papers, yellowed with their age,
Be scorned, like old men of less truth than tongue,
And your true rights be termed a poet's rage
And stretchèd metre of an antique song.   12

But were some child of yours alive that time,
You should live twice, in it and in my rhyme.

My verse conveys only a fraction of your qualities.
If it were a full description, posterity would put it down
*   to poetic exaggeration.*
But, if you had a child, you would live in it, and in my verse.

1–4   In Shakespeare it pays to remember the literal meaning of the words.
'Heaven knows' in line 3 is a casual cliché for us, but it is not a phrase used
lightly in Shakespeare. After the beloved's 'high deserts' and 'a tomb' in
lines 2–3, 'heav'nly' and 'earthly' in 8 carry the thought that knowledge of
the beloved's deserts has reached the heights of heaven, and heaven therefore is well aware that in this verse they are buried in the grave. Just as a
tomb hides a life, and an epitaph reveals only a fraction of the deserts of the
dead, so S's verse hides the beloved's life and reveals only a fraction of his
parts, his qualities. 'Deserts' rhymes with 'parts' (11.2, 49.10). 'Yet' suggests 'even if it were full of the beloved's qualities, it *still* is just a tomb.'

Burrow (2002) has an excellent note on 'filled', proving that the Quarto reading 'fild' does not suggest any notion of 'filing'.

5–12 'If I could write the beauty of your eyes' – this is absurd, as S well knew. No man can write beauty. 'Write' is used to mean 'outline', 'draw' (*OED* 1a), 'a sense recorded as late as 1590, but only in the consciously archaic world of Spenser's *Fairie Queene*', according to Burrow (2002), quoting 2.8.43, which describes a shield 'Whereon the Faery Queenes pourctract was writ'. S is slipping into archaic language as though his poetry were already outdated. He is mocking his verse in order to show that it would not be believed unless the young man had a son, and this contempt is conveyed throughout lines 5–12. 'Fresh' is part of this line of argument. Even if he could write the graces of the young man in fresh poetry, the paper it was written upon would soon be yellowed with age, and they would call it 'an antique song', and say that 'This poet lies.' 'Antique' carries with it a touch of 'antic', of madness, as when Hamlet thinks fit 'To put an antic disposition on' at 1.5.173.

Line 6 highlights the ludicrous impossibility of writing beauty, by the grotesque juxtaposition of 'numbers number', where 'numbers' means poetic measures, verses, and 'number' means count. Repetition of a word in a different form is polyptoton. This is an acute polyptoton, the same word used not only in a different form but also with a different meaning. A similar trick is played in line 8, 'Such heav'nly touches ne'er touched earthly faces.' Here 'touches' are vivid details, and 'touched' refers to contact. The polyptoton comes in a telling symmetry, 'heav'nly touches ... touched earthly', and this chiasmus, ABBA, throws the central 'ne'er' into relief, 'Such *héav'nly tóuches* né'er *touched éarthly* fáces.' The heavenly 'tóuches' carry a stress, which is not granted when earthly faces are 'touched', and all this trickery gives a passing glimpse of an angel touching the young man's face.

Shakespeare the satirist is at work in what follows, the cruelty of 'old men of less truth than tongue', where he is putting a barb on a wordy old proverb, 'Old men and travellers may lie with authority.' The barb is the resemblance in sound between the two words of a pair (16.4, 10 and 11). 'Tongue' is all the more unkind because of the alliteration with 'truth', and the monosyllabic line contributes.

'A poet's rage' is not anger, but inspired lunacy, as when Theseus smiles at 'The poet's eye, in a fine frenzy rolling' in *MND* 5.1.12. *Furor poeticus* has a long history going back at least as far as Plato's *Phaedrus* 245. So this ancient lore will be dredged up by future generations when they read these sonnets, and they will condemn them as 'the stretchèd metre of an antique song'. A 'stretchèd metre' would then apply to lines of verse stretched because they are swollen with flattery. Again the sound may support the sense. After the shorter forms, *fill'd*, *touch'd*, *yellow'd*, *scorn'd* and *term'd*, 'the *stretchèd* metre of an antique song' sounds even more passé. It is also a dig at the long lines, fourteeners, used by earlier English poets such as Golding, quoted in the commentary on 60.1–4, and by Shakespeare's rival George Chapman, whose translation of Homer's *Iliad* was published in part in 1598, and complete in 1611 (see comment on Sonnet 86 and the sample quoted at the end of the comment on Sonnet 19).

13–14   This is the last 'procreation sonnet', and the procreation element here joins the theme of immortality through poetry. Without a child the beloved will perish – 'Who will believe my verse?' – but, with a child, the beloved will be alive, and be alive twice, in the child and in the poetry which will now be believed because the child's beauty will establish the beauty of the father. Burrow (2002) suggests that by 1590 'rhyme' could be used as a term of contempt: 'There is a modest shrug here to counterpoise the optimism. Cf. *rhymers* at 38.10.'

These sonnets present arguments. Often they raise a question or announce a topic in the opening lines, argue it and arrive at a conclusion in the final couplet. But groups of sonnets taken together may also present a developed argument. In Sonnet 15 he is engrafting the beloved on verse to effect his survival. In 16 the graft is barren, and he suggests a mightier way, that the beloved should have a child. Sonnet 17 ends by proposing the use of both methods. It is followed in 18 by an outpouring of love and a promise that his poetry will immortalise the beloved. Not that it is an easy undertaking. He knows what 'swift-footed Time' does 'To the wide world and all her fading sweets', but, despite Time's iniquities, 'My love shall in my verse ever live young' (19.5–6 and 13–14), but it will never again urge the young man to marry and have children.

Shall I compare thee to a summer's day?
Thou art more lovely and more temperate.

Rough winds do shake the darling buds of May,
And summer's lease hath all too short a date.   4
Sometime too hot the eye of heaven shines,
And often is his gold complexion dimmed,
And ev'ry fair from fair sometime declines,
By chance or Nature's changing course untrimmed.   8

But thy eternal summer shall not fade,
Nor lose possession of that fair thou ow'st,
Nor shall Death brag thou wand'rest in his shade,
When in eternal lines to time thou grow'st.   12
    So long as men can breathe or eyes can see,
    So long lives this, and this gives life to thee.

You are lovelier than a summer's day, and more temperate.
Summer days are short and may be spoiled by wind or heat or cloud.
Everything beautiful loses its beauty. But your summer will never fade.
    You will live for ever in these poems.

1–2 Men do not often praise their beloved for his or her temperance. S
does so here because it is one respect in which the young man is better than
a summer's day, which is liable to swing from one extreme to another.
Besides it does seem that there was something equable and steady about
him which S found attractive (5.2, 20.3–4). After the question comes the
general answer in one line, followed by six lines on the shortcomings of
summer, followed by six on the superiority of the beloved.

3–8 A summer's day is personified first as though it were a young man in
love with young darlings who are roughly treated. The personification
continues as S adds brevity to intemperance in the charge against summer.

He is now a tenant with a short lease on his accommodation. He has an eye, and a complexion, and the Elizabethan use of 'his' where we would write 'its' enlivens the verse by personifying summer. In line 7 'fair' is a noun meaning beauty, as in 16.11, and a broader indictment appears. Not only summer but every beauty declines. But the sun is still in the picture, since heavenly bodies decline when they set, 'The sun declines, day ancient grows' (OED (1607)), and it is still in the picture with 'course' in line 8. The sun has his courses in 59.6, 'five hundred courses of the sun'.

But now, at line 8, 'By ... Nature's changing course untrimmed', there is a glide to a new metaphor. Commentators take 'untrimmed' as meaning stripped of ornament. This does not fit the tight argument of the poem. Ornaments have nothing to do with the case. A more relevant meaning is in OED (trim 15), 'to adjust the (sails or yards) with reference to the direction of the wind or the *course* of the ship', as in Captain Smith (1624), 'Nor had we a mariner nor any had skill to trim the sayles.' Some chance or some change in Nature may disturb the trim of the sails and set a vessel off course. In human terms that might be absence or accident or age or illness. The nautical allusion first surfaced at 'course untrimmed' in 8, but in retrospect the sighting was at 'declines' in 7. Its first meaning in OED is 'to deviate (from the straight *course*)'.

9–14 The brevity of a summer's day prepares the way for the immortality of the beloved. The season has been dealt with in human terms, his darlings, his tenancy, his eye, his complexion. Now the man is dealt with in seasonal terms. The sun is often *dimmed* but the beloved's beauty shall *not fade*, but *grows* to eternity. All other beauties are *driven off course*, but the beloved *does not wander* in Death's shade. Elizabethans knew Psalm 23: 4, 'Yea, though I walk through the valley of the shadow of death ...' Summer's lease had 'all too short a date' in line 4, but the beloved shall not lose possession of the beauty he owns. The young man's 'possession' is here contrasted with 'summer's lease' in line 4, as in *TGV* 5.2.25–9, where Proteus pities the *'possessions'* of Thurio, 'that they are out of *lease*', and Julia 'that such an ass should *owe* them'. Summer's decline was described in 7–8, but by contrast the immortality of the beloved is prophesied in the resounding monosyllables of the last two lines. The whole glorious poem is a structure shaped to this point, the claim that the poet will confer immortality on the man he loves.

This claim began modestly in a horticultural metaphor in 15.14, 'I engraft you new.' In 16.1–2 it is downplayed, 'But wherefore do not you a mightier way | Make war upon this bloody tyrant Time?' The graft at the end of 15 turns out to be barren in 16.4. In 17.14 it reappears as one way to survive, and there is a better. Now at the end of 18 and 19 it becomes a confident commitment, '[Forget marriage and procreation.] These poems of mine will make you immortal.'

Duncan-Jones (1997)
[Line 8] encompasses both accidental and cyclical decay, 'untrimmed' suggesting both 'stripped of ornaments or trimmings' and 'set off balance'; for the second see *OED* trim 13a, 'to distribute the load of (a ship or boat) so that she floats on an even keel'. There may also be an allusion to menstruation, or 'monthly courses' (*OED* 27), in *nature's changing course*, implying that the youth transcends the physiological variability of female love-objects.

Devouring Time, blunt thou the lion's paws,
And make the earth devour her own sweet brood,
Pluck the keen teeth from the fierce tiger's jaws,
And burn the long-lived phoenix in her blood,   4
Make glad and sorry seasons as thou fleet'st
And do whate'er thou wilt, swift-footed Time,
To the wide world and all her fading sweets;

But I forbid thee one most heinous crime—   8
O carve not with thy hours my love's fair brow,
Nor draw no lines there with thine ántique pen,
Him in thy course untainted do allow
For beauty's pattern to succeeding men.   12

Yet do thy worst, old Time. Despite thy wrong
My love shall in my verse ever live young.

*Do what you will, devouring Time, to the world and all its beauties,
but do not carve wrinkles on my beloved's brow.*
   Let him be a pattern of beauty for future generations.
No. Do your worst. He will live and always be young in my poetry.

1–7 The idea of Time as devourer of things ('*tempus edax rerum*' in Ovid,
Metamorphoses 15.234) is not new. (A sample of Arthur Golding's translation of Ovid comes at the end of this note.) Why then are the lines so
arresting? 'Those four lines alone should redeem Shakespeare's Sonnets
from the neglect that has fallen upon them. I know of no quatrain in
English poetry more heroic, more swelling, more original or more climac-
tically finished' (Donnelly (1859), in Rollins 1944).
   The main poetic thrust is in the particulars of Time's four victims, all of
them formidable *but yet* all undone by Time, all of them presenting vivid
pictures and dramatic incidents, and all tautened by implicit contrasts. The
lion is the king of carnivores, the great devourer, *but yet* devouring Time

may blunt his paws. Lions are cats, and their fearsome paws strike with the speed of a cat. Shakespeare would have seen them at the Tower of London. When the 'bloody Clifford' is about to murder the young Earl of Rutland, 'So looks the pent-up lion o'er the wretch | That trembles under his devouring paws' (*3H6* 1.3.13–14). At rest a lion's paws look plump and furry, but the claws within them are 'large, strongly compressed, sharp, exerted by muscular action when the animal strikes its prey' (*Encyclopedia Britannica* (1911) 738a). *But yet* the enfeeblement of age blunts them.

In the second line Earth loves her children. They are all sweet to her, *but yet* devouring Time makes her devour them. 'Earth to earth' in the Order for the Burial of the Dead in the Book of Common Prayer is a commonplace, but Shakespeare's expression of it is anything but. The word 'brood' occurs nine times in Shakespeare and in six of these it refers to nestlings. The earth is seen as a mother bird and hens under stress do sometimes eat their own eggs, and even their own chicks. It is difficult to exclude the literal meaning of 'sweet'. On this interpretation lines 1–4 offer two mammals and two birds.

In real life teeth are pulled, not plucked, and the pulling can be extremely difficult. In line 3 these are not the teeth of a submissive patient, but the sharp teeth of a great cat, 'Pluck the keen teeth from the fierce tiger's jaws.' The effortless ease of plucking has already made a poetic point in 14.1. With this victim too there is an implicit contrast. Time easily plucks these teeth, *but yet* he plucks them from ferocious jaws. In old age even the tiger, like man, is 'sans teeth, sans eyes, sans taste, sans everything' (*AYL* 2.7.166).

According to legend, at any one time there is only one phoenix living, feminine in some authors, masculine in others. How then can the species be preserved? The answer here adopted is that each phoenix dies in flames after 500–600 years, and her successor is born from the ashes. She lives for many years, *but yet* in due course even she will be the victim of Time. Some discuss whether 'burns in her blood' means that she burns while alive, or burns while in the full vigour of her life. Neither. It rather describes the blood spurting from her burst arteries into the flames. Shakespeare may have seen it gushing from martyrs as they burned at the stake. According to Pliny, *Natural History* 10.3–4, the phoenix has purple plumage with a gleam of gold round its neck, and rose-coloured feathers standing out in its blue tail. To avert the eyes from the burning of this splendid bird in its own blood is to dowse the poetry. All this is not routine classicising. Londoners would see a phoenix. When James I entered London in pomp on 15 March 1604, on Thomas Dekker's spectacular Nova Arabia Felix arch at Cheapside he 'found himself imaged as a beaming, well-feathered Phoenix who had given "to a new Arabia, a new spring"' (Honan 1999, 304).

Death by fire is the fate of the phoenix in Lucian and Lactantius, but this is not the only version of the story. In Herodotus 2.73, Ovid's *Metamorphoses* 15.392–402 and Pliny, it collects fragrant herbs to build a nest, on which it sits until it dies. Then from its bones and marrow is born a maggot from which grows a chick which will be the next phoenix. Shakespeare has chosen the other version because it is a more vivid demonstration of the violence of time, because it suggests an improving moral, and because it avoids the maggot.

Part of the power is in the music. In 'blúnt thou', the command is enforced by the reversal of the usual iambic beat, answered by the command in line 3, 'plúck the keen teeth', which can hardly be spoken without baring them, an effect intensified in 'the fíerce', which again jolts the ear by demanding a stress on 'fierce', which the iambic expectation would place on 'the'. 'Plúck the kéen téeth' is followed by 'And búrn the lóng-líved' where alliteration of -l- speaks to the assonance of -ee-, leading to the climactic finish 'burn' and 'blood' enclosing 'the long-lived phoenix' in assonance and alliteration.

8–12 Let swift-footed Time do what he wants to all life, to the passing seasons, to the whole world and its fading pleasures, but S forbids him one most heinous crime – he must not disfigure the beloved, 'O carve not with thy hours my love's fair brow, | Nor draw no lines there ... ' He is using monosyllables and a double negative. He means it. Time is a carver whose chisels score wrinkles in the brow, seen in the next line as lines drawn with an antique pen. The pen is old because Time himself is old (13), and it is antique because the network of wrinkles on the brow of beauty, once so smooth, can be so intricate as to be grotesque, like Golding's 'antique song', as quoted below. 'The pox of such antic, lisping, affecting phantasims,' says Mercutio in *RJ* 2.3.26–7.

13–14 S is well aware that this is nothing but bluster. He knows that Time accepts no stipulations, that wrinkles will come on his beloved's face, that there can be no exemption. Time will do what he wants, with or without permission. All that was a pose, and meant to be seen as such. Its rhetorical function is to fashion a setting for the climax in the couplet, the defeat of an invincible, vicious old tyrant, a claim hammered home mostly in Anglo-Saxon monosyllables, with a defiant emphasis on 'éver' against the iambic beat of the verse.

Ovid ruminates on the ravages of time in *Metamorphoses* 15.232–6. My italics highlight some resemblances with the Shakespeare. The first translation is mine, and I append a sample of Arthur Golding's (1567), as printed in Booth's (1977) appendix 2, 'the stretchèd metre of an antique song' (17.12):

flet quoque ut in speculo rugas adspexit aniles
Tyndaris, et secum cur sit bis rapta requirit.
tempus edax rerum, tuque, invidiosa vetustas,
omnia destruitis vitiataque dentibus aevi
paulatim lenta consumitis omnia morte.

Seeing an old woman's wrinkles in her glass, even Helen
weeps and asks herself why she has been carried off twice.
You, devouring Time and you, envious years,
destroy all things, and *consume* all things, grinding them
with the *teeth* of age, little by little, in lingering death.

And Helen when shee saw her aged wrincles in   255
A glasse, wept also: musing in herself what men had seene,
That by twoo noble princes sonnes shee twyce had ravisht beene.
Thou tyme, the eater up of things, and age of spyghtefull teene,
Destroy all things. And when that long continuance hath them bit,
You leysurely by lingring death consume them every whit.   260

A woman's face with Nature's own hand painted
Hast thou, the master-mistress of my passion;
A woman's gentle heart, but not acquainted
With shifting change, as is false woman's fashion;   4
An eye more bright than theirs, less false in rolling,
Gilding the object whereupon it gazeth;
A man in hue, all hues in his controlling,
Which steals men's eyes and women's souls amazeth.   8

And for a woman wert thou first created,
Till Nature as she wrought thee fell a-doting,
And by addition me of thee defeated
By adding one thing to my purpose nothing.   12

    But since she pricked thee out for women's pleasure,
    Mine be thy love, and thy love's use their treasure.

Your face, heart, eye and form are as beautiful as a woman's,
   but you are true, a man admired by men and women.
Nature was creating you as a woman when she fell in love with you
   and added to her creation a part which is nothing to me.
Let women use and treasure your love, but I pray that you love me.

1–8 The first four couplets make four statements. The beloved has the face of a woman without the aid of cosmetics, the heart of a woman without a woman's changeability, an eye brighter than a woman's but not flirtatious, and the hue, that is the form, of a man, admired by men, adored by women.

Women's faces are often painted by cosmetics, but Nature is the beloved's beautician. Now, in a phrase 'that has probably generated more heat than any other in the Sonnets' (Evans 1996), S, as though amazed, faces the fact that his mistress is a man, 'the Master Mistris of my passion', as written in the Quarto. This is the only one of the 154 sonnets in which every line has an extra eleventh syllable, 'feminine rhymes', so called from the French, where *rimes féminines* end in the feminine suffix with -e-. '*Féminines*' has four syllables in French verse. Henri Weber in *La Création poétique en France au XVIe siècle* shows that the alternation of *rimes masculines* and *rimes féminines* was practised from early in the sixteenth century. The term 'feminine rhyme' is recorded in *OED* as used by Samuel Daniel in 1603 in his *Defence of Rhyme*. Shakespeare must have known the term. As S greets the beginning of this love, he contemplates the feminine qualities of the young man he loves in 14 lines which have their own feminine qualities. The only sonnets which approach this are 87, where he contemplates the end of this same love ('Farewell, thou art too dear for my possessing'), and 152, the last of his poems to the Black Lady. In the first ecstasy of love and in its despairing ends the master poet is deep in a poetic technicality.

The beloved has a woman's gentle heart, but women's hearts are changeable and false and follow fashion. How is this nonsense to be explained? It is not as though the Shakespeare of the plays is a conspicuous misogynist. In his plays as in life men are more faithless in love than women, and here is a poet of supreme intelligence and self-awareness condemning women's 'shifting change'. Virgil may be partly to blame. Every educated Elizabethan would have known Mercury's warning to Aeneas as he commanded him to desert Dido in the *Aeneid* 4.569, that woman is a thing always unstable and changeable, '*varium et mutabile semper femina*'. 'Shifting' would be a clever translation of *varium*. But even if we could be certain that Shakespeare knew this passage, that would not explain why he thought of it here. The explanation may be in the last line. 'Use' has often a bitter taste in the Sonnets, as in line 14. 'Thy love's use' in this context may activate the associations of the word in 134.10–12.

The beloved's eye is brighter than a woman's, so much brighter that everything it lights upon is turned to gold. For this theory of vision, see the commentary on 114.7–8. The beloved is therefore like the sun who kisses green meadows with his golden face, 'Gilding pale streams with heavenly alchemy', in 33.3–4, or like Page's wife who, according to Falstaff, 'examined my parts with most delicious oeillades; sometimes the beam of her view gilded my foot, sometimes my portly belly' (*MW* 1.3.53–5). Nor does the beloved roll his eyes as women do to convey false messages. Most of the commentators take 'rolling' to mean 'roving'. But there does not appear to be any example of this meaning in Shakespeare or anywhere else. 'To roll' means 'to turn round the eyes in different directions with a kind of circular motion' (*OED* 7), and that is a vivid suggestion of flirtatious eye play. 'Her wanton eyes, ill signs of womanhed | Did roll too lightly' (Spenser, *Faerie Queene* 3.1.41–2).

The beloved is 'a man in hue', and 'hue' referred not only to colour but also, until the middle of the seventeenth century, to form and appearance. To say the beloved is a man in form comes close to contradicting the first two lines of the poem, and it is easy to guess why S did so. Not every man would like to be complimented for having a woman's face. These lines 7–8 make it quite clear that, although the beloved has the qualities of women, there is no doubt that his form is manly.

'All hues in his controlling' could be taken in several ways, but most probably it means that he possesses all the qualities of female and male, and as such he charms both men and women. Men stare at his beauty as though he were a woman, and it steals their eyes, and women, having gentle hearts, according to lines 3–4, not only stare but are amazed, a very strong word in Shakespeare, sometimes almost 'stupefied' as in *Luc* 446, 'She, much amazed, breaks ope her locked up eyes.' This is an important element of the plot of the Sonnets. Shakespeare knows from the beginning that the man he has come to love is attractive to men and to women (see below on 13–14).

The relative pronoun 'which' can be either personal ('Our Father, which art in heaven') or impersonal. Here it is probably the man that steals, having all the qualities of male and female, so that he controls both.

9–12 From his consideration of the beloved as being like a woman, S moves to a theory of his creation. According to Ovid in *Metamorphoses* 10.243–97, Pygmalion made a nude statue of a woman, fell in love with it, and the goddess Venus brought it to life for him. Similarly mother Nature was making the beloved as a woman, but fell in love with her, 'fell a-doting', and decided to make her into a man by adding male genitals, thus adding something which assisted her purpose but not S's. It is tempting to read, or just to speak, line 12 as 'By adding one thing to my purpose nó thing'. 'Th' was closer to 'd' and 't' than now, according to Kerrigan (1986), so 'nó thing' improves the rhyme with 'doting'.

13–14 If a selection is made from a list by piercing names with a pin, the persons selected are said to be pricked. Nature has pricked, chosen, the beloved for women's pleasure, but she has also equipped him with a prick. 'Prick' suggesting penis occurs in *H5* 2.1.33 and in *RJ* 1.4.28 and 2.3.104–5, where Mercutio announces that 'the bawdy hand of the dial is now upon the prick of noon.'

In the last words of this poem S prays that this young man may love him, 'Mine be thy love', even as he accepts that the man he loves will make love to women, and 'thy love's use their treasure'. After line 13 the word 'use' should be read in the light of the obscenity in 134.10. There could be two explanations of the misogyny in lines 1–5 and 13–14. The first is that his new love for a man has led him to revise his views on women. The second is a premonition that the young man he loves will be unfaithful to him with women. The importance of this premonition is stressed by its position, ending the octet at 8 and the whole poem at 14.

As is shown by the extracts quoted below, this hymn of praise to a young man can be read as proof or as disproof of S's homosexual love. It is typical of the Sonnets, a passionate but not revealing declaration. The first 17 urge a young man to have children, but contain glimpses of the beginnings of S's love for him in 8.1, 10.13, 13 throughout, and 15.13. Sonnet 18 is a rapturous declaration of love, ending with a promise that the beloved will be immortal in S's verse. This promise is repeated in 19, and now in 20 he contemplates the fact that he is in love with a man. Even so early in the love plot, there are premonitions of infidelity. S has no illusions. He knows what will happen, but when it does in Sonnets 33–6 there begins a descent into misery and bitterness.

These poems do not offer a history of a love affair. They tell us nothing about Shakespeare's love life. Poets are not historians and are not giving evidence on oath. But the Sonnets are arranged in an order that *suggests* a history. Nothing is known about the beloved or about the Black Lady of Sonnets 127–52 except the few touches and veiled hints in the poems. They should be read not as a case history but as a plot.

Shakespeare was a playwright, and when the Sonnets were being written the London theatres were more often closed than not, because of outbreaks of plague. The sonnet sequence is a drama with three main characters in the eternal triangle, with episodes, conversations and soliloquies, with acts and scenes, gaps and repetitions, and with a plot enacted behind gauze curtains, with lies, false trails, self-contradictions, and many other common features of drama and of daily life. He promises to make the beloved's name immortal (81.5), but never reveals it. Above all, the Sonnets are not imagined letters, but are presented as utterances spoken by S, and what they say has all the power, range, immediacy and subtlety of the living words in Shakespeare's plays. Sonnet 20 furthers this plot by this declaration of love by one of the characters. It is also a conclusion to the first act of the drama.

This poem is of such importance in the sequence that some early comments are appended:

George Steevens (1788) in Bate (1997)
It is impossible to read this fulsome panegyrick, addressed to a male object, without an equal mixture of disgust and indignation.

Chalmers (1799) in Rollins (1944)
[20 has] no appearance of obscenity, if it be chastely examined, by a chaste mind; taking the words, as they were then understood, without listening to the suggestions of *platonism*.

S.T. Coleridge (1803) in Rollins (1944)
... he knew that so strong a love would have been made more completely a thing of permanence and reality, and have been blessed more by nature and taken under her more especial protection, if this object of his love had been at the same time a possible object of desire – for nature is not soul only. In this feeling he must have written the twentieth sonnet; but its possibility seems never to have entered even his imagination. It is noticeable that not even any allusion to that very worst of all possible vices ... [occurs] in all his numerous plays.

Richardson (1840) in Rollins (1944)
One of the most painful and perplexing [poems] I ever read ... I could heartily wish that Shakespeare had never written it.

Harris (1909) in Rollins (1944)
The sextet ... absolutely disproves guilty intimacy [between Shakespeare and Pembroke], and is, I believe, intended to disprove it.

Douglas (1929) in Rollins (1944)
Shakespeare exculpates himself, in the eyes of any reasonable being, quite definitely and quite unconsciously. Obviously it never occurred to him that anyone would put a bad interpretation on his love and adoration for 'Master W.H.'

Booth (1977) on line 7
Several Renaissance meanings of *hue* are pertinent in this context: (1) form, shape, appearance; (2) complexion; (3) color; and perhaps (4) apparition, phantasm, specter ...

Kerrigan (1986) on line 2
The hint of eroticism flusters interpreters and drives them into extremes. Some save Shakespeare's reputation by reading the line as a literary joke ('you, praised in this love poem (one sense of the word *passion*) like the conventional sonnet mistress, are nevertheless male'), while others, of coarser fibre, prefer 'you, the seductively androgynous object of my homosexual lust'.

Kerrigan (1986) on line 12
Critics who argue that this disposes of homoeroticism misconstrue teasing incon-
sequence as unambiguous statement, though the weight of the verb defeated in
line 11 cannot be overlooked.

Duncan-Jones (1997)
The placement of this anatomical sonnet at 20 may allude to a traditional
association of this figure with the human body, equipped with 20 digits.

Vendler (1997)
Bizarre as it may appear, the poem seems to have been created in such a way as
to have the individual letters of the word *h-e-w-s* (the Quarto spelling) or *h-u-e-s* in
as many lines as possible ... The list of available letters (not words) in each of the
lines (Quarto spelling) is as follows: hews, hues, hews, hews, hews, hew[z], hews,
hews, hews, hews, he[ ], hues, hews, hues (with a phonetic pun on *use*). The *h*
needed for *hews* is contributed in line 8 by *amazeth*, thereby explaining perhaps
the *-eth* endings. *Hew* is climactic in line 7 because it is the word with which the
master/mistress controls almost all the other lines. The high proportion (2.7 per
cent) of w's ... is also explicable by the necessity of making *hew* as often as
possible.

Burrow (2002)
[The term 'feminine rhyme'] was first used in England by Samuel Daniel (*c.* 1603).
Feminine rhymes often occur at sexually suggestive moments, as in *Hero and
Leander* 555–8. I print the whole passage from the Penguin Classic of Marlowe's
poems as *Sestiad* 2.61–76. The tone suggests a knowing use of the feminine rhyme
in half of the lines in this extract:

> Albeit Leander, rude in love, and raw,
> Long dallying with Hero, nothing saw
> That might delight him more, yet he suspected
> Some amorous rites or other were neglected.
> Therefore unto his body hers he clung;
> She, fearing on the rushes to be flung,
> Strived with redoubled strength; the more she strivèd,
> The more a gentle pleasing heat revivèd,
> Which taught him all that elder lovers know
> And now the same 'gan so to scorch and glow,   70
> As in plain terms (yet cunningly) he craved it;
> Love always makes them eloquent that have it.
> She, with a kind of granting, put him by it,
> And ever as he thought himself most nigh it,
> Like to the tree of Tantalus she fled,
> And, seeming lavish, saved her maidenhead.

๛ 21 ๕

So is it not with me as with that Muse,
Stirred by a painted beauty to his verse,
Who heav'n itself for ornament doth use,
And every fair with his fair doth rehearse, 4
Making a couplement of proud compare
With sun and moon, with earth and sea's rich gems,
With April's first-born flowers and all things rare
That heaven's air in this huge rondure hems. 8

O let me, true in love, but truly write,
And then believe me my love is as fair
As any mother's child, though not so bright
As those gold candles fixed in heaven's air. 12

   Let them say more that like of hearsay well,
   I will not praise, that purpose not to sell.

I am not like the poet who compares his mistress to heaven itself
   and all the beauties under it.
I love truly. Let me write the truth, and then believe
   my love is as fair as anybody's, but not as bright as the stars.
Others can parrot their clichés. I will not praise. I'm not selling.

1–8 This poem is a satire on foolish love poetry. It is not clear whether
'that Muse' is one poet or a whole class of silly love poets, but the tone is
clearly sarcastic. 'Stirred' is equally sardonic, and 'painted beauty' is to be
measured against 'A woman's face with Nature's own hand painted' in the
first line of the previous sonnet. In line 3 these writers have the impudence
to use heaven as an ornament, and then in 4 they compare their painted
beloved with all the other beauties under the sun. '*Rehearse* is here pejorative:
the other *Muse* goes through the motions, repeating – someone else's? – words
mechanically, like an actor in rehearsal' (Kerrigan 1986). The metre adds its
mocking overtone, 'And ev'ry fáir with hís fair doth rehearse'.

Derision continues in line 5. A 'couplement of proud compare' is a pairing [consisting] of an arrogant comparison, and the word 'couplement' is pompous, used elsewhere in Shakespeare only on the lips of the boastful blundering pedant Don Armado in *LLL* 5.2.528, as he takes farewell of a king and a princess, 'most royal couplement'. The next three lines are best read as three expanding pairs covering sun and moon, then coming down to earth and sea ('Full many a gem,' according to Thomas Gray, 'The dark unfathomed caves of ocean bear'), and then soaring again from the earliest flowers of April to all things rare under the sky. Contempt continues with 'all things ráre | That heaven's áir', ringing with the jingle of 4 and the verse endings of 5, 7, 10 and 12. The climax is 'rondure', a very rare word not required elsewhere by Shakespeare. It posits the stellar system as a vast sphere with the earth in its centre and 'heaven's air' around it, a hem edging the 'huge rondure'. It may be no accident that *la rondeur de la terre* would be unremarkable in French. Shakespeare often associates France with foppery. 'Roundure' tells this same story. It is used in Shakespeare only at *KJ* 2.1.259–62, where the king is threatening the 'roundure' of the 'old-faced walls' of Angers, and contrasts them unfavourably with the 'rude circumference' of island Britain.

9–14 'I am no orator as Brutus is, | But, as you know me all, a plain blunt man | That love my friend.' So said Antony with many monosyllables in the great showpiece of false rhetoric in *JC* 3.2.212–14, knowing perfectly well that he was far more eloquent than Brutus. S plays the same card here, with 'O let me, trúe in love, but trúly write', just write truly. This is the same strategy as Leander applied in line 71 of the poem quoted at the end of the note on the previous sonnet, 'in plain terms (yet cunningly)'. In the next line there is another eloquent repetition, the polyptoton of 'me my', mimicking line 4, and here too the verse accent adds an edge, 'And then believe me mý love is as fair'.

In line 10 he presents the same modest and therefore credible persona as does the final couplet of Sonnet 130, 'And yet by heav'n I think my love as rare | As any she belied with false compare.' He does not say that his beloved is the best, only that there is none better, establishing his honesty by admitting that stars are brighter. The stars are 'those gold candles fixed in heaven's air'. Besotted lovers call the stars candles in Shakespeare. Bassanio does so in *MV* 5.1.220 when in trouble with Portia:

> Pardon me, good lady,
> For by these blessed candles of the night,
> Had you been there …

And Romeo does so at 3.5.9, trying to leave Juliet when she does not wish to be left, appeasing her with metaphor:

> Night's candles are burned out, and jocund day
> Stands tiptoe on the misty mountain tops.

13–14 'That like of hearsay well' is a sarcastic understatement. These do not simply enjoy hearsay. They love it.

Commentators report the proverb 'He praises who wishes to sell.' Shakespeare sharpens the dagger. The mistresses of these inane poets have a price, 'To things of sale a seller's praise belongs' (*LLL* 4.3.238).

Sonnet 130 has the same theme and tone as Sonnet 21. Each is a programme poem tilting at trite and exaggerated praise, and distinguishing that from S's own truthful practice. Who were the target poets? Commentators suggest that the meteorology of 6, 8 and 12 may be hinting at Sidney's Stella, a pseudonym for his mistress in his sonnets entitled *Astrophil and Stella*. Astrophil in Greek would be the lover of a star, and in Latin *stella* is a star.

It is surprising to read this attack upon images based on natural phenomena in a poet who is a master of this resource, and has just deployed it unforgettably in Sonnet 18. But then this is a poet who uses every resource to the full, and is happy to point out how others botch them.

This is the first sonnet not addressed to the young man. All the others so far, even 5 and 19, praise him or attempt to persuade him, and are presented as contributions to a conversation with him. Sonnet 21, on the other hand, is Shakespeare's open address to readers. It is also the first sonnet after the declarations of love in 18–20, a programme poem, a prologue to the next act of the drama, demolishing pretentious exaggerations in the work of contemporary poets (compare 130). It also hints at a confirmation of the premonitions in 20.8 and 13–14. There are rival poets and they may well turn out to be rival lovers.

My glass shall not persuade me I am old
So long as youth and thou are of one date,
But when in thee time's furrows I behold,
Then look I death my days should expiate.   4

For all that beauty that doth cover thee
Is but the seemly raiment of my heart,
Which in thy breast doth live, as thine in me.
How can I then be elder than thou art?   8

O therefore, love, be of thyself so wary
As I, not for myself, but for thee will,
Bearing thy heart, which I will keep so chary
As tender nurse her babe from faring ill.   12

Presume not on thy heart when mine is slain.
Thou gav'st me thine not to give back again.

My mirror will not persuade me I am old while you are young,
but when you become wrinkled then I look for death.
For your beauty covers my heart, which lives in your breast
(as yours in mine). How then can I be older than you?
So care for yourself, as I will care for your heart in my breast.
When my heart is killed, do not imagine yours will be returned to you.

1–4   He has looked in the mirror and seen wrinkles, as he will do in 62.10,
but he will not be persuaded that he is old while the beloved is young, while
'youth and thou are of one date'. When he sees wrinkles in the beloved's
face, then he looks at death coming to end, to 'expiate', his days. Elsewhere
expiation involves atonement, purging of guilt. How does that work here?
Is he glancing back at his past life, and thinking of his sins, or is it simply
that expiation is associated with death?
     The key to this sonnet is the famous line of Sir Philip Sidney, quoted at

the end of this commentary, 'My true love hath my heart, and I have his.' This is, in Vendler's words, 'one of the received Renaissance symbols of reciprocity' (Vendler 1997), and Shakespeare has pondered its anatomical implications. If B (the Beloved) has S's heart, where would he keep it? In his breast, obviously. But that does not mean that B would have two hearts, because his own heart is now in S's breast. But if S's heart is in B's youthful body, how old is S? Surely as old as the body which covers his heart. This is the problem explored in 1–2. Lines 3–4 then prophesy, reasonably, that S would be looking to die when he saw wrinkles on the young man's face, a sign that the body which covered his heart was growing old.

5–8   When this collection of sonnets was published in 1609, Shakespeare was 45 years old, and claiming to be in love with a youth perhaps 25 years younger than himself. Of course he is older than the young man, and no mental gymnastics can change that. His escape from this difficulty is to argue in line 8 that he is young because his heart lives in a youthful body, 'How can I then be elder than thou art?'

Line 7, 'Which in thy breast doth live, as thine in me', echoes the monosyllabic simplicity of Sidney's 'My true love hath my heart, and I have his.' 'As thine in me' is the first firm indication that the young man loves S in return, and this is confirmed in 'Thou gav'st me thine' in the last line. This conceit is therefore moving the plot of the sonnets along.

9–12   'You must care for yourself [since you carry my heart], just as I shall look after myself because your heart is in my body. I will nurse it like a baby, keeping it carefully' ('chary' is an adverb, meaning 'carefully', as in *OED* 8). The lovers are both to avoid risk-taking, on journeys, with their health, in quarrels, whatever. But there is also a delicate instruction to the youth to 'be wary', to avoid bad company perhaps, and not to engage in sexual adventures. S *asks* the young man to be wary, *but promises* that he himself will be careful with the beloved's heart. He knows he will be faithful, but we have seen already at 20.8 and 13–14 and in 21 traces of a premonition that the young man may not.

13–14   The stage is set for the final couplet. 'Presume not on thy heart when mine is slain' is often read as though S is thinking of his death, but the word is 'slain' not 'dead'. His heart will be slain when the young man ceases to love him. This dark close uses the image of heart exchange to say, 'When I received your love, the terms were that I would keep it and never cease to love you, and I shall die if you kill mine by ceasing to love me.'

Sidney's poem is in *Eclogues* 3 in Katherine Duncan-Jones, *Sir Philip Sidney: Selected Poems* (1973), 45.

> My true love hath my heart, and I have his,
> By just exchange one for the other given.
> I hold his dear, and mine he cannot miss:
> There never was a better bargain driven.   4
> His heart in me keeps me and him in one;
> My heart in him his thoughts and senses guides;
> He loves my heart, for once it was his own;
> I cherish his because in me it bides.   8
> His heart his wound receivèd from my sight;
> My heart was wounded with his wounded heart;
> For as from me on him his hurt did light,
> So still, methought, in me his hurt did smart;   12
>   Both equal hurt, in this change sought our bliss:
>   My true love hath my heart, and I have his.

The differences are revealing. Sidney restates the notion in half a dozen ingenious antitheses balancing heart and heart, all with verbal cleverness, but little emotional depth or detail, and little development of argument except that from line 9 he turns back to look at the history of their love. Sonnet 22 is more dramatic, and presents a coherent argument. In 1–4 S will never look in his mirror and find that he has grown old while the young man is still young. Lines 5–8 explain why, visualising the anatomy of the heart exchange and its effects. Lines 9–12 promise fidelity, and ask the young man to do the same (a hint that he expects squalls), and lines 13–14 explain that the loss of love would lead to his death. The development of the conceit is less mechanical in Shakespeare, more personal, and the poem has a more dynamic logical shape. It begins at one point and ends at another. Most importantly, Sidney's poem is an analysis for public consumption, whereas Shakespeare's seems to be an account of thoughts that went through S's head on a specific occasion, 'on looking in my mirror'. It is addressed to the person he loves, and has a place and purpose in the drama of that love.

Duncan-Jones (1997), headnote
This sonnet celebrates the loving dependence of the speaker on his friend and his appropriation of his friend's youthful beauty.

As an unperfect actor on the stage
Who with his fear is put besides his part,
Or some fierce thing replete with too much rage
Whose strength's abundance weakens his own heart,　　　4
So I for fear of trust forget to say
The perfect ceremony of love's rite,
And in mine own love's strength seem to decay,
O'ercharged with burden of mine own love's might.　　　8

O let my looks be then the eloquence
And dumb presagers of my speaking breast,
Who plead for love and look for recompense
More than that tongue that more hath more express'd.　　　12
　　O learn to read what silent love hath writ.
　　To hear with eyes belongs to love's fine wit.

Like an actor who forgets his words because of stage-fright or a wild beast
　　weakened by rage, so am I struck dumb and weakened by love.
Let my looks speak for me more eloquently than my rival's fluency.
Learn to read what love has written on my face. Love's wit hears with eyes.

1–8   In the first simile, in lines 1–2, S is like an actor, and the resemblance
is expounded in lines 5–6. In the second simile, in lines 3–4, he is like a wild
beast, and that resemblance is expounded in lines 7–8.

　　To make a simile stick, poets adjust the description on both sides of the
line, as shown by the italics:

　　　As an *unperfect* actor on the stage
　　　Who with his *fear* is put beside his part　　　2
　　　...
　　　So I for *fear* of trust forget to say
　　　The *perfect* ceremony of love's rite.　　　6

Such correspondences sometimes help to solve problems. An *unperfect* actor could be simply an incompetent, but in line 5 S *forgets*, and in *MND* 1.2.101, when Bottom is briefing his cast, by 'perfect' he means word-perfect, 'Take pains; be perfect.' So here an unperfect actor is one who forgets his words. Again, the lover's *fear* of trust is a difficult phrase for which half a dozen explanations have been put forward. The actor's fear is that he will freeze or flop, that the audience will not be convinced by, will not believe in, his performance. The lover's 'fear of trust' is fear of [the task of winning] trust and it makes him forget his words. In line 2 'besides his part' is like our phrase 'beside the point', 'missing the point' (*OED* B4c). The actor besides his part forgets his lines as S forgets the words of love.

In the second simile S compares himself to an animal weakened by rage. ('Some fierce thing' makes it sound very ferocious):

> Or some fierce thing, *replete with too much* rage
> Whose *strength*'s abundance weakens *his own* heart,   4
> ...
> And in *mine own* love's *strength* seem to decay
> O'ercharged with burden of *mine own* love's *might*   8

Apart from the verbal repetitions italicised, the links between simile and what it illustrates are strengthened by the correspondences between 'weakens' and 'decay', between 'heart' and 'love', between 'whose strength's abundance' and 'my own love's might', and by the fact that 'rage' can refer to sexual passion, as in *Luc* 424, 'the rage of lust'.

Two similes are not enough for Shakespeare to describe his failure to express his love. In 6 he moves to metaphor, 'I ... forget to say | The perfect ceremony of love's rite.' He has become a worshipper who stumbles over his words. S includes an eloquent compliment in this account of his uneloquence. His love is a sacred rite. The beloved is his god (110.12).

9–14   These last six lines are full of paradoxes. 'O let my looks be then the eloquence' is the first. Shakespeare knew that *eloqui* was Latin for 'speak out', and looks do not speak out. In 10 presagers are heralds who go before to make announcements, but these presagers are dumb, and yet plead. Another paradox follows at 'my speaking breast', and another when these looks of his now look for reward, and do so *more* passionately than the tongue, which has said *more*, and said it *more* often. 'More' occurs three times in line 12, and, whatever each one exactly means, they surely satirise the volubility and repetitiveness of S's rivals. This is another glimpse of the cloud of infidelity on the horizon, as in Sonnets 20 and 22.

Secret signs between lovers are a favourite theme with Ovid. See J. C. McKeown's 1987 commentary on *Amores* 1.17 and 19, '*vultum que loquacem*' and '*verba sine voce loquentia dicam*', 'speaking face' and 'I shall say words which speak without voice', where McKeown cites 16 other examples. In this sonnet to hear what is not spoken requires 'love's fine wit', and this is expressed even more paradoxically in the last line, 'to hear with eyes'. Shakespeare's elaboration of this conceit is not indulgence in the smoke of rhetoric for its own sake. It demonstrates love's subtle intelligence in action, a love so intense and mysterious that it goes beyond the possible.

In line 9 'looks' is an emendation. The Quarto reads 'books'. 'Let my looks be my eloquence' is eloquent; 'let my books be my eloquence' is feeble. The sense is strangely limp if S is advising the man he loves to read his books. Nor does the beloved need to be told to *learn* to read (13). That would belong to common literacy, not 'to love's fine wit'. 'To hear with the eyes' is also unconvincing if it means to read S's books. A dozing printer may have read ahead quickly and changed 'looks' to 'books', misled by line 13. In secretary hand -b- and -l- could easily have been confused by the compositor who printed line 14 as 'To heare wit eies belongs to loues fine wiht.'

The eloquence of looks is well understood in *Luc* 99–100, where 'parling' means speaking:

> But she that never coped with stranger eyes,
> Could pick no meaning from their parling looks.

Duncan-Jones (1997) on line 10
dumb presagers silent indicators: to 'presage' normally carries connotations of foretelling the future, but in Venus and Adonis (457) Shakespeare applies it to Adonis' silent blush, an 'ill presage' of the words he is about to speak.

∽ 24 ∾

Mine eye hath played the painter and hath stelled
Thy beauty's form in table of my heart.
My body is the frame wherein 'tis held,
And pérspectíve it is best painter's art.   4

For through the painter must you see his skill
To find where your true image pictured lies,
Which in my bosom's shop is hanging still,
That hath his windows glazèd with thine eyes.   8

Now see what good turns eyes for eyes have done—
Mine eyes have drawn thy shape, and thine for me
Are windows to my breast, wherethrough the sun
Delights to peep, to gaze therein on thee.   12

Yet eyes this cunning want to grace their art:
They draw but what they see, know not the heart.

*My eye has acted as a painter and portrayed your beauty in my heart.
My body is the frame, and eye's supreme art is perspective,
because you see his skill by looking through him to your portrait hanging
in the shop windows of my breast. Their glass is your own eye.
My eyes have drawn you, for me your eyes are windows to my breast,
and the sun peeps through them to delight in your portrait.
But eyes lack something to improve their art —
they draw only what they see. They do not know the heart.*

1–4   Sonnet 22 explored implications of the conceit 'My true love hath my
heart, and I have his.' Sonnet 24 makes another journey from the same
point. S's eye is a painter and this painter/eye has done a portrait of the
beloved on the table of S's heart. A table is a board, so in our terminology
the painting is a portrait on board. This is a physiological impossibility.
Eyes do not paint, nor are hearts painted on, but all is comprehensible after

the exchange of hearts in 22.5–12, only here it is not a heart lodged in a lover's breast, but the beloved's portrait in the lover's heart. The Quarto reads 'steeld' in the first line, but painters do not engrave with a steel point, whereas 'stell' means 'portray, depict', for example in *Luc* 1444, where in a 'well-painted piece' there is 'a face where all distress is stelled'. Besides, 'stelled' rhymes with 'held' here in 4, and with 'dwelled' in *Luc* 1446.

Lines 3–4 carry a pun. The frame of the portrait is S's frame, his body (59.10). Because this is the first recorded use of the word to denote a picture frame, some take the frame as an easel. 'Wherein' may tell against that. A picture is held *on* an easel, but *in* a frame. Besides, it is just possible to imagine a frame in a breast, but not the legs of an easel.

The supreme virtuosity of the painter/eye is 'pérspectíve', 'a representation which looks right from only one point of view', otherwise known as anamorphosis, and it is described in *R2* 2.2.16–20:

> For sorrow's eye, glazèd with blinding tears,
> Divides one thing entire to many objects—
> Like perspectives, which, rightly gazed upon,
> Show nothing but confusion; eyed awry,
> Distinguish form.

The object lying on the floor in Holbein's *The Ambassadors* in the National Gallery looks like a stick of French bread. Rightly gazed upon, from below left or above right, it is a skull, the hollow bone, *das hohle Bein*.

5–8 To see the skill of the portrait in S's bosom there is no point in looking directly at S's chest. You have to look through the painter, namely his eye, and from there the line of vision will go awry down into his bosom where the picture hangs. That is perspective, and it is the supreme art of painter/eye. This interpretation, one of many current, is supported by the first word of line 5, '*For* through the painter must you see his skill.' Lines 5–6 explain what has gone before.

In 23.5 there suddenly intruded a metaphor of a forgetful worshipper. Here in 24.7–8 S's bosom suddenly becomes a shop, and in its windows hangs the portrait. The simplest explanation of this conceit would start with line 5, where 'must you see' is addressed to the beloved. When he looks at his own portrait displayed in the shop which is S's bosom, the beloved's own eyes are the glazing of the shop windows.

9–12 Eyes have done favours to eyes. S's eyes have painted the beloved in his own breast – to paint someone's portrait is to do them a favour. But what favour have the beloved's eyes done for S? An explanation might begin from the notion that lovers gazed into each other's eyes and saw minute reflections of themselves. They 'looked love's babies'. *OED* cites from 1593 'that babie which lodges in womens eies' and from Burton's *Anatomy of Melancholy* (1621) 'They may kiss and coll, lye and look babies in one anothers eyes', where 'coll' is cognate with French *col*, 'neck'. Shakespeare himself refers to this idea in *KJ* quoted on 53.5–13. So in 9–10 S will be able to look into the beloved's eyes and see himself, including the beloved's portrait in his breast, and the sight is so enchanting that even the sun delights to take a peep at it. This image of a peeping sun is a humorous compliment to round off a tortured conceit, and make a dramatic setting for the darkness of the last line.

Booth (1977) says that 'the sonnet is carefully designed to boggle the reader's mind (make his eyes glaze)', and he contributes to that bogglement a dazzling panorama of views of this passage. Shakespeare has taken the poetic cliché quoted in the note on Sonnet 22, and, as in 22, has tested it towards destruction by exploring its anatomical implications.

13–14 To want is to be without (26.6), and eyes are without the cunning 'to find the mind's construction in the face' (*Mac* 1.4.11-12).

This is not the first of recent sonnets to end with a premonition of betrayal.

Seymour-Smith (1963)
… a confused sonnet. According to Miss M. M. Mahood, 'The resultant image is pure Bosch.'

Let those who are in favour with their stars
Of public honour and proud titles boast,
Whilst I, whom fortune of such triumph bars
Unlooked for, joy in that I honour most.   4

Great princes' favourites their fair leaves spread
But as the marigold at the sun's eye,
And in themselves their pride lies burièd,
For at a frown they in their glory die.   8

The painful warrior, famousèd for might,
After a thousand victories once foiled,
Is from the book of honour rasèd quite,
And all the rest forgot for which he toiled.   12

Then happy I that love and am beloved
Where I may not remove, nor be removed.

Let the lucky ones boast of their public honour and titles.
  I delight in what I myself honour most.
Courtiers glory in the prince's smile and die at his frown,
  like marigolds opening in the sun and closing in the shade.
Warriors are fêted when victorious and forgotten when defeated.
I am happy that I love and am loved by one from whom I cannot move
  or be removed.

1–4 'Those who are in favour with their stars' have achieved honours and
titles, but the under-sense is that they have not earned them. S does not
grieve because Fortune debars him from such triumphs. This is to take a
sceptical view of astrology, as in 14.5 or as in *TS* 4.6.40–2, when Petruccio
bids Kate to embrace an 'old, wrinkled, faded, withered' man, 'for her
beauty's sake', and Kate, now all obedience, does so, saying:

Happy the parents of so fair a child,
Happier the man whom favourable stars
Allots thee for his lovely bedfellow.

Lines 3–4 are normally punctuated differently:

Whilst I, whom fortune of such triumph bars,
Unlooked for joy in that I honour most.

'Unlooked for' then goes with ' joy', 'I joy unexpectedly', or with 'I', 'I who am unexpected'. Neither of these makes convincing sense. With the comma after 'Unlooked for' as above, S is saying that he has never had public triumphs and never wanted to. The Quarto has no comma in 3–4.

'Honour' in 4 is not a limp repetition of 'honour' in 2 but an active contrast – 'others boast about their public honour; I delight in what I myself honour.' Such repetitions mark the logic in many of the sonnets – such as 'Devouring ... devour' in 19.1–2. Here 'public honour' in 2 is the reward of the warrior enrolled in 'the book of honour' in 11; 'proud titles' points to the 'pride' and 'glory' of the courtiers in 7–8; 'triumph' in 3 to 'victories' in 10; and 'joy' in 4 to 'happy' in 13.

5–8 The above summary separates the courtiers from the marigolds, but the sonnet merges them, as when in 5 courtiers spread fair leaves. Here leaves are petals as at *1H6* 4.1.92–3, where a man wearing a white rose upbraided Basset about the rose he wore, 'Saying the sanguine colour of the leaves | Did represent my master's blushing cheeks.' In 6 it is not marigolds that react to eyes, but courtiers, flaunting their splendour in the eye of their prince. In 7 it is not courtiers who bury their pride in themselves, but marigolds that fold in the brilliant side of their petals when the sun is obscured, 'in themselves their pride lies burièd'. In line 8 the marigold does not die when the sun goes in, but 'goes to bed wi' th' sun, | And with him rises, weeping', [wet with dew] (*WT* 4.4.105–6). But for some courtiers in Elizabethan England the monarch's frown meant death.

9–12 The warrior is painful because pain is the price of victory, and he is 'famousèd', but soon rejected. S smiles at his pretensions by inventing the verb and using it only here. In the Quarto line 9 ends not with 'might' but with 'worth', which must be wrong because it does not rhyme with 'quite' in 11. 'Fight' is another possible correction. S had no chance of triumphs, the warrior wins a thousand, and they are soon forgotten. Line 10 begins imposingly, 'Áfter a thousand victories', imposing for its exaggeration and because it is the only opening inversion in the poem. 'Once' unstressed could be read as meaning 'As soon as he is defeated', but in view of Shakespeare's penchant for pointed contrasts, it should surely be read with emphasis against the metre, 'ónce', on one occasion, puncturing the inflated figure of 'a thousand', 'Áfter a thousand victories, ónce foiled'. 'The book of honour' from which the warrior's name is erased is not army records. It is a metaphorical book, like 'the leaf of pity' in TA 4.3.115–18:

> Let not the virgin's cheek
> Make soft thy trenchant sword; for those milk paps
> That through the window bars bore at men's eyes
> Are not within the leaf of pity writ.

The victorious warrior, after one defeat, 'is from the book of honour rasèd quite'. 'Rasèd' means 'erased', but war often included the razing to the ground of the cities of the defeated. So here there is a suggestion that after one defeat the victorious warrior is treated as he treated the cities he captured.

13–14 The poem began with courtiers, warriors and S. The body of it dealt with courtiers and warriors. Now the conclusion comes back to S. The warriors and courtiers were 'proud' and 'famousèd', but were then rejected. S on the other hand loves, and that love is immovable. The conclusion is a powerful epigram, 'I that *love* and am *beloved*', like '*amant amantur*' of the two lovers in Catullus 45, 'they love, are loved'. In the last line that polyptoton is answered by another, 'Where I may not *remove* nor be *removed*.' There is no room for doubt.

From where can he not remove, nor be removed? Those who have read 22.7, and remembered it in 24, will know that he is in his beloved's breast. Most powerful of all is the stark contrast with the gloom at the close of the preceding poem. But again those reading the sonnets in order will sense that this is a fond hope, as will soon be confirmed in 33–6. The self-delusion at the end of 25 is even darker than the doubt at the end of 24.

Wyndham (1780) in Rollins (1944)
No lines could have been penned more apposite … to the fall and disgrace of Essex after his military failure in Ireland. [Rollins adds that Wolfgang Keller (*Shakespeare's Werke*, 1916, 15, 511) correctly remarks that such interpretations as the foregoing of statements based on universal experience are always somewhat hazardous.]

ᛋᚩ 26 ᚳᚱ

Lord of my love, to whom in vassalage
Thy merit hath my duty strongly knit,
To thee I send this written ambassage
To witness duty, not to show my wit,   4

Duty so great which wit so poor as mine
May make seem bare, in wanting words to show it,
But that I hope some good conceit of thine
In thy soul's thought, all naked, will bestow it;   8
Till whatsoever star that guides my moving
Points on me graciously with fair aspéct,
And puts apparel on my tattered loving,
To show me worthy of thy sweet respect –   12

Then may I dare to boast how I do love thee,
Till then, not show my head where thou mayst prove me.

Lord of my love, to you I send this written embassy, not to display my wit,
but to attest my duty,
which is greater than my wit can express, but I hope you may remember it
till some day when I may deserve your respect.
Then I may boast of your love, but till then I will not show my face
where you can put me to the test.

1–4 Such is the towering merit of the beloved, that S sees himself as a
vassal addressing his feudal *lord*, and sending him an *ambassage*, the work
of an ambassador, an embassy. The word implies a deputation testifying in
person. A written ambassage is therefore a paradox. Its purpose is to
witness duty, not to show wit, but line 4 does exactly that – another
paradox. The game continues in line 5, in which a *great* duty exposes his
poor wit. Vassalage and ambassage are both rare words in Shakespeare, and
they make an outrageous rhyme. 'Embassage' is used in a stream of
high-spirited conceits by Benedick in *MA* 2.1.251–2, where he offers to

perform any imaginable service 'to fetch you a hair off the Great Cham's beard, to do you any embassage to the pigmies', anything rather than hold three words' conference with the harpy, Lady Beatrice. These two high-blown archaic words carry a tone of legal solemnity, as does the knitting of duty in line 2 and in *Mac* 3.1.17–18, where Banquo's duties 'Are with a most indíssolúble tie | For ever knit'. 'Duty' is his feudal duty as a vassal, here insisted upon in 2, 4 and 5 in this feudal context. Duty in love is devotion and service. For 'bestow' meaning 'stow away, lodge', see *CE* 1.2.77, 'answer me | In what safe place you have bestowed my money.'

5–12   In 4–5 S confesses the poverty of his wit in a virtuoso display of it. It is so poor that it may make his duty seem *bare*, because he does not have the words to express it. He has one hope – that the beloved may in his heart take a kindly view and store it away until S be able to earn his respect and put some *apparel* on the *tattered*, beggarly duty, all *naked*, which is all S can at the moment express. The word order is difficult. This interpretation stretches the syntax, but it connects the four words italicised, and makes them all refer to the seeming poverty of S's present expression of duty and of love. In line 8 'it' is this naked duty that the beloved is asked to form a good conceit of and store away till a better day.

The 'star that guides my moving' suggests the pole star, 'the star to every wand'rng bark' in 116.7. 'Aspect' is properly a technical term of astrology, referring strictly to 'the way in which, from their relative positions, the various planets look upon each other, but popularly transferred to their joint look upon the earth' (*OED* 4). S imagines not Saturn aspecting Jupiter, say, but a gracious star aspecting himself. 'Points' in line 10 may also belong to the language of astrology, as in 14.6.

13–14   When that day comes, he may dare to boast of his love, but until then, dressed in rags like a tramp, and speaking in bare monosyllables, he will not lift his head, or as we would say 'show his face', when the beloved is present to put him to the test.

The servitude of love, *servitium amoris*, can be traced back to Latin love elegy, but no Latin poet explores it with such density of wit, such complex-ity of metaphor, and such purchase on the individual's situation. S is conscious of his social and financial inferiority, he claims dullness of wit with a coruscation of it, he praises the beloved as he belittles himself (it would require a flight of fancy by the beloved, a generous conceit, to store up S's duty in the hope that it would gain in value). He hopes that his condition will improve, but modestly says that would not be because of any merit, but only as a matter of luck (9–10). He would love to tell the world of his love, but as things are he is afraid to lift his head in company, in case the beloved looks at him and assesses his condition. The repetitions of 'show' in 4, 6, 12 and 14 may imply, so quietly that it need not be heard, that S has more merit than some who have more to show, and that the day may come when he will produce some decent work.

Weary with toil I haste me to my bed,
The dear repose for limbs with travail tired,
But then begins a journey in my head,
To work my mind when body's work's expired.   4
For then my thoughts from far where I abide,
Intend a zealous pilgrimage to thee,
And keep my drooping eyelids open wide,
Looking on darkness which the blind do see,   8

Save that my soul's imaginary sight
Presents thy shadow to my sightless view,
Which like a jewel hung in ghastly night
Makes black night beauteous and her old face new.   12

  Lo, thus by day my limbs, by night my mind,
  For thee, and for myself, no quiet find.

Weary with the toil of travel I rush to my bed, and then my mind
  begins to travel, hastening to you as I gaze open-eyed at darkness,
except that my mind's eye sees a phantom of you beautifying the night.
Body has no rest by day, mind has none by night.

1–8 S is on a long and exhausting journey, and he hurries to bed every
night 'with travail tired'. In Elizabethan English 'travail' is sometimes
travel and sometimes toil. Here, with reference to his journey, it is travel,
but with reference to the journey in his head it is toil. It works his mind
(4). When his thoughts 'intend a pilgrimage' to the beloved, this does not
mean that they propose to go on a pilgrimage. They actually do go on a
pilgrimage (*OED* intend 6, 'to proceed (on a journey etc)'). A pilgrimage is
a journey, usually long, to a sacred place as an act of devotion, so this is a
tribute to the beloved, a passing statement of reverence like 23.6, and it is
reinforced by 'zealous'. Zeal is often religious. In *R2* 5.3.105–6 the prayers
of the Duke of York are 'full of false hypocrisy; | Ours of true zeal'. It is

a long journey for S's thoughts, far from where he is now lodging, and as they travel his eyes are heavy, but they remain open (this is no dream), and, as though he were blind, all he sees is darkness.

9–12   And yet his mind in 4, his thoughts in 5, and his soul's imaginary sight, the eye of his imagination in 9, see in this total blackness, and what they see is a shadow presented to his unseeing view, a miracle explained by the meaning of 'shadow' in *OED* 6a, a phantom. But there is in nature something that can be seen in the dark. In *TA* 2.3.226–7, when Martius falls into a black pit, he can recognise the dead body of Bassianus because 'Upon his bloody finger he doth wear | A precious ring that lightens all this hole', and Romeo praises Juliet who 'seems to hang upon the cheek of night | As a rich jewel in an Ethiope's ear' (1.5.44–5). The vision is of a carbuncle, a stone 'of a red or fiery colour', garnet, ruby or sapphire, anciently believed to glow in the dark, a notion no doubt helped by the Latin *carbunculus*, meaning a live coal. Here, in 'a jewel hung in ghastly night', 'ghastly' is usually explained as terrifying, horrible, deathly, but fear, horror and death have no place in this poem. Rather, night is ghastly because it is the time associated with ghosts and phantoms (*OED* 2).

In line 12 this phantom of the beloved 'Makes black night beauteous and her old face new', opposing 'old' to 'new', and 'black' to 'beauteous'. 'Black' is proverbially ugly, 'I am black, but comely, O ye daughters of Jerusalem' (Song of Solomon 1: 5), an idea explored in Sonnet 127. Night has long been seen as old and female, as in Hesiod, *Theogony* 116–25, where ' from Night came forth Day and Aither, whom she conceived and bore, joining Erebus in love'. Chaos and 'sable-vested Night, eldest of things, | The consort of his reign', sit enthroned together in *Paradise Lost* 2.962–3.

13–14   The final couplet summarises the sonnet. 'Limbs' here and in line 2 is not simply a convenient metrical variation on the 'body' of line 4. A long journey in Elizabethan times, particularly on horseback as in Sonnets 50 and 51, would make the limbs ache by evening. The rhetorical density of this summary is complex. To say that limbs find no quiet by day and mind finds none by night is clear, but 'For thée, and fór mysélf' adds another pair. By day there is no rest for limbs because of himself, his travel, by night there is none for mind because of the beloved.

Shakespeare often thinks in opposites. This sonnet, for example, has more than a dozen contrasts – weary/haste, limbs/head, mind/body, drooping/wide, blind/see, imaginary/sight, sightless/view, shadow/jewel, black/beauteous, old/new, day/night, limbs/mind, thee/myself.

❧ 28 ☙

How can I then return in happy plight
That am debarred the benefit of rest,
When day's oppression is not eased by night
But day by night and night by day oppressed,   4
And each, though enemies to either's reign,
Do in consent shake hands to torture me,
The one by toil, the other to complain
How far I toil, still farther off from thee?   8

I tell the day, to please him, thou art bright
And dost him grace, when clouds do blot the heaven.
So flatter I the swart-complexioned night
When sparkling stars twire not, thou gild'st the even. 12

But day doth daily draw my sorrows longer
And night doth nightly make grief's length seem stronger.

Day and night I cannot rest. How can I come back happy? Day and night
* are enemies but have formed an alliance to torment me.*
I flatter them by telling a dull day that you make it bright,
* and telling a starless night that you gild the evening.*
But every day makes sorrows longer and every night makes grief greater.

1–8 In Sonnet 27 S was on his travels. He now asks how he could possibly
come back in a happy condition, oppressed as he is by the toil of travel
during the day and by visions of the beloved at night. The endless round
of misery is represented by repetitions in lines 3–4, 'day ... oppression ...
night ... day ... night ... night ... day ... oppressed'. The oppressors are
tyrants (5), each ruling his own kingdom, each the enemy of the other, and
encroaching on the other's boundaries. The personification is made visible
as the two kings shake hands in 6 to make a truce to join in torturing their
victim. Day tortures him by the toil of travel (27.1), and night tortures him

to [make him] moan that the farther he goes as he toils, the farther he is from his beloved.

9–12   One reaction to tyranny is to flatter the tyrant (149.6–12). Here, 'when I tell the day, to please him, thou art bright', 'him' is the day and 'thou' is the beloved. When day is dull and the sky is blotted out, S assures day that he is not dull because the beloved's brightness makes him beautiful, gracing him. When night is grim and starless he flatters him by telling him that evening is gilded by the beloved. Here 'night', not 'evening', is required by logic, but 'even' is imposed by rhyme. There is a compensation. The evening star is the brightest star in the sky.

In the tyrant metaphor, night has suffered a sex change from the negress night of 27.12, and he is now not black, but 'swart-complexioned'. S is laying on the flattery, but he knows that a starless night is not pretty. 'Swart' is always disparaging in Shakespeare, for example in *KJ* 2.2.46, 'Lame, foolish, crooked, swart, prodigious'. 'Twire' (meaning 'peer'), too, is disrespectful. It occurs only here in Shakespeare. It has a humorous tone in John Fletcher's *Women Pleased* (1605): 'I saw the wench that twir'd and twinkled at thee the other day.'

This whole torture chamber scene has enabled S to insert into the poem a flash of praise of the beloved, whose brightness graces a dull day and gilds a dull evening.

13–14   Torturers are not often deflected by flattery. Day draws S's sorrows longer, and 'draws' is a strange word for 'draws out'. Is day using a rack? Night makes this long suffering seem nightly more intense. Again, as in 3–4, repetition represents the misery of separation, drudgery and insomnia, with 'day' and 'night' in 9 and 11 followed by 'day doth daily', 'night doth nightly', all made to seem even longer by the repeated rhymes in lines 1, 3, 9 and 11, and the extra syllable at the end of 10 and 12. The reading of the Quarto, 'length seeme stronger', is emended by many editors to 'And night doth nightly make grief's strength seem stronger.' The easy emendation comes too pat. The Quarto reading surprises and demands extra thought. Every day of his absence prolongs his misery, and every long night makes his misery more acute. Similar density occurs, for example, in the final couplets of 25 and 27. All three endings have more active content than this jingling emendation of 28.14.

ଈ 29 ଔ

When in disgrace with Fortune and men's eyes,
I all alone beweep my outcast state,
And trouble deaf Heav'n with my bootless cries,
And look upon myself and curse my fate,   4

Wishing me like to one more rich in hope,
Featured like him, like him with friends possessed,
Desiring this man's art and that man's scope,
With what I most enjoy contented least.   8

Yet in these thoughts myself almost despising,
Haply I think on thee, and then my state,
Like to the lark at break of day arising
From sullen earth, sings hymns at Heaven's gate.   12
 For thy sweet love remembered such wealth brings
 That then I scorn to change my state with kings.

When I think of my disgrace and misfortune, I weep and curse my fate,
envying those better off than myself,
but when I think of you, I sing at the gates of Heaven,
 glorying in my wealth.

'Sonnet 29 is the first of the great sonnets,' writes Evans (1996), 'followed immediately by the second.' It consists of four lines of misery, followed by four lines of envy, then a sudden thought introducing six lines of ecstasy. How does the poetry work?

1–4 The account of misery works by its density. To be in disgrace with men's eyes is to be disapproved of, deplored, by society, with distaste registering in people's eyes. To be in disgrace with fortune is to suffer so much that Fortune is felt as a disapproving critic, particularly if it has an initial capital letter as in the Quarto. In 2 S is all alone, an outcast, and weeping, and in 3 he is troubling 'deaf Heav'n'. If Heaven is deaf he is not troubling it, nor is there need to say that his cries are useless, but the contradiction and the unnecessary adjective both add to the pathos. This line is not easy to read. 'Deaf Heav'n' has a 'hovering accent', according to R. M. Alden (1916) in Rollins (1944). The iambic rhythm would expect 'And trouble déaf Heav'n with my bóotless críes', which is absurd. A reading which respected the sense would be more like, 'And tróuble déaf Héav'n with my bóotless críes'. Does this lurch in the metre suggest despair? The structure of 2–4, 'I beweep and trouble and look and curse', adds pathos or pseudo-pathos. This sonneteer/dramatist is well capable of the language of self-pity.

5–8 These lines present envy in the very accents of the envious man. He wishes he were 'like to one more rich in hope, | *Featured like him, like him* with friends *possessed*'. He is with what he '*most enjoys contented least*', the italics picking out the two ABBA constructions. Chiasmus is now varied by antithesis, ABC ABC, 'Desiring *this man's art* and *that man's scope* '. He envies everybody. In lines 2–4 the effect of an inventory of complaints was conveyed by monotony in a list of four main verbs, 'beweep' and 'trouble' and 'look' and 'curse'. In 5–9 the hint of self-mockery is conveyed by variety in the list of participles, present tense in 5, 7 and 9, past tense in 6 and 8 – 'wishing', 'featured', 'possessed', 'desiring', 'contented', 'despising'. The flavour of an endless list of complaints is heightened by the monotony in the metre. Editors put a mark of punctuation at the end of every line in these first ten. The Quarto has a comma after every line except 4, where it ends the quatrain with an absurd full stop.

9–14 In all this misery he happens to think of the beloved, and wretchedness is transformed into rapture. 'Haply', he says, to preserve the impression that he is recording a stream of thoughts. But was it just chance that made him think of the beloved. His misery had reached its climax in line 8, 'With what I most enjoy contented least', and at that moment, when considering what he enjoyed most in life, he finds himself asking if he is discontented with the beloved. Certainly not. The poem pivots on the word 'haply' and becomes a drama, first scene gloomy, second scene ecstatic.

One of the most joyous sounds in nature is the morning song of the lark, and its joy is all the greater by contrast with the sullen dampness of the earth from which it rises, just as the joy in the sonnet is all the greater for the abyss of gloom which precedes it. The strength of this poetry depends on its accuracy of detail. Larks build their nests on the ground, and soar singing at sunrise from the dew-soaked grass.

The logic is tight, as the last three lines contain a multiple refutation of the misery of the first eight. He was all alone (2) and not with friends possessed, but now he remembers the person he loves. He troubled 'deaf Heav'n' with bootless cries, but now his state sings hymns at Heaven's gate, and the discord of 'deaf Heav'n' is resolved in the music of line 12. Even the sound of 'Heaven' is different from the sound of 'Heav'n'. He wished himself 'like to one more rich in hope', and was almost despising himself, but now 'thy sweet love remembered such wealth brings | That then I scorn to change my state with kings.' 'State' binds the argument together in lines 2, 10 and 14, the first state outcast, the second changing, the third royal.

Another source of vitality in this poetry comes from the fact that Shakespeare wrote mostly for the theatre, for the human voice. Eight lines present misery, desolation, envy, self-pity and self-mockery – and then he happens to think of the beloved. The upward surge comes in lines 11 and 13, the only lines in the poem which do not end with a break in sense:

> and then my state,
> Like to the lark at break of day arising
> From sullen earth, sings hymns at Heaven's gate.

Some editors put a comma after 'arising' and not after 'earth'. This is poor sense:

> and then my state,
> Like to the lark at break of day arising,
> From sullen earth sings hymns at Heaven's gate.

His state does not sing hymns from sullen earth.

In her Introduction Duncan-Jones (1997) argues convincingly that Shakespeare was probably not given opportunity to read the proofs of his Sonnets in 1609, and certainly the punctuation offered by the printer often destroys the sense and cripples the rhythm.

๑ 30 ๙

When to the sessions of sweet silent thought,
I summon up remembrance of things past,
I sigh the lack of many a thing I sought,
And with old woes new wail my dear time's waste.   4

Then can I drown an eye unused to flow,
For precious friends hid in death's dateless night,
And weep afresh love's long since cancelled woe,
And moan th'expense of many a vanished sight.   8

Then can I grieve at grievances foregone,
And heavily from woe to woe tell o'er
The sad account of fore-bemoanèd moan,
Which I new pay as if not paid before.   12

But if the while I think of thee, dear friend,
All losses are restored and sorrows end.

When I think about the past, I grieve over my failed ambitions
and wasted life.
I weep for my dead friends, knowing that I shall never see them again.
I count all my grievances, and suffer for them as intensely as ever.
But if I think of you, dear friend, all losses are restored and sorrows end.

1–4 Sonnet 28 reviewed Sonnet 27 on the sufferings inflicted by day and
night, in the light of a metaphor of two torturing kings. Sonnet 30 reviews
Sonnet 29 on the change from misery to elation, in the light of a legal
metaphor, 'When to the sessions of sweet silent thought'. Thus far the
reader might think that these sessions were simply occasions when S sat
brooding. But the next three words change that. The two terms 'summon'
and 'sessions' collide to spark a metaphor. Sessions are sittings of a lawcourt, and this association is confirmed by 'remembrance'. The Queen's
Remembrancer was an officer of the Exchequer responsible for the collec-

103

tion of debts due to the sovereign (*OED* 1b, including a citation in 1607). This is therefore a debtor's court, S is the President of the Court, and he is reviewing the record of debts and losses incurred during his own life. A score of terms contributes to this legal fiction.

In line 4 the waste of the time allotted to him for life is all the more criminal because it is 'dear', meaning valuable, as confirmed by 'Farewell! Thou art too dear for my possessing' in 87.1. 'Dateless' hints at a *sine die* contract, as in 18.4, where 'summer's lease hath all too short a date', and in *RJ* 5.3.114–15, where Romeo calls upon his lips to 'seal with a righteous kiss | A dateless bargain to engrossing death'. The indictment mounts through 'long since cancelled' and 'expense'. 'Grievances' are often legal in Shakespeare, as in *2H4* 4.1.167–8, where a schedule contains 'general grievances, | Each several article herein redress'd'. 'Foregone' and 'fore-bemoanèd' have the flavour of legal jargon. 'Foresaid' is so used half a dozen times in the plays, as in *MM* 2.1.104, where in a burlesque lawsuit Froth admitted to 'cracking the stones of the foresaid prunes'. 'Telling' means counting, as when 'Every shepherd tells his tale | Under the hawthorn in the dale' in Milton's *L'Allegro*. The indictment concludes with 'account', 'pay', 'paid', 'losses' and 'restored'.

These legalisms and financial technicalities do not drag down the lyric flight. To see love through this strange glass is not to diminish it.

There is an obvious objection to this line of interpretation – that many of these terms are in frequent use without any sense of their legal connotations. Any one of these words, by itself, in a non-legal context, would be read easily as a dead metaphor. It costs nothing to 'pay' attention. But the interpretation stands because each term supports every other. So here in 10 'heavily' is a dead metaphor, used without any sense of physical weight, whereas at 50.11 it most certainly has that overtone, as S describes how 'heavily' the burdened horse answers the spur with a groan.

So much for the ruling metaphor. The first line has two surprises. Being silent, these are untypical law courts. And lawsuits are not sweet to any but lawyers. In the third line, when he *sighs* because he does not have what he *sought* to have, he is pretending that 'sought' is the past tense of 'sigh'. Polyptoton is the juxtaposition of the same word in different forms. The play on 'sigh' and 'sought' might even be called a pseudo-polyptoton.

The alliteration of -s- could be effective in the 'sessions of sweet silent thought'. In line 4 alliteration of -w- mimics the wailing (as in 9.4–5), and the three adjective and noun pairs add to the sense of weary repetition, 'And with *old woes new wail* my *dear time*'s waste'. So far this is 'a wailful sonnet' (*TGV* 3.2.69).

5–8   From things to persons. S is not given to tears, but his eyes can drown
for friends who have died, but it is 'eye', not 'eyes', with the poetic singular
to heighten the tone, and the friends are not simply dead but hidden in
night, in a night that will never end. He mourned them when they died,
but the mourning ceased, cancelled a long time ago, only to be renewed in
this remembrance, and the poetry is given a characteristic edge by the clash
of opposites, at 'weep *afresh* love's *long since* cancelled woe'. Since the dead
friends are 'hid in death's dateless night', they are the 'vanished sight' of
line 8. In 3 and 8 'many a' is spoken as two syllables, slurring the -y- into
the following vowel, and the repetition signals the great number of losses
he has suffered, 'many a … many a'.

9–12   From persons to grievances. Their multiplicity is conveyed in the
polyptoton parade in four lines in succession (if 'from woe to woe' is
allowed), all together intensifying the picture of obsessive brooding. The
monotony is heightened by triple alliteration in line 9, 'grieve at grievances
foregone', with triple assonance in line 10, 'from woe to *woe* tell *o'er*' where
the sound is so vivid that it has the ring of self-mockery, intensified by its
echoes at the end of the next line, in '*fore*-bem*oan*èd *moan*'.

13–14   These twelve lines of misery mock his own self-pity, but there is
no humour in what follows. The graph is the same as the graph of Sonnet
29, with the difference that the last six lines of 29 rise to a rhapsodic climax.
Some agree with Martin (1972, 105–6), who finds the last couplet of 30 to
be weak, perfunctory, trite and giving an appearance of intellectual collapse. Agreed, the last six lines of Sonnet 29 convey the sublimity of S's joy,
but the last two of Sonnet 30 suggest with a different eloquence how a
mountain of failure, bereavement and self-recrimination is removed simply by the thought of the beloved. The power is in the simplicity. The
indescribable is expressed in simple monosyllables, and the intensity is
increased by the fact that this is the first time in the sequence that the young
man is addressed as 'dear friend'.

At first hearing lines 3–12 may sound like a long tale of woe, saying the
same thing half a dozen times in different ways. This is not what it is. His
first remembrance is the desires he failed to achieve – 'I sigh the lack of
many a thing I sought'. The second is the precious time he has wasted, 'my
dear time's waste'. He then weeps for friends who have died, and loves he
will never see again. The fifth remembrance is of past grievances, injustices

he has suffered. All of this makes up an account which he has already grieved over and which he still has to keep on paying.

T. R. Price (1902) in Rollins (1944), on Sonnet 103.13–14
Alliteration rises to its highest use in sonnets 141–50, and sinks to its lowest in sonnets 41–50. Ten are free from alliteration, seven (30, 85, 116, 129, 135, 146, 148) rise above the rest in what may almost seem excess of alliterative art.

Vendler (1997)
Shakespeare here, as in many other sonnets, takes pains to construct a speaker possessing a multilayered self, receding through panels of time. We might give such temporal panels the names 'now', 'recently', 'before that', 'yet further back', 'in the remote past' … In receding order, before the weeping 'now' (T5, where T = Time), there was the 'recent' dry-eyed stoicism (T4); 'before that', the frequent be-moanèd moan (T3) of repeated grief; 'further back in the past', the original loss (T2) so often mourned; and 'in the remote past' T1, a time of achieved happiness or at least neutrality, before the loss.

[Vendler often finds deep meanings, and they are not always there. Her argument is that the earliest phase is the distant past, where one layer of the constructed speaker was happy or neutral. But this is not in the text. Second and third are the original loss and the bemoaning of it. But there has been many a loss and many a bemoaning intermixed over a long period of his life. These are not two temporal panels, but two experiences, each many times repeated. Fourth is 'a recent dry-eyed stoicism', based upon the information in line 5 that his eye is now flowing, although it once was 'unused to flow'. This does not establish a chronological panel, but makes it clear that he never was a weeper, but he weeps now when he remembers things past. This poem is a backward look over his life, but there are no temporal panels, and no painstaking creation of a multilayered self in five phases. S is saying rather, with incomparable eloquence, that, even when he is remembering how much he has lost and suffered throughout his life, the thought of his dear friend always puts an end to his suffering and sense of loss. Vendler's chronology is an invention.]

Thy bosom is endearèd with all hearts
Which I by lacking have supposèd dead,
And there reigns Love and all Love's loving parts
And all those friends which I thought burièd.   4

How many a holy and obsequious tear
Hath dear religious love stol'n from mine eye
As int'rest of the dead, which now appear
But things removed that hidden in thee lie.   8

Thou art the grave where buried love doth live,
Hung with the trophies of my lovers gone,
Who all their parts of me to thee did give.

That due of many now is thine alone.   12
    Their images I loved, I view in thee,
    And thou, all they, hath all the all of me.

Your breast is enriched by the hearts of all those I have loved.
  I thought them dead, but there they still live and reign.
Many a tear was drawn from my eyes as interest owed to the dead
  under false pretences, because they are not dead but hidden in you.
You are their grave and all the parts of me they took are now in you.
Therefore what I owed to many is all yours. You house all their features.
  You are all of them and have all the all of me.

1–4 In Sonnet 30 S lamented the lack of friends who had died. In Sonnet
31 he finds that after all they are not dead, but are preserved in his new
beloved. They are not 'hid in death's dateless night' (30.6), but 'hidden in
thee lie' (31.8). The poem plays with a conceit of past lovers buried alive in
a new lover's breast, after Sonnets 22 and 24 yet another exploration of 'My
true love hath my heart, and I have his.'
    In 30.4 'dear' meant 'valuable'; in 30.13 it meant 'loved'. So here the

beloved's bosom is 'endearèd', is made more valuable and is also more loved because it contains the hearts of all S's past lovers. This is a strange conceit. It is one thing for S's heart to live in his beloved's breast as in Sonnet 22, but it is a different matter if the beloved's breast houses the hearts of all S's previous lovers, dead and alive. Fanciful as this is, it corresponds to a genuine experience, the sense that a new beloved contains all the good qualities of all previous incumbents. In line 4 he calls them friends, but 'love' is mentioned seven times in this poem, three times in the previous line. They were friends in the sense that the young man is a friend at 30.13, 42.10–13 and often throughout the Sonnets.

There in the beloved's breast are the hearts of all his previous lovers, and with them are 'all love's loving parts'. This mysterious phrase is explained in line 11. S had given parts of himself to previous lovers, and in line 3 these parts are now gathered, and all are preserved in the new lover's breast, and there they reign as in a palace.

5–8   In 5 'many a' is two syllables, and S is repeating from 30.6–8 the important statement that he has in the past known many friends. 'Obsequies' are funeral rites, and in 5 'obsequious' (three syllables) means 'dutiful in regard to the dead', as in *Ham* 1.2.90–2, 'bound | In filial obligation for some term | To do obsequious sorrow'. The combination of 'holy', 'obsequious' and 'religious' suggests that S wept at the funerals of those he had loved. These tears were given as interest paid to the dead for the love they had loaned to S, but it now turns out that the payments were made under false pretences, 'stol'n', because those are lovers who are not dead, 'which now appear ... hidden in thee'.

9–11   In line 9 it seems for a moment that the conceit has collapsed. Lines 2, 4 and 6–8 make it abundantly clear that the past lovers are not deceased but have only changed their abode, but now love is buried in a grave. This is not a blunder but a paradox, 'Thou art the grave where buried *love* doth *live*.' The crucial word is the last. The lovers presumed dead are all buried in the beloved, but that is a grave in which they are all alive.

This grave is a tomb like the tombs in English churches, commemorating in stone carvings the trophies of the dead, as in *TA* 1.1.385, 'Till we with trophies do adorn thy tomb'. What these trophies might be is suggested by *Ham* 4.5.212, 'No trophy, sword, nor hatchment o'er his bones', where a hatchment is a coat of arms. The word is altered from 'achievement'. 'Can storied urn or animated bust,' asks Gray in his *Elegy in a Country Churchyard*, 'Back to its mansion call the fleeting dust?' The beloved's breast is the living grave of all S's former lovers, and is hung with their honours, perhaps including all the parts of himself which S had given to them, which they have handed over to the beloved, who now has all the love S ever gave. The beloved is a tomb. Love is a familiar subject in poetry, but Shakespeare sees it in lights which are anything but familiar.

12–14 'What I owed to many is now yours alone. I loved them, and now I see images of them in you. You are all of them, and possess all the all of me.' Such is the richness of the beloved that his bosom contains all those whom S has ever loved before. This declaration requires 'all' four times, and two monosyllabic lines, 11 and 14.

Quiller-Couch (1896)
For mere subtlety of thought Sonnet 31 seems to me to be unbeaten by anything that I can select from the poetry of the [nineteenth] century.

Duncan-Jones (1997)
The young man is universally loved, and in the congress of those who love him the lonely poet imaginatively discovers his lost (dead) friends.

Burrow (2002)
The dominant mood here is of a triumph over death through the friend, but there is also a faint suggestion (anticipating the jealousies later in the sequence) that the poet has lost all his former lovers and thinks they are dead because they have switched their affections to the friend.

℘ 32 ☜

If thou survive my well-contented day
When that churl death with dust my bones shall cover,
And shalt by fortune once more resurvey
These poor rude lines of thy deceasèd lover,   4
Compare them with the bett'ring of the time,
And though they be outstripped by every pen,
Reserve them for my love, not for their rhyme,
Exceeded by the height of happier men.   8

O then vouchsafe me but this loving thought:
'Had my friend's Muse grown with this growing age,
A dearer birth than this his love had brought,
To march in ranks of better equipage.   12

But since he died and poets better prove,
Theirs for their style I'll read, his for his love.'

If you happen to look at this feeble verse after I am dead and buried,
preserve what I have written, though later poets will be better.
Spare a thought for me – 'If he had lived to share this improvement,
he would have produced better work,
but, since he died too soon, I'll read his lines because he loved me.'

In Sonnet 31 he thought about his past lovers now dead. Now in Sonnet 32 he imagines how the beloved will think about him when he himself is dead. The key to this sonnet is that it is totally insincere. Shakespeare (and S) know that this is superlative work. It is enough to look at the final couplets of Sonnets 17, 18 and 19. This poem is full of self-abasement and appeals for pity, beginning, 'When that churl death my bones with dust shall cover', and he adds to the poignancy of the scene by calling earth dust, to evoke the order for the burial of the dead in the Book of Common Prayer, 'earth to earth, ashes to ashes, dust to dust'. In lines 1–3 he talks as though he doubts whether the beloved will ever look at his poems again,

'If thou survive ... And shalt by fortune once more resurvey | These poor rude lines of thy deceasèd lover', implying, 'if you happen to cast an eye over them again'. When 'These póor rude línes' (where a stress on 'rúde' would elegantly slow down the iambic beat) are compared with later improvements, 'the bett'ring of the time', they will be 'outstripped', and his rhyme will be 'exceeded by the height of happier men'. In line 9, 'vouchsafe me but this' makes it clear that he is not asking much. This analysis of the special pleading explains 'well-contented' in line 1. When he dies he is not going to complain. He knows he is of no consequence.

1–8   So much for an interpretation of the tone of voice of the poem. Now for details. In line 7, 'Reserve them for my love', 'reserve' means preserve (85.3), and 'for my love' could mean because of your love for me', or 'because of my love for you'. Here the latter sense fits the argument of the poem. He is presenting himself as an unhappy lover humbly begging just for a loving thought in line 9, not as one who can take for granted that he is loved. Much more affecting to beg a favour because one loves than to beg it because one is loved. In lines 11 and 14 too, 'his love' is love he feels, not love he receives.

9–12   The 'growing age' in 10 repeats the 'bett'ring of the time', and here again there is an expressive disturbance of metrical expectation. Iambic rhythm would run 'Had mý friend's Múse grown wíth this grówing áge', but sense requires something like 'Had my friend's Múse grówn with this grówing áge', where the unexpected accent makes 'grówn' swell into 'grówing'. The beloved is now asked to think that, if S had lived, his Muse would have brought him a more valuable progeny than these jejune verses. Poetry seen as offspring is a familiar metaphor, developed for instance in 38.11–14, and here it offers a play between 'bear' and 'brought', as in 'O had my mother borne so hard a mind, | She had not brought forth thee, but died unkind', in VA 203–4. For such 'pseudo-polyptoton', see 30.3.

In 12, had he lived to improve with the improvement of the times, his lines would have 'marched in ranks of better equipage'. The salient sense of the word 'equipage' here is 'military garb, accoutrements', so the picture is of lines of verse as ranks of soldiers on parade in splendid uniforms, as in Thomas Nashe (1589) referring to the poet Thomas Watson, 'whose Amintas may ... march in equippage of honour, with any of our ancient poets'. S's poems would then have grown to be warriors in more splendid array than the poor rude lines which were all that he would leave behind him when he died. Here lines of verse drift into lines of soldiers on parade, just as in 16.9 they became genealogical lines of descent.

This interpretation takes this as a love poem, playing the humility card, hoping to be contradicted, and insisting on love throughout, in 4, 7, 9, 11 and finally, with monosyllabic intensity, in 14.

Evans (1996)
Ingram and Redpath suggest that Sonnet 32 reflects Shakespeare's recognition that he was living in an age of extraordinary literary growth ('the bett'ring of the time' (5), 'this growing age' (10)) and was uncertain (as yet) of his future reputation. Perhaps so, but one should allow for the convention of an ironic personal depreciation or mock modesty in the sonnet tradition.

Burrow (2002)
Verse is here no longer the instrument of immortality: it needs to be read affectionately by its addressee in order to have permanent value.

ᔎ 33 ᦔ

Full many a glorious morning have I seen
Flatter the mountain tops with sovereign eye,
Kissing with golden face the meadows green,
Gilding pale streams with heav'nly alchemy;   4
Anon, permit the basest clouds to ride
With ugly rack on his celestial face,
And from the fórlorn world his visage hide,
Stealing unseen to west with this disgrace: 8

Ev'n so my sun one early morn did shine
With all triumphant splendour on my brow;
But out alack! He was but one hour mine,
The region cloud has masked him from me now.   12

    Yet him for this, my love no whit disdaineth,
    Suns of the world may stain, when heav'n's sun staineth.

A bright morning often means a dull day.
Just so my sun shone briefly on me, and has now gone behind the clouds.
I do not blame him. If the sun in heaven fades, earthly suns may do the same.

1–8 The poem opens with the description of a day's weather. In *VA*
856–8, 'The sun ariseth in his majesty', and its light touches the eastern
mountains so 'That cedar tops and hills are burnished gold.' When here the
sun flatters the mountain tops, this may activate a contemporary sense of
'flatter', to caress. Booth (1977) quotes from *OED* (1599), 'Trout is a fish
that loveth to be flattered and clawed in the water.' After caressing the
mountain tops, the sun then kisses green meadows with his golden face,
rises a little more and gilds rivers, turning water to molten gold. Rivers are
the lowest of the three, the palest, the last to catch the light and the best to
reflect it. But only too often clouds low on the horizon, 'basest clouds',
blow up and obscure the sun, which may never be seen again that day. The

'ugly rack' is a mass of high cloud driven before the wind. This is not an unusual order of events and Shakespeare has observed it.

But these lines are not only a weather report. The sun is pictured in a metaphor as a glorious king, who flatters the highest in the land by turning his royal gaze, his 'sovereign eye', upon them at his daily levée. A monarch might also condescend to kiss a subject, not of course with the lips, but by offering his cheek, 'kissing with golden face', and when he does so, as though by a miracle of alchemy performed by heaven, the palest and humblest subjects might turn to gold. The alchemist aspires to change base metal into gold, but a monarch may allow baser elements to come between him and his people, who will be abandoned and never again see his face. He may 'permit the basest clouds to ride | With ugly rack on his celestial face' like black knights riding between himself and his subjects, and bringing rack and ruin to the realm. The king who loses touch with his subjects leaves 'the forlorn world', slinking away in disgrace, in a line with six sibilants. 'Disgrace' means dishonour, and 'dis-grace' something which destroys grace, a disfigurement, here caused by the 'ugly rack'.

Ransom (1938) in Rollins (1944) is far from the truth: 'this sun is weakly imagined; rather it may be said to be only felt, a loose cluster of images as obscure as they are pleasant, furnished by the half-conscious memories attending the pretty words.'

9–12 The first eight lines are a landscape and a metaphor. At 'Ev'n so' they become a simile. In the metaphor the sun *is* a monarch. In the simile he is *like* the beloved. To make the comparison valid the simile is locked into what it illustrates by corresponding details. 'A glorious morning' in the first line is caught up in lines 9–10 by 'one early morn' with 'triumphant splendour'; the world is left 'forlorn', and so S exclaims 'out alack!'; the sun does not last long, 'Anon' it is obscured, so the beloved 'was but one hour mine'; the beloved fell into low company, the 'region cloud', presumably London society, so the sun allows 'the basest clouds to ride | With ugly rack on his celestial face'. S often takes as harsh a view of the beloved's friends as Prince Harry did of his own tavern cronies in *1H4* 1.2.194–200:

> Yet herein will I imitate the *sun*,
> Who doth *permit the base* contagiou*s clouds*
> To smother up his beauty from the world

and then he schemes to be 'more wondered at' by abandoning his old drinking companions

> By breaking through the foul and *ugly* mists
> Of vapours that did seem to strangle him.

Repeatedly the face is the bonding element between the image and its explanation. It is mentioned in lines 3, 6 and 7, and picked up by 'brow', a brilliant link to the mountain tops of line 2, offering a picture of the sun gleaming on a domed forehead. The final correspondence is in 'masked'. Masks go on faces.

13–14   Determined not to sour this love, S struggles not to blame, to disparage or 'disdain' the beloved for deserting him. 'Stains' is used to mean loses colour in *OED* (1579), 'purple dye will never stain.' If the sun in heaven stains, darkened by base clouds, earthly suns also may stain in bad company. The lament is rounded off by a glowing compliment. The young man is a sun on the earth. Shakespeare could well have ended with his usual verb forms, but he had an ear. 'Disdains' and 'stains' have nothing like the weight of sound in

> Yet him for this, my love no whit disdaineth,
> Suns of the world may stain, when heav'n's sun staineth.

There may have been premonitions of doubt at 20.14 and 23.12, but this is the first clearly audible rift in the lute in the plot of the Sonnets. The cause is not defined in detail, but there is no doubt that the beloved is neglecting S and consorting with undesirable company.

Duncan-Jones (1997, 10–11) suggests that Shakespeare was called away from London to Stratford after he had submitted the text of the Sonnets to the printer. 'Such a sequence of events would help to account for the mediocre printing of the text and the apparent absence of authorial proof-correction.' This shabbiness shows clearly in the Quarto version of this sonnet. Line 8, for instance reads 'Stealing un eene to west with this dsgrace', and the last word in the poem is printed 'stainteh'. More important are mistakes in punctuation. The compositor's rough practice is to punctuate at the end of almost every line regardless of the sense. Here, for instance, only line 7 lacks final punctuation, thus blocking the flow of sense at the end of lines 1, 5 and 9 and providing a meaningless semicolon at the end of line 3. Vendler's transcription copied above articulates the argument of the poem: commas ending lines 2 and 3 and a semicolon ending the beautiful landscape of the first quatrain at 'alchemy' before the contrasting clouds arrive in line 5. This second quatrain ends with a colon after 'disgrace', before the application of the simile. Here again, at line 10 the semicolon marks a contrast, this time between beauty in 9–10 and the loss of it in 11–12.

Why didst thou promise such a beauteous day,
And make me travel forth without my cloak,
To let base clouds o'ertake me in my way,
Hiding thy brav'ry in their rotten smoke?   4

'Tis not enough that through the cloud thou break
To dry the rain on my storm-beaten face,
For no man well of such a salve can speak
That heals the wound and cures not the disgrace.   8

Nor can thy shame give physic to my grief;
Though thou repent, yet I have still the loss.
Th'offender's sorrow lends but weak relief
To him that bears the strong offence's cross.   12

   Ah! but those tears are pearl which thy love sheds
   And they are rich and ransom all ill deeds.

Why did you promise a lovely day
   and then let clouds overtake me on my road?
It's not enough that you dry the rain on my face. Nobody could speak well
   of a cure that heals the wound but leaves the scar.
Nor does your shame cure me. I still suffer the loss.
   The criminal's repentance is small comfort to the victim.
Ah, but your tears are so lovely that I forgive you everything.

Sonnet 33 is a dozen lines of a lover's complaint based upon the metaphor of sun and cloud, and it ends by providing an absurd excuse for the fickleness of the beloved. Sonnet 34 is also a dozen lines of a lover's complaint, starting from the same metaphor of sun and cloud but moving to four or five other metaphors merging one into another, with vividly mounting indignation, and again the poem ends in a reconciliation, but there are differences. In 33 S is musing to himself. In 34.13 he is speaking to the beloved, and the beloved is reacting. 'Ah! but those tears' makes 34 a dramatic scene:

S: Why did you leave me after all those promises?

B: I admit I left you, but now I'm back.

S: That's not enough. The damage is done.

B: I'm sorry.

S: Being sorry doesn't give me back what I have lost.

> *B weeps.*

S: Oh, don't weep. Your tears are so beautiful I forgive you everything.

1–4   The opening feints at a domestic scene in which a man is grumbling because he has been tricked into going out without a raincoat. But readers of Sonnet 33 will know that the sun being addressed in line 4 is S's beloved. The promise of a beauteous day in Sonnet 34 is the 'glorious morning' of 33. The base clouds of 34 have already been seen in 'the basest clouds' of 33.5, the sun's bravery in 34 is its 'triumphant splendour' of 33.10, and the sun that breaks through the base clouds in 34.5 is again the beloved. Here too the weather is a metaphor for love.

In literal terms the poems say that, when love began, it was all serenity, promise and trust, but now the beloved has deserted him. 'Base clouds' with 'rotten smoke' are the low company of 33.5–6 and 12. Smoke is vapour, mist, in *1H6* 2.2.27, 'smoke and dusky vapours of the night', and it is rotten like 'the reek o'th' rotten fens' in *Cor* 3.3.125.

5–8   It is no great help that the beloved comes back to dry S's tears, in the metaphor 'To dry the rain on my storm-beaten face'. Being sorry is not enough. Lines 7–12 explain why, using different metaphors. The first is medical. The beloved has come back with a salve, an ointment, presumably remorse, and healed the wound, but he has not cured the disgrace. Here dis-grace is part of the metaphor in the sense suggested for the word in 33.8, namely 'deprivation of grace or beauty, disfigurement, deformity'. The remorseful return has eased the pain of the wound, but the damage is permanent, like a scar or a limp, and remorse cannot physic it. Once love is flawed, it can never be perfect.

9–12   Here begins a metaphor of crime and punishment. Shame and repentance are all very well, but they do not cure the victim's grief. The offence carries a punishment of crucifixion, yet the cross is not borne by the offender but by his victim. There is a glimpse of another innocent victim. Men sin, and Christ bore the cross as a ransom for their sins.

13–14   After this indictment S sees tears of remorse on the cheeks of the man he loves, and sees them as tears of pearl, 'A sea of melting pearl which some call tears' (*TGV* 3.1.223), pearl rich enough to 'ransom all ill deeds'. The metaphor of ransom now merges with the crime and punishment of lines 11–12. A ransom is normally a payment for the release of a prisoner, but sometimes it is 'a sum of money paid to obtain pardon for an offence', as for example in Sonnet 120.14, and in *TGV* 5.4.74–5, 'If hearty sorrow | Be a sufficient ransom for offence'. Here in 34.14 the ransom is paid in tears, atonement for an offence against love. This is the graph which gives drama to Sonnets 29, 30 and 33, in all of which a long complaint is followed by a couplet in which all discontent is dissolved in praise of the beloved. The greatest and commonest offence in love is infidelity, and that is the most likely cause of grief in this poem. S knows it but at this point is too diplomatic to be explicit.

Vendler (1997)
After the sixth line the meteorological metaphor disappears, and the metaphorical appeal undergoes startling changes, as follows:
A.   Medicine (*salve, heals, wound, cures, physic*);
B.   Pain, both social and emotional (*disgrace, shame, grief, loss, sorrow, relief, bear[ing'a] cross*);
C.   Religion (*repent, cross, ransom*);
D.   Sin, meaning ethical offense (*offender, strong offence, ill deeds*);
E.   Pearl (*pearl, rich, ransom*);
F.   Love.
Though these categories roughly follow one another, each begins in a line where the former is still present, or recurs after another has just begun ... Shakespeare's strategy here thus affords us a map of a mind resorting over time from one of its compartments to another in order to find adequate metaphorical expression for a shocking experience.

ഔ 35 ര

No more be grieved at that which thou hast done:
Roses have thorns and silver fountains mud,
Clouds and eclipses stain both moon and sun,
And loathsome canker lives in sweetest bud.   4

All men make faults and even I in this,
Authórising thy trespass with compare,
Myself corrupting salving thy amiss,
Excusing thy sins more than thy sins are.   8

For to thy sensual fault I bring in sense.
Thy adverse party is thy advocate,
And 'gainst myself a lawful plea commence.

Such civil war is in my love and hate   12
    That I an áccessáry needs must be
    To that sweet thief which sourly robs from me.

Do not condemn yourself. Everything has faults,
even I in excusing yours and so committing greater sins myself.
Your fault is of the senses, mine of the mind.
You rob me, and I am forced to be an accessary after the crime.

1–4 The beloved has behaved badly, and lines 2–4 parade five excuses.
Analogical arguments are never valid, but these are obviously flimsy, the
feeble stuff of handle-turning love poetry, already satirised in Sonnet 21. A
specimen is given at the end of the note on Sonnet 130.

5–8 Now comes the hard truth. He has been authorisíng the beloved's sin
by comparisons, and comparisons are invalid. He has been corrupting
himself [by] salving the beloved's amiss, and has been excusing his sins,
[which is] more of a sin than the sins themselves. In line 6 'authorising' is

probably to be stressed on the second syllable, as in 'His rudeness so with his authórised youth' in *LC* 104.

Some editors insert a comma after 'corrupting', and so make the four present participles into a straight list of S's four faults, authorising, corrupting, salving, excusing. The difficulty about this is that 'myself corrupting' standing by itself is not clear. How is he corrupting himself? Besides, this makes 7–8 repetitive. 'Salving thy amiss' is the same as 'excusing thy sins'. The punctuation offered above suggests an answer, 'Myself corrupting' by 'salving thy amiss', by forgiving his sin. This gives S three sins in three lines, each qualified in the second half of its line. However lines 6–8 are understood, the gravity of the charge sheet is increased by the run of these four present participles.

In line 8 the Quarto reads 'Excusing their sins more than their sins are', but this makes difficult sense. After 'thy trespass' and 'thy amiss', what is needed is 'thy sins'. The Quarto often reads 'their' in places like this where 'thy' is necessary (13 times as listed by Booth (1977) on 26.12, including 46.13–14). If 'thy' is read, the line argues that forgiving sins is a greater sin than committing them – a harsh doctrine, to forgive is worse than to commit.

9–11 The beloved's sin was sensual, therefore not so heinous as his own, which is of the mind [and therefore willed and calculated]. This now becomes a lawsuit. The beloved has committed an offence against S. S brings in sense as a witness, but paradoxically the accuser becomes the defending counsel, and rejects the accusation. The paradox is sharpened by the echo of -ad-, 'Thy ádverse párty is thy ádvocate'. The offence is theft. The beloved took what belonged to S and gave it to others (14). This is the sensual fault. Baldly, the young man has been making love elsewhere. But S does not speak baldly. He dare not quarrel.

12–14 'Odi et amo,' says Catullus 85 in a similar situation, 'I hate and love'. This same war is being waged in line 12, and hatred is a new development in this love story. The legal metaphor is not clearly established until line 10, but in retrospect it is beginning to surface with 'authórising trespass' in line 6, and 'corrupting' and 'amiss' in line 7, and it continues in the last two lines, where S realises that by defending the beloved he is making himself an áccessáry after the fact in a case of theft.

Shakespeare often thinks in contrasts. Here this tendency is not simply an idle habit of thought, but rather an obsession with the deep pain that summarised his love and hate in 12. Aspects of this appear in 4, a 'loathsome canker lives in sweetest bud'; in 7–8, 'Myself corrupting salving thy amiss'; and in 'Excusing thy sins more than thy sins are.' In 9–10 'sensual' clashes with 'sense', and 'adverse' with 'advocate', and the last clash ends the poem, 'that sweet thief which sourly robs from me'.

Sonnets 33–5 are an episode in the plot. In Sonnets 33 and 34 S gives the reader a veiled account of his betrayal, and each poem ends with a compliment and a reconciliation. In Sonnet 35 he starts by excusing the beloved's misconduct, and admitting that the excuses are false, then he argues that his own behaviour is a greater offence. There is no compliment or reconciliation, only the painful understanding that he loves and hates the same person at the same time, and the realisation of his own dishonesty, 'More perjured I | To swear against the truth so foul a lie' (152.13–14) is his farewell to love, and 35.5–8 is a presentiment of it.

❧ 36 ☙

Let me confess that we two must be twain
Although our undivided loves are one.
So shall those blots that do with me remain,
Without thy help by me be borne alone.   4

In our two loves there is but one respect
Though in our lives a separable spite,
Which, though it alter not love's sole effect,
Yet doth it steal sweet hours from love's delight.   8

I may not evermore acknowledge thee,
Lest my bewailèd guilt should do thee shame,
Nor thou with public kindness honour me,
Unless thou take that honour from thy name.   12

But do not so: I love thee in such sort
As thou being mine, mine is thy good report.

In love we are one, but in life we must be two.
In that way I shall bear responsibility for my own faults.
This does not damage our love but leaves us less time for its delight.
From now I must not shame you by acknowledging you in public.
If you showed me kindness, my faults would dishonour you,
and I so love you that you are mine, and your good name is mine.

1–4 In the form of the Solemnisation of Matrimony as laid down in the
Book of Common Prayer the celebrant may read the words of St Paul in
his Letter to the Ephesians 5: 28–31: 'So ought men to love their wives as
their own bodies. He that loveth his wife loveth himself. For no man ever
yet hated his own flesh … For this cause shall a man leave his father and
mother, and shall be joined unto his wife, and they two shall be one flesh.'
For 'two' in the Authorised Version, the Geneva Bible reads 'twain'. In
their love it is as though S and the beloved are one, in a form of marriage.

This is not a dead formality nor simply a frigid Renaissance conceit, but folk wisdom. Honan (1999, 22) finds such Elizabethan posies engraved on the flat inner surfaces of rings: 'NOT TWO, BUT ONE, TILL LIFE BE GONE'. But in life, as revealed by Sonnets 33–5, the beloved has been unfaithful. S still loves and the endings of 33–5 make it quite clear that he wishes to continue to love, so here he produces a formula of continuance: 'In our loves we are one; in our lives we must be two' – a pact whereby they will continue to love, but each will be free to live his own life. Line 3 introduces a new element in the drama of the Sonnets. S too has genuine faults, differing from the rhetorical faults of 35. Part of this proposed pact will be that S shall take full blame for 'those blots that do with me remain' (3). He does not explain these blots, nor his 'bewailèd guilt' (10), the guilt he so regrets.

5–8   The first two lines are a guide to the reading of 5–6. Lines 2 and 5 say that their two loves make them one. Lines 1 and 6 say that their two lives must be separate. That bird's eye view of the lines pays no attention to 'respect' and 'spite'. Superficially they add an extra contrast – 'twain/one', 'loves/lives', 'one/separable' and now 'respect/spite'. Whatever form spite may take (probably the malice of Fortune (37.3)), it is 'separable', it is capable of separating their lives. In that case the one respect in their two loves (5), 'love's sole effect' (7), could be the respect in which they hold each other. They spend fewer hours together sharing the delight of love, but that does not impair their love's unifying effect. The spite separates, and the respect unites. Adjectives often have a condensed sense in Shakespeare.

Booth's note on 5–6 begins, 'These lines exemplify Shakespeare's habit of using language with a special precision that gives both a precise meaning not quite demonstrable in the syntax and a wealth of additional meaning as well' (Booth 1977). The rest of his note explores this wealth, writing at great length on the force of 'respect', listing eleven different senses of the word as used elsewhere by Shakespeare, all of which 'are in one way or another pertinent to the particulars of this sonnet'. He then speaks of the 'developing, evident, but never quite developed statement', which he paraphrases as 'Our love makes us one person though unfortunately we must live separately.' He calls this 'a free translation, a paraphrase that does unavoidable violence to the lines, diminishing them in the name of sanity.' It may approach insanity to try. 'In love we are one, united by respect; In life we must be two, separated by spite.'

9–12   The first eight lines have proposed a *laissez-faire* 'love', a pact S has been driven to by the young man's infidelity and by his own bitterly regretted guilt, the stains he will continue to carry (lines 3 and 10). Suggestions abound. Has he also been unfaithful in shameful circumstances? Has he committed adultery? Has he been found guilty of a crime? Or is he exaggerating his offence in aspiring to mix with a social class higher than his own? Some commentators suggest that his 'bewailèd guilt' is that he is an actor consorting with an aristocrat. That would make some sense of lines 8–12, but not of 3–4. Besides, the word 'guilt' is perhaps a little severe. It is not a serious offence to be an actor. Nobody knows what he has done wrong, but one thing is certain: Shakespeare did not wish it to be known. One great advantage for him in writing this discontinuous drama is that he does not have to supply strict lines of cause and effect. These are flash sights of different situations, each in 14 lines, and their effect is increased by the intervening darkness. The diversity in readers' reactions over the centuries shows the success of the technique.

Whatever his offence, S will never be able to acknowledge the young man in public because it would shame the man he loves. The beloved will never be able to speak kindly to S in public, because to confer that honour would diminish his own.

13–14   The climax, as so often, is largely monosyllabic. Strict logic requires, 'Since you *are* me, your reputation is mine.' But that would make the last line of the sonnet contradict its first. Shakespeare avoids contradiction and achieves point by the wording, 'thou being mine, mine is thy good report', a rhetorical flourish with a chiasmus ('thou … mine … mine … thy'), and a polyptoton of 'thou … thy'. As so often the logic is driven home by the metre. The iambic rhythm expects 'As thóu being míne, mine ís thy góod repórt', but the argument calls for something more vigorous and natural, 'As thóu being míne, míne is thy góod repórt.'

This poem is a tortuous play on an arithmetical conceit, but it is not empty cleverness. Agony of the intellect comes with the agony of love. This poem is typical of the Sonnets in making a dramatic scene out of a phase in an intense love. It also advances the plot of the Sonnets. We now know there have been faults on both sides.

As a decrepit father takes delight
To see his active child do deeds of youth,
So I, made lame by Fortune's dearest spite,
Take all my comfort of thy worth and truth.   4

For whether beauty, birth, or wealth, or wit,
Or any of these all, or all, or more,
Intitled in thy parts do crownèd sit,
I make my love ingrafted to this store.   8

So then I am not lame, poor, nor despised,
Whilst that this shadow doth such substance give,
That I in thy abundance am sufficed,
And by a part of all thy glory live.   12

   Look what is best, that best I wish in thee.
   This wish I have, then ten times happy me.

As a decrepit father takes delight in his child's prowess,
   so, crippled by misfortune, I take comfort in your worth and truth.
For I graft my love on to all your supreme qualities.
I am then no longer unfortunate, but feed on the abundance
   of the plant on which I am grafted.
I wish whatever is best to be in you. My wish is granted,
   and I am therefore ten times happy.

S finds comfort in the beloved as an old man delights in the successes of his young child. He himself is decrepit; the beloved is young. He is lame (3, 9); the beloved is active (2). He is poor (9); the beloved has wealth, store, abundance (5, 8, 11). He is despised (9); the beloved is glorious.

1–4 'Fortune's dearest spite' is that spite of hers which hurts him most, which is most costly, damaging, direst, as in 'thy dear exile' in *R2* 1.3.145,

126

and in 'God of his mercy give | You ... true repentance | Of all your dear offences' in *H5* 2.2.176–8. After the beloved's faithlessness in 33–5, this praise of his worth and truth seems to protest too much. It is as though the lover is saying his beloved is true in order to make him so.

5–8   This desperation shows in the inventory of the beloved's qualities, six of them in lines 4–5, paired by initial alliteration, béauty and bírth, wéalth and wít, coming after wórth and trúth, where the alliteration is final. In line 6, whether any of these, or all of them, or all these plus others not listed, sit crowned on thrones among the beloved's royal 'parts' (a man's parts are his qualities), S engrafts his love on to that stock, 'thy abundance' (11). The pedantic precision of line 6 suggests that he finds it difficult to come to terms with the vast inventory of the glories of the beloved.

9–12   When he grafts his love on to that rich stock, then he is neither lame nor despised, the victim of spite, as he was in line 3 and 36.6, nor poor, because now he shares in the beloved's wealth, and 'poor' is given emphasis as the only syllable in this poem which demands to be stressed, although it does not carry the metrical beat. Startlingly a shadow now gives substance, and the explanation is in line 8. A graft is a shoot inserted into a parent tree, from which it derives its sustenance. It needs to be kept cool and moist until it takes. So S lives in the shadow of the beloved and takes his sustenance from its abundance. The shadow gives substance.

13–14   'Look what' means 'whatever', as in 77.9–10. Since he is feeding on the substance of the beloved, naturally he wishes the beloved to contain all that is best, 'that best I wish in thee'. Lines 4–7 make it clear that this wish is fulfilled, and therefore he is not only happy, but ten times happy with the nourishment he is receiving.

Vendler (1997)
We find in Sonnet 37 more *th*'s than chance would usually allow ... Every line except the third displays at least one *th*, and several display more than one ... Line 3, the exception, takes on in the Quarto the form of a joke: it possesses a *th*, indeed, but reversed to *ht* in *despight*. [Some joke. I count 22 in this sonnet and the same number in 38, 39 and 40.]

ᔒ 38 ᘓ

How can my Muse want subject to invent
While thou dost breathe, that pour'st into my verse
Thine own sweet argument, too excellent
For every vulgar paper to rehearse?   4

O give thyself the thanks, if aught in me
Worthy perusal stand against thy sight,
For who's so dumb that cannot write to thee,
When thou thyself dost give invention light?   8

Be thou the tenth Muse, ten times more in worth
Than those old nine which rhymers invocate,
And he that calls on thee, let him bring forth
Eternal numbers to outlive long date.   12

   If my slight Muse do please these curious days,
   The pain be mine, but thine shall be the praise.

How can I be short of subjects when you inspire my verse,
   a subject far too good for run-of-the-mill scribblers?
If I achieve anything worth your reading, the credit is yours.
   Any fool could write poems to you, when you light the way.
Be the tenth Muse, ten times better than the old nine,
   and let him who calls upon you write immortal verse.
If my slight Muse please our fastidious critics, I will have the pain,
   but you will have the praise.

1–4 Invention (Latin *inventio*, finding) is a rhetorical term meaning 'the finding of topics to be treated or arguments to be used' (*OED* 1d). It occurs five times in the Sonnets at 38.8, 59.3, 76.6, 103.7 and 105.11, in each of these except 59.3 in conjunction with 'argument'. 'Thine own sweet argument' is therefore part of this rhetorical play. In Cicero, *Partitiones Oratoriae*, the young Cicero asks his father what argument is, *'Quid est*

128

argumentum?' and his father replies, 'Argument is what is invented credible for persuasion', *'Probabile inventum ad faciendam fidem '*. Shakespeare knew his rhetoric. The title of Cicero's treatise just cited is the basis of Demetrius' joke when Wall has said his piece in *MND* 5.1.165, 'It is the wittiest partition that ever I heard discourse, my lord.' *Partitio* is the division of a speech into sections.

Argument here means subject matter. It is a cliché that the Muse breathes inspiration into the poet, but here the cliché is given life as the beloved breathes himself as subject matter into S's verse, 'You and love are still my argument' (76.10), a subject far above the powers of poetic hacks.

5–8 If anything S writes were to stand up to the beloved's scrutiny as worth reading, 'Worthy perusal stand against thy sight', the thanks are due to the beloved himself. Nobody is so stupid that they could not write poems to the beloved, since he lights their search for arguments, their invention. S's own search for flattering arguments leads him perilously close to inconsistency, 'Your qualities are a subject too high for ordinary versifiers, but any fool can write your praises when you light his way.' This may be a slip by the poet, but it is more likely a cheerful risk, or a calculated display, by the poet/lover/orator. Two compliments are still two compliments, even if they contradict each other.

9–12 'Some say there are nine Muses: how careless! Look – Sappho of Lesbos is the tenth' (Plato in the *Palatine Anthology* 9.66). Following this hint, S makes the beloved the tenth Muse, ten times more valuable than the old nine. If this means that he is ten times more valuable than all the old nine put together, the beloved is 90 times more valuable than any one of them. The cheerful compliment is laced with satire at the words 'Than those old nine which rhymers invocate'. 'Invocate' is a mock-pompous hyper-Latinism for 'invoke', used elsewhere in Shakespeare only twice, and then for the invocation of the ghosts of kings (*1H6* 1.1.52 and *R3* 1.2.8). Shakespeare uses 'rhymers' only once, and that contemptuously, in *AC* 5.2.210–12, where Cleopatra contemplates what she would have to suffer in a Roman triumph, when 'saucy lictors | Will catch at us like strumpets, and scald rhymers | Ballad us out o' tune' ('scald' means scurvy, mean, paltry).

Child-bearing as a metaphor for poetic composition appears in 32.11, 'A dearer birth than this his love had brought', and in 59.3–4, where our brains, 'labouring for invention, bear amiss | The second burden of a former child'. In 72.13 'I am shamed by that which I bring forth', and in

103.1 'Alack, what poverty my Muse brings forth'. So here the poet exhorts poets to call upon this tenth Muse to help them bring forth lasting verse, to assist at the birth of what will not soon die.

13–14 If S's slight Muse should please the finicky critics of the day, the pain (glancing at the pangs of childbirth) will be his, the praise will belong to his beloved. In line 9 his Muse, the beloved, is supremely valuable; in 13 the Muse that is S's unaided poetic gift is puny.

Classical Background

This sonnet is saturated by classical thinking on poetic inspiration, as treated notably by Plato in his *Phaedrus* 245 and *Ion* 533–4, but this note will concentrate on Horace's use of these ideas. In lines 2–3 the beloved's breath pours its sweet argument into the verse. In Horace, *Odes* 2.16, Fate has given Italian Horace the subtle breath of the Greek Camena, '*spiritum Graiae tenuem Camenae*', where Camena is the Muse of Italy; in *Odes* 4.6, Apollo has given him the breath of song, '*spiritum carminis*'; in 2.19 his breast is full of Bacchus as the god of poetry '*plenoque Bacchi pectore*'; in 3.4 the infant Horace was one whose soul, whose breath, was not without gods, '*non sine dis animosus infans*'.

The 'slight Muse' in 13 is another classical recollection. Horace, too, pretended that his Muse was slight, *tenuis*, in *Odes* 2.16 just quoted, as did Virgil in his first *Eclogue*, where Tityrus sat under a beech tree practising on a 'scrannel pipe', *tenui avena*. The translation is Milton's in *Lycidas* 124. Apollo's advice to Tityrus in *Eclogues* 6.1–5 is to feed his sheep fat and *draw down* [from the distaff] a fine-spun thread of song, '*pinguis pascere oportet oves, deductum ducere carmen*'. This concern with the delicate, the fine-spun, the slight, is part of the aspiration of Latin poets to rival the refinement and subtlety of Hellenistic Greek poetry like that of Callimachus. Shakespeare knows about this, as the silly pedant Holofernes reveals at the beginning of the fifth act of *Love's Labour's Lost*, '*Novi hominem tanquam te*, I know the man as well as I know you,' he says of Don Adriano di Armado. 'He *draweth* out the thread of his verbosity *finer* than the staple of his argument.' Since the staple is the constituent filament of a thread, Don Adriano's argument is not strong.

Another resemblance between Horace and this sonnet (it may be no more) is the number game in lines 9–10. Horace too enjoys number games. The Cerberus who puts down his ears at the end of *Odes* 2.13 has 100 heads and no doubt 200 ears, but Cerberus with the golden horn who rubs his tail against Mercury's feet and legs and licks them in 2.19 has a three-tongued mouth. How many heads? At the end of 2.16 a *hundred* flocks and cows are mooing, a mare fit to pull a *four*-horse chariot is whinnying and Grosphus is wearing *double*-dyed purple. Horace would have smiled at the number ten in line 9 followed by the number nine in line 10. There is so much numerical play in the sonnets that some might even add up this juggle of 10 + 9 + 9 + 10 and look narrowly at 'numbers' in line 12.

There is more. In *Odes* 4.3 Horace addresses his Muse (as Shakespeare does in this sonnet). Melpomene could grant dumb fish the song of the swan, as Shakespeare's tenth Muse could grant the power of song to the dumb at 38.7, and all Horace's poems are the Muse's gift, '*totum muneris hoc* tui *est*'. Any pleasure he gives is hers, '*si placeo* tuum *est*', like '*thine* shall be the praise' at the end of the sonnet. And why these 'curious days'? Is it sheer coincidence that a cliché of Latin literary criticism was to praise Horace for his *curiosa felicitas*, his felicity in the handling of detail? It looks as though somewhere in the labyrinthine mine of Shakespeare's brain there was a recollection of this ode of Horace. And why should there not be? Deep calls to deep.

Vendler (1997) on line 1
Shakespeare is in the *Sonnets* an astonishingly nonclassical poet.

ᔒ 39 ᔆ

O how thy worth with manners may I sing,
When thou art all the better part of me?
What can mine own praise to mine own self bring,
And what is't but mine own when I praise thee?   4

Even for this let us divided live,
And our dear love lose name of single one,
That by this separation I may give
That due to thee which thou deserv'st alone.   8

O absence, what a torment wouldst thou prove,
Were it not thy sour leisure gave sweet leave
To entertain the time with thoughts of love
(Which time and thoughts so sweetly doth deceive),   12
    And that thou teachest how to make one twain
    By praising him here who doth hence remain.

I cannot praise you, because you are the better part of me,
    and it is ill-mannered to praise what is mine.
Let us live separate lives, and then I shall be able to praise you as you deserve.
Absence would be torment except that it gives me leisure
    to think loving thoughts, and teaches me how to make one into two,
    by praising him here when he is not here.

1–4 'The better part of me' is not original. On Horace, *Odes* 1.3.8, Nisbet
and Hubbard (1970) suggest that its origin may be found in Aristophanes'
speech in Plato's *Symposium*, and trace examples of it through Greek and
Latin literature to this sonnet and 74.8, and to *Paradise Lost*. The Victorian
vulgarism 'my better half' they find first in Sidney, *Arcadia* 3.280.

'It is bad manners if I praise you because you are the better part of me,
and a man cannot praise what is his own.' This is not a profound idea. How
does Shakespeare make it poetry? This is one of a score of sonnets which
start with the exclamation 'O'. These are not private broodings, but

addresses to the beloved, here introducing three passionate questions. Another couple of dozen sonnets have an exclamation in line 9, the point where there tends to be a dramatic turn in the argument. This sonnet has exclamations at the beginnings of both lines.

The glowing compliment in line 2 raises the emotional temperature and hints at a lofty spiritual dimension of love. If praise of the beloved is praise of himself, line 3 implies that the beloved *is* himself. This is playing with the conceit of the union of lovers, which has already been put to work in Sonnets 22 and 36. The invention continues in line 4. 'And what is't but mine own when I praise thee?' Mine own property? The better part of mine own self? Mine own praise? The ambiguity is part of the poetry, and the question is skirting round the bald statement, 'I am you.' Valentine goes the whole way in *TGV* 3.1.170–2, 'And why not death, rather than living torment? | To die is to be banished from myself, | And Silvia is myself.' So too in *CE* 3.2.66, 'I am thee'.

Crucially, although the language is highly wrought, this is still a natural speaking voice, urgently making its point. The metre is part of that effect, perhaps:

> What cán mine ówn práise to mine ówn sélf bríng,
> And what ís't but mine ówn when Í práise thée?

The force of the argument increases when 'mine ówn ... mine ówn ... mine ówn' is driven home by the one potent word 'thee'.

5–8 This is why they must part, and their love cease to be called a unity. Strictly it is not their love that will cease to be called a unity, but the two persons. The same notion lies behind Sonnet 36.1–2:

> Let me confess that we two must be twain
> Although our undivided loves are one.

The beauty of this separation is that it is now possible for S to praise the man he loves without being so ill-mannered as to praise himself.

9–14 Line 12 is bracketed in this edition to suggest that it is love which sweetly beguiles time and thoughts. With this punctuation the syntax of lines 9–14 is as follows: 'O absence, what torture would you bring were it not (1) [that] thy sour leisure passed the time with thoughts of love (which sweetly deceives), and (2) that thou teachest how to make one into two.'

133

The first benefit of absence is that it allows S to enjoy thoughts of love. The second is that praise becomes possible. The beloved 'doth hence remain'; they are two. S can therefore praise him, but in doing so he senses his presence. He is 'here'. The essence of the poem is that S values this love so highly that he desperately needs to manufacture a consolation for any break in it.

The poem contains a tantalising ambiguity. In 5–8 the two seem to be divided, and the separation is a matter of their emotions, a break in their loving unity. In 9–14 this seems to change to physical absence. S is here, and the beloved is hence. The needle oscillates between absence and estrangement in other sonnets, for example 41, 97 and 109.

℘ 40 ℘

Take all my loves, my love, yea, take them all—
What hast thou then more than thou hadst before?
No love, my love, that thou may'st true love call;
All mine was thine before thou hadst this more.   4

Then if, for my love, thou my love receivest,
I cannot blame thee for my love thou usest.
But yet be blamed, if thou thyself deceivest
By wilful taste of what thyself refusest.   8

I do forgive thy robb'ry, gentle thief,
Although thou steal thee all my poverty;
And yet love knows it is a greater grief
To bear love's wrong than hate's known injury.   12

Lascivious grace, in whom all ill well shows,
Kill me with spites yet we must not be foes.

O my love, take all my love[r]s. You then have no more love than before,
because none of them gives you true love. You already had all mine.
I don't blame you if for love of me you take my mistress,
but I blame you for choosing to love her and refusing me.
I forgive you for stealing what little I had, although a wrong done by a lover
is crueller than an injury done by an enemy.
You lecherous beauty, every wrong you do seems right. Kill me if you like,
but let us not be enemies.

This is a bitter play upon the word 'love'. It occurs ten times in the first
dozen lines in several different senses. Another difficulty is that the poem
cannot be understood without the help of the next two sonnets. The plot
unfolds as we read, but not always in chronological order. It is as though
we are eavesdropping on what one person is saying to another, and gradually piecing the story together. Sonnet 40 refers darkly to some act of

infidelity by the beloved with some person or persons loved by S. Sonnet 41 will reveal that S's mistress has made advances to the young man whom S loves, and he has responded. In 42.1–4, S will grieve because the young man has his mistress, but not as much as he grieves because his mistress has the young man. In 42.5–8 he will try to console himself by assuming that the young man and his mistress love each other because each of them loves him. This is the first mention of a mistress in the Sonnets, although she may haunt 36.3 and 10. She may, and she may not, be the same person as the Black Lady of 127–52.

1–4 In view of all this, 'loves' in the first line means lovers, and the juxtaposition of 'loves' and 'love' is the crux of the argument – 'You are my love. You can take not just this mistress of mine, but all my other loves.' The repeated command in the first line is made all the more bitter by the fusillade of monosyllables. In the first four lines only 'before' is not a monosyllable. The heartfelt tone is heightened, by 'yea', which comes with all the greater force because it must be spoken with emphasis although it does not carry the metrical stress, 'Take áll my lóves, my lóve, yéa, táke them áll.' The line might be read without stress on the second 'take', 'yéa, take them áll'. A reader might even go as far as Prospero's bitter words in *Tem* 1.2.82–3, 'or changed 'em | Or else new formed 'em'. The play on 'love' is continued in line 3, where 'love' refers twice to the emotion, and once to the beloved. The argument hinges on the word 'more'. 'If you take all my loves, what more do you have? You had all my true love [and this 'more' of yours is nothing of the sort].' But if the young man had all S's love, S had none for his mistress. The undercurrent of misogyny is flowing here as in 42.1–4.

5–8 S now considers the possibility that the beloved took S's mistress out of love for S, 'for my love'. This is not a likely history, but it is put forward in 41.7–8 and 42.6. Kerrigan (1986) observes S's tactics, seeing that 're-ceivest' largely absolves the youth by making him a passive agent. In line 5 the beat of the verse on the first 'my' and the second 'love' marks out the sense, 'Then if, for mý love, thou my lóve receivest'. The first 'love' means the beloved's love for S, and the second is S's mistress, 'Then if you make love to my mistress because of your love for me'.

Having received S's mistress, the young man is *using* her, a loaded word, as at 20.14 and 134.10, and he blames his mistress, not the young man, but in the same breath he corrects himself, 'But yet be blamed'. The charge is not that the beloved yielded to the woman's charms, but that he deceived himself by wilfully sampling with the woman the sexual pleasures he had refused to grant to S. Self-deception is an inexact description of the young man's offence. Inconsistency would be nearer the mark. The young man refused S's advances, but is now wilfully tasting the dish with S's mistress.

Part of this elaborate play of mind, emotion and language is the hidden variation in the repetition of 'thyself' in the same place in lines 7 and 8. In line 7, 'thou thyself deceivest', the beloved is deceiving himself. Line 8 refers to what the beloved himself is refusing. The first is the reflexive pronoun, object of the verb, the second is the emphatic pronoun, subject of the verb.

The bitterness in the first four lines was expressed in monosyllables. Now his cynical view of this affair, and particularly of the woman's part in it, is expressed in four rattling -est feminine rhymes in 5–8, as though to mark the arrival of a feminine threat to his love for the young man. See 42.5–8 and also Burrow (2002), quoted at the end of the note on Sonnet 20.

9–12   These four lines are one paradox after another, all of them looking at facets of the love–hate relationship introduced in 35.12. The beloved is a 'gentle thief', like the Black Lady, who will be a 'gentle cheater' in 151.3. In line 10, 'thou steal *thee* all my poverty', 'thee' is an indirect object of the verb, 'for thyself', as in 10.13. He has stolen *for himself* S's poverty, what little S possesses, namely his mistress. S has received no riches of that sort from the young man. All that he had was the poverty of the love he received from the woman. 'Knows' in 11 is in some strange play with 'known' in 12. The next paradox is that hurt caused by a lover is harder to bear than injury done by an enemy.

13–14   'Grace' is beauty, and in the natural course of events is sometimes lascivious. But grace is often the grace of God, and therefore 'lascivious grace' is blasphemous, and the shock is made more severe by the emphasis required on 'well' against the metre, 'all íll wéll shóws', the same effect as met in the first line with 'yea'. After 'hate' in 35.12 and 'spite' in 36.6, now comes the supreme paradox of love's betrayal, 'Kill me with spites yet we must not be foes.' S will accept whatever the beloved does to him, but he cannot think of surviving in a future in which they will be enemies.

In Sonnet 39 the argument was tortured and sophistical, a believable version of the sort of feelings an intense and intelligent lover might experience. With its tenfold play on 'love', Sonnet 40 is even more cerebral, brooding on the hurts of love.

Booth (1977) on line 5

For, *love*, and *receivest*, each has several appropriate and syntactically available meanings here; some of their many combinations are these: (1) if, out of affection for me (for love of me), you take my mistress; (2) if, because of my affection for you, you courteously welcome my mistress; (3) if, for yours (as your possession – you being *my love*, my beloved), you take my mistress; (4) if, in place of my affection, you take my mistress; (5) if you understand my mistress to be my true-love; (6) if you understand what I feel for my mistress to be love; (7) if, because of my affection for you (or yours for me), you accept (or suffer) my affection. Overtones of two pertinent contexts of *receivest* reflect dishonorably on the transaction: (a) such agents as tax collectors, toll collectors, and stewards were called 'receivers' (see *OED*, s.v. 'receive', I.1 and 'receiver'); (b) 'receiver' was also used as we use 'receiver of stolen goods' (*OED*, s.v. 'receive' I.1.c and 'receiver').

Those pretty wrongs that liberty commits
When I am sometime absent from thy heart,
Thy beauty and thy years full well befits,
For still temptation follows where thou art.   4

Gentle thou art, and therefore to be won,
Beauteous thou art, therefore to be assailed,
And when a woman woos what woman's son
Will sourly leave her till he have prevailed?   8

Ay me, but yet thou might'st my seat forbear,
And chide thy beauty and thy straying youth,
Who lead thee in their riot even there
Where thou are forced to break a twofold truth: 12
  Hers by thy beauty tempting her to thee,
  Thine by thy beauty being false to me.

Your misbehaviour fits your youth – wherever you go you are tempted.
Because you are well born, kindly and beautiful, people target you,
  and, when a woman woos, no man leaves till he has won her.
Still, you might have kept off my territory, but youth and beauty
  led you astray and made you break two contracts.
  Your beauty tempted her, and made you false to me.

1–4 The first eight lines of this sonnet are an attempt to manufacture excuses for the beloved's infidelity. First, by calling infidelity 'pretty wrongs', he tries to adopt a tolerant, sophisticated tone. These charming lapses are said to occur when S is absent from the beloved's heart, meaning when the young man forgets his love for S. 'Absence' is the theme of 39.9–14, and absence here in line 2 merges into estrangement. The beauty and the years 'befits' the wrongs, accords with them, where 'befits' is the common Elizabethan usage of a singular verb with plural subject, as, for example, at 101.3 and 112.1. This is some sort of excuse,

139

implying that the cause is youthful heedlessness, not any deeper breach of love.

'Sometime' charitably suggests that of course these infidelities do not happen very often. Even then, the blame does not attach to the beloved but to the fact that 'still temptation follows where thou art', one who is young and beautiful is always being tempted.

5–8 In lines 5–6 the wording is more subtle. 'Gentle thou art' suggests that the beloved is of noble blood, and therefore courted by many. It also suggests that he is not rough and uncouth, but kind, and therefore likely to attract sexual overtures and too kind to rebuff them. The variation in metrical stress from 'thérefore to be won' to 'theréfore to be assailed' carries the intonation of a persuasive speaking voice. This principle is advanced, *sotto voce* and with a different variation, by Suffolk in *1H6* 5.5.34–5: 'She's beautiful, and therefore to be wooed; | She is a woman, therefore to be won.' Here the expressive variations are the cynical omission of 'and' in line 35, and change from 'she's' to 'she ís'.

The final excuse for the beloved's philandering is that no man can resist a woman's advances. But the observation which ends the first eight lines of the poem is much more pointed than that. To imply that men cannot be expected to resist women because their mothers were women is such nonsense that it is an excuse which excuses nothing. The very sound seems to guy the idea '*w*hen a *w*oman *w*oos *w*hat *w*oman's *s*on | *W*ill *s*ourly leave her'.

Then to suggest that a man who leaves when a woman is trying to seduce him is behaving 'sourly' is equally ridiculous, and it comes as such a shock to hear that no man will leave a female assailant until *he* is victorious that some editors change 'he' to 'she', forgetting the old joke about the woman who pursued a man until he caught her.

A military metaphor creeps in at 'therefore to be assailed', and continues in 'prevailed' in line 8. In retrospect it may even add a warlike tinge to 'therefore to be won'.

9–14 In Sonnet 40.1–4, S implied that the loss of his mistress did not hurt him badly, because he did not truly love her. He tried not to blame the beloved but did blame him, and now in 41, after desperate attempts to invent excuses, he is honest about his hurt. He can deceive himself no longer. 'Ay me,' he sighs, 'you might still have kept off my property.' 'Might'st ... forbear' and '[might'st] chide' refer to past time, 'You might at least have spoken sternly to your Youth and Beauty.' He is identifying the same culprits as in line 3, but now the dramatist visualises them as characters, '*Who* lead thee in their riot' (11), young bloods whom the beloved should have kept under control. Instead he allows them to lead him astray and take him on a rampage into his own home, 'even there' into his estate, his 'seat', breaking two things precious to him, 'a twofold truth'. Lines 9–12 then hang together in this metaphor of young hooligans stray-ing into the grounds of a private house, but commentators find a more brutal metaphor, from horse-riding, by quoting Iago in *Oth* 2.1.294–5: 'I do suspect the lusty Moor | Hath leapt into my seat, the thought whereof | Doth, like a poisonous mineral, gnaw my inwards.'

The twofold truth consists of the mistress's truth, her contract of love with S, and the beloved's truth, his contract with S. The beloved's beauty has led him to him break them both. S is still trying to excuse him, to put the blame on his beauty and youth, who 'forced' him to behave as he did, but we have read so many feeble excuses from S in this and recent sonnets that there is no doubt about his final bitterness. In lines 1–8 he attempts or affects to forgive and argue away the beloved's offence, but the truth is suddenly felt in 9, 'Ay me', and the last four words of the sonnet carry the pain.

ॐ 42 ॰

That thou hast her, it is not all my grief,
And yet it may be said I loved her dearly;
That she hath thee is of my wailing chief,
A loss in love that touches me more nearly.⁣   4

Loving offenders, thus I will excuse ye—
Thou dost love her because thou know'st I love her,
And for my sake ev'n so doth she abuse me,
Suff'ring my friend for my sake to approve her.⁣   8

If I lose thee, my loss is my love's gain,
And losing her, my friend hath found that loss.
Both find each other, and I lose both twain,
And both for my sake lay on me this cross.⁣   12

    But here's the joy, my friend and I are one.
    Sweet flattery! Then she loves but me alone.

It makes me unhappy that you have taken my mistress,
   but much more unhappy that she has taken you.
I will excuse you both — you love her for my sake because I love her,
   and she loves you for my sake because I love you.
If I lose him she gains. If I lose her he gains. They both gain,
   I lose both, and they inflict this torment on me for my sake!
Ah! But the joy is that I and my beloved are one.
   Sweet delusion — she loves only me.

1–4 The balance is set up with 'That thóu hast hér' echoed by 'that shé
hath thée'. 'Dearly' gains force by the extra syllable of the feminine rhyme,
and because it is the first word in the sonnet which is not a monosyllable.
Dearly as he loved her, he loved the other more – not the first whiff of
misogyny in the Sonnets. See 20 and 40.

142

5–8 'Loving offenders' implies that they have offended by loving each other, an offence because both of them had given their love to S. He coolly sees no inconsistency in requiring fidelity from each, while he is loving both. Sonnet 41 searched in vain for an excuse for the infidelity of the beloved. Now S searches for an excuse for both of them:

> Thóu dost love hér becáuse thou knów'st Í love her,
> And for my sáke ev'n só does shé abúse me,
> Súff'ring my fríend for mý sake to appróve her.

If the iambic beat is heard, the variation of stress between 'my' and 'mý' in 8 is as rational here as in 40.5, 'Then if for mý love thóu my lóve recéivest'. 'The feminine rhymes *excuse ye ... love her ... abuse me ... approve her ...* may draw attention to the unmanageable complexity of the situation' (Duncan-Jones 1997), but 'feminine rhymes often occur at sexually suggestive moments' (Burrow (2002) at the end of my commentary on Sonnet 20).

So the young man loves S's mistress for S's sake, because he knows that S loves her (6). In the same way his mistress abuses S's trust and love, by allowing the young man for S's sake to approve her, and some commentators suggest that this means that she allows S's friend to speak highly of her. This cannot be right. The commonest meaning of 'to approve' in Shakespeare is to test, as in *MND* 2.2.74–5, 'On whose eyes I might approve | This flower's force in stirring love'. For S's sake she permits the young man to try her out and the young man used her (40.6). The manoeuvre is seen at its coldest in 110.10–11, 'Mine appetite I never more will grind | On newer proof, to try an older friend.' Here in 42 it is bitterness masquerading as forgiveness.

9–12 'My love' in 9 refers to the woman. The whole conundrum is a construction of excusing and complaining, loving and abusing, finding and losing, the losses rising to five in lines 9–11, and climaxing in line 12, where his beloved and his mistress are lifting the cross on to his back, and sending him off to carry it through the streets to his own crucifixion, and all for his own benefit. 'For my sake', he says in 7, 8 and 12, each time in a different place in the line, and rising to a cruel climax in 12. He knows he is deluding himself. Line 12 makes it unmistakable.

13–14 'Kill me with spites; yet we must not be foes' (40.14). Whatever the beloved does, S will find some way, however tortuous and desperate, of accepting it. So here in line 13 he recalls the notion he explored in Sonnets 22, 36 and 37, and gave up in 39.5, that he and the beloved are one in love, and therefore that in loving the young man his mistress is loving him and only him. Again he knows he is deceiving himself with false comfort, 'sweet flattery'. It is not unusual for a disappointed lover to find consolation in absurd fantasies.

Lines 1–4 are addressed to the beloved, line 5 to the mistress and to the beloved, but lines 6–9, where the mistress is spoken of in the third person, show that it is the beloved he cares about. In the last four lines S is speaking to himself. Such switches of addressee could not have happened in real life. The poem is a drama in the mind, and this is of course not the maunderings of William Shakespeare but the self-delusion of a dramatic character.

Anon. (*Fraser's Magazine* (1855), 52, 429) in Rollins (1944)
This sonnet must be accepted as the expression of a friendship existing in the imagination alone, and thus carried to excess as an expression of *jeu d'esprit*. Even although a man were really guilty of the base pusillanimity of such sentiments, he can hardly have been so destitute of the sense of shame as to proclaim them to the world.

Rollins (1944)
Gregor (1935) tells us that such superhuman forgiveness as that in 42 must bring forth the deepest loneliness of a spiritual art. This, he adds, is the much-sought-for key to the poet's psyche, but for me the key opens no secret doors.

When most I wink, then do mine eyes best see,
For all the day they view things unrespected,
But when I sleep, in dreams they look on thee,
And darkly bright are bright in dark directed.   4

Then thou, whose shadow shadows doth make bright,
How would thy shadow's form form happy show
To the clear day with thy much clearer light,
When to unseeing eyes thy shade shines so!   8
How would (I say) mine eyes be blessed made
By looking on thee in the living day,
When in dead night thy fair imperfect shade
Through heavy sleep on sightless eyes doth stay!   12

    All days are nights to see till I see thee,
    And nights bright days when dreams do show thee me.

My best seeing is when I am asleep and dream of you.
Since your dream form, your shadow, makes shadows bright,
*   what joy it would be for my open eyes to see you in daylight,*
*   since your dream form stays on my closed eyes at night.*
Till I see you days are nights, and nights are days when I dream of you.

1–4 'Although I wink, I am not blind' is the proverb, and here Shakespeare puts it through its paces. To wink is to have the eyes closed (unseeing in 8, sightless in 12), and it is when S's eyes are most closed that he sees best. This poem is a Chinese box of such paradoxes and riddles, but the basic argument is simple: 'I see best when I see you in my dreams, but what bliss it would be to see you in the light of day.' All day he sees nothing he respects, and even here there is a twist. Shakespeare knew perfectly well that the literal sense of 'unrespected' is 'unlooked back at'. Nothing he sees when awake is worth a second glance.

    Line 4 is a rhetorical *tour de force*. When he is asleep, his eyes are 'darkly bright', they shine brilliantly in the dark. 'Bright in dark directed' adds to this the notion that their light pierces the darkness as they are directed like a searchlight to see the beloved. The eyes project light in the act of vision at 20.6, 33.4 and 114.7–8. Here the language dazzles by chiasmus, 'darkly bright ... bright dark'.

5–12   When the beloved's shadow makes shadows bright, 'shadows' has its normal meaning, but 'the beloved's shadow' is his phantom, his image (27.10) seen in dreams. It is so bright, this shadow, that it makes shadows shine!

The two exclamations ending 8 and 12 both express the sentiment that the sight of the beloved would be better than the dream vision. How happy a show would be made in the clear light of day by the beloved's real form, when his dream phantom shines so brightly at night! That is presented in four lines so complex as to be surreal. Line 6 is almost another chiasmus. In 'thy sh[ad]ow's form form happy show', but the first 'form' is a noun, the second a verb.

Line 7 might have read 'To the clear day with its much clearer light', but it is limp to say that day is much brighter than night, and the Quarto reads not 'its' but 'thy', and that gives a characteristic tautness. The much clearer light is light pouring from the beloved (4 and 7–8), and it is much clearer than the clear light of day. The comparison is made more vivid by the polyptoton of 'clear ... clearer', and that would be highlighted by the metrical stress where it is not expected, on 'clear', 'To the cléar dáy with thý much cléarer líght'. This is not to dictate how the verse should be spoken, but to stress the importance of hearing it.

In line 8 a shadow shines, and shines to unseeing eyes, and, as though that were not surreal enough, the very sound of the verse, particularly its last three words, is strange, 'When to unseeing eyes thy shade shines so'. In some authors this might be inept and ugly. But this is Shakespeare.

So weird is all this that he says it again, and says it clearly, 'How would (I say) mine eyes be blessed made ... ' This second exclamation contrasts 'dead night' with 'living day'. It contrasts 'thee' with 'thy ... imperfect shade', almost another chiasmus, 'thee day night thy'. Line 1 spoke highly of night vision, but now, although what he sees at night is lovely, it is imperfect. The dream shadow stays on his eyes through sleep, but his sleep is heavy, and his eyes are sightless. Line 12, like the earlier exclamation in 8, ends with shimmering sounds, 'sleep on sightless eyes doth stay'.

13–14   Days are nights because he has no respect for what he sees in the days, and the nights are days, and bright days, because he sees the beloved

—yet another lurking chiasmus, 'days nights nights days'. At night 'dreams show thee me', yet another puzzle. When I show you the way, 'you' means 'to you'. So this poem seems to end 'when dreams show me to thee' — which is absurd. 'Show me thee' would have rhymed 'thee' with 'thee' in the previous line. Perhaps Shakespeare saw the difficulty and decided to let it stand, as a final optical surprise in this poem of many illusions.

'Till I see thee' could mean just for the next few hours, but Sonnets 44, 45 and 48 deal with a period of prolonged absence. This poem has all the greater emotional weight if that long separation has already begun. Absence in 39.7 and 41.2 hints at something more cruel than physical separation.

Rollins (1944) on lines 13–14
Those who regard monosyllables as harsh in poetry should notice the twenty that are here piled up.

G. K. Hunter (1953) in Jones (1977)
Here 'darkly bright are bright in dark directed' is not merely a piece of wordplay but also a triumphant dance of words expressing the lover's delight. The emphatic 'thee' in line 3 and 'thou' in line 5, impress on us the fact that the poem for all its conceits is a love poem directed towards a beloved object. The contrasts between the radiance of dream and the drabness of reality, the brightness of the beloved and the brightness of the sun, remain expressive of an emotional situation.

Booth (1977), 203
The rhetorical devices are these (some examples qualify for more than one label):
antithesis: *wink, see* (line 1); *bright, dark* (4); *shadow, form* (5, 6); *living day, dead night* (10, 11); **antistasis** (repetition of a word in a different or contrary sense): *bright* the adjective, *bright* the adverb (4); *shadow shadows* (5); *form form* (6); *clear, clearer* (7); **epizeuxis** (repetition of a word with no other word between) *shadow shadows, form form*; **diacope** (repetition of a word with one or a few words in between): *bright, are bright* (4); *see till I see* (13); **polyptoton** (repetition of words from the same root but with different endings): *darkly, dark* (4); *shadow, shade* (5, 6, 8, 11), etc.; **antimetabole** (inversion of the order of repeated words): *darkly bright, are bright in dark* (4); and rhetorically unclassified **word plays**: a sort of fusion of **antithesis** and an **antistasis** of ideas (compare 134.9, note — on **ideational puns**): *dark*, meaning 'darkness', 'night' (4), with *fair* meaning 'beautiful' (11) and the noun *light* (7) with the adjective *heavy* (12); and words that in combination suggest **oxymoron** (miniature paradox) but are used in senses that are logically compatible: *shade shines* (8) where *shade* means not 'darkness' but 'image'.

❧ 44 ☙

If the dull substance of my flesh were thought,
Injurious distance should not stop my way,
For then despite of space I would be brought
From limits far remote, where thou dost stay.   4
No matter then although my foot did stand
Upon the farthest earth removed from thee,
For nimble Thought can jump both sea and land
As soon as think the place where he would be.   8

But ah! thought kills me that I am not Thought,
To leap large lengths of miles when thou art gone,
But that, so much of earth and water wrought,
I must attend Time's leisure with my moan,   12
    Receiving naught by elements so slow
    But heavy tears, badges of either's woe.

If my body were made of thought, I should travel to you in a moment.
  Thought could jump the distance, no matter how far.
But my body is made of earth and water, and travels slowly.
  Earth makes me heavy, and water makes me weep.

The philosophical background to Sonnets 44 and 45 is the theory of the four elements, dear to the early Greek philosophers. According to this doctrine (expounded by Ovid in *Metamorphoses* 15.239–44 and earlier by Lucretius, cited at the end of this commentary), at the making of the universe earth, water, air and fire emerged from primeval chaos. Earth, being heaviest, sank to the bottom, water rested on it, air rose above them, and fire rose higher still. Aether, which glows in the heavens, is its purest form. By comparison human flesh is a dull, sluggish substance, a compound of earth and water. Of passion, mind and soul there were various explanations, but in 45.1 and 3 Shakespeare takes the view that mind consists of air, and passion of fire. The braggart Bourbon's horse 'is pure air and fire, and the dull elements of earth and water never appear in him, but only in patient stillness while his rider mounts him' (*H5* 3.7.21–3).

1–8   If the substance of S's flesh were thought, that is air, he would always be able to be with his beloved. Distance could not injure him by keeping him away, and space could not be an obstacle. From limits far remote he would be brought [to] where the beloved stays, even if he were standing on 'the farthest earth removed', where our word order would demand 'the earth farthest removed'.

'Jump' in line 7 is surprising. The obvious word would have been 'leap', not this rough colloquialism. But 'leap' is needed in line 10 to add to the lightness of the alliteration in 'leap large lengths of miles'. Not that 'jump' is simply a second best to avoid repetition. The earthy term goes well with 'foot' and 'stand' and 'nimble'. Thought is personified and visualised, and in line 8 'he' is a man. If Shakespeare were Thought, although his 'foot' were to 'stand' on land far removed from the beloved, he too, like 'nimble' Thought, could 'jump' anywhere. Sea and land would not impede him (7). After all, they are only water and earth, the sluggish substances in the human body, and Thought is made of finer stuff. This lightness is expressed in 8–10, the only three consecutive monosyllabic lines in the Sonnets. Puck was a sluggard. He needed forty minutes to 'put a girdle round about the earth' (*MND* 2.1.175–6). Thought jumps where he wants to be as soon as he thinks of it.

9–14   But S is killed by the thought that he is not Thought. From line 12 it appears that Time is his master or king (in 16.2 'a bloody tyrant'). S, being made 'of earth and water', must wait in misery till the king has leisure to give audience to his complaint, and even then he gains nothing from his petition but heavy tears, made heavier by the unexpected stress on 'bádges', heaviness being the badge of earth and tears being badges of water, salt because of the sea, as the sonnet drags to a halt with 'moan ... so slow ... woe'.

'Naught' is a conjecture for 'naughts' in the Quarto, which some editors print, pointing to the possible pun with noughts referring to the figure 0. Shakespeare enjoys puns more than most, but here the pun does not work. Receiving nothings (0 + 0 + 0) but tears does not make good sense.

Lucretius, *De Rerum Natura* 5.495–508

> So then the mass of earth compacted, its weight stopped
> it moving, and as though it were all the slime in the universe
> it oozed together and sank to the bottom like dregs.

Then the liquid atoms of sea, then air, then aether-bearing fire
were all left pure, each lighter than the other, and aether,
liquidest and lightest of all, floated above the winds of air.
It does not mingle its liquid body with those restless breezes,
but lets them whirl in hurricanes and riot in sudden squalls,
while it glides on bearing its fires in a changeless stream.
That the aether can flow in one steady progress is proved
by the Pontus, which flows with unchanging current,
ever maintaining the steady single tenor of its gliding.

[Shakespeare probably knew this passage. See *Oth* 3.3.456–63:
    Never, Iago. Like to the Pontic Sea,
    Whose icy current and compulsive course
    Ne'er knows retiring ebb, but keeps due on
    To the Propontic and the Hellespont,
    Ev'n so my bloody thoughts with violent pace
    Shall ne'er look back, ne'er ebb to humble love,
    Till that a capable and wide revenge
    Swallow them up.]

℘ 45 ℞

The other two, slight air and purging fire,
Are both with thee, wherever I abide,
The first my thought, the other my desire.
These present-absent with swift motion slide.   4

For when these quicker elements are gone
In tender embassy of love to thee,
My life, being made of four, with two alone
Sinks down to death, oppressed with melanch'ly   8

Until life's composition be recured
By these swift messengers returned from thee,
Who ev'n but now come back again assured
Of thy fair health, recounting it to me.   12

    This told, I joy; but then no longer glad,
    I send them back again, and straight grow sad.

Thought / air and desire / fire are always with you, moving so quickly
  that they are here and there at the same time.
When they are with you, my other elements sink to melancholy and death.
When they come back assuring me that you are well, I am restored, I rejoice,
  send them back to you, and am sad again instantly.

1–4   In Sonnet 44 flesh is made of dull, heavy elements, earth and water,
whereas thought is nimble and swift. Here thought is air, slight, that is fine,
rarefied (*tenuis*, thin, being used of air and of wind in Lucretius 3.232 and
4.901), and desire is fire, which purifies the souls of the dead not only in
Christian Purgatory, but also in the Underworld in Virgil, *Aeneid* 6.742,
where the stain of evil is burned out by fire, '*exuritur igni*'. Wherever S is,
his airy thought and fiery desire are with the beloved.

5–8   When air and fire are with the beloved, S is deprived of the two light elements, and therefore sinks to melancholy and death. 'Sinks' is a glance back at the weight of flesh in the theory of the four elements, and the heaviness of earth and water, in 44.14. In Shakespeare 'mélanchóly' is always four syllables, but that produces an extra syllable in line 8, and the resulting feminine ending would not rhyme with 'from thee' in line 10. It should surely be read as 'mélanch'ly, a pronunciation commonly attested in Elizabethan verse. W. S. Walker (1860) in Rollins (1944) compares *How a Man May Choose a Good Wife from a Bad* (1602), 'Then thus resolv'd, I straight will drink to thee | A health thus deepe, to drowne thy Melancholy.'

9–12 The return of air and fire restores S's four components, and cures him of the melancholy that had afflicted him in their absence. 'Recure' was once a common word meaning 'restore and cure', for example 'A smile recures the wounding of a frown' in *VA* 465. The medical term supports the reference to melancholy, a depression sometimes leading to death, caused, according to the theory of humours, by a surplus of black bile (see commentary on 91.5).

13–14 The absence of the beloved causes pain, but it also provides the temporary pleasure of thinking about him and desiring him. This is not a bad summary of the poem, but by what miracle is this abysmal platitude fashioned into a witty and poignant poem? Part of the answer is that it takes the four elements of ancient philosophy, earth, water, air and fire, and personifies the first two as dull miseries reducing S to melancholy when he is left alone with them. The other two spend their time busily rushing backwards and forwards, and their visits give him bursts of joy. These '*quicker* elements' go in 'tender embassy'. They are '*swift* messengers', and they '*ev'n but now* come back again assured' of the beloved's health, report it, and are then sent back. The italics show how quickly they move, how they '*with swift motion slide*', how they are '*present-absent*', so swift that at any one moment they can be in two different places at the same time. '*Straight*' is a witty word, as in 89.3. He often thinks of the man he loves, but, when he does, in an instant he remembers the distance between them and is desolate.

෨ 46 ෩

Mine eye and heart are at a mortal war
How to divide the conquest of thy sight:
Mine eye, my heart thy picture's sight would bar,
My heart, mine eye the freedom of that right. 4

My heart doth plead that thou in him dost lie,
A closet never pierced with crystal eyes,
But the defendant doth that plea deny
And says in him thy fair appearance lies. 8

To 'cide this title is impanellèd
A quest of thoughts, all tenants to the heart,
And by their verdict is determinèd
The clear eye's moiety and the dear heart's part, 12
  As thus: mine eye's due is thy outward part,
  And my heart's right, thy inward love of heart.

Heart and eye are fighting over the spoils of victory.
  Neither will concede to the other the right to see your picture.
Heart claims you lie in him, where eye has never penetrated.
  Eye says your beauty lies in him.
A jury of thoughts is summoned and they have reached a verdict —
  eye's due is your outward; heart's right is the love of your heart.

1–4 S's eye and heart are engaged in a fight to the death. The spoils of war are the right to see a picture of the beloved. Eye would not allow heart to view it, and heart would not grant that right to eye. Their war soon becomes a lawsuit. 'Bar', 'freedom' and 'right' speak of the courts, and the rest of the sonnet is full of the language of litigation. The underlying sense is not absurd. Heart cannot see beauty and eye cannot conceive it.

5–8 Heart advances his plea, speaking first as a plain, blunt man, in monosyllables, then moving on to a lofty image. The disputed property is stored in a closet, almost always in Shakespeare (despite *OED* 3a) a private room, but in *Mac* 5.1.6, and probably here, it is a cabinet for personal property, a private repository, sealed and inaccessible to the eye. The closet of the heart is contrasted with eyes clear as crystal (6). 'Go clear thy crystals,' says the gallant Pistol to the Hostess as she weeps at his departure (*H5* 2.3.50). The wordplay in the sonnet may be more complex. In an anatomical treatise of 1594, the pericardium, the membraneous sac which contains the heart, was called 'the little closet of the heart' (*OED* 6a). (Thersites plays on the pia mater membrane in *TC* 2.1.73). But there is more than wordplay, and it emerges in the last line of the sonnet, like Duncan's rueful reflection quoted at the end of the note on Sonnet 24, and in young Elizabeth's distress in protesting her innocence to her sister Queen Mary in her famous letter of 1556, when she wished there were 'good surgeons for making anatomies of hearts'.

These four lines are a clash of two litigants. Heart pleads that the beloved lies in him, where eyes have never pierced; eye denies the plea and says that 'your fair appearance' lies in him. The court scene uses the speaking voice, particularly at the repetition of 'in hím', each time with the accent, and each time stressed by coming before its verb, but in eye's reply pressing up towards the beginning of the line, 'No, in me, not in you'.

9–14 To resolve the dispute, a quest is empanelled. A quest is a jury at *R3* 1.4.179–80, 'What lawful quest have given their verdict up | Unto the frowning judge?' Since thoughts are in the heart, and this is 'a quest of thoughts', with all its members tenants of one of the contending parties, it is a packed jury, yet it scrupulously balances the interests of the litigants. A 'moiety' is strictly a half 'in legal or quasi-legal use' (*OED* 1), more loosely any portion. So the jury decides the legally determined share of the spoils of war, first for the eyes, 'clear' because they see clearly, and also because the legal issue is clear; second for the heart, 'dear' because it deals with precious feelings. Legalisms continue into the final couplet with 'due' and 'right'. To look back now at line 9, 'To 'cide this title' may be part of the same game. Shakespeare frequently suppresses the first syllable of compound words (Abbott (1870), section 460, lists nearly a score of examples), but 'cide' for 'decide' is attested only here in English. Is this guying the weirdness of legal jargon?

And is there a more subtle satire? As Vendler (1997) writes, 'We sense a rabbit-out-of-the-hat preciosity in the last three lines, when they are read as legal verdict.' Perhaps there is a flavour of the law in 'As thus', best spoken with lips pursed and tips of the fingers pressed together. These last two lines are shaped to show that the jury has given equal weight to each side of the case. 'The *clear* eyes' moiety' is echoed in 'the *dear* heart's part', and 'mine eyes due ... thy outward part' is echoed in 'my heart's right, thy inward ... heart'. The 'preciosity' of the tone and the balance of interests are audible even in the rhyme scheme. Only here in these 154 sonnets are the rhyming words of the last two lines repeated from the quatrain that precedes, here producing a sequence of five lines ending 'heart', ('determinèd'), 'heart's part', 'part', 'heart'. Something approaching this occurs only in 3 and 135. And if these rhymes can be held to be mocking the repetitiveness of legal language, it may be that the game begins even at lines 5–8, which end with the jingle of 'lie', 'eyes', 'deny', 'lies', and even in the forced rhyme of 'impanellèd' with 'determinèd' (compare also 26.3, 46.11, 57.4). The jury of tenants of one of the appellants is improperly constituted, but they follow proper legal procedures and come to a just and technically sound verdict. 'Moiety' in 12 is part of the game. The suggestion is that it is used in its strict technical sense of 'half'. The eyes shall have right of access to the outward part of the beloved, his visible aspect; the heart to the love deep in the beloved's heart.

The poem is a witty *tour de force*, particularly as a vivid law report, but with all the wit and rhetoric there is also feeling. Beauty is an important element in love, in its conception and its continuance, but the very last line, the climax of the legal play, is more than play. Heart's access to the inward love in the beloved's heart, without visual aid, is the serious climax of the poem. 'A strife is grown between virtue and love' in Sidney's *Astrophil and Stella* 52, but there the personification is less acute, and the settlement is frivolous, 'Let virtue have that Stella's self; yet thus, | That virtue but that body grant to us' but only on condition that virtue grants the body to Sidney. Shakespeare improves that joke for the end of Sonnet 128.

The Quarto of Sonnet 46 ends:

> The cleere eyes moyitie, and the deare hearts part,
>   As thus, mine eyes due is their outward part,
>   And my heart's right, their inward loue of heart.

First, 'their' in lines 13 and 14 does not make satisfactory sense. 'Their' and 'thy' are often confused in the Quarto, as in 35.8 and lines 3 and 8 of this very sonnet. Second, some editors transcribe 'eyes' as a plural, but it must be written with an apostrophe, making it a singular noun. In lines 1, 3, 4, 7, 8 and 12, the eye is referred to as a combatant in the singular. In line 6 'eyes' is not eye, the opponent of heart, but the eyes of men in general. It gives no support to the plural 'mine eyes' in 13.

✥ 47 ✥

Betwixt mine eye and heart a league is took,
And each doth good turns now unto the other.
When that mine eye is famished for a look,
Or heart in love with sighs himself doth smother,   4
With my love's picture then my eye doth feast,
And to the painted banquet bids my heart;
Another time mine eye is my heart's guest
And in his thoughts of love doth share a part.   8

So either by thy picture or my love,
Thyself away are present still with me.
For thou no farther than my thoughts canst move,
And I am still with them and they with thee;   12
   Or if they sleep, thy picture in my sight
    Awakes my heart, to heart's and eye's delight.

Eye and heart have signed a peace treaty.
   When eye is hungry for a sight, heart invites him along to share thoughts;
   when heart is sighing, eye invites him along to view your picture.
So you are with me when you are absent, because my thoughts are always
   with you, and, when I sleep, your picture in dreams wakes heart to share
   eye's delight.

1–8 Which is stronger? Love of the beloved's beauty or of his inner nature? Eye and heart fought a war about this in Sonnet 46, and took their dispute to law. In Sonnet 47 a treaty of mutual assistance has been struck. An eating metaphor now takes over. When eye is desperately hungry for a sight of the beloved, he 'shares a part' of the thoughts heart feasts upon (7–8). When heart, being in love, is smothering himself with sighs (4), he is invited to a 'painted banquet' (5–6), to share the picture of the beloved which appeared in 46.3.

9–14 The result of this pact between former enemies is that, when the beloved is absent, he is present, 'Thyself [being] away are present'. The beloved cannot move faster than S's thoughts, as graphically described in Sonnets 44 and 45, and so the beloved is always in S's heart. When thoughts are stilled in sleep, eye sees a dream picture of the beloved as in 43, and wakens heart to share in his delight. S's love is of the eye, and of the heart.

The conceits and sophistries of Sonnets 44–7 are built upon mysteries of love, the parts played by presence and absence, appearance and reality, flesh and spirit, the senses and the mind, the stock in trade of many earlier and contemporary poets; but none of Shakespeare's predecessors writes with his intelligence, eloquence, humour, imagination of scene and argument, and mastery of the speaking voice – 'doth good turns now unto the other ... famished for a look ... with sighs himself did smother.'

How careful was I when I took my way
Each trifle under truest bars to thrust,
That to my use it might unusèd stay
From hands of falsehood, in sure wards of trust!   4

But thou, to whom my jewels trifles are,
Most worthy comfort, now my greatest grief,
Thou, best of dearest and mine only care,
Art left the prey of every vulgar thief.   8

Thee have I not locked up in any chest
Save where thou art not, though I feel thou art,
Within the gentle closure of my breast,
From whence at pleasure thou mayst come and part.   12

And even thence thou wilt be stol'n, I fear,
For truth proves thievish for a prize so dear.

When I left I put all my trifles into store for safety.
I value you far more, but left you at the mercy of thieves,
free to come and go, locked up only in my breast, and even from there
I fear you will be stolen. Truth itself is a thief for such a prize.

1–4   When he left home he was most careful to put all his valuables under
lock and key, but the verb is 'thrust', indicating haste and impatience at all
the bric-à-brac he had to stow away, 'each trifle'. He was keeping it under
bars for his own use and out of the hands of burglars. The bars for his jewels
(5) are presumably steel bands reinforcing jewel boxes or caskets. The
wards of trust would then be the secure places for his valuables, but they
might also refer to locks, 'wards' being ridges inside a lock and the incisions
on the key that fits it (*OED* 24, citing *Luc* 303, 'The locks between her
chamber and his will, | Each one by him enforced, retires his ward', where
'retires' means 'withdraws'). Keats used this technicality to effect in his

lines 'On Sleep', set by Benjamin Britten in his *Serenade for Tenor, Horn and Strings*, suiting the music to the deftness and the hush:

> Turn the key deftly in the oilèd wards
> And seal the hushèd casket of my soul.

5–8 These lines describe, with some self-mockery, the anxious care he takes of 'each trifle', and contrast his failure to set a guard over the supremely precious beloved, whose value is conveyed by the swell of the voice at the elaborate addresses in 6–7, including 'most', 'greatest', 'best', 'only'.

9–12 He has not locked the beloved in any chest except his own. He feels the beloved in his heart. The pun on 'chest' occurs also at *Luc* 761, where after Lucrece is raped she beats her breast and bids her heart to find 'Some purer chest to close so pure a mind'. A steel-barred chest would be very different from 'the gentle closure' of line 11. There would be nothing harsh about the closure applied to the beloved in S's breast. It would be an open prison (12).

13–14 S is afraid that the young man will be stolen even from there. He is so dear, so loved *and* valuable, that even honesty is a thief for such a prize.

That is a run through the metaphor of the poem, but its power comes from the intensity of suffering in the underlying literal sense. The young man has already been unfaithful to him in Sonnets 33–6 and 40–2, and this shows in line 3, where he thrusts each trifle under *truest* bars 'That to my use it might unusèd stay | From hands of *falsehood*'. The polyptoton of 'use' and 'unusèd' points the bitter sexual sense, already met in 40.6, and the 'hands of falsehood' are the hands of seducers. In line 6 the beloved, once his 'Most worthy comfort', is now his 'greatest grief' by reason of his infidelities. In line 8 there is a dig at the low company the beloved is now keeping (see also 33.5–12) and an even uglier fear that he is not the prey of *any* vulgar thief, but 'of *every* vulgar thief'. In line 12 'at pleasure' hints at such pleasures as 41.7–14 and 58.2 and 14, and the utter darkness of this may cast a shadow back over line 10. He fears that the beloved is not in his heart at all, but even now straying as he had already strayed at 41.10. The paraphrase above has the cliché 'come and go', but the terrible last word of line 12 is 'part'.

The final expression of fear carries a compliment to the beloved. Even honest men and women will become thieves for such a treasure. S fears he will be betrayed by a person who had been *true* to him till now. Readers of Sonnets 41 and 42 will know that the person who once stole S's beloved was S's own mistress. 'Truth proves thievish for a prize so dear', and she is the thief, or one of them.

A huge intelligence is at work in these poems, giving them their intensity and tautness. Here, in this typical example, 'careful' in line 1 is picked up by 'care' in 7; 'hands of falsehood' in 4 by 'thievish' in 14; 'dearest' in 7 by the last word, 'dear'; trifling jewels are set against the priceless beloved in 5–8, where 'comfort' is set against 'grief', and his unique importance to S against the low company he is now keeping. Throughout the obsession with falsehood and truth takes many different forms, with 'truest bars', 'hands of falsehood', 'sure wards of trust', 'every vulgar thief', 'thou art not, though I feel thou art', 'come and part', 'stol'n', 'truth proves thievish'.

℘ 49 ℂ

Against that time (if ever that time come)
When I shall see thee frown on my defects,
Whenas thy love hath cast his utmost sum,
Called to that audit by advised respects,   4

Against that time when thou shalt strangely pass
And scarcely greet me with that sun thine eye,
When love converted from the thing it was
Shall reasons find of settled gravity,   8

Against that time do I ensconce me here
Within the knowledge of mine own desert,
And this my hand, against myself uprear
To guard the lawful reasons on thy part.   12

    To leave poor me thou hast the strength of laws
    Since why to love, I can allege no cause.

Against that time, if ever it come, when you will frown at my faults,
   when you will decide to stop loving me,
against that time when you will pass me in the street,
   when you will find good reason to change,
against that time I fortify my position, knowing my deserts,
   raising my hand against myself, to defend the justice of your case.
You are within the law if you leave me. There is no cause for you to love.

This rough summary brings out the massive triple structure of argument in the first dozen lines, and the great shock after the very different 'against' in line 11. It also highlights a dramatic slide from a possible future with 'if', to a certain one in lines 5 and 8, an anxious present in line 9, and back to a bleak future in lines 13–14.

1–4 To explain 'cast' in line 3 commentators consult *OED* and find twelve senses for the word, each with subsections. They then pick and mix. In this context, however, the word has nothing to do with dicing, nothing to do with the sky becoming overcast, nothing to do with forecast, or reject, or cast aside, or snakes. In this financial context, with 'sum' and 'audit', 'cast' has the sense which survives in astrology in the casting of horoscopes. It means to calculate, as in *2H4* 5.1.17, when Davy presents the note for shoeing and plough irons, and Shallow's response is 'Let it be cast and paid.' A word may have a wide spread of meaning, but that does not mean that its whole spread is working in every context. In that last sentence the interpretation of 'spread' is not illumined by thoughts of marmalade or muck.

The legal metaphor continues with 'advised respects'. In *KJ* 4.2.209–15 'it is the curse of kings to be attended | By slaves', who take it upon themselves

> on the winking of authority
> To understand a law, to know the meaning
> Of dangerous majesty, when perchance it frowns
> More upon humour than advised respect.

So Falstaff enjoys the legal flavour of 'advise', as he makes his excuses for absence to the Lord Chief Justice at *2H4* 1.2.135, 'As I was then advised by my learned counsel in the laws of this land-service, I did not come.'

5–8 In 36.9–12 he accepts that because of some guilt or other he may no longer acknowledge the beloved in public, nor may the beloved show him any kindness. Here he visualises that scene more vividly. The beloved will pass him as though he were a stranger (see 89.8 and 110.6), and scarcely greet him even with his eye, where the repeated rhythm of 'strangely pass | And scarcely greet' doubles the blow. This gloom is then deepened by the vision of the beloved's eye shining with the splendour of the sun, but no longer shining on S. All this added to the frown in the second line shows a lover terrified at the thought of a cold look. And the cold look is justified. The 'advised respects' of line 4 are now reinforced by the 'settled gravity' in line 8. 'Settled' is a live adjective. It activates the literal sense of gravity.

9–14 S's response follows in a military metaphor. He occupies a small fort, a sconce, 'Within the knowledge of mine owne desart', and the Quarto spelling shows that 'desart' is a perfect rhyme for 'part'. The reader might expect his deserts to be substantial, the fort to have a sturdy rampart round it, and his arm to be robust, since 'uprear' is used of substantial fortifications, like the 'high uprearèd and abutting fronts' that separate 'two mighty monarchies' in the great Prologue to *H5*. Now comes the shock, when he raises his hand to attack himself, and defends not himself but the beloved. For once the punctuation in the Quarto is useful. The comma after 'hand' encourages the reader to hear the shock of 'against myself'. The legal metaphor now returns. The defendant becomes the prosecuting counsel, as in 35.10, 'Thy adverse party is thy advocate', raising his hand to testify that the beloved's reasons are lawful, and asserting their strength against the poverty of his own case. The first quatrain ended with 'advised respects', the second with 'settled gravity', the third with 'lawful reasons'. This regular insistence shows that he has absolutely no doubt that the fault is his, and the beloved is entirely in the right,

13–14   and he marshals monosyllables to say so in 13–14. In this court of law he can show no cause why the young man should love him. Many lovers have said this and some have felt it, but not many have made such a poem out of it.

Servaes (1906) in Rollins (1944)
Has self-torturing love ever conceived words more horrible?

Vendler (1997)
The beloved's former *love* has decomposed verbally into *leave* and *laws*; and we witness the awful descent from *love* through the declension *frown, cast ... utmost sum, audit, strangely pass, scarcely greet me*, and *shall reasons find of ... gravity* all the way to *leave. Leave* has an odd plausibility as an imagined past tense of *love*, as if by spiritual word-shift.

How heavy do I journey on the way
When what I seek, my weary travel's end,
Doth teach that ease and that repose to say,
'Thus far the miles are measured from thy friend.'   4

The beast that bears me, tirèd with my woe,
Plods dully on to bear that weight in me,
As if by some instínct the wretch did know
His rider loved not speed being made from thee.   8

The bloody spur cannot provoke him on,
That sometimes anger thrusts into his hide,
Which heavily he answers with a groan
More sharp to me than spurring to his side,   12
    For that same groan doth put this in my mind—
    My grief lies onward and my joy behind.

I travel heavy, and journey's end will teach my repose to say,
    'You are now X miles further from the one you love.'
My horse plods on, burdened by the weight of misery in me,
    as though he knew I did not want to speed from you.
His groan is sharper to me than the spur to him,
    because it reminds me that I travel from joy to misery.

1–4   During a long day in the saddle, a rider may well imagine conversations with his horse, or with anything else, even with the rest he is going to enjoy when he arrives. So here S imagines that the end of his day's journey will teach the ease and repose to say to him, 'You are now that much further away from your friend.' These poems are full of personifications, but only a dramatist would make ease and repose speak.

There is no important difference between ease and repose, but this is not a versifier's padding. The poem is built upon the monotony of travel, and the reader might well find himself nodding in time with the regular iambic

164

beat and the repetition. But there is a cunning music to it, 'Doth téach that éase and thát repóse to sáy'. Polyptoton is the repetition of a word in a different form. The difference in stress between the first 'that' and the second is a subtle form of polyptoton, noticed already at 6.10 and 41.5.

5–8   On a long journey the traveller may fantasise that his conveyance, horse, boat, bicycle, even car, has a personality of its own, and is sharing his experience. The rider carries a weight of woe, and the horse groans heavily (11). The boredom of travel is represented by alliteration, repeated rhythm and assonance, 'the *m*iles are *m*easured', 'The *b*east that *b*ears me … *b*ear that *w*eight in me'. Metre contributes to the boredom. The standard iambic rhythm plods on as marked, 'Plods dúlly ón to *b*éar that wéight in mé', but 'Plods' cries out to have its own stress to slow down the movement as the verse 'Plóds dúlly ón'.

9–14   This will never do. The rider reacts with a sudden spurt of irritation against the poor wretch. Not for the first time anger thrusts the spur into his hide (the language is rough) and draws blood. The horse is so thoroughly personified by this time that he answers – with a groan – and so weighed down is he with his master's woe, that he answers heavily. The horse feels with the rider, and the rider now feels with the horse, whose groan is 'More sharp to me than spurring to his side', reminding the master that he has left joy behind and is heading for grief.

   This poem conveys with some humour the tedium of a long day in the saddle. Mile by mile the rider broods, stages conversations between his journey's end and the repose it will bring, and between that repose and himself, but most of all it suggests the relationship between horse and rider on a long weary journey.

Vendler (1997)
Nowhere is the obsessiveness of love better exemplified in the *Sonnets* than in the speaker's response to his bloodied horse's groan. He feels a sharp pang, but not for the horse; all that the horse's pain means to him is a reminder that further pain is in store for himself. We are meant, I think, to wince at this tenacity in private grief in the presence of the horse's pain.

ഇ 51 ര

Thus can my love excuse the slow offence
Of my dull bearer when from thee I speed—
'From where thou art why should I haste me thence?
Till I return, of posting is no need.'   4

O what excuse will my poor beast then find
When swift extremity can seem but slow?
Then should I spur though mounted on the wind.
In winged speed no motion shall I know.   8
Then can no horse with my desire keep pace.
Therefore desire, of perfect'st love being made,
Shall neigh, no dull flesh, in his fiery race.

But love, for love, thus shall excuse my jade,   12
   'Since from thee going he went wilful slow,
    Towards thee I'll run, and give him leave to go.'

My love for you excuses my horse for going slow when I'm riding away,
   by saying, 'Why should I hurry? I'll hurry on the way back.'
What excuse will he have on the way back when any speed can seem slow?
   I'd use the spur if mounted on the wind. If flying,
   I'll think myself motionless. No horse can keep pace
   with my desire. It shall neigh and run like fire.
But my love shall excuse my horse, 'He went slow going away from you,
   so I'll turn him loose and run to you myself.'

1–4   In Sonnet 50 the horse, in sympathy with his master, went slowly
away from the beloved. That is 'the slow offence' of 51.1, meaning 'the
offending slowness'. Inversion of adjective and noun is a common trick in
these poems, as in line 6, where 'swift extremity' means 'extreme swift-
ness'. The horse answered with a groan in 50.11–12. Now in 51.3–4 S's love
gives it an excuse, 'Why should I hurry away from you? There's no need

for hurry till I'm on the way back.' To post is to travel quickly, originally with relays of horses from post to post, but that sense is not active here.

In line 3 'thence', meaning 'from there', is the peg on which hangs 'From where'. 'Why should I hurry from there where you are? There is no need to go post-haste until I'm on the way back.'

5–11 On the way back to the beloved, the greatest imaginable speed can then only seem slow. Though mounted on the wind, S would then put spur to it. Spurring hurt the horse in 50. 9–12, but it would not hurt the wind. Though going at the speed of flight, S will think he is stationary, 'Then can no horse with my desire keep pace.' 'Then' in 5, 7 and 9 stresses the urgency, and the strange variations in 5–12 add impatience to the imaginings – 'will', 'can', 'should', 'shall', 'can', 'Shall', 'shall', speeded up at the swift 'I'll' in 14.

'Perfect'st' in line 10 is a modernisation of the Quarto reading 'perfects', a spelling cited by Evans (1996) in three contemporary or near-contemporary poets as a shortened form of 'perfectest', starting with Michael Drayton (1593) in *Eclogue 5*, 'unperfect are the perfects colours.' Nothing can be more perfect than what is perfect, but when Claudio knows that he has won the hand of Hero in *MA* 2.1.287–8 he is at first struck dumb, then explains, 'Silence is the perfectest herald of joy. I were but little happy if I could say how much.' In both these passages as in the sonnet the superlative of 'perfect' uses the irrational to suggest the impossible. S could mount the wind and put spur to it. He could fly and his desire is made of perfectest love.

What next? Could he reach towards a further absurdity? Easily. Not only is his desire faster than a horse, but S imagines a race, which desire will win. Desire is no dull horse flesh, like the plodder of 50.6, but will neigh in his fiery race. In 45.1–3 thought is fire, and fire is unimaginably swift. 'His' is standard for 'its' and also standard is Shakespeare's exploitation of the word in personifications. Desire has become a stallion, and anyone who has heard a stallion neigh when he scents the mares will enjoy this outrageous line. Desire has every right to neigh, like the amorous stallion in *VA* 265, 'imperiously he leaps, he neighs, he bounds', and in 307 'he looks upon his love and neighs unto her.' A poet who imagines a rider sticking his spurs into the flanks of the wind is not going to balk at the lustful stallion giving a neigh 'like the bidding of a monarch' (*H5* 3.7.27–8). Shakespeare had heard that sound.

The Quarto reads 'naigh' and there are many suggestions, well summarised by Burrow (2002), who favours the dull emendation 'weigh'. A straw in the wind in favour of 'neigh' is that there are several details in Sonnet 50 which anticipate details in Sonnet 51, the speech of ease in 50.4 followed by the speech of love in 51.3–4, and 13–14, 'dully' answered by 'dull' twice, 'the beast that bears me' by 'bearer', 'the wretch' by 'the poor beast', and also 'speed from thee' and 'spur' in each poem. 'Neigh' in 51.11 is a loud response to the groan of the horse in 50.11.

12–14   Lines 5–6 ask a question and 13–14 answer it. Given the ineffable speed of this conveyance, my love for you, which excused my wretched horse's slowness on the way out, will excuse it now on the way back, and 'give him leave to go'. It seems love will turn him loose and leave him to find his own way home. 'Why should my love for you be so forgiving? Because of the love the horse displayed in deciding *of its own free will* to go so slowly when I was leaving you.' In other words, '[My] love, [in exchange] for [the jade's] love, shall thus excuse my jade, "Since from thee going he went *wilful* slow".' A jade is a sorry worn-out horse, so called here with a touch of affection. 'Poor jade' occurs four times in the plays. S will run home himself with the speed of desire as documented in 45.1–4, and as fast as the 10 monosyllables of 51.14.

ᔥ 52 ᔥ

So am I as the rich, whose blessèd key
Can bring him to his sweet up-lockèd treasure,
The which he will not every hour survey
For blunting the fine point of seldom pleasure.   4

Therefore are feasts so solemn and so rare,
Since, seldom coming in the long year set,
Like stones of worth they thinly placèd are,
Or captain jewels in the carcanet.   8

So is the time that keeps you as my chest
Or as the wardrobe which the robe doth hide,
To make some special instant special blest
By new unfolding his imprisoned pride.   12

    Blessed are you, whose worthiness gives scope,
    Being had to triumph, being lacked to hope.

I am like a rich man who does not look at his treasures too often
   in case that takes the edge off his enjoyment.
Holy days are highly valued because they are spaced over the year
   like precious jewels in a golden neckband.
Just so the time that keeps you from me is a wardrobe.
   It is a great event when I open it to unfold the robe it conceals.
To have you is to triumph, to be without you is to hope.

1–4 S and his beloved are compared to the rich man and his sweet treasure, and 'sweet' is a stock epithet of the beloved (note on 70.4). When he will not every hour survey it, there is a hint of a smile at the expense of the miser with a compulsion to visit his hoard, as in Plautus, *Aulularia*, and Molière, *L'Avare*.

    The taut eloquence of line 4 is best demonstrated by worthy attempts to paraphrase it, 'for fear of dulling the keenness of pleasure, which is sustained by infrequency'. In many poems in this collection there is a line that registers in the memory, sometimes for no reason we can understand, sometimes for its sound, perhaps like line 8 of this sonnet. Here in 4 there are at least four features which may be contributing: the striking use of an adverb to qualify a noun in 'seldom pleasure' (see note on 7.2); the characteristic clash of opposites in 'blunting' and 'fine'; the compact metaphor carried in three terms, 'blunting' and 'fine point'; and the need to read not 'thé fine póint', but 'the fíne póint', which brings the line to its peak in the centre.

5–8   After that simile, 'So am I as the rich', comes another, 'My times with you are like the holy days in the year.' But this second comparison is differently shaped. 'Therefore' is the peg on which is hung the clause which begins at 'Since'. '*Therefore*', *for this reason*, are holy days celebrated with due ceremony and valued so highly, 'so rare', *since* they are thinly spaced throughout the year. This had a topical resonance for Shakespeare's contemporary readers. In the early years of Elizabeth's reign 'the collapse of the Catholic Church in England was releasing the full effect of the European Renaissance and Reformation ... Lost with the old faith were Catholic dirges and trentals, the sets of thirty requiem services ... as well as extreme unction and purgatory and satisfactory masses. Holy days had been cut in number from over a hundred to twenty-seven' (Honan 1999, 7).

This analogy of the holy days is now illustrated by the simile of the carcanet, a neckband of precious metal studded with jewels. 'Captain jewels' clearly refers to the chief, the principal jewels, and sounds as though it ought to be a technical term of jewellery. There is no evidence of this, and though 'captain' for 'chief' in an impersonal sense did occur in the sixteenth and seventeeth centuries, as in *OED*, 'sound sleepe, the captaine cause of good digestion' (1581), it is a rare use. It therefore looks as though this may not be a dead metaphor. These 'stones of worth' would be arrayed on a neckband, standing out like captains parading in front of the rank and file, the metal of the carcanet. In John Nichols's account of the long progress of Queen Elizabeth in 1572, she received 'one rich carkanet or collor of gold haveing in it two emeraldes' (*The Progresses and Public Processions of Queen Elizabeth I* (1788–1823)). These would have been the captains.

For a simile to be persuasive, it has to resemble what it illustrates. Holy days are 'seldom coming in the long year set', and *setting* is a technical term of jewellery, so preparing the way for the simile, where captain jewels are *set* [at intervals], 'thinly placèd' in the carcanet.

9–12 This poem has a string of comparisons, articulated by 'So ... as' in the first line, 'Like' in 7, and 'So ... as my chest | Or as the wardrobe' in 9–10. A wardrobe is a room, not recorded as a piece of furniture by *OED* (citing Hepplewhite) until 1794. Here the wardrobe which wards, protects, the robe, is defined immediately in line 10 as 'which the robe doth hide'. The glide from 'ward' to 'hide' is important. S does wish he could see his beloved more often, but he is hidden. In 11–12, when the festive day comes round, the unfolding of that special robe confers a special blessing. It is a '*new* unfolding', as though he is seeing the man he loves for the first time. The beloved is S's pride, but that pride has been imprisoned. To S his absence is as grievous as his incarceration would have been. The poem is attempting to take a positive view of absence, but truth will out, and here it undercuts the whole argument. He is whistling to keep his spirits up.

13–14 There have been six or seven images in these 12 lines, some developed, some fleeting, the rich man looking at his treasure, the sharp point of pleasure's dagger, the holy days spaced throughout the year, the setting of precious stones in a neckband, army captains on parade, a robe taken from a chest for a festive day, and the chest is its prison, just as for S the absence of the beloved is the beloved's prison. Now the bare literal truth, the beloved is blest, worth so much to S that his presence is a source of pride and a cause for triumph, and his absence is a cause for hope of his return. The rhetoric and the music of the last line are enriched by a metrical variation between 'Being had', where 'Being' is one syllable, and 'being lacked', where it is two (compare 50.3).

For an argument to stand in logic, a problem has to be stated, it has to be worked through, and a conclusion has to be reached. This demands repetitions of words and of concepts to hold the structure together. So here 'blessed' or 'blest' in 1, 11 and 13; so 'rare' in 5 and 'seldom' in 4 and 6; so 'up-lockèd', 'keeps', 'hide' and 'imprisoned'; so 'pride' and 'triumph'; so 'rich', 'treasure', 'rare', 'worth', 'jewels' and 'worthiness', and here 'blessèd' could reappear, since it often refers to wealth. These sonnets are heavy with repetitions because they present logical arguments.

What is your substance? Whereof are you made,
That millions of strange shadows on you tend,
Since every one hath, every one, one shade,
And you, but one, can every shadow lend?   4

Describe Adonis, and the counterfeit
Is poorly imitated after you;
On Helen's cheek all art of beauty set,
And you in Grecian tires are painted new;   8
Speak of the spring and foison of the year,
The one doth shadow of your beauty show,
The other as your bounty doth appear,
And you in every blessed shape we know.   12

In all external grace you have some part,
But you like none, none you, for constant heart.

What are you made of that you are attended by millions of shadows?
Everyone else has only one.
Portraits of Adonis or Helen would be copies of you, Adonis a poor one.
Spring is a shadow of you, and the bounty of autumn is yours.
You have a share of every beauty, but none has your constancy of heart.

1–4 The Quarto and most editions have a comma after 'substance'. This
edition prefers the question mark. Baffled, S asks the same question twice,
'What's your material? What are you made of that you have a million shadows?' As his beloved walks down the street, say, he 'lends', supplies (we would
say 'throws'), not one, but a million shadows, and they are strange shadows,
not shadows of himself. This puzzle becomes even more baffling when the
shadows are said to tend. 'To tend' is to serve as a slave, as in 57.1–2:

Being your slave, what should I do but tend
Upon the hours and times of your desire?

Apart from its normal meaning, a shadow can be an attendant, a lackey, as in *OED* 8a, citing Stephen Gosson (1579), 'Though the pryde of their shadowes (I meane these hangebyes whome they succour with stipend) cause them to be somewhat il talked of abroade.' The word 'tend' thus turns the black silhouette which is the normal shadow into a lackey, suggesting that the beloved is a man of substance tended by a retinue of millions of servants.

This still does not solve the opening problem, and lines 3–4 vividly explore it, savouring the detail, with repetitions which suggest what a miracle it is and how difficult to understand, 'every one hath, every one, one shade, | And you, but one, can every shadow lend' – where 'but one' means '[being] only one'. These two lines are suitably complex; 'every one hath, every one, one' is shadowed in 'you ... one ... every'. Line 4 is a strange shadow of line 3.

5–12   A portrait of Adonis, the beautiful boy loved by the goddess of love and a paragon of youthful male beauty, would be a poor imitation of the beloved. 'Describe him' means 'depict him, draw him'. The verb was commonly used in Shakespeare's day meaning to draw, as in our 'describe a circle'. So this line means 'if anyone were to do a portrait of Adonis, it would be a poor imitation of you.' The syntax is not unusual, a command, standing as a vivid conditional clause, followed by a statement often introduced by 'and', as in 'Laugh and the world laughs with you.' If Ella Wheeler Wilcox had written, 'If you laugh the world laughs with you, if you weep you weep alone', it would not have appeared in dictionaries of quotations. This construction is given vigour by the present tenses, 'Is ... imitated' and 'are painted'. Neither of these works of art really existed, but S speaks as though they were there before his eyes.

Helen is the paragon of woman's beauty. 'Was this the face that launch'd a thousand ships?' (Marlowe, *Doctor Faustus* 1332). Shakespeare, pouncing on the minute detail, caps that verse (compare 8.13–4) by focusing on the cheek. Lavish all the skill of the painter's art to depict her cheek, and what is painted is a new portrait of the beloved, this time in a Greek headdress (Shakespeare never uses 'tire' to mean clothes in general). A portrait of Helen, the most beautiful of women, would be a new portrait of the beloved.

From a pair of paragons of human beauty to a pair of seasons, with the same vivid syntax, 'Speak of the spring ... ' The gaudy spring (10.1) for all its colours is a black-and-white drawing of the beloved. This uses yet another meaning of 'shadow', a representation, as in *TGV* 4.2.122, where

Proteus asks Julia for a portrait of her, 'And to your shadow will I make true love.' Autumn is the season of *foison*, plenty, pro*fu*sion, and its bounty looks like the beauty of the beloved. Line 12 summarises: in every shape blessed [with beauty] we see the beloved.

13–14   In line 2 he has millions of shadows. In 13 there is something in every beauty, which the beloved also has, 'In all external grace you have some part' (13). 'Grace', like 'blessed', suggests benefactions of the gods. 'God Send Grace' was the motto of the royal burgh of Sanquhar, now replaced by 'On, Sanquhar on'. In the last line, S takes one further step. Every beauty has something which the beloved has, but the beloved has something seen nowhere else, an inner beauty, a constant heart. 'External' is there to point its opposite, the heart. There is no difference in meaning between 'you like none' and 'none [like] you', but the repetition lends great emphasis, and also ties the sound of the argument to lines 3–4. These sonnets are often ring compositions – the end often looks back to the beginning. In the first four lines S's bafflement is conveyed with repetitions, halting syntax and chiasmus; in the last line the mystery is fully explained, but S's wonderment remains, conveyed with repetitions, halting syntax, and chiasmus, 'But you like none, none you, for constant heart.' Kerrigan (1986) is more succinct: 'The last line resolves the sonnet in the rhythms of lines 3–4.'

The word 'shadow' in different senses is the thread that leads through this maze, and it also delighted Shakespeare in Sonnet 43 and in *KJ* 2.1.497–504, where the Dauphin tells his father King Philip that he loves the Lady Blanche:

> in her eye I find
> A wonder, or a wondrous miracle,
> The shadow of myself formed in her eye;
> Which, being but the shadow of your son,   500
> Becomes a sun and makes your son a shadow.
> I do protest I never loved myself
> Till now enfixèd I beheld myself
> Drawn in the flatt'ring table of her eye.

In 499 'The shadow' is the reflection, which is a representation of the prince. Because it shines from her eye, this 'shadow' becomes a sun, which shines upon the king's son, with such brightness that he 'makes', throws, a shadow. If the Elizabethan audience understood this conceit as they heard it, their ability to understand spoken English far exceeds our ability to understand it written.

After several sonnets in which S has aired his premonitions of the young man's infidelity, and after 35, 40, 41 and 42, where we are told that infidelity has already taken place, this last line is a shock. As an ironic jibe it does not make satisfactory sense. It would be better to read it partly as a lover's wishful thinking, partly as an amorous tactic, praising the beloved for a quality the lover wished he would develop. Perhaps, too, there is a suggestion that a lover's pact has been sealed, that they have agreed that there will be no more infidelity. Whatever, Shakespeare is setting the scene for the drama of the next betrayal.

Duncan-Jones (1997)
The fair youth is claimed as the archetype or defining image of all beauty, whether human or natural, male or female; but according to the Platonic idea of externals as a shadow of inward realities, he is (apparently) praised above all for moral excellence.

Vendler (1997)
There seems an arbitrary pattern in vowel/diphthong + n – an/en/on/oun (eighteen such phonemes) – running through the poem, perhaps as a reflection of the millions of strange shadows cast by the object.

❦ 54 ❧

O how much more doth beauty beauteous seem
By that sweet ornament which truth doth give!

The rose looks fair, but fairer we it deem
For that sweet odour which doth in it live.   4
The canker blooms have full as deep a dye
As the perfumèd tincture of the roses,
Hang on such thorns, and play as wantonly
When summer's breath their maskèd buds discloses.   8
But, for their virtue only is their show,
They live unwooed and unrespected fade,
Die to themselves. Sweet roses do not so;
Of their sweet deaths are sweetest odours made.   12

And so of you, beauteous and lovely youth,
When that shall vade, my verse distils your truth.

Beauty seems more beautiful if true.
The rose is fair but we think it fairer because of its fragrance.
Canker roses are as beautiful, but they have no perfume.
When they die they die, but roses live on distilled.
So when your beauty fades, my verse distils your truth.

1–2 It would be natural to think of beauty as an ornament to truth, but
here truth is the ornament to beauty. Hence the exclamation mark.
    The note on the last two lines of Sonnet 53 ended by arguing that the
praise of the beloved's constancy is not what it seems to be. That is
confirmed by the warning against inconstancy which now fills Sonnet 54.

3–12 This sonnet compares the beauty and truth of the beloved with the
beauty and fragrance of roses. To make the comparison work, lines 3–12
on roses contain terms which fit human life. The sweet odour of the rose
in lines 4, 6, 11 and 12 corresponds to the sweetness of truth in line 2. Roses

have a dye in line 5, and tincture in line 6; in *OED* a tincture is a 'a dye, pigment, *spec.* used as a cosmetic', the 'false painting' of 67.5. Roses play wantonly in line 7, and 'summer's breath their maskèd buds discloses', just as the warm whispers of a lover (at a masked ball), may persuade a dancing partner to doff the mask and disclose the features. 'Virtue' in line 9 is a technical term for the effect of herbs (it is a standard paragraph heading in Nicholas Culpeper's *Herbal* of 1653), and the virtue of the beloved, his truth in 2 and 14, is what this sonnet is about. Canker roses 'live unwoo'd and unrespected fade, | Die to themselves', and the application to human life is clear. At line 9 begins a new point of resemblance between roses and the beloved. The preservation of the fragrance of flowers by distillation of their petals supplies an image in 5.9–14 and 6.1–4, there used to persuade the young man to preserve his beauty by having a son. Here in 54 the distillation of rose oil, the attar of roses, a vastly expensive luxury, is an image for the preservation of the beloved's truth in S's verse.

Vendler (1997) finds that the adjectival repetition of 'Sweet', 'sweet' and 'sweetest' in 11–12 'mimics the increasing concentration of distillation'. Surely not. In distillation the first drop is as strong as the last, but the heady perfume that fills this poem rises in line 12 to the superlative adjective 'sweetest', taking the verse beat on its first syllable, whereas 'sweet' in 11 and 12 has to do without.

13–14 In 'When that shall vade', 'that' must be the beauty and loveliness of the beloved referred to in the previous line. The Quarto reading 'vade' is an archaic verb meaning 'go, depart' (Latin *vadere*). The young man's beauty will vade, just as canker roses fade in line 10. Shakespeare has achieved correspondence *and* avoided repetition, so honouring the resemblance *and* the difference between flower and man, while making music by the alliteration, 'When that shall vade, my verse ... '

In the last line the Quarto reads 'by verse distils your truth', but this involves a strange use of the verb 'to distil'. Distillation is mentioned a score of times in Shakespeare and the spirit never distils – it is distilled. So here truth does not distil. It is rather 'my verse' which distils the beloved's truth and immortalises it. Besides, 'by verse' might advance the claims of poets in general, and that is not S's way. From Sonnet 15 onwards, when he talks of verse granting immortality, the verse he means is his own. This interpretation sets the scene for the triumphant claims of Sonnet 55.

Shakespeare takes liberties with syntax, as for example with the verbs in 51.5–12. Here again in line 14, 'When that shall vade, my verse distils your truth', the present tense of 'distils' does not accord with the future tense of 'shall vade', but his imagination leaps ahead to visualise what *is happening* when beauty shall die, as though the beloved were already dead, and this is happening even as he speaks. Another advantage is that the slight illogicality sounds like a natural speaking voice.

S speaks of the truth of his beloved as a fact, but he has already revealed that it is not, as noted at the end of Sonnet 53. Here too the poem ends with a compliment which is an appeal. The truth of the beloved at the beginning and end of 54 links it to the constancy which ends 53. 'My verse' at the end of 54 links it to 'this powerful rhyme' at the beginning of 55.

The above division of the poem into 2–10–2 is an attempt to highlight the argument. Another division would show the sonnet as a stepped podium, 2 lines on beauty – 2 on roses – 6 on canker roses – 2 on roses – 2 on the beauty of the beloved.

Duncan-Jones (1997), on line 11
They die alone; they are their own dye, furnishing no colour or value to others; and, possibly, they experience orgasm in solitude.

ஐ 55 ௧

Not marble nor the gilded monuments
Of princes shall outlive this pow'rful rhyme,
But you shall shine more bright in these conténts
Than unswept stone besmeared with sluttish time.   4

When wasteful war shall statues overturn
And broils root out the work of masonry,
Nor Mars his sword nor war's quick fire shall burn
The living record of your memory.   8

'Gainst death and all oblivious enmity
Shall you pace forth. Your praise shall still find room
Ev'n in the eyes of all posterity
That wear this world out to the ending doom.   12
   So, till the judgement that yourself arise,
   You live in this and dwell in lovers' eyes.

No monument will live longer than this poetry.
  It will make you shine brighter than any dirty old stone.
War will overthrow statues and destroy buildings,
  but neither sword nor fire will burn this living record.
You will stride out against death and oblivion, praised till the end of time.
  Until you rise at the Last Judgement, you live in the eyes of lovers.

1–4   The power of this verse to confer immortality was touched upon at
the end of Sonnet 54, and is the proud promise which fills Sonnet 55.

What marble and what monuments did Shakespeare have in his mind's
eye? 'Monuments of princes' with gilded lettering would be seen in
churches and cathedrals, such as that of Henry V in Westminster Abbey
or, nearer Shakespeare's home, the noble effigy of King John in the chancel
of Worcester Cathedral. Vertical stones are not swept nor are table grave-
stones in cemeteries. So the unswept stone of line 4 is inscribed stones on
the church floor, but, when a church is tended by sluttish cleaners,

memorial paving slabs will be begrimed with dirt. The culprit in this sonnet is a slut called time. The beloved will shine more brightly 'in these conténts', in the contents of these sonnets, than the names of princes will shine on marble inscriptions or gold lettering. This verse is called powerful because it is being matched against the power of princes.

5–8   It is only too obvious that war is wasteful in the sense that it is a waste of life and in particular of youth, but in this context the primary sense is that it creates ruin, in the literal sense of Latin *vastare*, 'ruin, devastate', as when the Goth did fix his eye 'upon the wasted building ... a ruinous monastery' in *TA* 5.1.21–3. 'Of all phases of architecture in Shakespeare, ruins carry the strongest emotional quality', according to A. H. R. Fairchild (1937) in Rollins (1944), an assessment borne out by 'Bare ruined choirs where late the sweet birds sang' in 73.4. The dissolution of the monasteries in the 1530s left its mark on the English landscape and on Shakespeare's imagination. The iconoclasts tore down statues, including effigies of the powerful, and when monks resisted there were 'broils', skirmishes, in holy places, as religious houses were destroyed. Ruined masonry was a common sight in Shakespeare's England.

'Mars his' is an archaic form of the possessive, and often used with Mars, for example with 'idiot', 'gauntlet', 'helm' and 'heart' in *TC* 2.1.55, 4.7.61, 4.7.139 and 5.2.167. Perhaps Shakespeare did not like the sound of 'Mars's'. The sword of war hacked the breasts off statues of virgins in the Lady Chapels at Ely and Worcester, and abbey churches were fired all over England. Swords do not burn anything, but fire and sword often work together, as they do here in line 7. 'Quick' and 'living' interact. Although fire is quick in that it is swift, it is also living, as in 'the quick and the dead', but this living fire of war will not burn the living record preserved in this verse.

9–14   War continues in lines 9–10. In 'oblivious enmity', enmity is not oblivious; what is meant is 'hostile oblivion'. This is another example of the inversion of noun and adjective noted at 51.1 and 6. The enemies are death and oblivion, but the beloved boldly paces out in front of the battle line as a champion to challenge them.

The obvious picture would be the solid world wearing out the eyes of men, but here eyes will wear out the world until the Last Judgement. A similar surprise occurs in Horace, *Odes* 1.11, where the obvious picture would be the sea wearing out the shore, but instead of coastal erosion the storm wears out the sea on the pumice pebbles that oppose it on the South

Italian beach, '*oppositis debilitat pumicibus mare*'. In line 12 'doom' as judgement occurs in 145.7, where the lover's tongue, 'ever sweet, | Was used in giving gentle doom'.

This poem speaks with the certainty of an assured prophecy. The pitiful paraphrase offered above uses the tame word 'will', but 'shall' rings out in lines 2, 3, 5 and 7, and twice in line 10, but then in lines 12 and 14 the vast future of this poem, all posterity, is expressed as a present certainty, 'You live in this and dwell in lovers' eyes.'

Poems stand or fall by their adjectives, and usually fall. But here they are all load-bearing. Monuments may be *gilded*, but they will not shine as *bright* as the contents of these poems. Princes are powerful, but not as *powerful* as this rhyme. Time is a *sluttish* cleaning lady, begriming stone that should have been swept. War is *wasteful* in that it lays waste. Fire is *quick* because it destroys quickly, and also because it seems to be alive, but it will not burn this *living* record, and '*oblivious* enmity' encourages the reader to realise that it is the hostile power of oblivion that would strive to make the world forget the beloved.

ஐ 56 ଔ

Sweet love, renew thy force; be it not said
Thy edge should blunter be than appetite,
Which but today by feeding is allayed,
Tomorrow sharpened, in his former might.   4
So, love, be thou: although today thou fill
Thy hungry eyes ev'n till they wink with fulness,
Tomorrow see again, and do not kill
The sp'rit of love with a perpetual dullness.   8

Let this sad interim like the ocean be,
Which parts the shore where two contracted new
Come daily to the banks, that when they see
Return of love, more blest may be the view.   12

   As call it winter, which being full of care,
   Makes summer's welcome thrice more wished, more rare.

Love, be like appetite, appeased today, renewed tomorrow.
  Though yesterday you fill your eyes until they close, see again tomorrow.
  Do not kill love by unrelieved dullness.
Let this interval be like the sea which parts two lovers,
  who come every day to the shore and are blest by seeing each other,
like the return of summer after winter's gloom.

1–8 'Sweet love, renew thy force' seems to be addressed to the emotion
of love, but no sooner is it spoken than the focus is shifting to the beloved,
'be it not said | Thy edge should blunter be than appetite.' In line 5, the
beloved is clearly meant, and there is no difficulty about the notion that he
has an edge. Lord Angelo, for instance, has one in *MM* 1.4.59–60, and 'doth
rebate and blunt his natural edge | With profits of the mind, study, and
fast'. The metaphor runs through the first eight lines – a 'blunter' 'edge' in
2, 'sharpened' in 4 and 'dullness' in 8. It has already occurred unforgettably

in 52.4, 'For blunting the fine point of seldom pleasure', and will recur in 103.7–8.

The beloved is asked to renew his force, the implication being that his energy [as a lover] has flagged. His edge should be like appetite, satisfied today, but sharp again tomorrow, as strong as before. In line 5, 'That, my love,' he says, 'is what you should be like.' The comparison between loving and eating is then developed. If the lover *fills* his *hungry* eyes so full that 'they wink' (close, that is, as at 43.1) 'with fullness', it is as though he has over-indulged and fallen asleep, but when the next day comes he should open them and see again, not kill the spirit of love with unrelieved dullness. Sight is important in love in lines 6–7 and 11–12, as at 104.2. Love is linked to the feeding metaphor by 'tomorrow' in lines 4 and 7. It is clear from line 8 that it is the *spirit* of love which should be daily renewed. 'Spirit' is a monosyllable, something like 'sprit', as in sprite and sprightly. 'Perpétual' slurs -ua- into one syllable.

9–12   In the second simile S proposes that this sad interval in their loving, 'this sad interim' (pronounced 'int'rim' and spelt *Intrim* in the Quarto), should 'like the ocean be | Which parts the shore' where two new lovers come daily to the banks to see each other. This ocean is therefore a strait or narrow inlet or the estuary of a river. In Shakespeare 'bank' can refer to the seashore, as in *2H6* 3.2.82–4, where Queen Margaret was 'nigh wrecked upon the sea, | And twice by awkward winds from England's bank | Drove back again.' But the scene in the sonnet irresistibly recalls the story recently retold by Christopher Marlowe in *Hero and Leander* (1592–3). There every night Leander swims across the strait of the Hellespont to Hero's tower and swims back before dawn. Shakespeare has used the myth, and adapted it to fit his own poem. Hero and Leander made love nightly, but S hopes only to see the one he loves, and the sad interim in his love affair seems to be caused by his beloved's lack of interest.

13–14   The Quarto reads 'As call it winter', a harsh irregularity in the syntax, but defensible, as conveying the flavour of living speech, 'Let it be like the ocean, as [though one might] call it winter'. Most editors emend to 'Or call it winter', perhaps rightly.

Literally, 'more rare' means more unusual, but the return of summer is a regular event. The commoner meaning of 'rare' is precious (52.5), but it has added piquancy here when applied to what cannot be more or less rare in its literal sense.

Some have found an inconsistency in the argument. Evans (1996), for example, writes, 'the separation theme does not arise naturally out of the appetite/love analogy of the preceding lines, where there is little or no suggestion of impending temporal or spatial division, only the danger of satiety.' This is surely unfair. The first eight lines plead with the young man to return to loving after satiety. The rest of the poem supports the plea by arguing that resumption of pleasure after deprivation is intense. The 'separation theme' of 9–12 is not a theme; it is, like the argument from the seasons in 13–14, a simile. Their separation is 'like the ocean' which divides lovers. It is the essence of a simile to compare one thing with something different.

The first eight lines show S believing that his beloved has lost his desire to see him. There could be an explanation of this which S does not contemplate, that the beloved has had enough, and never wants to see him again. As the plot develops in the next two poems, S will soon learn, with great grief, that the beloved is taking up with other companions, and in 61.14 he will not think highly of them. Here in Sonnet 56 the young man's love seems to be losing its edge and the older man is trying to explain this in terms least wounding to himself. Reality will soon take over. 'This sad Intrim' is a sad phrase.

ॐ 57 ॐ

Being your slave, what should I do but tend
Upon the hours and times of your desire?
I have no precious time at all to spend,
Nor services to do till you require;   4

Nor dare I chide the world-without-end hour
Whilst I, my sovereign, watch the clock for you;
Nor think the bitterness of absence sour
When you have bid your servant once adieu;   8

Nor dare I question with my jealous thought
Where you may be, or your affairs suppose,
But like a sad slave stay and think of nought
Save, where you are, how happy you make those.   12

   So true a fool is love, that in your will,
   Though you do anything, he thinks no ill.

I am your slave, and my only task is to attend upon you.
Nor dare I complain about how slowly time passes as I wait for you,
*   nor dare to feel aggrieved when you leave me,*
nor dare I ask what you are doing. My only thought is how happy you make
*   those you are with.*
Love is a fool that sees no ill-will in anything you may do.

In Sonnet 56, S longs to be loved and to be with the beloved more often. It
is as though the beloved has protested, 'Am I expected to spend all my time
with you?' In Sonnet 57, S retreats, acknowledging that he has no rights
over the beloved. In 58 he will retreat further.

1–4   In the second line the phrase 'hours and times' is not padding. All the
times he will be required and all his *hours* of waiting will be picked up in
what follows. He has 'no precious *time* at all' of his own, and he waits 'the

world-without-end *hour*', now singular instead of plural, since any one *hour* of waiting is an age. S is a slave tending upon his master, and he has no time of his own which he values, 'no *precious* time at all to *spend*'.

5–8 He does not dare scold his beloved for all the endless hours he has to wait for him, watching the clock 'world without end'. It seems like eternity. Shakespeare must have heard the phrase many times as a boy, four or five times at Morning Prayer every day when the priest intoned, 'Glory be to the Father, and to the Son: and to the Holy Ghost', and the congregation answered, 'As it was in the beginning, is now, and ever shall be: world without end. Amen,'

In line 6 the beloved is not only his master, he is his king, 'my sovereign'. Neither slave nor courtier dare grumble when kept waiting. Metaphor apart, S dare not scold the beloved, because those who think themselves inferior in a love affair are afraid of reprisals. But he does not even dare mention the possibility of scolding, only 'the world-without-end hour' of waiting. The skeleton of thought is: 'Nor dare I chide ... Nor [dare I] think bitterness sour ... Nor dare I question.' He is so abjectly afraid of offending that he dare not think that black is black, white white, or bitterness sour. The implication is clear. Bitterness *is* sour and the beloved's behaviour *does* cause him great pain. He has succeeded in saying it while saying that he dare not say it. 'When you have bid your servant once adieu' could be innocent and toneless, but there is a subtext, 'It's easy for you, but I suffer.' 'Adieu' can be casual. Time grants Troilus only one hasty farewell from Cressida, 'He fumbles up [farewells] into a loose adieu | And scants us with a single famished kiss' (*TC* 4.4.45–6), and there is 'too cold an adieu' in *AW* 2.1.51.

9–12 Master has gone off for a social evening, or so we may deduce from 48.10–14, 58.9–12 and 61.14. Meanwhile the servant does not dare even to think jealously 'Where you may be'. But the words are more potent than that. He does not question with his own thought. He does not even dare to make that contribution to his own private debate. Nor dare he imagine the absent beloved's affairs (10). The word is not recorded of amours until 1704 (*OED* 3, citing Richard Steele, 'to marry a Woman after an affair with her'), but S again lets it be known what he suspects by saying he dare not ask. Line 12 confirms this, 'But ... think of nought | Save ... how happy you make those' where you are. Lines 11–12 contradict 9–10. He dare not question, but he sits there wondering. Stricken as he is, he includes a word of praise with the complaints he says he dare not make. It is as though he is trying to console himself by thinking selflessly what a joy the beloved must be giving to others.

The first line of this poem opens with the standard inversion of metrical beat in the first two syllables, 'béing' for the iambic 'beíng'. In this poem there are only two other syllables which might be stressed against the metrical accent, and these are both expressive, 'world-without-énd hour' in 5, where 'énd' seems to prolong the agony of waiting, and 'But like a sad sláve stay' in 11, where the dragging syllable of 'slave' could sound even slower by the alliteration of -s- and the assonance of 'slave stay'.

This poem is a precarious gambit in the rhetoric of love. To say 'I dare not ask myself where you are or what you are doing there or who you're with' is a complaint inviting the retort, 'Have I to get your permission for everything I do?' Sure enough, that retort comes along between this sonnet and the next, drawing the anxious denials at 58.1–2 and 14.

13–14 A fool in Shakespeare is often a professional entertainer. Lear, for instance, had a true, a loyal fool. In that sense the final couplet preserves the theme of the sonnet, harking back to 'slave' in line 1, and 'sovereign' in line 6. Love is then the loyal jester who serves his king and who is not entitled to think ill of him whatever he does. But a true fool is also an absolute idiot, and in that sense love makes the lover unable to see the vices of his beloved. This ambiguity makes a fitting end to this devious argument. It seems to be saying that love has so affected S that he cannot think ill of the beloved whatever he may do, and that is not a direct accusation. But it also suggests that love has reduced S to such stupidity that he cannot see that the beloved is behaving badly, and that is bitter.

If this were a letter to a lover, it would be a monument of deception, including perhaps self-deception. But, if the Sonnets are a discontinuous drama, this is a speech crafted by the dramatist, exploring the jealousy and deceit and self-deception of which lovers are capable. That turns the poem into an appeal in which S extols his own patience, begs the beloved for pity, begs to be appreciated, and begs for a denial of the innuendoes in lines 10, 12 and 14, where 'anything' shows that he knows the truth. This act of submission follows naturally after the appeal for the resumption of love in Sonnet 56. It will be followed in Sonnet 58 by total submission.

Burrow (2002)
The Quarto capitalizes 'Will', which may indicate a pun on the male or female sexual organs, as well as anticipating the pun on the poet's name in e.g. 136.

❧ 58 ☙

That god forbid that made me first your slave
I should in thought control your times of pleasure,
Or at your hand th'account of hours to crave,
Being your vassal bound to stay your leisure.   4

O let me suffer, being at your beck,
Th'imprisoned absence of your liberty,
And patience tame to suff'rance, bide each check
Without accusing you of injury.   8

Be where you list your charter is so strong
That you yourself may privilege your time
To what you will; to you it doth belong
Yourself to pardon of self-doing crime.   12

   I am to wait, though waiting so be hell,
   Not blame your pleasure be it ill or well.

May the god who made me your slave forbid me to rule your pleasures,
   or beg an account of how you spend your time.
Let me accept your absence. When you are free, I am in prison.
   Let me tame my patience, and accept every rebuff.
Be where you wish. You have full jurisdiction, can sanction anything.
   It is your right to pardon your crimes.
I wait in hell, and do not criticise your pleasure, good or ill.

1–4   Slave, times, hours and stay announce that this poem continues the
argument of Sonnet 57. In 57 it was 'Being your slave'; here it is 'Being your
vassal' and 'being at your beck'. The beloved's hours and time dominated
the first six lines of 57, and the theme is taken up in 58.2 and 3. 'Sad slave
stay' in 57.11 anticipates to 'bound to stay' in 58.4.

   In 57 S grumbles when the beloved leaves him to join other company.
Sonnet 58 opens with an expostulation, 'May the god [of love] forbid', as

though the beloved had accused S of wishing to control his pleasure, and had asked if he has to give a written account of everything he does, an account 'at your hand'. In 57.9–12, S had said that he dared not think jealous thoughts about the company the beloved was keeping. The beloved must have protested, and now S retreats, 'Be where you list … *you yourself* may privilege *your* time | To what *you* will'.

There is a slight irregularity in the syntax – 'god forbid I should control … or [god forbid me] to crave'. Again the roughness sounds like the impetus of real spoken English.

5–8   In 57.7 S had mentioned the bitterness of absence, and now he makes an even more abject statement of his suffering. While insisting that he is at the beloved's beck and call, he admits in 6, a line of Shakespearean density, that his master is at liberty to be absent, but insists that it is an 'imprisoned liberty'. The liberty of the beloved is imprisonment for S, whereas in 52.12 separation was imprisonment for the beloved. In line 7, S begs to be allowed not just to tame his impatience, but to go even further and tame his patience to accept suffering, 'suff'rance'. Biding each check is a matter of putting up with disappointment after disappointment with no recriminations. He will not accuse the beloved of 'injury' (here injustice), but the implication is that the beloved is guilty. The tactic is to convey subjection and at the same time a sense of injured merit.

9–12   In 57.9–12 S had said that he dared not think jealous thoughts about where the beloved might be. Between sonnets the beloved must have assumed that, by not daring to question, S was questioning. S now denies this with emphasis, 'Be where you list. You are completely free.'

In 57.6 the beloved was accepted as king. Here S invokes the constitution. The beloved enjoys a [royal] charter, [royal] privilege and [royal] right of pardon. Now it is out in the open, no ambiguity, no innuendo. The beloved has the right himself to pardon the crimes he himself has committed, a *carte blanche* so extreme as to be a condemnation. The repetition of 'self' is pointed by the metre, 'Yoursélf to párdon of sélf-dóing críme', where the stress on the second 'sélf' is unexpected, like the stresses on 'end' in 57.5 and on 'slave' in 57.11.

13–14   The rhetoric of 9–12 is in 'you … your … you yourself … your … you … you … Yourself', and the bitterness comes in 'I am to wait'. In 57.5–6, while saying that he did not grumble, S grumbled about the hours of waiting he had to endure. Between sonnets the beloved must have protested, and again S capitulates, 'I am to wait, though waiting so be hell.' And again his tactic is to be meek while making it clear how much he suffers.

Sonnet 56 implied that there had been a time of ardent love, followed by an intermission. In begging the beloved to renew that love, S supposed or pretended to suppose that the intermission was caused by the beloved's satiety. Either this was the young man's excuse which he is supposed to have offered before the sonnet began, or it was a fancy in S's mind, to save himself from darker suspicions. In Sonnet 57 there is no word of it. Now in Sonnet 58 S sees that the man he loves has other friends and other pleasures. For reasons of fear and amorous tact, in 57 he stopped just short of a cry of misery and an explicit protest against the beloved's behaviour, although as the poem proceeded it came nearer to being both. He ended it by thinking no ill. In Sonnet 58 he has realised the truth. He starts by restating his total subservience, but, as in 57, his misery intensifies as the poem proceeds, and in the last three lines goes all the way. The young man is guilty of a crime against love, and S is in hell, accepting 'ill or well' [but knowing it is ill]. On this interpretation these three sonnets are richly dramatic, a playlet in three short scenes with one speaker heard and the other's words understood between.

Empson (1984)
[reading line 7 'And patience tame, to sufferance bide each check']
And patience tame expresses petulance by its contraction of meaning ('suffer tame patience'; 'be patience-tame' as in 'iron-hard'; and 'tame patience' as in *bide each check*) followed by a rush of equivocal words, clinched with *belong*, which has subject both *your time* and *to pardon*, and implies, still with sweetness and pathos (it is an extraordinary balance of feeling), 'that is all I could have expected of you.'

℘ 59 ℛ

If there be nothing new, but that which is
Hath been before, how are our brains beguiled,
Which, lab'ring for invention, bear amiss
The second burden of a former child!   4

O that recórd could with a backward look,
Ev'n of five hundred courses of the sun,
Show me your image in some antique book,
Since mind at first in character was done,   8
That I might see what the old world could say
To this composèd wonder of your frame.

Whe'er we are mended, or whe'er better they,
Or whether revolution be the same,   12
    O sure I am the wits of former days
    To subjects worse have giv'n admiring praise.

If there be nothing new under the sun, we deceive ourselves,
    labouring to be original but producing what has already been produced.
If only I could find your picture in an old book, so that I could see
    what writers of the day said about your wondrous beauty.
Whether or not they were better writers than we are, O sure I am
    the old poets praised beauties less beautiful than you.

1–4 'There is no new thing under the sun. Is there any thing, whereof it
may be said, See, this is new? It hath been already of old time' (Ecclesiastes
1: 9–10, in the chapter ordained to be read at Evening Prayer every year on
29 October). This principle is applied to poetic composition, here seen as
child-bearing. Our brains are in labour, striving to give birth to something
new, but being pregnant for a second time with a child which has already
been born once, they 'bear amiss | The second burden of a former child'.
For poetic composition seen as child-bearing, see commentary on 38.11.

5–10 He wishes fervently, with an exclamation, 'O that recórd could', that he could look back even 500 years and find the beloved's image in some old book. 'Ev'n' is a compliment, implying that records would have to go back a very long way to have any hope of finding such a likeness. Five hundred is chosen presumably because it is an impressive round number (it would also include some of the miraculous art work in medieval illuminated manuscripts). But the number is often explained with reference to the Great Year discussed in Plato, *Timaeus* 39D, the period between two times when the planets would all be in the same position with reference to the fixed stars. On this interpretation the 'revolution' of line 12 would be the return of the planets to their former position. This idea is mentioned by several Greek and Latin writers, but one difficulty is that I know of no trace of it anywhere in Shakespeare. Another is that in his massive commentary on Cicero, *De Natura Deorum* 2.52 (Harvard University Press, 1955–8), A. S. Pease lists a score of definitions of the length of the Great Year, from 30 to 36,000 years, but no figure between 365 and 600. Nevertheless the mention of 'revolution' in line 12 makes it possible that the Great Year is lurking in lines 6 and 12 of this sonnet.

Lines 5–8 do not flow smoothly. Perhaps the connection runs, 'If only the record going back 500 years could show me your portrait [done] in some old book [at some time] since [the human] mind was first done in character ...' The idea seems to be that the art of portraiture can convey character. He is thinking not only of the physical beauty of the beloved, but also of the beauty of his mind and nature. 'I paint him in the character,' says Menenius in *Cor* 5.4.27, meaning 'to the life'. So here S would like to see the image of the beloved, done to the life long before the beloved was born. If he could find such a thing, he would be able to look up the old poets and see what they wrote about that wonderful composition, the 'composèd wonder of your frame', and he would then know whether they were better poets than his own contemporaries ('mended' means amended, improved). 'Composèd wonder' for 'wonderful composition' is the common inversion of noun and adjective, as seen in 55.9.

11–14 In the Quarto the three occurrences of 'whether' are spelt 'whether ... where ... whether', but metre requires each of the first two to be a monosyllable, and 'whe'er' is an Elizabethan spelling of the word. There is a strange effect of climax in line 12 when it has to be pronounced *differently*, as two syllables, though 'revolution be *the same*'.

Sonnet 59 has posed two problems. 'Do Elizabethan poets simply repeat the work of their predecessors?' and 'How do Elizabethan poets compare with their predecessors?' Neither question is seriously tackled, because the real point of the sonnet is not to discuss literary history, but to invent a new setting for praise of the beloved in lines 10 and 13–14.

Lines 5–10 expressed a wish that he could find in some old book the picture of a beauty identical to the beloved, and then read what poets had written about it in order to compare old poets with new when describing the same object. The rest of the argument is implied in lines 11–12, 'I do not know if we are better than the old poets, but I am sure of one thing – that the old poets praised beauties who were inferior to my beloved.' This is his position in 53.5–11 and 106.9–14. Only here he does not pitch it so high, but praises by understatement, as in 130.13–14.

Other editions break the sense not after line 10 but after 12. If 11–12 are taken as above with what follows, a more lively argument is produced.

Some commentators take 'character' in line 8 as referring to the written letters of the alphabet, as paraphrased by Evans (1996), 'Since thought was first expressed ("done") through writing ("character").' The argument would then run, 'If I could find your image described in words in some old book, I would know whether the old poets were better than those of today.' But how would he know that an old poet was writing about an identical beauty? This method of testing does not work. Besides, 7 and 10 speak of an 'image' of the beloved's 'frame'. Surely the obscure line 8 refers in its complex way to the same image which he wishes to be shown in line 7, not to a verbal description.

❧ 60 ☙

Like as the waves make towards the pebbled shore,
So do our minutes hasten to their end,
Each changing place with that which goes before
In sequent toil all forwards do contend.   4

Nativity, once in the main of light,
Crawls to maturity, wherewith being crowned,
Crooked eclipses 'gainst his glory fight,
And Time that gave doth now his gift confound.   8

Time doth transfix the flourish set on youth,
And delves the parallels in beauty's brow,
Feeds on the rareties of nature's truth,
And nothing stands but for his scythe to mow,   12

    And yet to times in hope my verse shall stand,
    Praising thy worth, despite his cruel hand.

The minutes of our life hasten to their end like waves breaking on the shore.
We are born, mature, decline and die.
Time ruins beauty, and yet my poems in praise of you will defy his cruelty.

1–4   These four lines owe something to Ovid's *Metamorphoses* 15.177–85,
here in Golding's translation (1567), in Burrow's (2002) modern spelling:

In all the world there is not that that standeth at a stay.
Things ebb and flow: and every shape is made to pass away.
The time itself continually is fleeting like a brook.
For neither brook nor lightsome time can tarry still. But look   200
As ev'ry wave drives other forth, and that that comes behind
Both thrusteth and is thrust itself: Even so the times by kind
Do fly and follow both at once, and evermore renew.
For that that was before is left, and straight there doth ensue

Another that was never erst. Each twinkling of an eye   205
Doth change.

Ben Jonson, writing 'To the Memory of my beloved, the Author Mr.
William Shakespeare', reported that Shakespeare had 'small Latin and less
Greek'. This is unlikely. He clearly had a deep and loving understanding
of the rhetoric and wit of Ovid's Latin. Here in Sonnet 60 he seems to have
had the original in mind. In Golding's translation at 203 the times 'fly and
follow', and in Ovid 'follow' is *sequuntur*, which appears in the 'sequent
toil' of the sonnet.

But differences are more important than similarities. Shakespeare has
transposed Ovid's river scene to a pebbled seashore. The advantages are
that he can open with a robust old English nautical term. Tides and ships
'make', meaning progress, as in *OED* make 65a and 90b.

Our minutes 'hasten' as waves 'make'. He has also added an implied
sound effect, the grinding of waves breaking over pebbles. But the crucial
difference is that the waves of a brook pass, whereas the waves of the sea come
to an end at our feet. Ovid's argument is cosmological – time is ever passing.
S's point is that we live and die. He needs his waves to come to an end.

5–8 Astrologically nativity is the moment of a baby's birth, but, when it
is said to crawl, that moment has become a baby. The *sea* image continues
in 'once in the *main* of light', but now the child is beginning to be compared to the sun. When it has reached its zenith, it is opposed by eclipses,
as a human being at his peak is attacked by age. The astronomy is faulty.
Solar eclipses do not wait until midday, and crookedness is not a feature of
them. Rather they occur when three bodies are in a straight line. They
could be called 'crooked' only in the sense that light would have to bend
to get round the obstruction. 'Crooked' applies more accurately to the
human scene. The disasters of age make us 'deformèd, crookèd, old, and
sere' in *CE*4.2.19. So minutes move on, men are born, reach maturity, and
age, and die; and line 8 summarises all this with an eloquent polyptoton,
'Time that *gave* doth now his *gift* confound.' This edition prints 'Time'
with a capital, eased towards the personification by the word 'his' (see note
on 18.6).

9–12 The personification continues in four aspects. Two of these are
clearly agricultural, delving parallels, that is digging furrows, and scything
standing crops. What of transfixing the flourishes set on youth? The first
definitions of flourish in *OED* include 'the blossom on a fruit tree' and

195

'luxuriant growth', citing in 1619 'the tree is first seene in the budde, then in the flourish, and after in the fruits.' To transfix is to pierce. So, in this agricultural context when time transfixes the flourish of youth, the picture is of a parasite boring holes in petals. If, then, the agricultural context is active at some level in lines 9, 10 and 12, when Time feeds on the rarities of nature in 11, he is devouring choice edible fruits. But these are the produce not simply of nature but of nature's truth. Truth is relevant because the truth of the beloved has already been prominent in 14.11, 37.4 and 54.14. This whole quatrain then takes its power from the image of growing things, some explicit, others underlying, all images for the beauty of the beloved and its demise.

13–14   The metaphor is not exhausted. In the triumphant monosyllables of line 13 'stand' is not a feeble repetition but a working part, as is clearly heard if the line is read with emphasis on 'verse': 'nothing stands but for his scythe to mow, | And yet to times in hope my vérse shall stand.' By the plural 'times', Time the present destroyer is thwarted and this poetry will survive to other times, to times yet to come. Our minutes *hasten* to their end in line 2, and yet this verse will *stand*. The poem contemplates eternal change, decay and death, in order to arrive at a double destination, praise of the beloved and a claim of immortality for this poetry.

Duncan-Jones (1997), on line 2
'Our minutes' plays upon 'hour-minutes', the total of minutes in an hour being suggested by the sonnet's number.

❧ 61 ☙

Is it thy will thy image should keep open
My heavy eyelids to the weary night?
Dost thou desire my slumbers should be broken
While shadows like to thee do mock my sight?   4
Is it thy spirit that thou send'st from thee
So far from home into my deeds to pry,
To find out shames and idle hours in me,
The scope and tenor of thy jealousy?   8

O no, thy love, though much, is not so great.
It is my love that keeps mine eye awake,
Mine own true love that doth my rest defeat,
To play the watchman ever for thy sake.   12
  For thee watch I, while thou dost wake elsewhere
  From me far off, with others all too near.

Is it your will that your image keeps me awake? Do you want to break
my sleep by sending phantoms of yourself? Do you send your spirit
to pry into my doings, and all because of your jealousy?
O no, your love is not so great. It is my love that makes me watch for you,
while you wake elsewhere, 'from me far off, with others all too near'.

1–8 He is sleepless, kept awake by a dream of the beloved. His eyelids are
heavy, the night is weary, and the metrical beat stresses the adjectives, 'My
héavy eyelids to the wéary night'. 'Ís it thy wíll' and 'Dóst thou desíre'
introduce two-line questions, capped by four lines beginning 'Ís it thy spírit
… ?' as his anger swells into the third question. 'Thy image' and 'shadows
like to thee' are dream apparitions mocking his sight, but in lines 5–8 he
asks if the young man is actually sending his own spirit, and sending it to
spy on him. Can his jealousy have such 'scope', such range? Is this the
character, the 'tenor' of it? This is a tirade against the beloved, 'thy', 'thou'
or 'thee' ringing seven times in the first five lines.

9–12 Lines 1–8 are the fatuous broodings of a man who cannot sleep, an insomniac's stream of consciousness. At 'O no' he pulls himself up. Now comes the truth which he knew all along, and it begins with three lines heavy with monosyllables. The cause is not the beloved's love for him, but his love for the beloved. In 10–11, 'my', 'mine', 'Mine' and 'my' make the point, which is strengthened if the first 'my' is stressed against the iambic beat, 'It is mý love ...'

He started by asking three questions. He has now the answers. It is himself and not the beloved who is the jealous lover (57.9), the 'shames and idle hours' are not his but the beloved's, and the beloved does not love him enough to spy on him. In 57.9–14 and 58.9–14 he protested about the beloved's behaviour, but now he goes an inch further, 'thy love, though much, is not so great.' But how great is it? Is he deluding himself? Can the beloved really love him if he behaves like this? S is trying a dangerous gambit. He dare not say outright that the beloved does not love him. That would be an invitation the beloved might accept, and he might then walk away. The statement in line 9 is phrased in the hope that it will be denied.

The rhetoric and the drama swelled to the climax on 'jealousy' in line 8, the only word of more than two syllables in the poem. The balloon is immediately punctured at 'O no', and from now on the sonnet moves from foolish hope to bitter truth. A score of sonnets pivot with a dramatic exclamation in line 9 (for example 65, 71, 72, 76). 'O no' does what 'Ay' does in the most famous soliloquy of all, in *Hamlet* 3.1.67, when he is considering the advantages of suicide, and suddenly realises that he is deceiving himself:

> To die, to sleep.
> To sleep, perchance to dream. Ay, there's the rub,
> For in that sleep of death what dreams may come ... ?'

13–14 What is the sense of 'watch' in 'For thee watch I'? Burrow (2002) offers three possibilities: '(a) keep lookout to protect your property; (b) stay awake; (c) keep watch to see if you are coming.' The answer is given by 'watchman' in line 12. S is not guarding property, and not simply staying awake. He stays awake watching for the return of the beloved, who is on a *wake*, a drunken party, as in *Ham* 1.4.9–10, 'The king doth wake tonight and takes his rouse, | Keeps wassail ...'

It would be a sin to paraphrase the last line of the sonnet, which Vendler (1997) calls 'the scorpion's sting in its tail'.

ઝ 62 ભ

Sin of self-love possesseth all mine eye
And all my soul and all my ev'ry part,
And for this sin there is no remedy,
It is so grounded inward in my heart.   4

Methinks no face so gracious is as mine,
No shape so true, no truth of such account,
And for myself mine own worth do define
As I all other in all worths surmount.   8

But when my glass shows me myself indeed,
Beated and chopped with tanned antiquity,
Mine own self-love quite contrary I read:
Self so self-loving were iniquity.   12

  'Tis thee, myself, that for myself I praise,
  Painting my age with beauty of thy days.

I suffer from the sin of self-love, irremediable because deep-seated.
No face is so lovely as mine, no form so true, no truth so valuable,
*   and my own worth is beyond all others.*
But when I look in the mirror and see my battered old face, I reinterpret:
*   such self-love would be a sin.*
It's you I'm praising, not me. I am painting myself in your youthful colours.

1–4 His own self-love claims every part of him, 'áll mine eye | And áll
my soul and áll my év'ry part'. It is an irremediable disease, deep-seated in
the heart, and spread all through him.

5–8 He now goes into detail. His self-love applies to his features, his
figure, his judgement of truth, and generally his own worth. In short, he is
better in every respect than everyone else. The word 'all' appears five times
in lines 1, 2 and 8, and the message is hammered home by other repetitions,

'no ... so ... as', 'no ... so', 'no ... such', 'true ... truth', 'my self mine own', 'worth ... worths', in lines 5–8. The exaggeration is meant to be detected. Nobody could be so vain and confess it. A marker has been planted in line 5. 'Methinks' occurs four times in the sonnets and every time it introduces an untruth (14, 104, 112). When Hamlet is pretending to be deranged in 3.2.364–8, he claims to see a cloud in shape of a camel. 'By th'mass and 'tis: like a camel, indeed,' agrees Polonius, humouring him. 'Methinks it is like a weasel,' replies Hamlet.

9–12   But when S looks in the mirror he sees himself as he really is. The 'tanned antiquity' of his face suggests leather. Tanning is the conversion of hide into leather by steeping in an infusion of an astringent bark like that of the oak. So then, in retrospect, 'Beated' also suggests leather because tanners beat their hides with mallets to soften them. In this leathery context 'chopped' must have the sense of our 'chapped', as in *OED* chop 10 (1576), 'broken open in clefts or cracks', like cracked leather (citing 'The oven ... must be well playstred with fast and strong lyme, that the same chop not'). S has seen the leathery complexion of his lived-in face, and realised that to love himself would be an iniquity. As in 61, the first eight lines present a false picture, and in each poem line 9 begins an account of the truth.

13–14   It is not himself he has been praising, but the beloved. The great yearning of lovers is to merge in each other, to become one, and S approaches or achieves this union elsewhere in the Sonnets (see notes on 39.3 and 42.13). So, when he is praising himself, and the praise clearly does not fit, this is because he is praising not his own decrepitude, but the youthful beauty of his beloved, ''Tis thee, my self, that *for* my self I praise', in other words: 'It is you, my self, that I praise *instead of* my self.' He is even addressing the beloved as 'my self'. Ingenuity is required to turn from love of self in 1–8 to praise of the beloved. Line 13 provides it.

❧ 63 ❧

Against my love shall be as I am now,
With time's injurious hand crushed and o'erworn,
When hours have drained his blood and filled his brow
With lines and wrinkles, when his youthful morn   4
Hath travelled on to age's steepy night,
And all those beauties whereof now he's king
Are vanishing or vanished out of sight,
Stealing away the treasure of his spring –   8

For such a time do I now fortify
Against confounding age's cruel knife,
That he shall never cut from memory
My sweet love's beauty, though my lover's life.   12
   His beauty shall in these black lines be seen,
   And they shall live, and he in them still green.

In anticipation of the time when my beloved will be as old as I am now,
   and will have lost his beauty,
I now build a fortification to preserve it in these lines.

1–8 In 62.10, S saw his own face as a hide 'Beated and chopped with tanned antiquity'. Now he imagines the hand of Time crushing the beloved and wearing him out. What sort of hand is this? Is he imagining the beloved as a crumpled old rag? No reader could possibly give the normal iambic rhythm to the end of this line, 'crushed ánd o'erwórn', and no other line in the poem ends as this one must, 'crúshed and o'erwórn'. The variation in rhythm leaves no doubt. Beauty will be literally crushed.

In line 3 the contrast between draining and filling is typical – the Sonnets are full of contrasts. Here, for instance, friction of opposites causes the spark also in lines 4–5 and 13–14. To fill a smooth surface with hollows is a surprise, heightened by the run-on of the sentence from lines 3–4. There is no checking the busy advance of hours as they march in monosyllables along line 3 to wrinkles in line 4.

In line 5 the Quarto reads 'trauaild'. In Elizabethan English 'travel' and 'travail' were interchangeable spellings, so morn both journeys and labours to night. In so doing it becomes the sun, plunging steeply from the sky, reeling from the day, as in 7.10. In 60.6 the sun at his zenith is crowned in glory, and here too he becomes a king and his beauties are now courtiers. Their gradual disappearance is expressed in graded tenses, 'are vanishing, or vanisht out of sight' (as the Quarto has it), just as the landscape vanishes when the sun travels 'on to age's steepy night'. The poet treasures the precise phases of loss and of ageing, as in the autumn scene in Sonnet 73.2, 'When yellow leaves, or none, or few, do hang | Upon those boughs'. When the splendid courtiers one by one desert their king, they are not above taking some of the royal treasures with them, just as the beloved's beauties steal away the treasure of his spring, his youth.

In lines 7–8 metre again corresponds to sense when 'vánished out of síght' could echo 'tréasure of his spríng', and these are the only two lines which have that racing close. In the Sonnets it is common to hear an inversion of rhythm in the first two syllables (tum-te for te-tum), but it occurs only once in this poem in the climactic line at the end of the octave, 'Stéaling away the treasure of his spring'.

9–14 S is fortifying against age's knife, which can cut a memory out of the human brain. It is also an assassin's knife. It could kill the beloved, but cannot destroy his beauty. This is a miracle. Miracles astonish, and so does the colour contrast in the final couplet. 'Green indeed is the colour of lovers', according to Armado in *LLL* 1.2.83, but beauty living in black and being green is a shock, and it is sharpened by the monosyllables. The beloved's spring ended line 8; his green ends line 14.

Metaphor is the heart of poetry, according to Aristotle in *Poetics* 22. The great gift of the poet is to see resemblances. Mixed metaphors are usually disasters, fair game for writers of parodies, and for Fowler's *Modern English Usage*, 'The Avon and Dorset River Board should not act like King Canute, bury its head in the sand, and ride rough-shod over those who live by the land and enjoy their fishing.' Sonnet 63 is a series of metaphors and some of them are mixed, but great poets make mixed metaphors work, here partly because different elements in the series cohere, the injurious hand and the cruel knife, the morn and the sun, the spring and the green, and because they connect important things, beauty, ageing, death and love, with violence, politics and wealth, and with the sun and the seasons.

When I have seen by time's fell hand defaced
The rich proud cost of outworn buried age;
When sometime lofty towers I see down razed,
And brass eternal slave to mortal rage;   4

When I have seen the hungry ocean gain
Advantage on the kingdom of the shore,
And the firm soil win of the wat'ry main,
Increasing store with loss and loss with store;   8

When I have seen such interchange of state
Or state itself confounded to decay,
Ruin hath taught me thus to ruminate—
That time will come and take my love away.   12

    This thought is as a death, which cannot choose
    But weep to have, that which it fears to lose.

When I have seen ruined tombs and towers and tarnished brasses,
when I have seen sea gain from land and land from sea,
when I have seen such interchange and decay, I have realised
    that I shall lose my love.
This is death to me, and I can only weep to have what I fear to lose.

1–4 There are ten descriptive adjectives in the first four lines, whereas in the last six there is only one, 'confounded'. In lines 1–4 what is rich, proud, lofty, eternal, is annulled by its opposite, which is fell, defaced, outworn, buried, razed, mortal. This gush of adjectives demonstrates the pomp of man's monuments. The dearth of adjectives in 9–14 demonstrates the bleak reality of decay and death.

    'Cost' is extravagance. The ostentatious tombs of the second line would be on religious sites. Line 4 refers to brasses on church floors and commemorative inscriptions in brass on church monuments, sardonically said to be *eternal*, although they are slaves to *mortal* passions. In this context, 'sometime lofty towers', towers that once were lofty but are now razed to the ground, are surely to be seen primarily as the bell towers of churches and monasteries. Such ruination would have been a feature of Shakespeare's England around 70 years after the dissolution of the monasteries. He himself mourns 'bare ruined choirs where late the sweet birds sang' in Sonnet 73.4. All this defacement is the work of time, but in 'defaced' and 'down razed' there is a suggestion that time has been helped by vandalism and violence in the dissolution of the monasteries,

5–8   When he has seen 'the *hungry* ocean gain | Advantage on the kingdom of the shore' the ocean is annexing the territory of a neighbouring kingdom. He then sees 'the *firm* soil win [advantage on the kingdom] of the wat'ry main'. The adjectives are not empty ornaments. The sea is *hungry* as it gnaws the land, and *terra firma* counter-attacks successfully because it is *firm* soil struggling against what is *watery* (two syllables, 'watry', as the Quarto spells it). The familiar opposition of adjectives dramatises the contest. The metre contributes. 'Firm' in line 7, like 'proud' in 2, would not carry the iambic stress, but each word demands emphasis, and that slight irregularity gives them both extra weight.

Lines 5–6 describe the action of the sea. Lines 7–8 describe the action of the land. In line 8 it is the land which increases holdings at the low tide, and land which loses territory at the high. The motion of the contest is represented in sound, 'store with loss and loss with store', and also by the chiasmus, 'store ... loss ... loss ... store'. Shakespeare has seen the tide coming in and going out, and pondered on the tides in the affairs of men.

9–12   His organising intelligence arranges decay (D) and interchange (I) with some cunning in this poem, D in 1–4, I in 5–8, ID in 9–10. In 1–10 the DIID order (chiasmus) combines clarity and variety, but more importantly it ends the sequence with decay, to make a peg for the ruin which is the sombre conclusion of the poem. This strategy conceals a logical difficulty. The sonnet is aiming at decay and death as bearing upon his inevitable loss of the beloved, and lines 1–4 and 10 offer relevant examples. But the unending interchange of 5–8 and 9 does not apply to the beloved. The losses of land and sea are regularly repaired, but when the beloved is lost he will not return. The logic falls, but the poetry stands. 'Increasing store' and 'interchange of state' in 8–9 are not relevant, but a clever patch covers the flaw with 'Or state itself confounded to decay'.

'State' in lines 9 and 10 is primarily simply 'condition', but the condition of land and sea is that they are both kingdoms (6), enjoying therefore royal state, as S himself contemplated, for a moment at least, in the final phrase of Sonnet 29, 'That then I scorn to change my state with kings.'

Four lines in 1–12 begin with 'When'. This builds up suspense, as in Sonnet 63. 'What happens to him when he has seen these things?' The answer comes in a climax, 'Rúin hath taught me thus to rúminate', wordplay at a serious moment, and heightened by the metre. This is the only line in this poem which must open with the standard opening inversion, and it stands out in reading.

On lines 5–7 commentators cite Ovid's *Metamorphoses* 15.261–3, in Arthur Golding's translation lines 287–9:

Even so have places often*tymes* ex*chaunged* they*r* e*state*
For *I have seene* it sea which was *substancial* ground alate,
Ageine where sea was, *I have seene* the same become dry lond.

My italics suggest resemblances between Golding and the sonnet. Just as in Sonnet 60, Ovid is remembered, and just as in Sonnet 60 Shakespeare uses Ovid for his own purpose. Ovid's argument is that nothing in the world perishes; its parts simply interchange. In *Metamorphoses* 15.256–7, being born is beginning to change into something else, and dying is ceasing to be that. So, when Ovid says he has 'oftentymes' seen where sea has changed into land and land into sea, he is not talking about the tide but about changing coastlines. This is clear in Golding's version, and clear in the Latin in D. E. Hill's close translation, 'I have myself seen what once had been the most solid earth become water, I have seen lands made out of sea, and sea shells far from ocean, and an old anchor has been found on mountain tops.' What S has seen is the tide coming in and going out. The poets are expounding two different arguments, and it is not surprising that they use different analogies, and not surprising that Ovid was not thinking of tides. The Mediterranean is not tidal.

13–14 What is the 'which' that cannot choose but weep? Not thought, not death, because neither thought nor death can weep. And what is 'it' in the last line? The syntax is cryptic but the meaning is all the more powerful for its density and unpedantic freedom. The dramatist knows what can be said. How much weaker to be clear, 'This thought is to me as a death, and it makes me unable to choose to do anything but weep to have that which I fear to lose.'

In these last three lines there are only two words of more than one syllable. Monosyllables form the stiletto which so often ends these poems, for example in the last two or three lines of most of them between Sonnets 60 and 69. (In Sonnet 69.12 'flower' is a monosyllable.) The comma supplied above in the last line is an attempt to suggest that the ending becomes even more dramatic if the iambic pulse is varied by a gentle accent on 'that', namely, 'cannot choose | But wéep to háve, thát which it féars to lóse', where 'fears to lose' effectively echoes the rhythm of 'weep to have'.

Booth (1977)

This poem is full of words regularly used with sexual connotations. No sexual sense is active at any given point in the poem, but the cumulative effect of the diction is to invoke a vague aura of reference to male helplessness to postpone the moment of sexual climax and the general collapse and sexual helplessness that follows sexual emission; note proud (see 151.10, note – sense 4), buried, down razed (and 'down raised'), rage (see 13.12, note), store, confounded (see the notes to 26.1–14, 59.9–12, 60.9, and 151.1,2,13), death (see 'dye' in the example quoted from Donne in 154.9, note), which cannot choose, weep, and have (see 87.13, note).

ഒ 65 ര

Since brass, nor stone, nor earth, nor boundless sea,
But sad mortality o'ersways their power,
How with this rage shall beauty hold a plea,
Whose action is no stronger than a flower?   4

O how shall summer's honey breath hold out
Against the wrackful siege of battering days,
When rocks impregnable are not so stout
Nor gates of steel so strong but Time decays?   8

O fearful meditation! Where alack
Shall Time's best jewel from Time's chest lie hid?
Or what strong hand can hold his swift foot back?
Or who his spoil of beauty can forbid?   12

O none! unless this miracle have might,
That in black ink my love may still shine bright.

Nothing is strong enough to resist mortality. How shall beauty survive?
O how shall summer hold out against the siege of Time?
Where shall beauty hide? How can Time be thwarted of his spoil?
The only hope is that my love may survive in these poems.

1–4   Why brass, stone, earth and sea in Sonnet 65? Because brass eternal is
slave to mortal rage in 64.4, stone is defaced and razed to the ground in 64.3,
sea and land are inconstant in 64.5–8. Now Sonnet 65 opens with a summary of the power of this mortality and rage over the same four victims.
The two sonnets are companion pieces. In Sonnet 64 ruin and interchange
make S ruminate and drive him to tears; in Sonnet 65 the weakness of
beauty in its war with time drives him to a 'fearful meditation', but he finds
in the end a possibility of hope. The different conclusion and different
imagery make a different poem.
    In 65.2 mortality is a gloomy monarch holding under his sway four

powerful subjects who resist but cannot survive. He is also capable of violent anger in line 3, and that is vented against beauty, another of his subjects, in a lawsuit, and her plea cannot be sustained. The action that she has raised is feeble, 'no stronger than a flower', and this comparison leads on to another.

5–8 The argument now glides to summer, not its flower but what is even more evanescent, its fragrance. Against something so delicate is arrayed Time, the great ally of mortality, and not just Time. Every separate day is a soldier in his besieging army, and the beleaguered citadel is the fragile fragrance of a flower.

In paraphrase we might write 'summer's fragrance'. 'Summer's honey breath' is a measure of the gulf between paraphrase and poetry. Such a feeble citadel cannot hope to resist a siege in which destructive, 'wrackful', battering rams daily pound its feeble wall. 'Rocks impregnable' glance back to the stone of the first line, but not even the rock foundations of a great fortress could resist this onslaught. 'Steel gates' may be a poetic exaggeration, but great oak gates reinforced by steel bands, and swung on huge steel hinges, must have been a familiar sight in Elizabethan England. Even the sound is forbidding, -s- and -t- more than a dozen times between 'not' and 'Time', all this armament arrayed against 'summer's honey breath'.

9–12 The imagery changes with two exclamations and three rhetorical questions in lines 9–12. Beauty has become a jewel (two syllables), and Time is a miser, perhaps a usurer, who has loaned the jewel and is determined to reclaim it in order to store it away in a chest for himself. And suddenly he is a runner no man can slow down, such is the rush of monosyllables in line 11. Aristophanes' *Frogs* 100 mocked Euripides for giving a foot to time, but other poets have sided with Euripides and found poetry in the metaphor. The monosyllabic music of this line is reproduced by William Blake in his own series of questions, asking who but God could have made the tiger, 'And when thy heart began to beat, | What dread hand? and what dread feet?' (Blake is thinking of real feet. In Blake's day a blacksmith could manoeuvre his white-hot metal by a hoist operated by pedals.) Line 12 reverts to the siege. Time will take the citadel, and what follows the taking of a city is plunder. If beauty's the spoil, what follows is rape.

13–14 In these 14 lines the poet has presented a procession of metaphors, sharply visualised and subtly linked to one another. He also deploys a rich armoury of rhetoric, half a dozen questions spiced by exclamations, and 'shall' ringing through the poem and answered at the end by 'may', sounding the possibility of a miracle, a brightness in black, like the green black which ended Sonnet 63. 'Might' (13) could seem to come pat, a filler to rhyme with 'night'. Not so. This 'powerful rhyme' (55.2) will need might to stand up against the passion and violence of the first 12 lines. As so often, Anglo-Saxon monosyllables give the power to the crucial last line. The author of this lyric was a dramatist.

ഔ 66 ♋

Tired with all these, for restful death I cry:

As to behold Desert a beggar born,
And needy Nothing trimmed in jollity,
And purest Faith unhappily forsworn   4
And gilded Honour shamefully misplaced,
And maiden Virtue rudely strumpeted,
And right Perfection wrongfully disgraced,
And Strength by limping Sway disablèd,   8
And Art made tongue-tied by Authority,
And Folly, doctor-like, controlling Skill,
And simple Truth miscalled Simplicity,
And captive Good attending captain Ill.   12

Tired with all these, from these would I be gone,
Save that to die, I leave my love alone.

This is a catalogue of 11 injustices, all expressed as generalities. But it is not
easy to make poetry out of a catalogue, and abstractions like faith, honour
and virtue are not so powerful as particulars and persons. The key to the
poem is 'behold' in the second line. This is not, after all, a list of abstractions, but a visible masque or pageant, seen as early as the trimming and
gilding of lines 3 and 5, and vividly confirmed in 8, 9, 10 and 12. S has
beheld them all. All the 16 items are characters mimed in an imaginary
procession, and to stress that point the above text gives each of them a
capital letter. As Ingram and Redpath (1978) write, 'In the Quarto some of
the personifications are capitalized, but with no apparent system. We have
capitalized all.'

1 'Desert' is an abstract meaning something like merit, worth. S is tired
  of seeing merit clad in rags because born poor.
2 A nothing is a person worth nothing, like Cloten in *Cym* 3.4.133–5,
  'that harsh, churlish, noble, simple nothing, | That Cloten, whose love
  suit hath been to me | As fearful as a siege.' 'Needy' means that he needs

or lacks all decent qualities. 'Look at that [good for] nothing strutting around in finery, with [lace and ermine] trimmings.' So the first two abuses are Desert in rags and its converse Worthlessness in gaudy trimmings, each an affront to justice.

3 'Faith' is a person who has given his word and kept it, expecting others to do the same, but has been betrayed and ruined, 'unhappily forsworn'.

4 'Gilded Honour' is a magistrate, priest or lord, wearing robes with gilt braiding (gilt not gold, therefore spurious). This honour is misplaced, so this fourth abuse, like the second, is the converse of its predecessor.

5 'Maiden Virtue' is a virgin ravished and turned into a whore.

6 Since the first four examples run in opposing pairs, after the feminine 'maiden Virtue rudely strumpeted', there is a temptation to take 'right Perfection wrongfully disgraced' as applying to an innocent man falsely accused and discredited.

7 'Strength' presents a picture of a strong man reduced to weakness because he has to trudge along behind a master so crippled that he sways as he walks. Burrow reports that James I had an ungainly walk caused by a childhood injury. 'Disab[i]lèd' has four syllables to make a lame rhyme for 'strumpeted' (For effective bad rhymes see on 46.11).

8 'Art made tongue-tied by Authority' on the lips of an Elizabethan dramatist might suggest the censorship exercised by the Lord Chamberlain over the Elizabethan theatre, for example by the Privy Council order of 28 July 1597 to pull down the theatres.

9 'Folly ... controlling Skill' is a pompous fool of an administrator, standing over a skilled practitioner and telling him how to do his job. 'Doctor-like' is contemptuous, 'with professorial pomposity', as Booth (1977) explains. In Latin and early English a doctor is a teacher. The bureaucrat adopts a didactic tone in patronising an expert.

10 'Simple' here is used in its first dictionary meaning, 'honest', but in this unjust world 'simplicity' is often taken to be mental deficiency. The simple, honest man is miscalled a simpleton. Some such play occurs also in 138.7–8.

11 A virtuous man, a prisoner of war, acts as slave to a worthless officer, the picture sharpened by polyptoton as 'captain' clashes with 'captive'. This is a variant on the stock figures of classical comedy, the boastful soldier and his parasite, Pyrgopolynices and Artotrogus in Plautus, *Miles Gloriosus*; Armado and Moth in *Love's Labour's Lost*; and Pistol and Nim in *The Merry Wives of Windsor*. The arrogance of Captain Pistol is the theme of a sublime tirade by Doll Tearsheet in *2H4* 2.4.135–44, ending, 'A

captain? By God's light, these villains will make the word "captain" odious; therefore captains had need look to't.'

13–14 If the last line read, 'I would wish to be gone from these except that if I died I would leave my love', this would be an obvious, sentimental end, but S adds 'alone', which would make sense if he thought he was leaving the young man desolate and helpless. He had no such illusions, as he has already made clear in 57, 58 and 61.14. As so often the Sonnets have to be read with their neighbours. 'Alone' leads into Sonnet 67, in which the beloved is alone, the only health and grace in a sick and sinful society.

The text is printed above in an extraordinary shape. This is done to show that the sonnet has an extraordinary structure, highlighted by Shakespeare by the near-repetition of lines 1 and 13–14, as 'Tired with all these, for restful death I cry' is gathered up by 'Tired with all these, from these ... Save that to die ... ' The weary repetitions underline S's yearning for death, and the intervening 11 lines all beginning with the same word suggest an infinity of injustices. The link between the first couplet and the last is reinforced by strange echoes. All four lines, and only these in the poem, begin with the metrical variant, 'Tíred with all thése ... Ás to behóld', unlike the standard iambic, 'And néedy Nóthing ... And púrest Fáith'. These emphases seem almost to pace the reading of the poem. The other strange link is the bold syntax of the verb 'to behold' in line 2 followed with a similar looseness of syntax, by 'to die' in line 14, glossed by Evans (1996) as 'by beholding' and 'by dying'.

Yet another articulation which subtly relieves the uniformity and heightens the drama is that lines 2–7 describe one character in each line, each representing an ethical value, whereas lines 8–12 are a denser list, in which each line mentions not only the victim but also the villain, and four of the five pictures move away from virtues and vices to talent tyrannised by arrogance. If this articulation is a small example of the commanding technique of this poet, an illustration of his inexhaustible imagination is the passage where Hamlet is contemplating suicide in 3.1.72–8. This is another sermon to the same text, but Shakespeare does not repeat himself:

> For who would bear the whips and scorns of time,
> Th'oppressor's wrong, the proud man's contumely,
> The pangs of disprized love, the law's delay,

The insolence of office, and the spurns
That patient merit of th'unworthy takes,
When he himself might his quietus make
With a bare bodkin?

'Patient merit' is not far from 'Desert' in the first line of the sonnet, and the insolence of office is not far from 'Folly, doctor-like' in line 10, but the sonnet conjures up different, more vivid pictures, as befits characters in a masque.

Booth (1977), on line 14
I leave my love solitary – without a companion. (Richard Sylvester suggests to me that 'I leave only my love' is also possible; that reading would reinforce the otherwise inherent notion of the beloved as the only earthly thing worthy of regret.)

Kerrigan (1986)
Alone solitary. But with a hint of word-play: the beloved is 'all one' ('just one, only a single thing'), but he nevertheless outweighs *all these*.

Duncan-Jones (1997)
I ... alone 'I leave my beloved lonely'; or 'I withdraw from my emotion of love'; or 'I desist from importuning my love-object'; or even 'I leave only my love, nothing else.'

Burrow (2002)
The Quarto capitalizes the personifications sporadically (Nothing, Folly, Truth, Simplicity are capitalized; faith, honour, virtue, perfection, strength, art, captive good are not). The poem reads more like a survey of abstract ills than a personification allegory, so the capitals have all been removed.

℘ 67 ℭ

Ah, wherefore with infection should he live,
And with his presence grace impiety,
That sin by him advantage should achieve,
And lace itself with his society?   4

Why should false painting imitate his cheek,
And steal dead seeming of his living hue?
Why should poor beauty indirectly seek
Roses of shadow, since his rose is true?   8
Why should he live, now Nature bankrupt is,
Beggared of blood to blush through lively veins?

For she hath no exchequer now but his,
And, proud of many, lives upon his gains.   12
    O him she stores to show what wealth she had
    In days long since, before these last so bad.

Why should he live in this sick world and grace sin by his presence?
Why should cosmetics steal his colour to make a feeble imitation?
    Why should he live when Nature has nothing else like him?
Because he is her only asset, and she keeps him
    to show how rich she used to be before these evil days.

1–4   The last word of Sonnet 66 was problematic. In what sense was S
reluctant to leave his beloved alone? Sonnet 67 solves the problem by
asking why the beloved should live alone in this sinful world (1–4), when
Nature 'hath no exchequer now but his' (11).

The wickedness of the times is described in a rush of metaphors in the
first four lines. It is *infection*, then *impiety*, given *grace*, divine favour, by
the beloved's presence, and the *sin* of the world would gain advantage from
it. He would adorn it like lace [trimmings on a garment], in a line hissing
with contempt.

5–10 The body of the sonnet consists of four questions beginning in lines 1, 5, 7 and 9. In the first four lines the beloved would be a sound and pious person in an infected and sinful world. As the questions speed up in lines 5–10 he would be the only true beauty in a world of painted faces. From sin to cosmetics and the bridge is '*lace*' in line 4, 'Why should he live on to adorn society? Why should he live to be a model for those who paint their faces?'

In line 7 'indirectly' suggests that others, being poor in beauty, realise their deficiencies and aim to achieve it by an indirect route, by imitating the beloved. They therefore steal 'roses of shadow', colourless imitations of his beauty, from his living colour [by applying rouge]. A rose of shadow would be false and black, not much of a rose. Line 8 might well be read with a stress on 'hís' against the beat. Why should the world seek 'Roses of shadow, since hís rose is true?'

'Advantage' in 3, 'steal' in 6 and 'poor' in 7 are the first intimations of a financial metaphor which appears in every line from 9 to 13.

Lines 9–10 pick up line 1, 'Why should he *live*, now Nature bankrupt is, | Beggared of blood to blush through *lively* veins?' Nature has now '*dead seeming*' achieved by rouge, whereas 'his *living* hue' (6) is caused by blood coursing through '*lively* veins' (10). The beloved's vascular system is not simply living, it is beating with life, and the alliteration in 9–10 makes it almost audible, 'bankrupt is, | Beggared of blood to blush'.

11–14 'Nature being bankrupt, why should he live?' Answer: 'For', because, Nature's treasury is empty and he is the only thing that keeps her alive (12). She has many beauties of a sort, and boasts of them, but they are false and valueless. Yes, she stores him up, as a surviving proof of the wealth she once enjoyed before the world descended to the depths described in Sonnet 66. The last line, like the first, looks back to 66, and, as so often, the poem arrives at its destination in a couplet heavy with monosyllables.

The argument took a surprising turn, from the beloved's piety to his beauty, a switch of thought disguised by the rhetorical structure. The four questions – 'wherefore', 'why', 'why', 'why' – seem to hang together, but the first, 'Wherefore should he continue to live in an infected world?', a question about the beloved's behaviour, looks back to 66. The other three questions are from a broader point of view, 'Why do human beings behave as they do?' It is this twist which enables the poem to move from the social satire of 66 and 67.1–4 to praise of the beloved's beauty in 67.5–12. He has found a new vehicle to carry his praise of the beloved.

℘ 68 ℘

Thus is his cheek the map of days outworn,
When beauty lived and died as flowers do now,
Before these bastard signs of fair were born
Or durst inhabit on a living brow,   4

Before the golden tresses of the dead,
The right of sepulchres, were shorn away
To live a second life on second head,
Ere beauty's dead fleece made another gay.   8

In him those holy antique hours are seen,
Without all ornament, itself and true,
Making no summer of another's green,
Robbing no old to dress his beauty new,   12

And him as for a map doth Nature store
To show false art what beauty was of yore.

His cheek is therefore a record of days when beauty was natural,
*   before people wore blond wigs cut from the dead.*
He has true beauty without robbing others, and Nature preserves him
*   to show what beauty used to be.*

1–4 Sonnet 66 ended with the thought of the beloved living alone in a
wicked world. Sonnet 67 continued that thought and imagined the beloved
as the only unpainted beauty in the world, preserved by Nature to demonstrate her former riches. Sonnet 68 continues the theme with 'Thus is his
cheek the map of days outworn'. A map is a small-scale representation, so the
beloved is a model in one person of a whole past age when beauty was natural.
    Line 3 begins a move from cosmetics to wigs, 'these bastard signs of fair'
born and inhabiting a living brow (for 'fair' meaning beauty, see 16.11).
Wigs are personified. They are born bastards, not beauty, but false rela-
tives, and they dare to lodge on a living brow. 'Cheek' in line 1 looks back

216

to the contrast between rouged cheeks and the beloved's 'living hue' of 67.5–10. 'Brow' in line 4 signals the move from cheek to head, from rouge to wig.

5–8 In wig-making the blond hair of corpses, which legally belongs to the grave, was shorn to have a second life on a living head, as in *MV* 3.2.95–6, where gold locks are 'the dowry of a second head, | The skull that bred them in the sepulchre'. 'Shorn' leads the satirist to sheep. The wig now becomes fleece shorn from a dead body to make the living 'gay', that is gaudy, showy, and the metre could suggest the absurdity. In line 8, in the climax of this satire, where a sheep's fleece is on the head of a belle or beau, occurs the only syllable in the sonnet that cries out to be stressed, although it does not carry the iambic beat, 'Ere beauty's dead fléece made another gay'. Another such expressive violation of the expected rhythm occurs with the beat on 'fair' and 'rank' in 69.12.

9–14 'These holy antique hours' are not just our 'good old days', because 'holy' harks back to the contemporary impiety of 67.2–3, and 'antique' to the 'days long since' of 67.14. What is 'itself' in line 10? Beauty? The beloved? Hours, thought of in the singular as time? Commentators differ, and Shakespeare might have been hard put to it to answer. He is writing with impetus, and not pausing over such questions, but beauty is the subject of the poem, mentioned in lines 2, 3 and 8, and it is that beauty of the beloved, 'itself and true', not the 'false painting' of 67.5 which is 'making no summer' and 'robbing no old'.

These present participles acquire emphasis as they open two successive lines with the standard metrical inversion, 'Máking' and 'Róbbing' (compare 33.3–4). 'Green' in 11 is obviously youth (see also 63.8 and 14).

Rollins (1944) quotes J. R. Planché's discussion of the 'Elizabethan periwig' or 'peruke', 'terms applied to a single lock' (perhaps on the brow, as in line 4) 'or a set of ringlets'. It is 'nothing more than false hair worn by men and women'. The heart of Sonnet 67 is a tirade against rouge; the heart of Sonnet 68 is a tirade against wigs, and each sonnet ends with the same ringing praise of the beloved.

❧ 69 ❧

Those parts of thee that the world's eye doth view
Want nothing that the thought of hearts can mend:
All tongues, the voice of souls, give thee that due,
Utt'ring bare truth, ev'n so as foes commend.   4
Thy outward thus with outward praise is crowned,

But those same tongues that give thee so thine own
In other accents do this praise confound
By seeing farther than the eye hath shown –   8
They look into the beauty of thy mind,
And that in guess they measure by thy deeds.

Then churls, their thoughts (although their eyes were kind)
To thy fair flow'r add the rank smell of weeds.   12
   But why thy odour matcheth not thy show,
   The soil is this, that thou dost common grow.

Your looks could not be improved. Everyone says so, even your enemies.
But those who praise dilute their praise. They see further, into your mind,
   by guesswork from your actions.
To your lovely flower they add the stench of weeds. Why does odour
   clash with appearance? The explanation is that you grow common.

1–5   The last three sonnets have praised the beloved, and particularly his
beauty. Now S contrasts that outward beauty, his 'show' (13) as perceived
by the eye, with the inward, his mind (9). 'Those párts of thée that thé
world's éye doth víew' is how the first line would sound according to the
iambic metre. It is inconceivable that anyone could read it like that. The
sense requires an accent on 'wórld's' – 'Those párts of thée that the wórld's
éye doth víew' – and that emphasis strikes a sinister note. 'The world's eye'
sees nothing that thought could improve upon, but what parts of the
beloved does the world not see? His outward appearance is commended
even by his enemies, another sinister note: the beloved has enemies. A third

negative note is struck in line 5, where his outward is crowned with outward praise. What about the inward?

Lines 2–3 offer a strange contrast when 'the thought of hearts' is set against 'the voice of souls', namely tongues.

6–10 And indeed the tongues that praise, and praise sincerely, from the heart (2), speak in different tones to confound that praise. 'Confound' means defeat, annul. It also means mix, confuse. Here the meanings merge. The praise of the externals is *annulled* by being *mixed* with criticism of the internal essence. These strange tongues see further than eyes, and are the voice of souls (3), and could therefore reasonably be expected to see into minds (9) because 'soul' and 'mind' are synonymous (see 27.9 and 13). These busy tongues report what souls see. Not content with that, in 9–11 they proceed to look, measure, have thoughts and eyes.

In 9 'They look into the beauty of thy mind', another dark suggestion. If those who praise externals confound that praise when they look into the beloved's mind, they cast doubt on its beauty. 'There's no art | To find the mind's construction in the face' (*Mac* 1.4.11–12), so how then can these tongues who praise see into the beloved's mind? Line 10 gives the answer. They use guesswork based upon the beloved's deeds, a sound method. Murky deeds, murky mind.

11–14 The tongues of observers spoke kindly about the outward appearance, but these tongues are churls, and their thoughts 'To thy fáir flów'r add the ránk sméll of wéeds'. The accents on 'fair' and 'rank' fall where the iambic stress would not fall. Fair flower, rank smell. The attack is given weight by the heavy accents. How churlish to criticise the beloved, to add the foul smell of weeds to the flower of his beauty – that would be the expected run of the thought. But no.

The tongues are right. Now comes the hideous truth which gathered in Sonnets 56–8 and rose to a gloomy comment in 61.14. The direct accusation has been looming since the first line of this dramatic poem, although line 11 seemed to be veering away from it by feinting to condemn the churlish critics. This feint is a dramatic touch which makes the final diagnosis all the more deadly. The flower of the beloved is beautiful but corrupt, its odour does not match its show, and the soil is that he is becoming common, is mixing with low company.

'Soil' is an emendation of the Quarto reading 'solye', presumably a misspelling of 'soyle', and after 'fair flow'r' and 'rank weeds' the 'soil' must continue the botanical image. If then 'the soil' suggests the ground in which the flower grew, there is another botanical metaphor in 'thou dost common grow.' The metaphor, not explicitly stated, but hovering, implies that the flower (of his beauty), has the stench of a weed because it grows not in the well-tended soil of a private holding but in ordinary soil, the soil of common land (see 137.5–6 and 9–10). 'The soil' could also be simply the blemish, the stain, on the beloved's character. The paraphrase offered above takes 'soil' as meaning explanation, cause, but 'soil' is not found in this sense. However, in the fourteenth to the sixteenth century, 'to soil' was a verb meaning to solve, to explain, and 'assoil' occurs meaning explanation, and that meaning would make excellent sense here, 'But why the odour matcheth not thy show, the explanation is that you are growing common.' There is no need to decide between these options, but what is clear is that the beloved's external beauty has an inner corruption because he has made himself cheap. He is sexually promiscuous.

After the passionate love and fulsome praise of Sonnets 62–8 and the acclaim in 69.1–4 this indictment comes as a shock. The lover has been forced to see the truth.

It is worth noting that the Quarto writes line 11 without a comma:

> Then churls their thoughts (although their eies were kind)
> To thy faire flower ad the rancke smell of weeds.

Possibly this could stand in the usage noted on 55.7, 'Nor Mars his sword', meaning 'nor the sword of Mars'. Then 'churls their thoughts' would mean 'the thoughts of churls', but it is better not to introduce these new characters into the poem. Surely the churls are the tongues so active in 6–10, 'Then [being] churls, their thoughts add the rank smell.' Hence the comma added above.

ɛɔ 70 ʆ

That thou art blamed shall not be thy deféct,
For slander's mark was ever yet the fair.
The ornament of beauty is suspéct,
A crow that flies in heaven's sweetest air.   4

So thou be good, slander doth but approve
Thy worth the greater, being wooed of time,
For canker vice the sweetest buds doth love,
And thou present'st a pure unstainèd prime.   8

Thou hast passed by the ambush of young days,
Either not assailed, or victor being charged,
Yet this thy praise cannot be so thy praise
To tie up envy, evermore enlarged.   12

   If some suspect of ill masked not thy show,
   Then thou alone kingdoms of hearts should'st owe.

It's not your fault you are criticised. Slander always targets beauty.
   Suspicion is beauty's ornament.
Slander confirms your worth, for canker loves the sweetest buds,
   and your springtime was untainted.
You escaped the ambushes of youth, either unattacked or undefeated,
   but praise will not tether envy. Envy is always free.
If your beauty were not masked by some suspicion of wrongdoing,
   you would rule the hearts of everyone.

1–4 Sonnet 69 ended with S delivering a bitter criticism of the beloved.
Now Sonnet 70 argues in his defence that it will be no fault of the beloved
that he is the target of slander. 'Thy' carries the metrical stress, 'shall nót
be thý deféct'. S is retreating from his position of 69.12–14 by pretending
that the criticism came not from himself but from envious slanderers.
   In line 3 'suspect' is suspicion. Suspicion is a crow, black and raucous,

like those in Holinshed's woodcut of Makben and Banquho (1577) as they ride to meet the three weird sisters. The beloved is a cloudless sky sweet with the fragrance of flowers.

5–8 'So thou be good' is a vivid form of the conditional clause, 'If you were good, slander simply proves that you are even better' [since it is the tribute paid to virtue]. S is retreating from his earlier criticism, but not quite so far as to say that the beloved is good. 'Being wooed of time' has raised many explanations from commentators, six in Booth (1977), for example. The best fit with what follows is 'courted by the age, by your contemporaries'. The argument would then run, 'If you were good, being courted by everyone, and slander attacked you, that confirms your goodness. For 'in the sweetest bud | The eating canker dwells' (*TGV* 1.1.42–3). The beloved has passed this stage and his beauty shows no worm in the flower, a striking retreat from 69.11–14. The tactic in Sonnet 69 was to accuse. The tactic in 70 is to discredit accusers.

9–12 He has safely 'passed by the ambush of young days', and the military metaphor continues in 10, when either the enemy has not attacked, or his charge has been victoriously repulsed. In 12 the enemy will be identified as envy. High praise cannot be guaranteed, it cannot be accorded 'so as to tie up envy', because envy is always at large, 'the many-tonguèd blatent beast' who breaks his iron chain and is 'evermore enlarged' free for ever, in Edmund Spenser's *Faerie Queene* 6.12.34–40. Line 10 is difficult to read. It is best to take 'either' as one syllable, 'Éith'r not assáil'd, or víctor béing chárged' (compare 'whe'er' in 59.11).

13–14 'If some suspect of ill masked not thy show' is another retreat from the indictment of 69.13–14, where bluntly the odour did not match the show. S has himself condemned the beloved, and now in 70 retreats from the condemnation as though it were gossip by others. He has said too much, and is now trying to unsay it, and so he ends with a compliment in an attempt to retrieve his position – 'Of course your reputation is clouded by suspicion. If it were not, all mankind would be in love with you. You would win the hearts of all, and be their king. You would 'owe', that is own, possess, sovereignty over all.'

Noyes (1927) in Rollins (1944) ['on contradictions in the so-called sonnet story':] [There are] flagrant instances as ... 70, where the escutcheon is praised for its spotlessness immediately after its grime has been explained in detail.

No longer mourn for me when I am dead
Than you shall hear the surly sullen bell
Give warning to the world that I am fled
From this vile world with vildest worms to dwell.   4

Nay, if you read this line, remember not
The hand that writ it, for I love you so
That I in your sweet thoughts would be forgot,
If thinking on me then should make you woe.   8

O if, I say, you look upon this verse,
When I perhaps compounded am with clay,
Do not so much as my poor name rehearse,
But let your love ev'n with my life decay,   12
    Lest the wise world should look into your moan
    And mock you with me after I am gone.

Stop mourning the moment my funeral bell stops ringing.
If you read this, forget the writer, for I love you so that I do not wish
    to cause you grief.
If you look at it when I am dead, do not even speak my name—
    the world would laugh at you.

1–4 'Never send to know for whom the *bell* tolls; It tolls for *thee*,' wrote
John Donne in *Devotions*, and the same stern note is struck with a different
message in the first quatrain of this poem. In Elizabethan England most
people knew their neighbours and lived within earshot of church bells.
When they heard the bell, they would know who was leaving the world.
At such times it would have been natural to think that we all have something in common with 'one sore sick that hears the passing bell' (*VA* 702).
The sound which is made audible in the last three words of the second line
would have been 'a ceaseless reminder of mortality to the sick' during the
plague of 1592–4 (Burrow 2002). On 31 December 1607 Shakespeare ap-

pears to have paid 20 shillings for 'a forenoone knell of the great bell' of St Saviour's, Southwark, for his actor brother Edmund (Duncan-Jones 1997).

As S contemplates the sound of his own funeral bell, he thinks of the world he would be leaving and how vile it is, as described in Sonnet 66, but the work of the worms will be even viler. The voice of doom is carried in the paired alliterations of 'mourn for me' 'surly sullen' and 'warning to the world', ringing on into 'vile world with vildest worms'. 'Vildest' is a common variant of 'vilest' and it makes the effect even weightier. Booth (1977) cites Henry Peacham's *The Garden of Eloquence* (1577), where the expansion of 'vile' to 'vilde' is taken as an example of paragoge, the addition of an extra sound in a word for metrical convenience, or simply to make the verse 'more fine'.

5–8   The hand of the writer is also the hand of the lover, and 'I love you so' is not our novelettish formula. 'So' is the peg on which the next two lines hang: 'I love you *in such a way* that I wish to be forgotten rather than cause you sorrow when I am dead.'

9–14   This lover has been deploying a combination of praise, pleading, accusation, retraction, denunciation of rivals, and his claim to be able to grant immortality. Now, after the outburst at the end of Sonnet 69 and the olive branch offered in Sonnet 70, he plays the pity card. In the Latin treatise on rhetoric, *Rhetorica ad Herennium*, of about 82 BC, some 26 means of arousing pity are recommended for the orator's armoury. Shakespeare the dramatist knew them all.

There is a subtle grading to his appeal. Being older than his beloved, he applies first the 'when I am dead' motif, and supports it in line 4 by a vivid evocation of his funeral, a pitiable declaration of his disillusionment with life, and the certainty of his putrefaction. He then reminds his beloved of the hand that wrote these poems, in particular that very line 6 (and later line 9), and begs to be forgotten for the most noble and selfless reasons – he does not want his beloved to remember him and be sad.

In line 4 he imagined the worms at work on his corpse. In line 10 they will have done their work and his body will be merged with clay. Line 5 began, 'Nay, if you *read* this line ...' After a swift compliment to the sweetness of the beloved (7), fearing that it may be going too far to entertain the possibility that the beloved should read his poem, he retreats to a humbler possibility – he might just look at it, 'O if, I say, you *look upon* this verse'. In line 11, where 'rehearse' means 'speak', he is fishing for a word of praise and reassurance. 'Nay' and 'O' at the beginning of lines 5 and 9 sharpen the impression that S is actually talking to the beloved. These are not lyrics for the reader, but utterances addressed to a lover. Vendler (1997) demonstrates this by providing a prose version of the poem expressed as five speeches by Poet interspersed by four responses from Beloved.

The end of the poem, as so often, recalls the beginning. 'This vile world' of line 4 has become in 13 'the wise world', because it has inquired into this moaning, and had the wisdom to see what a failure S has been. 'Moan' picks up 'mourn' from the first line, and the paired alliterations of 'the wise world', followed by 'moan | And mock', echo the paired alliterations of the tolling of the bell in 1–4.

When the bell has rung, when the worms have done their work and S is compounded with clay, he does not want the beloved even to mention his name, in case he expose himself to ridicule for moaning over such a nonentity – this grovelling from a poet who has already offered immortality to the beloved in Sonnets 18 and 19 and a dozen others. He does not suffer from modesty, but claims to do so. Perhaps he is writing for the sake of writing and does not worry about inconsistencies. Perhaps the sonnets are technical exercises on the theme, 'What can a lover say to the one he loves?' No one could read the first eight lines of this poem properly and believe such trivial explanations. These are poems exploring the ways of love, the things that could be felt and said and experienced by a lover. Shakespeare was a playwright, and his plays are built upon his experience of life. These sonnets are similar, a drama in 152 scenes with a broad arc of plot, but also with loose ends and inconsistencies, different versions of events, and different techniques of persuasion. In these respects they form a drama quite like life.

Burrow (2002)
The expected term of life is threescore years and ten; as Duncan-Jones notes, the 71st sonnet turns to thoughts of death.

ဢ 72 os

O lest the world should task you to recite
What merit lived in me that thou should'st love,
After my death, dear love, forget me quite,
For you in me can nothing worthy prove, 4
Unless you would devise some virtuous lie
To do more for me than mine own desert,
And hang more praise upon deceasèd I
Than niggard truth would willingly impart. 8

O lest your true love may seem false in this,
That you for love speak well of me untrue,
My name be buried where my body is,
And live no more to shame nor me nor you. 12
    For I am shamed by that which I bring forth,
    And so should'st you, to love things nothing worth.

*O, in case they demand to know why you loved me, just forget me
    when I die. You can't find virtue in me unless you overpraise.
O, in case your love should lead you into untruth, forget me rather than
    live on to shame us, me for what I produce, you for loving rubbish.*

1–8 The world that was capable of being inquisitive and mocking at the
end of Sonnet 71 continues in the same vein in Sonnet 72. There is a danger
that it may burden the beloved with the task of reciting S's virtues after he
is dead. To prevent this S advised, 'No longer mourn for me when I am
dead' (71.1), which is a peg on which he hangs the self-abasement which
fills this sonnet and is part of his strategy of playing for pity. Some editors
follow the Quarto in reading no punctuation after line 2, so that the sense
would be 'in case people ask you to tell them what merit I had displayed
that would make you love me after my death'. This is a strange question
for people to ask, but the greatest flaw in this punctuation is that it robs
line 3 of its eloquence, 'After my death, dear love, forget me quite.'
    It would be a hard task to declaim S's virtues because the beloved could

not prove that there had been any, not unless he told 'some virtuous lie'. At the end of Plato's *Republic*, Er dies and comes back to tell a myth of reincarnation, which is a noble lie, '*gennaion pseudos*', because it encourages the belief that virtue will be rewarded in a future life. In Horace, *Odes* 3.11, Hypermestra deceives her father by a splendid lie, '*splendide mendax*', in order to save the life of her bridegroom. Sidney Lee, in Rollins (1944), quotes Tasso, *Gierusalemme Liberata* (1581), '*magnanima menzogna*', translated by Edward Fairfax in 1600 as 'noble lie'. This is not to claim that Shakespeare was thinking of the passages in Plato or Horace or Tasso. Commentators are too ready to find classical allusions where there are only drifts of spray from the ocean of popular classicism.

S does not wish his beloved to tell virtuous lies for him. Truth is just, not generous but miserly, 'niggard'. In line 6 it helps to give 'fór' its iambic stress, 'to dó more fór me', and 'desert' is pronounced 'desart', rhyming with 'depart' in line 8 (as at 49.10). If praise is hung as in line 7, it is thought of as a tribute hung on a hearse or tomb, like the trophies of 31.10 or the scroll praising Hero which Claudio hangs on her tomb in *MA* 5.3.9.

9–14 'O lest' recalls the opening, and stays with truth and falsity. In line 10 'untrue' could be applied to himself, 'of me untrue', but it is not his truth, his fidelity, which is the subject of this poem, but his worthlessness and in particular the worthlessness of his verse. Better then to read 'untrue' as referring to the words of the beloved, '*your true love* may seem *false*, in that *you for love* speak *untruth* about *me*.' He does not want to be responsible for making the beloved tell lies. At 11 the appeal for pity is more blatant, 'My name be buried where my body is', and in the hail of monosyllables that follows the tone is even more abject. What he brings forth is his poetry, a common metaphor, as at 38.11–14. Although as recently as Sonnets 63 and 65 it was to be immortal, it is now worth nothing. He is using the same general tactic as in Sonnet 71, slighting himself, and begging to be refuted, and loved. The orator is at work, inventing persuasive arguments (see note on 38.1–3). There is no need for them to be consistent.

❧ 73 ❧

That time of year thou mayst in me behold,
When yellow leaves, or none, or few, do hang
Upon those boughs which shake against the cold,
Bare ruined choirs where late the sweet birds sang.　　4

In me thou seest the twilight of such day
As after sunset fadeth in the west,
Which by and by black night doth take away,
Death's second self that seals up all in rest.　　8

In me thou seest the glowing of such fire
That on the ashes of his youth doth lie
As the deathbed whereon it must expire,
Consumed with that which it was nourished by.　　12

　　This thou perceiv'st, which makes thy love more strong
　　To love that well, which thou must leave ere long.

You can behold autumn in me.
In me you see sunset, twilight, night.
In me you see the dying embers of a fire.
This you perceive and love me more, because you must soon leave me.

1–4 In the second line the obvious order would be either yellow, few or none (decreasing), or else none, few or yellow (increasing). The choppy order makes the line sound like a man brooding, and correcting himself, 'yellow, or none, [wait a minute] there are just a few'. Then, in mid-metaphor he sees the autumn wood as a ruined church (there were hundreds of these in England 70-odd years after the dissolution of the monasteries, many of them between Stratford and London). The branches shivering in the cold merge into the ruined arches of a choir, frequently foliated, 'decorated, especially carved with leaves', as glossed in Pevsner and Metcalf

(1985). The sweet birds merge into the monks who used to sing there, and they are also the old poet shivering in the cold and no longer able to write.

5–8   In 5–6 the cadence of 'twílight of such dáy' is echoed in 'fádeth in the wést', and the new metaphor of 9–12 will open with the same dying fall, 'glówing of such fíre'. This imposes a steady rhythm on the passage of time. Sun sets, twilight comes on, night removes day. Night creeps on moment by moment, monosyllable by monosyllable, and S is ageing, hour by hour, towards death. Night is death's *second* self, because of its stillness and its darkness. It seals up all in rest, as death seals coffins, but another sense of 'seal' may be active. 'Seel' is used of sewing up the eyes of hawks in training, as in *Mac* 3.2.47–8, 'Come, seeling night, | Scarf up the tender eye of pitiful day'. Shakespeare uses this metaphor also in *Oth* 3.3.214 and *AC* 3.13.113. 'Seel' in this sense is frequently spelt 'seal' in the sixteeenth and seventeenth centuries.

9–12   Now S is a fire dying on the ashes of his youth. 'His' is the common possessive adjective used both personally and impersonally (1.4). Here it brings the simile sharply into reality. 'His youth' is the early stages of the fire, 'its youth', but it is also the youth of the man. The fire glows on its embers as though they were its deathbed, and it is consumed by the fuel that nourished it. It is eaten by what it ate. But what was it that nourished S's youth and now consumes it?

13–14   'Thou perceiv'st' picks up 'thou mayst in me behold' from line 1, and 'In me thou seest' from lines 5 and 9. What the beloved sees makes his love more strong to love what he soon must lose, simply, 'the young man loves S all the more because he knows that S will soon die.' Why should S say this if it is true? To note with approval the nobility and selflessness of the young man's love? Implausible, after his outburst at the end of Sonnet 69. By stating this as a fact, S is begging the beloved not to deny it – 'You love me more than ever now that you know that I soon will be dead. Is that not so?' This is another volley in the barrage of appeals for pity which rumble through Sonnets 71 and 72. There he begged for pity because of the worthlessness of himself and of his poetry, here because of his advanced age. In 1609 he was all of 45.

'Thou must leave ere long' is a surprise. It is S who is about to leave the beloved. This twist is perhaps suggestive. S sees himself lying motionless in death, as the beloved walks away from his corpse. A poignant picture.

Empson (1947), 2–3

There is no pun, double syntax, or dubiety of feeling, in 'Bare ruined choirs, where late the sweet birds sang' but the comparison holds for many reasons; because ruined monastery choirs are places in which to sing, because they involve sitting in a row, because they are made of wood, are carved into knots and so forth, because they used to be surrounded by a sheltering building crystallised out of the likeness of a forest, and coloured with stained glass and painting like flowers and leaves, because they are now abandoned by all but the grey walls coloured like the skies of winter, because the cold and Narcissistic charm suggested by choir-boys suits well with Shakespeare's feeling for the object of the Sonnets, and for various sociological and historical reasons (the protestant destruction of the monasteries; fear of puritanism) which it would be hard now to trace out in their proportions; these reasons and many more relating the simile to its place in the Sonnet, must all combine to give the line its beauty, and there is a sort of ambiguity in not knowing which of them to hold most clearly in mind.

Duncan-Jones (1997), on line 2

Since Shakespeare was bald, a visual analogy may be implied between an almost-leafless tree and the almost-hairless head, a process which may in a specific as well as a general sense be viewed *in me*.

Duncan-Jones (1997), on line 13

Totally ambivalent: = either declarative of the existing strength of the youth's love, or carrying a note of hope: 'which (will) make your love more strong'; or simply descriptive, 'yours must be a very strong love, to be capable of being bestowed on a transient object.'

Anthony Hecht in Evans (1996), 8–9, on lines 13–14

… the continued love, especially in the face of a ravaged lover, is quietly heroic. Something of the deep risk of all mortal attachments is expressed, and we once again realise that to avoid such attachments may be the safer and more prudent course, but it is not to live life to its fullest, whereas to love means to expose oneself to every kind of grief.

Vendler (1997)

It has often been remarked that 'lose' would make better sense in the couplet than *leave*, but because everything, love included, is consumed by that which it was nourished by, Shakespeare enacts his analytic 'law of nourishment and consumption' by reconjugating the verb 'to love' so that it reads 'loving, leaving, leafless'.

ℬ 74 ℭ

But be contented when that fell arrest
Without all bail shall carry me away,
My life hath in this line some interest,
Which for memorial still with thee shall stay.   4

When thou reviewest this, thou dost review
The very part was consecrate to thee.
The earth can have but earth, which is his due;
My sp'rit is thine, the better part of me.   8

So then thou hast but lost the dregs of life,
The prey of worms, my body being dead,
The coward conquest of a wretch's knife,
Too base of thee to be rememberèd.   12

The worth of that is that which it contains,
And that is this, and this with thee remains.

Be assured my poetry will stay with you as a memorial when I die.
When you see this you see my spirit, the better part of me, and it is yours.
You have lost the dregs of my life. My body is worth nothing.
Its only value is the spirit within it, and that stays with you.

1–4 In 73.14 the beloved loves S all the more because he sees that he will
soon be dead. *But*, carrying on from there, when that happens he can be
sure that S will still be alive in these poems. Some editions change the
comma at the end of the second line into a semicolon, thus asking the
beloved to be contented when S dies. The comma offered by the Quarto
makes the request more realistic, 'Be contented [that] you will have my
verse as my memorial'. This construction appears, for example, at *JC*
3.1.242–3, 'we are contented Caesar shall | Have all due rites and lawful
ceremonies.'

When that fell arrest comes, S will be haled off by 'this fell sergeant

Death', who 'is strict in his arrest' in *Ham* 5.2.288–9, and the terms of this arrest forbid any form of bail. Money will not release him, and money is involved in the next line in the word 'interest', which is often used with a financial connotation (see 31.7). This suggests right of ownership as at *R3* 2.2.47–8, 'Ah, so much interest have I in thy sorrow | As I had title in thy noble husband.' So S's life has some right over this line of verse, and line 4 suggests that the owner is exercising it by leaving the poetry as a bequest to the beloved. But the sonnet does not say 'in this poetry' but 'in this line', namely line 3. This is the commonplace poetic singular, but, common as it is, it has here particular force. It is as though S is actually working on this poem for the beloved, and suddenly thinks as he writes this very line that it will be read by the beloved some day after he is dead. This same moment of composition is caught in 71.5 and 9.

5–8 When the beloved looks at it again, he looks at S's spirit. In the present tenses here and again in line 9, S is imagining that he is already dead. His spiritual part is consecrated to the beloved, because his love is spiritual. The religious connotation is sharpened by the use of 'consecrate', equal to 'consecrated'; *OED* cites, for example, 'when our Lorde is consecrate in the fourme of bread' (1507). This connotation is supported in what follows, 'The earth can have but earth', which invokes the order for the Burial of the Dead, 'Earth to earth, ashes to ashes, dust to dust', but the holy text is not put to holy use. S's spiritual part is not going down or up a Christian path, it is going to live on with the beloved in his surviving poetry. The earth will have his due, the body, the earthly part. 'His', being personal and impersonal, as for example in 1.4 and 73.10, makes the earth like a human creditor, the lesser beneficiary in this will.

9–12 Now that his body is dead it is slighted in monosyllables, 'So then thou has but lost the dregs of life, | The prey of worms.' What is the body? A cowardly wretch can stab you and put an end to it with a knife, like the knife which killed Christopher Marlowe in a Deptford tavern on 30 May 1593; he too was a poet and his spirit lives on in his poetry. 'Coward' occasionally occurs as an adjective, for example 'coward cries' in *KL* 2.2.219 and 'coward lips' in *JC* 1.2.124. The body could then could be a cowardly conquest by a wretch's knife. This may be too simple. Ingram and Redpath (1978) have a weighty analysis of possibilities. In line 12 follows another denigration of the body, as being too base a thing to be remembered by the beloved.

232

13–14   The only value of the body is what it contains, the spirit, and that is preserved in these poems, and 'with thee remains'. The end of the poem refers back to line 4, 'with thee shall stay'. The closing couplet sounds like the conclusion of a strict and cogent logical argument:

> The worth of *that* is *that* which it contains
> And *that* is *this*, and *this* with *thee* remains.

In Sonnets 71–4, S is playing from the pity suit of cards. In 71 he wants the beloved to forget him and his 'poor name' lest he be mocked for mourning such a nonentity. In 72 he offers the same advice with a different slant, 'When I am dead do not praise me, because that would be a lie. What I produce is worthless.' In 73 his self-denigration continues. He is a pitiable old man and soon will die, and the young man loves him all the more because of it. Now 74.9–12 offers a corrective to all this self-contempt, by denigrating his body but proudly asserting the power of his poetry. In 71.9 he was tentative, 'O if (I say) you look upon this verse'. In 74.5 he is more confident, 'When thou reviewest this'.

The differences could be explained by seeing the Sonnets as a disconnected string of rhetorical exercises bearing no relation to any real experience in S's life. Another approach would be to suppose that they are a jumble of assorted love poems. But these four sonnets, for instance, take four different views of the same situation, and they are developing views each inching the plot forward. This is a drama in sonnet form. If it had been written in blank verse with three characters, it would have been a play presenting a shrewd picture of love's diplomacy, but the sonnet form releases the dramatist from the tyranny of explicit continuity. Apart from a few soliloquies the Sonnets are utterances addressed by S to a lover who does not speak, but whose response and whose behaviour can often be deduced.

Duncan-Jones (1997), on line 11
A much-discussed line: momentarily it may seem that the poet anticipates self-slaughter, but it is more likely that the *wretch* whose sharp instrument has taken possession of the speaker's body is personified death … However, the tone is confusing, both because it is not clear whether *coward* applies chiefly to the terror of the dying man or to the 'cowardly' attack made upon him, and because Shakespeare often uses *wretch* in terms of pity or tenderness.

So are you to my thoughts as food to life,
Or as sweet-seasoned show'rs are to the ground,
And for the peace of you I hold such strife
As 'twixt a miser and his wealth is found,   4

Now proud as an enjoyer, and anon
Doubting the filching age will steal his treasure;
Now counting best to be with you alone,
Then bettered that the world may see my pleasure;   8

Sometime all full with feasting on your sight,
And by and by clean starvèd for a look;
Possessing or pursuing no delight
Save what is had or must from you be took.   12
    Thus do I pine and surfeit day by day,
    Or gluttoning on all, or all away.

You are to my thoughts as food to life, as rain to the ground,
* as wealth to a miser.*
He and I sometimes show off our treasure, and sometimes keep it secret.
Sometimes I feast on the sight of you, sometimes I'm starved.
* My only pleasure is from you. Every day I either gorge or pine away.*

1–4 After the breach in Sonnet 69 and the tentative attempts to heal it that
have followed, in the first two lines of Sonnet 75 S seems to be saying that
he can't go on living without the beloved, a sense supported by the similes
of food and showers. As food is essential to life, and showers are essential
to the ground, so you are to my thoughts – but the argument of the sonnet
is completely different.

    The point of the poem is to ponder contradictions in S's love. The miser
simile in lines 3–4 is expounded immediately in 5–8, the food simile in
9–14. No more is heard about the showers. According to Booth (1977), line
3 'passeth all understanding'. Since the miser simile in 3–4 is expounded in

5–8, that is where the explanation should be sought. For neither S nor the miser is there serene enjoyment of their treasure, because of strife between desire to display and desire to enjoy in private. Instead of finding the peace that love can bring, S is suffering internal war. 'For the peace of you' therefore seems to mean for the peaceful enjoyment of your love.

5–8 Other details are shared between miser and lover. Line 6 applies properly to the miser, but is easily transferred to the lover. They both suspect everyone in the world of being a thief with an eye on their treasure. In lines 7–8 the words are applied to S, but are easily transferred to the miser. S is sometimes counting [it] best to be alone with the beloved, sometimes [counting it] better than best to flaunt his pleasure in public. Misers like to count their treasure.

9–14 These lines leave the miser and expound the food simile of the first line. S is sometimes full with feasting on the sight of the beloved, and by and by starved for a look at him, a condition expressed in 56.3–4, and here in 11–12 with a glance at a metaphor of possessing and pursuing. Whether pursuing or possessing, his only delight is in the beloved. Sonnet 129.11 gives the same metaphor a more bitter taste.

The final couplet returns to food. Either he is pining for it or full of it. Either he is gluttoning on all the beloved offers or there is nothing, 'or all away'. The presence of the lover is a feast; his absence is starvation.

Shakespeare is a master of rhetoric. The poem is a list of swings from one extreme to another, and items in the list are so similar as to run the risk of becoming monotonous, but, unlike the summary at the head of this note, the sonnet varies the introductory words, 'now and anon' (5), 'Now' and 'Then' (7–8), 'Sometime' (9) 'And by and by' (10), in 11 simply 'or', in 13 'and', in 14 'Or … or'. This virtuosity is crowned in the final couplet by the chiasmus, 'pine and surfeit, (AB), 'Or gluttoning on all, or all away' (BA), with another chiasmus embedded in 'gluttoning all … all away'. Chiasmus is a common shape of words and also of thought in the Sonnets. In lines 3–8, for example, 3 is devoted to S and 4 to the miser, but the miser is dealt with in 5–6 and S in 7–8. Lines 5–6 describe display and solitary enjoyment, but 7–8 describe solitary enjoyment and display.

The rhetorical play is not exhausted. In 9–10 'all full' has its antithesis in 'clean starvèd'. Lines 11–12 form a more complex antithesis, by which he *possesses* no delight except what is *had*, or *pursues* no delight except what *must be taken*. 'By and by' (10) is strangely echoed in 'day by day' (13). It

235

is a long agony. There are those hammering monosyllables in 1, 3 and 12, the run of them broken in 13–14 by 'surfeit' and the gross word 'gluttoning', which stands out also because 'glutton' never occurs as a verb in Shakespeare and is very rare elsewhere.

The same poem that is full of rhetorical fireworks also shows some examples of rough and ready grammar. In line 6 the miser is 'doubting', but in line 7 the reader has to adjust because it is S who is 'counting'. The end of the note on 5–8 has to supply three words to fill out the sense. Again, at the end of the poem, 'or all away' is grammatically baffling, but clear and forcible like all these other irregularities. Perhaps there is even a touch of the colloquial in 'all full', and 'clean starvèd'. This master of rhetoric is also master of speech as it is spoken.

The informality in this poem, including the failure to develop the simile of the showers in the second line, is in such marked contrast to the polish and lucidity of the triple structure in Sonnet 73 and the tight argument of Sonnet 74 that Shakespeare may be deliberately giving a flavour of untidiness to Sonnet 75 to prepare for the crushing self-criticism of Sonnet 76. He often links sonnets with their neighbours, and this might just be an ingenious new way of doing so.

Anthology sonnets tend to be lucid and smooth, but many others are more rugged and difficult to understand. A simple explanation might be that the poet has polished some poems and not others, but a more fruitful suggestion might be that some of the poems present a simple argument, while others deal with more complex, more shifting situations, and respond to them with more sudden movements of the mind, and with irregularities of language like those that occur in spoken English. Such unevenness is not a fault. It diversifies the tone, enriches the drama, and makes it more like life. Such unevenness is a characteristic of Shakespeare's mature writing.

Why is my verse so barren of new pride,
So far from variation or quick change?
Why with the time do I not glance aside
To new-found methods and to compounds strange?   4

Why write I still all one, ever the same,
And keep invention in a noted weed,
That every word doth almost tell my name,
Showing their birth and where they did proceed?   8

O know, sweet love, I always write of you,
And you and love are still my argument.
So all my best is dressing old words new,
Spending again what is already spent.   12

For as the sun is daily new and old,
So is my love still telling what is told.

Why is my verse so uninventive, so monotonous, why so dated?
Why is it all the same, so that every word carries my signature?
Answer – I always write about you, putting old words in a new dress.
As the sun is new and old every day, so I tell what I have already told.

1–4 Typically, the first two lines deny variation and contain it. 'Of' and 'or' could not be spoken with an accent. 'Bárren of néw príde' disturbs the iambic rhythm, and the disturbance is repeated in '… -átion or quíck chánge', and this line ending does not occur again in the poem. This gives emphasis to 'new' and 'quick', neither of which would bear the iambic stress. 'New pride' is the modern style described in line 4. 'Quick change' could refer to swift successions of tone, style and subject matter, but 'quick' also means 'live', and the metrical emphasis points towards that meaning. Lack of life would go with the barrenness of the first line.

Why with the time, i.e. following the fashion of the day, does he not look aside from his set path at 'new-found methods and compounds strange'? These strange compounds are probably compound adjectives, which were rife in some contemporary writers. Evans (1996) gives examples of the growth of this fashion at the end of the sixteenth century, and King Ferdinand pours out half a dozen in his parody of amorous bombast in *LLL* 1.1.227–46, including 'a most preposterous event, that draweth from my snow-white pen the ebon-coloured ink'. Booth (1977) argues that 'the juxtaposition of *methods* and *compounds*, in the context of ... . barrenness activates the specifically medical meanings of both words.' A method was a specific course of treatment for a particular disease, according to *OED* 1, citing 'Every kynde of dysease hath his owne Methode' (1541), and compounds were compounded drugs as opposed to simples (*OED* 2, and see *AYL* 4.1.16). The three schools of classical medicine were called Dogmatic (*OED* B.1), Methodic (*OED* B.1) and Empiric (*OED* B.1, and see *AW* 2.1.121).

5–8 Lines 1, 3 and 5 begin 'Why', 'Why', 'Why', as his sense of failure mounts. In 'Whý wríte I stíll áll óne, éver the sáme' the monosyllables could carry distaste and impatience, where 'éver' stands out as a bisyllabic word, and as a variation to the iambic expectation 'evér'. However the line is read, it clamours to be spoken naturally, not as doggerel. Here as in lines 1–2 the verse refutes itself, demonstrating variation even as it confesses monotony. Invention and argument (10) are technical terms of Latin rhetoric, defined by Cicero in his *De Inventione* 1.9 as 'the discovery of valid or seemingly valid arguments to render one's case plausible'. This poet knows his rhetoric, and Sonnet 38.1–3 offers the best comment:

> How can my Muse want subject to *invent*
> While thou dost breathe, that pour'st into my verse
> Thine own sweet *argument*?

Now a new metaphor emerges as verse is clad in a familiar weed, meaning dress (see 2.4), and there is also a sly hint at the absurdity of keeping invention, which is by definition new, in old clothes. So familiar is the weed 'that almost every word doth tell my name' and now poetry is seen as the child of the poet (38.11–14). 'Barren' in the first line deploys the same metaphor. In lines 7–8 every word he fathers is like its parent (even speaks like him). They all speak his name, showing 'where they did proceed', meaning where they came from. In *H5* 3.5.15 the constable of France also uses 'where' as equal to 'from where', '*Dieu des batailles!* Where have they this mettle?' On 'proceed', which is common in the Bible, Booth (1977) cites the communion service in the Book of Common Prayer, 'I believe in the Holy Ghost, The Lord and giver of life, Who proceedeth from the Father and the Son.' This mock modesty is the cover for a critique of his poetic rivals.

9–12 The emotional tone rises through the three questions of lines 1, 3 and 5, and now they receive their answer in 'O know, sweet love, I always write of you.' The plain language makes us hear the tone of voice, and the eloquence of simple English continues the attack upon 'methods new and compounds strange'. Simple as it is, it has its own command of rhetoric, in four words an exclamation, a command, an address and an endearment, and the intensity is carried into the algebra of line 10, 'love … I always … you, | … you … love … still my', where 'still' is a clever link to 5, a line spoken in the same plain and passionate tone. As he admits that he repeats himself, he repeats the word 'still'. He is dressing old words new, a return to the clothes metaphor of line 6, and the repetitions continue in 'Spending again what is already spent.' Duncan-Jones (1997) believes this may suggest that his words could be like 'sexual emissions from an almost-exhausted source'. Surely not.

13–14 The justification follows with 'For'. His poetry is repetitive, but so is the sun [and who dare fault the sun?]. All his best work was 'Spending again what is already spent' in line 12; now his love is still saying what it has been saying for the last 10 lines. The thrust of the argument is not to boast that his work is like the sun, and not only that the beloved is like the sun, but also to suggest that the sun is repetitive, and is not criticised for it. Why should S be? There is such richness in the sun and in the beloved that their praises could never be exhausted.

ᔓ 77 ᔓ

Thy glass will show thee how thy beauties wear,
Thy dial how thy precious minutes waste,
The vacant leaves thy mind's imprint will bear,
And of this book, this learning mayst thou taste: 4

The wrinkles which thy glass will truly show,
Of mouthèd graves will give thee memory;

Thou by thy dial's shady stealth mayst know
Time's thievish progress to eternity;   8

Look what thy memory cannot contain
Commit to these waste blanks, and thou shalt find
Those children nursed, delivered from thy brain
To take a new acquaintance of thy mind.   12
   These offices, so oft as thou wilt look
   Shall profit thee, and much enrich thy book.

Your mirror will tell you how your beauty wears, your sundial how time
*   wastes away, this book will preserve your mind's imprint.*
Wrinkles will remind you of graves.
The shadow on the sundial will show time stealing to eternity.
Commit whatever memory cannot hold to this book, which will nurse it
*   and deliver it later to your mind as a new acquaintance.*
Every time you look at it, it will profit you and increase in value.

1–4 The beloved's mirror will show him how his beauty wears. His
sundial will show him his precious minutes wasting away. The 'vacant
leaves' are the blank pages of a book which S is now giving him. It is a
diary, daybook or commonplace book, like the tables Hamlet calls for
when he learns that his uncle has murdered his father and married his
mother (1.5.106–9):

240

O villain, villain, smiling damnèd villain!
My tables. My tables – meet it is I set it down
That one may smile and smile and be a villain.

The diary is concerned with time but, unlike the mirror and the sundial, it
will not wear or waste away, but will profit the beloved in years to come.
From this book he will be able to taste this learning, namely the contents
of 5–12 – that all things are short-lived, except the wisdom he will preserve
in the book. 'Imprint' is metaphorical. It does not, of course, imply that
the book will ever be printed. It is there to contrast with 'wear' and 'waste'.
These pages will last because they bear the stamp of his mind.

5–6   With characteristic lucidity glass, sundial and book are explained in
that order. By keeping a daybook he will learn three things, and they will
profit him (14). The mirror will 'truly show' his wrinkles. There will be
no room for doubt, he will see them, and they will remind him of gaping
graves because of their shape. They will be slits, trenches in 2.2, furrows in
22.3, delved parallels in 60.10, and the resemblance to graves is made all the
more cruel by the word 'mouthèd'. They are open mouths, waiting to devour.

7–8   'Dial' could refer to a clock or a watch, but '*shady* stealth' rules that
out. The *shadow* of the rod of the sundial moves stealthily, every precious
minute, and will continue to eternity. In Elizabethan English 'stealth'
could refer to stealing (*OED* 1), as in *TA* 3.4.30–1, 'I know my lord hath
spent of Timon's wealth | And now ingratitude makes it worse than
stealth.' This sense is activated in 'Time's thievish progress'.

9–14   'Look what' means 'whatever', as at 9.10. As the beloved goes
through life, he will have valuable experiences and thoughts which he has
no hope of being able to remember, but if he commits them to the book,
it will deliver them for a second birth. For 'delivery' in this context see *Oth*
1.3.368, 'There are many events in the womb of time, which will be
delivered.' These brain children will be new acquaintances for his older
mind. As children perform profitable offices to aged parents, the book will
profit the beloved every time he looks at it. The waste blanks and the later
increase in value (10 and 14) are apologies for the modesty of the gift.
    Many commentators take 'These offices' (13) to include the duties of
looking in the mirror and observing the movement of the shadow on the
sundial. The last word of the sonnet tells against that.

This is an occasional poem, (purporting to be) an enclosure sent with the present of a notebook for the beloved. It is not clear what the mirror and the sundial have to do with the book. One explanation is that one parcel contained all three, but '*Thy* glass' and *Thy* dial' suggest that the mirror and the sundial are both already in the young man's possession. A more likely link is that all three have to do with time. In days to come the mirror and the sundial will announce a cruel message to the beloved, but this daybook will be an improving asset, like lost children rediscovered by an aged parent.

It would be hazardous to try to fit this poem into the plot of the Sonnets, but the mirror and the sundial are warning the young man that what he values at the moment will not last. In that context, the daybook or diary given by the older lover may be a witty and tactful suggestion to his young friend not to devote himself totally to the pleasures of the hour, but to take a more reflective view of life, not to grow common (69.13–14) and 'be anchored in the bay where all men ride' (80.10), but to live wisely and, of course, to be faithful in love.

Vendler (1997)
Like Sonnets 10, 36, 37 (if we allow for the playful reversal in *spight*), 54, 69, 128, and 131, sonnet 77 registers a *th* in every line ... The repetition of the single sound *th* (principally through deictics and possessives) seems to be one of Shakespeare's self-testing games, but here it also reflects the sonnet's principal figure, which is incremental repetition.

ॐ 78 ୡ

So oft have I invoked thee for my Muse,
And found such fair assistance in my verse,
As every alien pen hath got my use,
And under thee their poesy disperse.   4

Thine eyes, that taught the dumb on high to sing,
And heavy ignorance aloft to fly,
Have added feathers to the learned's wing,
And given grace a double majesty.   8

Yet be most proud of that which I compile,
Whose influence is thine and born of thee.
In others' works thou dost but mend the style,
And arts with thy sweet graces gracèd be,   12
   But thou art all my art, and dost advance
   As high as learning, my rude ignorance.

I have so often called upon you as my Muse and received such valuable help
   that others have taken to doing the same.
Dumb and ignorant as I am, your eyes taught me to soar and sing,
   and have given strength and majesty to the learned.
You should take most pride in what I write. You mend the art of others,
   but are all my art, raising my ignorance as high as their learning.

1–4   The assistance he has received from his beloved is 'fair', primarily as
a wind may be fair behind a sailing ship. It is favouring help. But the notion
of the presence of a fair helper is also hovering. 'Every alien pen hath got
my use' means that everybody else, even total strangers, has acquired my
habit of invoking you as their Muse, writing *under* your name as they spray
their poetry about. 'Disperse' is contemptuous, never again used of any
form of publication or distribution of literature in Shakespeare, and 'poesy' too, as in the effusions of the pompous pedant Holofernes in *LLL*
4.2.120–4, 'You find not the apostrophus, and so miss the accent. Let me

supervise the canzonet. Here are only numbers ratified, but for the elegance, facility, and golden cadence of poesy – *caret*. Ovidius Naso was the man' (where *caret* means 'there is none').

5–8   As usual in these poems, the logical structure is firm and clear. Lines 1–2 on S himself are developed in 5–6, 9–10 and 13–14; the intervening lines deal with the learned poets. But in this majestic company S does not at first presume to refer to himself. He waits till the last three words of the poem to reveal that he himself is 'the dumb' and 'heavy ignorance'. The dumbness arrives in line 5, the only monosyllabic line in the sonnet, as though once he could only manage words of one syllable.

The beloved's eyes have taught the dumb to sing on high and ignorance to fly aloft. Love began in the eyes in 104.2, 'When first your eye I eyed', and continued gazing, 'Thine eyes I love' in Sonnet 132.1. Here they are personified, 'Have added feathers to the learned's wing | And given grace a double majesty.'

It would be wise to take S's humility with a pinch of salt. Despite the heavy load of ignorance he carries, he sings and soars aloft, but no information is given about the altitude attained by the learned. Their wing, on the other hand, is a fine poetic singular (although it is not easy to fly with one wing), and the beloved's eyes have added feathers to it, as a falconer imps a wing, 'adds feathers … so as to … restore or improve the powers of flight'. The sly hint is that imping is usually a treatment for a damaged bird, as in *OED* 4, citing 'Imping his broken wings with better plumes' (1618). George Herbert gloried in this same metaphor in *Easter Wings*, 'For if I imp my wing on thine | Affliction shall advance the flight in mee' (*Notes and Queries* 39 (1992), 448–52, 489–90). Unlike S, who is dumb, heavy, ignorant and rude, i.e. uneducated, the learned have grace and majesty, but majesty, particularly when doubled, is no aid to levitation.

Honan (1999, 84–5) suggests that Shakespeare was probably married in the church at Temple Grafton where four years later the vicar John Frith was described as 'an old priest & Unsound in religion', whose chiefest trade was to cure hurt or diseased hawks, 'for which purpose manie doe usuallie repaire to him'. Shakespeare knew about hawks (see 73.8).

9–14   The beloved should take more pride in what S compiles than in the work of the learned, who required less teaching. The bird metaphor still stirs. *Pilare* in Latin is 'to pluck', as in the proverb in Petronius 43.4, *malam parram compilavit*, 'he has plucked a bad owl', meaning that he has caught a Tartar, has had a nasty experience. In Latin *compilare* means to plagiarise. 'Compile' in *LLL* 4.3.131–4 has a similar mocking tone as the King, with a lovely double negative, teases Longueville whom he had just caught reading his sonnet to Maria:

> Longueville
> Did never sonnet for her sake compile,
> Nor never lay his wreathèd arms athwart
> His loving bosom to keep down his heart?

When S writes, he is simply plucking the feathers out of other people's work. It is strange that the pupil of the Muse condemns himself as a plagiarist, but at this point in the argument he is playing down his powers. The more he denigrates his own gifts, the greater credit to the Muse who taught him to soar.

'Influence' in Shakespeare is almost always astrological, 'planetary influence', as in *KL* 1.2.123. So Timon of Athens (5.1.61) had a 'starlike nobleness' which 'gave life and influence' to his friends, and here the hint of that image is reinforced by the hint of the horoscope in 'born of thee'. Line 10 is therefore a compliment to the star quality of the beloved. In 11–12 he 'mends the style' of these other poets, and their arts are 'gracèd' with his sweet graces, where the 'double majesty' at the end of line 8 is repeated in the polyptoton 'graces gracèd', but what he has done for S is a far greater achievement. He has raised the work of dumb, rude ignorance to these same heights. S has no arts, only the beloved, 'Thou art all my art', but the three arts in 12–13 quietly overtrump the 'double majesty', and double graces of the learned. There is also a little extra art for the ear. 'Thóu art áll my árt' has a subtle variation in the stresses on 'art'. He is not as rude and ignorant as all that.

The metaphor of flight continues in 13–14, where 'advance' means 'raise', as in George Herbert quoted above on line 7.

In one witty poem he has cruelly satirised learned poets, built an edifice of self-praise buttressed by mock modesty, and has praised the beloved in almost every line.

The identity of these learned poets is much discussed, and many names have been put forward, but Bate (1997, 14–18) builds an imposing case for Robert Greene, one of the Cambridge-educated dramatists, the 'University Wits'. These included Christopher Marlowe, George Peele, Thomas Nashe as well as Greene. These poets tended to die in poverty, partly because actors paid writers a pittance for their work, but also, according to Greene, because one of the actors has set himself up as a writer: 'Yes, trust them not: for there is an upstart crow, beautified with our feathers, that *with his Tiger's heart wrapped in a Player's hide*, supposes he is as well able to bombast out a blank verse as the best of you; and, being an absolute *Johannes fac totum*, is in his own conceit the only Shake-scene in a country.' There can be no doubt that Shake-scene is Shakespeare. The quotation is a parody of *3H6* 1.4.138, 'O tiger's heart wrapped in a woman's hide!' A *Johannes fac totum*, a jack of all trades, could describe a player who is also a writer. Besides, when Greene died in a shoemaker's house in London in 1592, Hostess Isam, the shoemaker's wife, said that on his deathbed he 'called for a pot of Malmsey' and then scribbled a letter to his abandoned wife: 'Doll, I charge thee by the love of our youth, and by my soul's rest, that thou wilt see this man paid: for if he and his wife had not succoured me, I had died in the streets. Robert Greene.' Falstaff was to die in Hostess Mistress Quickly's tavern, crying out for sack and no doubt remembering Doll Tearsheet (*H5* 2.3. 26–30).

Given these possible contacts between Greene and Shakespeare, the 'upstart crow' in Greene's denunciation of Shakespeare is worth considering. It is the upstart crow, *cornicula*, who has dressed himself up in the feathers of all the other birds in Horace, *Epistles* 1.3, as Shakespeare the actor has taken to writing plays, 'beautified with our feathers'. *Cornicula* is a pitiful little crow, and 'upstart' is Greene's shrewd translation of the diminutive form. S does not refute the charge, but instead pictures the University Wits who have taken to dedicating their verse to the beloved as raptors who have had their wings imped by the eyes of the beloved, while poor S plucks feathers from wherever he finds them to piece together his own verse. 'Compile' is part of the riposte of this upstart actor to the University Wits. His rhetorical pyrotechnics and his display of Latin learning demonstrate that this grammar school boy has an easy command of university wit and learning. The beloved's sweet graces have graced their *arts*, 'But thou *art* all my *art*' is trouncing them at their own game. So much for 'my rude ignorance'.

๛ 79 ๛

Whilst I alone did call upon thy aid,
My verse alone had all thy gentle grace,
But now my gracious numbers are decayed,
And my sick Muse doth give another place.   4

I grant, sweet love, thy lovely argument
Deserves the travail of a worthier pen,
Yet what of thee thy poet doth invent,
He robs thee of, and pays it thee again: 8
He lends thee virtue, and he stole that word
From thy behaviour; beauty doth he give,
And found it in thy cheek; he can afford
No praise to thee, but what in thee doth live.   12

Then thank him not for that which he doth say,
Since what he owes thee, thou thyself dost pay.

While I was the only poet to invoke your aid, I was the only good poet,
but now there is another, and my poetry is enfeebled.
I grant your beauty deserves a better pen than mine,
but everything he gives you in his poems he takes from you.
So don't thank him. He owes you a debt, and you are the one that pays it.

Vendler (1997) calls this a rewriting of Sonnet 78. Not so. In 78 S praised
the beloved as the inspiration for poetry, his own most of all. In Sonnet 79
he praises the beloved on the ground that all the beauty in a rival's verse is
stolen from the beloved. An obvious weakness in this case is that Sonnet
78 suggests that S would be open to the same attack, 'thou art all my art'. The
two arguments do not sit comfortably together, but S is not deterred. Each
structure supports praise of the beloved. They do not need to fit together.

1–4   The logic is highlighted by the repetition of 'alone' in the same place
in lines 1–2 and the play upon 'grace' and 'gracious'. In Sonnet 78 'grace'

and 'graces gracèd' were associated, ironically, with S's learned rivals, but now he drops the irony, and claims that his own verse had once 'gentle grace'. The target here is a single rival poet (7), as S finds his own 'gracious numbers' are decayed, and his Muse is sick, like a feeble old woman ousted by a younger rival.

5–12 Here begins the direct flattery. 'Argument' is subject matter (see 38.1–3), and the beloved is lovely. 'Thy lovely argument' is therefore the subject of my poetry, your beautiful self (see 76.10). Now S moves to the attack, there follows a cataract of 'thy', 'thee', 'thou', 'thyself'. Contempt is particularly audible in the sarcasm of 'what of *thee thy* poet doth invent' (7). This is not invention, but theft. He has the effrontery to pay you *back* what he has robbed you of, 'he pays it thee *again*'. He lends you virtue and gives you beauty, having stolen them both from you. Clearly he has none of his own. He can provide you with nothing but what is yours, 'he can afford | No praise to thee, but what in thee doth live.'

A point of principle arises in line 11. There Duncan-Jones (1997), commenting on 'cheek', writes 'synecdoche for the beauty of the youth's whole form, as in 68.1'. Synecdoche is part for whole as in 'a fleet of fifty *sail*'. Another approach to this problem is to look closely at the word. '*Cheek*' in 53.7 trumps 'the *face* that launched a thousand ships' and in 67.5 and 68.1 it is 'the map of days outworn'. Here 'cheek' recalls previous mentions and is a glancing tribute to the *natural* beauty of the beloved; but it also evokes the colour and form and loveliness of a living face. Duncan-Jones might be faulted for failing the detail; those who focus on it are in danger of over-interpreting. The same problem arises in 80.6, where 'sail' may be more than 'ship'.

13–14 No thanks are owed to this rival poet, and the last three lines clinch the argument with a paradox in the last line when all the 'he's and 'thee's and 'thy's come to harbour in 'what he owes *thee, thou thyself* dost pay.' The poet owes the beloved, the beloved pays. The beloved was, in effect, gentle, gracious, sweet and lovely. He deserves a worthier poet than S and he has one. This is the combination of self-depreciation and praise of the beloved, which is the basic strategy of Sonnets 71–3 and 76–9, culminating in praise of the beloved's virtue and beauty coupled with an attempt to deprive the rival poet of any credit for praising them, and to insinuate *en passant* that he is guilty of theft and fraud (8, 9 and 14), as the poem ends in a rush of financial terms, perhaps eight in eight lines.

≫ 80 ≪

O how I faint when I of you do write,
Knowing a better sp'rit doth use your name,
And in the praise thereof spends all his might
To make me tongue-tied speaking of your fame.   4

But since your worth (wide as the ocean is)
The humble as the proudest sail doth bear,
My saucy bark (inferior far to his)
On your broad main doth wilfully appear.   8
Your shallowest help will hold me up afloat,
Whilst he upon your soundless deep doth ride;

Or being wracked, I am a worthless boat,
He of tall building and of goodly pride.   12
    Then if he thrive and I be cast away,
    The worst was this: my love was my decay.

I swoon when I write about you, knowing that a better poet
* is putting out all his strength, and making me tongue-tied.*
But the ocean of your virtue bears both my little boat and his galleon,
or if I founder I'm no loss. The worst of it was that my love was my decay.

1–4 The worthier pen of 79.6 is now a better spirit. Those who have read
about the frauds practised by the rival poet in 79.7–14 will not be taken in.

5–10 The beloved's worth is wide *as* the ocean, but the simile immediately glides into a metaphor when that worth actually becomes the ocean,
'your broad main', bearing great galleons and tiny lighters. Up until the
seventeenth century a bark, or barque, was a small ship, often a flat-
bottomed rowing boat used for work in shallow water, and that strict sense
is indicated here in the contrast with the tall building (12) of the rival's ship.
A tall ship needs a deep keel. In the note about synecdoche, part for whole,
in Sonnet 79.11, an example was 'sail' for 'ships'. To explain 'the proudest

sail' in 80.6 as an example of synecdoche would fall short of the truth. The phrase evokes the heart-stirring sight of a tall ship in full sail standing out from shore on the broad main, top gallants and all. One sees the sails and not the hull. Speak not of synecdoche. S's Saucy Sue, on the other hand, has the effrontery wilfully to show herself on the vast ocean of the beloved's virtues. All a bark needs is a shallow inshore water, whereas the rival is riding the unsounded, unfathomable deep. The English view of the defeat of the Armada in 1588 was that the little ships of Drake and Collingwood had routed the towering Spanish galleons with their high bows, stern castles, and lofty superstructures (Mattingly 1959, 189).

11–14 If I am 'wracked', shipwrecked, no great loss, whereas he is a proud, tall, well-built ship. So much for the metaphor. Being applied, it means that S is out of favour with the beloved, and would be content with only a few tokens of affection (9). 'I' in 11 would not bear the iambic stress, but demands to be emphasised to bring out the contrast with 'He' in 12, which, is stressed by the inversion common at the beginning of the line, 'Í am a worthless boat, | Hé of tall building and of goodly pride.'

Then, in that case, 'if he thrive and I be cast away, | The worst was this: my love was my decay.' The sharp change of tense and mood is dramatic. Regular syntax would require 'if he thrive ... the worst *would be* ... ' But so vividly does S imagine this outcome that he talks as though it had already happened. He has already been cast away, and his greatest grief is that his love has brought about his downfall. 'My love' is presumably S's love for the beloved, but it teasingly contains the possibility that it was the beloved himself who caused S to decay.

The metaphor may still be alive. If his bark is 'wracked', shipwrecked, and he is 'cast away' (Antonio had 'an argosy cast away coming from Tripolis' in *MV* 3.1.94), it may be because of the decay of its timbers (see 79.3).

In Sonnet 78 heavy irony is heaped upon a number of learned poets. In 79 the beloved is praised and a single rival poet is undermined by accusations of theft. Here in 80 the beloved is again praised (5, 8 and 10), the rival poet is lauded in overblown terms as 'a better sp'rit' complete with confidence, pride and magnificence (6, 10 and 12), and S himself is belittled, tongue-tied, humble, inferior, impertinent, just keeping afloat while the rival rides upon the soundless deep. In short, S is worthless. Here as in many sonnets, for example 71–4, self-abasement is an appeal for pity, a hope of praise, and an artillery platform for a bombardment on the enemy.

ஐ 81 ௸

Or I shall live your epitaph to make,
Or you survive when I in earth am rotten,
From hence your memory death cannot take,
Although in me each part will be forgotten.　　　4
Your name from hence immortal life shall have,
Though I, once gone, to all the world must die.
The earth can yield me but a common grave,
When you intombèd in men's eyes shall lie.　　　8

Your monument shall be my gentle verse,
Which eyes not yet created shall o'er-read,
And tongues to be your being shall rehearse,
When all the breathers of this world are dead.　　　12

　　You still shall live, such virtue hath my pen,
　　Where breath most breathes, ev'n in the mouths of men.

Whether I survive you, or you survive me, death cannot erase your memory,
　　though I shall be completely forgotten. Your name will be immortal.
　　I must be in a common grave, but your tomb will be in men's eyes.
Your monument shall be my verse. Eyes shall read it, and tongues shall
　　speak of you when men now breathing are dead.
You will live where breath is strongest, in the mouths of men.

1–8　The first 'or' is the equivalent of our 'whether' as in 'Tell me where
is fancy bred, | Or in the heart, or in the head?' (*MV* 3.2.63–4). The brutal
description of S's body lying rotten in the ground is part of his strategy of
presenting himself in a pitiable light. He has done this repeatedly in recent
sonnets, and continues to do it here in lines 4, 6 and 7. In line 3 'From
hence' seems to mean 'from the world', and in line 5, after 'immortal life',
its likeliest meaning is 'from this moment on'. After 'rotten' in line 2, 'in
me each part' seems to refer to each of his bodily parts, but he is also playing
down his talents, his qualities, as in 'a man of parts'.

The immortality conferred on the beloved by S's verse is a frequent theme, but here it is conferred not on him but upon his name. This is a name S never reveals and clearly never intended to reveal. That being so, it is unlikely that it will ever be known. According to Leishman (1961, 33), there is 'a certain deliberately chosen hermeticism or hieroglyphicalness which pervades Shakespeare's Sonnets, as though he were trying to ensure that no reader should be able to discover from them the identity of the person addressed.'

Shakespeare was confident that his own verse would live on, and is about to say so in lines 5 and 9–14. In the world's eyes, 'to all the world', he himself would not die, but at this moment his strategy is to stress his own worthlessness. The earth can offer him only a common grave. This could mean simply an ordinary grave, but it also suggests a mass grave with no headstone, as though he were a pauper or criminal or plague victim. The first seven lines of this poem are therefore false, a rhetorical build-up to the riddle of line 8. How can a man be entombed in eyes? The deceased who lies in men's eyes is likely to be an aristocrat, with his effigy lying at eye height on a splendid table tomb. S seems to be implying that the beloved's monument will be no ordinary or common grave like his own, but a grave worthy of a nobleman.

There is an elegant order. If S is the speaker and B is the beloved, it runs SBBS BSSB, and the last six lines are full of the poetic immortality that S will give B.

9–12   His tomb will be men's eyes, and the monument on it will be this gentle verse. In 79.2 S had pretended that it had lost all the 'gentle grace' that the beloved had given it. Now he asserts its nobility. 'Gentles, perchance you wonder at this show,' says Quince in *MND* 5.1.126, addressing the royal court of Theseus. Generations yet unborn will read this poetry. But instead of any pat phrase like 'future generations', this poet embarks on a weird conceit, involving tongues, breathers, breath, breathes and mouths. Lines 10–11 are very simple (but see Empson (1947) below). The eyes of men unborn will read the epitaph on this monument, and tongues to be will speak of the beloved's life, his *being*, when all men now living and breathing in the world are dead. 'Breathers' in 12 leads into the climax of the last line.

13–14   Such virtue has his pen that the beloved will live 'where breath most breathes', and where is that? 'Ev'n in the mouths of men.' This conceit is a variation on a favourite boast of Latin poets, going back to the epitaph of Ennius, who died in 169 BC, '*volito vivos per ora virum*', usually translated as 'I fly alive on the mouths of men', but perhaps *per* should be translated as 'through'. Romans tended to declaim their poetry.

Ivor Brown and George Fearon (1939) in Rollins (1944), on line 7
Shakespeare's grave was in the chancel [of the Stratford parish church], which was a place of honour ... The poet had a right to lie in the chancel, not because of his immortal verse, but as a lessee of tithes. As ever in England, property was more important than poetry.

Booth (1977)
The experience of understanding lines 1–8 (as opposed to what is understood from them) is one of so many simple alternations and alternatives to pairs of alternatives that the actual experience of plodding through them is like a physical experience of relationships that are literally metaphysical – an experience of perceiving stolidly physical patterns (of paired lines and pairs of paired lines) that are both reductively simplistic in their interrelation and too multifariously complex to think about.

Empson (1930)
Tongues can *over-read* as well as *eyes*, and this would leave either *being* the subject of *rehearse*, or both *tongues* and *eyes*. However *tongues* is particularly connected with *rehearse*, because the contrast of *your being* with *to be* ('in order to be') shows the transient I rehearsing your ideal *being*, lapping up your blood as it were. [Rollins comments, 'A passing strange note by a modern master'. He did not live to read Booth (1977) or Vendler (1997).]

Vendler (1997)
Central words in the poem are phonemically or graphically linked: the monument is an *immortal* and *gentle* one in which *memory* is *intombèd*, rehearsed by *men's mouths*. By such linkages are the poet's sentiments made to seem almost neurologically conclusive. In this sequence all *the m/o/n/u/m/e/n/t* responses, phonemic and graphic, are made to fire repeatedly (by my count, $m = 8$, $o = 5$, $n = 4$, $u = 2$, $e = 7$, $t = 5$).

ഇ 82 ര

I grant thou wert not married to my Muse,
And therefore mayst without attaint o'erlook
The dedicated words which writers use
Of their fair subject, blessing every book.   4

Thou art as fair in knowledge as in hue,
Finding thy worth a limit past my praise,
And therefore art enforced to seek anew
Some fresher stamp of the time-bett'ring days.   8

And do so, love; yet when they have devised
What strainèd touches Rhetoric can lend,
Thou, truly fair, were truly sympathised
In true plain words by thy true-telling friend.   12
    And their gross painting might be better used
    Where cheeks need blood. In thee it is abused.

You were not married to my Muse, so you are blameless
   if you read tributes other poets pay their lovers.
You are fair in mind as in form in judging that I cannot do you justice
   and looking for someone else – the new poets are better.
But when they have deployed all their rhetoric, your true beauty
   was already truly conveyed in true words by your true friend.
Their daubing would look better on cheeks short of blood.

1–4 The broad argument is clear: 'You are perfectly entitled to look for another poet to praise you, but although the new poets are much more florid, I am a truthful friend, and you don't need their exaggerations.' The difficulty is in the first four lines, and they have been interpreted in many different ways. 'You were never married to my Muse, so you are perfectly entitled "without attaint", that is without any kind of guilt, to look elsewhere, to scan the work of other poets and see what words they dedicate to their lovers.' He is not suggesting the beloved should consult book

254

dedications. Such formal addresses to patrons contain nothing relevant to praise of 'fair subjects'. He is thinking not of dedications but of love poems. It is praise of lovers that is 'blessing every book', every book has it, and S's beloved has been consulting other writers to see whether their work is more effective in this vital respect. In response S takes up a liberal stance. Marriage is a binding and exclusive contract. There is no such contract between the beloved and S's poetry. It would not be a form of adultery if the beloved read other poets, with a view to finding a better practitioner.

5–8 From this tolerance S now moves to praise. The beloved is fair in 'hue', which refers to appearance, form, as in 20.7, and he is also fair in 'knowledge', which is here closely connected with judgement, as in 14.1 and 9. In line 6 S adds self-depreciation to praise. The beloved has the judgement to know that his own worth is beyond the reach of S's poetic powers. He must look for 'a fresher stamp', new imprints, because poetry has moved on and is now much better than it used to be. 'The time-better-ing days' are these present days each of which improves upon time past. As usual, the self-criticism is heavy with irony, particularly in lines 4 and 8. In 'Some frésher stámp of the tíme-bétt'ring dáys', a stress on 'tíme' against the iambic rhythm could add a touch of sarcasm, as though the fashions of today could better time. 'Time' has a broad range of meaning. See 18.12, 60.13, 70.6, 76.3, 124.8 and 13, and particularly 32.5.

9–14 The beloved has S's blessing. Of course he must examine the work of other poets. But what he will find will be 'strainèd ... Rhetoric'. The above text keeps the Quarto's capital letter. It seems to add to the pompos-ity of the new poets. The beloved, who is truly beautiful, had already been truly and sympathetically understood in true plain words from a truth-tell-ing friend. These plain words contain a lush polyptoton, 'truly ... truly ... true ... true-telling', as S deploys strainèd Rhetoric in claiming to be a plain, blunt man with a small vocabulary. He is no orator as his rivals are. The point is perhaps sharpened by a weighty rhythm. Doggerel would be happy with 'In trúe, plain wórds, by thý true-télling fríend', but a more eloquent reading might be something like 'In trúe pláin wórds bý thý trúe-télling fríend'. Hood, as reported by Evans, notes that 'Shakespeare here shows that he at least can employ rhetoric in the service of genuine feeling.' He is also busy with innuendo. The insistence on his own truth carries a contrast with the 'strainèd touches' of others' Rhetoric. Let them keep their gaudy colouring for bloodless cheeks (67.5). 'Gross painting' is at last the insult direct, adding a scornful hint of brushstrokes to the 'touches' of line 10.

'Abused' at the end is not used in its sense of 'badly treated' but rather 'misused'. Their gross painting is misused in describing the glowing un-rouged cheeks of the beloved (see Sonnets 67, 68 and 79). Here again, a word might leap into life if 'abused' were read according to the sense and against the iambic expectation:

> And their gross painting would be better used
> Where cheeks need blood. In thee it is ábused.

This poem follows a graph from tolerance, praise of the beloved, ironic flattery of opponents, and self-abasement to self-assertion and denuncia-tion of rivals, all ingredients in the rival poets' sonnets between 78 and 86.

Shakespeare knew exactly what he was doing. A useful commentary is the speech by the most eloquent and unscrupulous of Shakespeare's ora-tors. In *JC*3.2 Antony praises 'the noble Brutus': 'And Brutus is an honourable man' (half a dozen times), 'But here I am to speak what I do know', 'I am no orator as Brutus is, | But as you know me all, a plain blunt man | That love my friend; and that they know full well.' Antony is calculating and insincere. S speaks the same language, much of it monosyllabic.

ᔰ 83 �

I never saw that you did painting need,
And therefore to your fair no painting set.
I found, or thought I found, you did exceed
The barren tender of a poet's debt.   4

And therefore have I slept in your report,
That you yourself, being éxtant, well might show
How far a modern quill doth come too short
Speaking of worth, what worth in you doth grow.   8

This silence for my sin you did impute,
Which shall be most my glory, being dumb.
For I impair not beauty, being mute,
When others would give life and bring a tomb.   12

    There lives more life in one of your fair eyes
    Than both your poets can in praise devise.

I never saw you needed painting. I thought you beyond price,
   a debt no poetic tribute could repay.
That is why I have been idle, so that your living self could show
   how far modern writers fall short of your virtues.
You have held this against me, but I glory in it.
   I do not damage your beauty. Others try to give it life and kill it.
There is more life in one of your eyes than your two poets can invent.

1–4 Using the evidence of his eyes, S never judged that the beauty, the
'fair' (see 16.11), of the beloved needed paint, the sort of word-painting laid
on by rivals in 82.13. The self-correction in line 3 is natural talk – 'I found,
or thought I did, that you were beyond praise.' 'Tender' is cited twice in
OED 1b in the sixteenth century, as 'an offer of money in discharge of a
debt'. A barren tender is a worthless offer, because a poet's debt for it is
vastly greater than the poor coinage he could offer in repayment.

5–8   This is his excuse for failing to report upon the beauty of his beloved, for sleeping on the job. He has neatly turned a fault into a compliment. In line 6 'being' is one syllable, 'being éxtant', as in 52.14. It is two in 10 and 11. He decided not to write, [in order] that the living form of the beloved should speak for itself, and beggar the efforts of contemporary poets. 'A modern quill' is contemptuous, as at 85.3. It is a feather far too short to do justice to the beloved's beauty. Besides, to call something 'modern' is usually a sneer in Shakespeare, as in *Oth* 1.3.108–9, 'these thin habits and poor likelihoods | Of modern seeming'.

In 'speaking of worth, what worth in you doth grow' the repetitive construction has been taken to indicate some hesitation on the poet's part, implying some question about the extent to which 'worth' does flourish in the youth. Impossible. The whole tenor of this poem is to praise the beloved as being above all praise. There can be no innuendo. This is the binary construction familiar from Greek and the Bible, 'I speak of worth, what worth in you doth *grow*' like 'I know thee who thou art', in Luke 4: 34, and it carries an extra compliment. He is speaking not only about worth in general, but about worth not static but dynamic, ever *growing*.

9–12   The beloved has taken this silence for a sin, but S glories in it, 'being dumb', echoed with deliberate inelegance at the end of the next line, 'being mute'. His silence does no harm to the beloved's beauty, whereas those who try to bring life to it bring a tomb. How different from S's gentle verse, the monument in which the beloved will find immortal life, 'such virtue hath my pen' (81.13). So much for the 'barren tender of a poet's debt'. The argument of Sonnet 83 is inconsistent with the argument of Sonnet 81. No matter. They are both good arguments. These poems are examples of the lover in action.

13–14   Life in line 12 sets up the epigram about living life in line 13. *One* of the beautiful eyes of the beloved has more life living in it than the praise his *two* poets can muster. In 78, 82, 85 and here in 83.12 there appear to be several rival poets; in 79, 80, 86 and here in 83.12 only one. Ingram and Redpath (1978) argue that it is not uncommon to find the plural 'used, especially in a petulant mood, even when only one person is in question'.

ᛞ 84 ᛡ

Who is it that says most which can say more
Than this rich praise that you alone are you,
In whose confine immurèd is the store
Which should example where your equal grew?   4

Lean penury within that pen doth dwell
That to his subject lends not some small glory,
But he that writes of you, if he can tell
That you are you, so dignifies his story.   8

Let him but copy what in you is writ,
Not making worse what nature made so clear,
And such a counterpart shall fame his wit,
Making his style admirèd everywhere.   12

    You to your beauteous blessings add a curse,
    Being fond on praise, which makes your praises worse.

The most long-winded could not say more than that you are you,
   and only you possess your qualities.
It is a poor author that cannot lend some glory to his subject,
   but one who writes that you are you, so dignifies his story.
If he just copies you, everyone will admire his wit.
You cheapen your beauty by doting on praise.

1–4   In spoken English an emphatic question might be 'Who is it *that* spilt the milk?', rather than 'Who is it *who* spilt the milk?' The repetition of 'who' is avoided by using the more impersonal 'that'. Similarly here, 'Who is it *that* says most …?' But there is a third clause, and here again Shakespeare avoids repetition by using yet another apparently impersonal form, '*Who* is it *that* says most *which* can say more?', meaning, 'Who can say more?'. 'Which' is sometimes used personally in Elizabethan English, witness 'Our Father, which art in heaven'. These elaborate repetitions are

259

S's way of saying that nobody, no matter how eloquent, could say more than 'you are you', and in putting it like this he mocks the longwindedness he condemns – yet another broadside aimed at the 'proudest sail' (80) and 'strainèd ... Rhetoric' (82) of rival poets.

Lines 2–4 have been simply explained by E. B. Reed (1923) in Rollins (1944), 'You, in whom is stored up the whole sum of your unexampled beauty', but this may not do full justice to the line. A less elegant version might come closer, 'you, in whom is walled up [and therefore unavailable for use] the supply of resources which should produce other examples, from which your equal could grow'. The beloved is a walled garden which includes specimens from which the beloved's equals might grow.

5–8   In 83.7 the quill was too short. Here penury, starved and thin, lives in the pen that cannot lend glory to its subject, so lean a pen that it has lost its -ury. Penury is the failure of one pen. 'You are you' is the 'rich praise' of the other.

9–12   The beloved is a model text to copy. All a poet has to do is imitate exactly what Nature has clearly written, and the 'counterpart', the copy, will win him fame for his brilliance, and everyone will admire his style.

13–14   The background to this poem is that in Sonnets 78–80 and 82–3 others are overpraising the beloved by devising 'What strainèd touches Rhetoric can lend' as opposed to S's 'true plain words' (82.10–12). Now comes the plain truth. The young man is 'fond on praise'. To be fond is to be foolish. By doting on fulsome flattery, he has made the praise he receives worse than the simple truth offered by S himself, that 'you are you'. Anyone who is too fond of praise encourages flattery. Witness the first scene of *King Lear*.

℘ 85 ℘

My tongue-tied Muse in manners holds her still,
While comments of your praise, richly compiled,
Reserve their character with golden quill
And precious phrase by all the Muses filed.   4

I think good thoughts, whilst other write good words,
And like unlettered clerk still cry 'Amen'
To every hymn that able sp'rit affords
In polished form of well-refinèd pen.   8

Hearing you praised I say ''Tis so, 'tis true',
And to the most of praise add something more,
But that is in my thought, whose love to you,
Though words come hindmost, holds his rank before.   12

   Then others for the breath of words respect,
   Me for my dumb thoughts, speaking in effect.

My Muse is silent while others write glowing praises.
I think, others write. They sing hymns, I cry 'Amen.'
They praise, I agree, and add more in thought, led by love.
So respect others for their words, me for thoughts unspoken.

1–4 The dramatist visualises the body language of his characters. S's Muse
is a tongue-tied girl, so afraid of being ill-mannered that she dare not move.
She is an outsider, standing nervously on the fringes of a brilliant and busy
company, which is richly dressed in fine language, 'richly compiled', but
is only a compilation of comments [not original or genuine but] plucked
out of previous writers (see 78.9). The usual meaning of 'reserve' in Elizabethan English is 'store, preserve' (see 32.7), and in Shakespeare 'character'
almost always refers to writing. So these comments, personified as scribes,
are storing their writing. This chimes with 'richly' in line 2 (riches are
stored), and implies that the writing is longwinded (see 84.1). It is also

pretentious. The Muses, all nine of them, are busy filing their precious phrases with golden pens (and perhaps even gilt lettering). Two details add to the satire. At this time 'comments' are often formal, systematic treatises, and 'quill' and 'phrase' are lofty poetic singulars. Perhaps, too, the Muses are busy sharpening their precious quills with their files.

5–8 'Other' is commonly used for 'others' (see 62.8). A clerk was a lay assistant to a clergyman. The clergyman conducted the services; the clerk led the responses, a procedure bitterly remembered by Richard II (*R2* 4.1.163–5):

> God save the King! Will no man say 'Amen'?
> Am I both priest and clerk? Well then, 'Amen.
> God save the King!' although I be not he.

S doesn't even *say* 'Amen.' His 'Amen' is a *cry*. As 'unlettered clerk' he is reverting to his satire on learned poets in Sonnet 78. His rivals are empowered to lead the worship, men of learning, able and imposing spirits, and S is ignorant and illiterate.

9–12 The clerk simile is ended. Now S turns to a literal account. He presents himself as a dullard, nodding his head and agreeing with everything his superiors say. The sycophantic Justice Shallow in *2H4* 3.2 is a great repeater of words and phrases, 'Certain, 'tis certain; very sure, very sure.' In line 10 comes the counter-attack. In 84.1 S had mocked, 'Who is it that says most which can say more?', and now he himself is adding something more, but the difference is that what he adds is thought, and suddenly there is a procession, in which his words come last, but his loving thought holds first place, in terms of time because thought is faster than any words, and in terms of value because of its strength and truth. This conjures 'a procession in which the poet's *words* are so undistinguished that they come at the rear, his loving *thoughts* are so puissant that they have a place in the front rank of marchers' (Kerrigan 1986).

13–14 It follows that the beloved should respect others for their words, but they are [mere] breath. He should respect S for his thoughts, which are dumb, but real. In 80.4 he became tongue-tied while speaking. Now again he is dumb, but speaks by 'effect', by his actions. Burrow (2002) cites a proverb, 'The effect speaks, the tongue need not.' S's inarticulacy, already demonstrated by monosyllables in lines 5 and 11, is now heard in the halting metre, 'Mé for my dúmb thóughts, spéaking in efféct.'

This poem contains a succession of amusing vignettes, the glitterati in 1–4, and the unlettered clerk in 5–8 crying 'Amen' to their great hymns of praise, the procession in 12, the speechless bumpkin in 9–14, all to mock S's rivals and assert the depth of his own love. Duncan-Jones (1997) enjoys the paradox whereby 'the reader is asked to accept a carefully elaborated sonnet as an image of inarticulate love.'

℘ 86 ℧

Was it the proud full sail of his great verse,
Bound for the prize of all-too-precious you,
That did my ripe thoughts in my brain inhearse,
Making their tomb the womb wherein they grew?   4
Was it his sp'rit, by spirits taught to write
Above a mortal pitch, that struck me dead?

No, neither he, nor his compeers by night
Giving him aid, my verse astonishèd.   8
He, nor that affable familiar ghost
Which nightly gulls him with intelligence,
As victors, of my silence cannot boast.
I was not sick of any fear from thence,   12

But when your countenance filled up his line,
Then lacked I matter. That enfeebled mine.

Was it his superb poetry that killed my verse before it could be born?
Was it his spirit, taught by spirits, that struck me dead?
No. Neither he nor his cronies stunned my poetry into silence,
nor did the ghost that misleads him nightly defeat me.
But when your face filled his verse, I was enfeebled.
I had nothing to write about.

1–6   Sonnet 80.5–12 poked fun at the better spirit whose verse in praise of
the beloved was the proud sail of a tall ship. It is now under 'full' canvas –
a majestic sight. This magniloquent opening couplet continues the mockery. The monosyllables of the first line fill the sail and swell the line. They
also depart from the iambic beat, perhaps 'Was it the próud fúll sáil of hís
gréat vérse?' The rival's great ship is bound for the prize of the beloved,
'all-too-precious you' – a sneer. The beloved is far too good for him.
     Recent scholarship summarised by Burrow (2002, 103–11) suggests that
Sonnets 61–103 were written around 1594–5. In 1595 Sir Walter Ralegh set

sail from Plymouth, bound for the precious prizes of gold and gems to be plundered on the Spanish main. Contemporary readers might have seen a connection and reflected in this sarcastic context that Ralegh was a great poet, and that S's rival was not.

In the next metaphor, as in 76.8, S sees his own thoughts as babies in the womb of his brain, and their term had come. They were ripe in the sense found in *R2* 2.2.10–11, 'Some unborn sorrow, ripe in fortune's womb, | Is coming towards me.' In Elizabethan times a hearse was a coffin or a grave, so the great verse of the rival has turned S's brain into a grave for his ripe thoughts, 'Making their tomb the womb wherein they grew'. It does not sound much of a change. The assonance of 'tomb', 'womb', 'grew' – all carrying the iambic beat – adds to the sarcasm. The author of this poetry knew it was not dead.

The scorn continues with 'sp'rit' (my spelling) and 'spirits', a polypto-ton, the same word appearing in different forms, here made more derisive by the metrical change whereby his rival's 'sp'rit' is a shrunken form of the immortal 'spirits', who taught him to write (see 144.2 and 4). 'Pitch' here may refer not to music, but rather to height. Scholars detect an allusion to falconry, 'pitch' being the height from which the falcon plunges for its kill, as in *2H6* 2.1.11–12, where the Lord Protector's hawks 'know their master loves to be aloft, | And bears his thoughts above his falcon's pitch.' The rival's writing is 'above a mortal pitch' even above the flight of a mortal falcon. Similarly Milton's song 'with no middle flight intends to soar | Above the Aonian mount' in *Paradise Lost* 1.14–15.

7–12 It was not his rival's great verse that silenced him, and it was not his cronies, his 'compeers'. 'Compeers' occurs as a noun only here in Shake-speare. *OED* 2b cites it as used contemptuously by Ben Jonson in 1610 in *The Alchemist* 4.4, 'your sooty, smoky-bearded compeers'. Neither the poet nor his cronies 'astonishèd' S's verse. The verb means more than 'struck dumb with amazement'. *OED* cites from 1530, 'astonish with a stroke upon the head', and from Philemon Holland in 1600, 'The one smote the king upon the head, the other astonished his shoulder.' In 86.6 therefore, when S's verse is 'astonishèd', it is actually struck, and answers the phrase with which it so forcibly rhymes, 'that struck me dead'. What comes from above a mortal pitch and kills is lightning, and there is a glimpse of a flash in lines 5–8. 'Astonish' is connected etymologically with the Latin word *attonitus,* which literally means thunderstruck, and that connection seems to be in Shakespeare's mind in *JC* 1.3.49–56, when

Cassius bared his 'bosom to the thunder-stone ... the cross blue lightning seemed to open | The breast of heav'n', and Casca protested:

> It is the part of men to fear and tremble
> When the most mighty gods by tokens send
> Such dreadful heralds to astonish us.

The rhetoric points the logic, 'Was it ... his great verse ...? Was it his sp'rit, by spirits taught ...? The two questions are immediately answered in 'No, neither he ... nor that affable familiar ghost ... ', but a third group of suspects has intervened, 'nor his compeers by night'. These helpers are discussed below in the note on the 'Classical background'. The commonest sense of 'gulls' (10) is 'deceives'. The ghost would then be deceiving the rival with false information. A less common meaning, but one that also fits the argument of the sonnet, is 'fill, stuff' as in *OED* 2 (1604), 'Let us gull ourselves with eating and quaffing.' In line 13 the rival's line is *filled* with the beauty of the beloved's face, and no doubt it was the beauty of the beloved which filled his sails in the line 1. It would go well with these fillings if the ghost stuffed him with false information in line 10.

At this time the 'University Wits', whose plays were heavy with Greek and Latin learning, were angered by writers with no academic qualifications. One target was Shakespeare, an actor who was poaching on their preserves (see commentary on Sonnet 78.5–8). A group among the University Wits went under the name of the 'School of Night' (including Sir Walter Ralegh, according to Bradbrook (1936)). The name was perhaps given because one of them, George Chapman, had written a long poem entitled *The Shadow of Night* (1594). Chapman has 'dreames of retirèd Night', which he feares are 'idle vaines | Of an unthriftie *Angel* | That *deludes* my simple *fancie*' (*Euthemiae Raptus* 947–8). Hence perhaps the stress on night in 86.7 and 10. Further, Chapman had claimed in 75–85 of that poem to have undertaken his translation of Homer's *Iliad* under the guidance of Homer's spirit. Hence perhaps the 'affable familiar ghost' of line 9. 'Affable' is normally explained as 'benign and friendly', giving the phrase an appropriate note of sarcasm by suggesting that Homer was a crony of Chapman's, but this interpretation fails to catch the learned etymology here paraded by Shakespeare, an example of counter-learning. In Latin *affabilis* means 'addressable, speakable to', as Milton knew when in *Paradise Lost* 7.41 Raphael, 'the affable archangel', conversed with Adam. Milton may well have had this sonnet in mind as he started writing Book 7; 'thou | Visit'st my slumbers nightly,' he says to Urania in 7.29, and 'more safe I sing with *mortal* voice' in 7.24. Sonnet 86.9–10 might well stick in the mind of a blind man composing his verse by night, wandering *nightly* where the Muses haunt, and dictating to an amanuensis in the morning.

'Familiar' may contribute to the sardonic tone. In *OED* 2 a familiar is defined as 'a demon supposed to be in association ... with a man', and there is a derisive flavour in a citation from 1585, 'A familiar sprit hee had ... in the likenesse of a catte' and in Talbot's sneer at the defeated Joan of Arc in *1H6* 3.6.8, 'I think her old familiar is asleep.' Neither the rival nor his familiar ghost can take the credit, as victors, for S's silence. S was not sick with fear from that quarter. (Perish the thought!)

13–14   The end returns to the beginning. When the proud full sail of the rival's line was filled by the beloved's countenance (a topic powerful enough to fill any sail), S was left without subject matter, and the enfeeblement of his verse, already mimicked in the rhythms of the last line of Sonnet 85, is represented here in the broken line, 'That enfeebled mine.' There is a similar effect in the last lines of 13, 82 and 109.

Classical Background

The above explanation of lines 5–10 assumes that the rival's compeers are friends who help him with his writing on night visits, and are different from the affable familiar ghost. Each of these is to be found in classical literature. The Latin poet Terence was highly influential in the development of comedy in and before the seventeenth century and was a staple element in grammar school instruction. In the prologue to *Heauton Timoroumenos* (*The Self-Tormentor*) he deals with a rumour spread by a rival poet that his work relied upon the talents of friends, rather than his own native wit. In his prologue to *Adelphoe* (*The Brothers*) he repeats the charge and does not deny that eminent persons, *homines nobilis*, constantly write with him. These noble men are aristocrats, peers in English. If there is anything in this speculation, it might add an extra sting to the 'compeers' in line 7 of the sonnet. Educated people might have picked up this allusion. University Wits certainly would, and it would not have pleased them. Another straw in this wind is that *affabilis* is by no means a common word in Latin. Its first recorded use is from Terence, *Adelphoe* 896.

Latin poets sometimes met 'affable' ghosts. Homer appeared in a dream to Ennius at the beginning of his epic the *Annales* and expounded the nature of things to him. Livy 1.19 and 21 tells the story of Numa, the second king of Rome (fifth century BC), and the goddess Egeria. Believing that he could not lead the early Romans to fear the gods without inventing a miracle, '*sine commento miraculi,*' as Livy puts it, Numa pretended that he had nocturnal meetings with Egeria, and was guided by her authority in setting up the rituals of Rome. She was therefore seen as an immortal who taught Numa by night, an affable familiar.

This is not to argue against the contemporary relevance of lines 5–12. On the contrary, it looks as though Shakespeare here, as at the end of Sonnet 78, is taking on the University Wits at their own game. Let them boast of their classical erudition and let them be helped by their aristocratic friends – he was not 'sick of any fear from thence'.

Ingram and Redpath (1978)

Many candidates have been suggested for the rival poet ... we are not concerned with such identifications in the present edition; though we may perhaps venture the opinion that the question cannot be decided on the available evidence. If, however, a convincing case were made out for Chapman being the rival poet, these difficult lines could be coherently interpreted. Line 1 would fit the fourteeners of his *Iliad*. Lines 5–8 would readily apply to his labours in translating the classics and his heavy reliance on past writers. 'Above a mortal pitch' would describe well the high epic style and theme of his great translation. And lines 9–10 might refer to his rhetorical claim in his *Tears of Peace* to have been constantly prompted by the spirit of Homer. The double reference to night, moreover, might allude to the motto of his poem *The Shadow of Night* (1594). [Its title page bore an interesting motto, *Versus mei habebunt aliquantum noctis*, 'My verses will have something of the night.']

George Chapman, *The Shadow of Night* (1594)

[knowledge] will scarce be lookt upon by others, but with invocation, fasting, watching; yea not without having drops of their soules like an heavenly familiar.

℘ 87 ℭ

Farewell, thou art too dear for my possessing,
And like enough thou know'st thy estimate.
The charter of thy worth gives thee releasing,
My bonds in thee are all determinate.

For how do I hold thee but by thy granting,
And for that riches where is my deserving?
The cause of this fair gift in me is wanting,
And so my patent back again is swerving.

Thyself thou gav'st, thy own worth then not knowing,
Or me to whom thou gav'st it, else mistaking;
So thy great gift, upon misprision growing,
Comes home again, on better judgement making.   12

      Thus have I had thee as a dream doth flatter,
      In sleep a king, but waking no such matter.

Farewell, you are far above me and have every right to leave me.
You chose to give yourself to me for no good reason,
   and so the gift must be returned.
Whether you underestimated yourself, or overestimated me,
   it was an error and is therefore annulled.
I was deceived by a dream. Now I am awake.

1–4 Shakespeare was a man of the theatre. Here, for instance, after 86
poems charting a complex course of love and jealousy, he begins the next
with 'Farewell'. He was also a master writer of the spoken word. 'And
like enough' is a colloquial understatement, spoken with a wry twist, as
in *1H4* 3.2.124–6, where King Henry says to his wastrel son Prince Hal,
'thou art like enough … To fight against me under Percy's pay', or at
4.4.1–7, when the Archbishop gives some letters to Sir Michael and Sir
Michael says, 'I guess their tenor', to which the reply comes, 'Like enough

do.' The beloved has made it perfectly clear how highly he values
nself.

'Dear' has three main senses – noble, loved and valuable. The first of
ese may be touched upon (the beloved seems to be S's social superior).
he second is vital. The literal truth is that S's love has cost him suffering
o intense (as tracked in 78–86) that he has to end it. The third sense
resounds in all the financial metaphors of the first 12 lines, as italicised in
this note. Such play with 'dear' occurs in other sonnets, for example at 30.4
and 13, and at 110.3, where he 'sold cheap what was most dear'. Here it
picks up 'all-too-precious' from 86.2. '*Dear*' and '*possessing*' introduce the
financial metaphor, and '*estimate*' confirms it, as in *AW* 2.1.179–80:

> Thy life is *dear*, for all that life can *rate*
> *Worth* name of life, in thee hath *estimate*.

A *charter* of the *worth* of a property would be a solemn contract which
certified its value, and this particular charter is a contract between S and
the beloved, hereinafter known as B. All the terms of this contract contain
releasing clauses which define the *bonds* which tie S to B. They are laid
down, decided, '*determinate*', as in 'my determinate sentence' *OED* (1541),
or as in a 1609 commentary on the Douai Bible where 'he confirmeth the
same determinate sentence of their punishment.' There is a 'determinate
voyage' in *TN* 2.1.9 and a 'determinate resolution' in *H8* 2.4.176. Commentators take the word to mean 'finished, expired'. There seems to be no
evidence for that meaning (but compare 'determination' in 13.6). Terms of
these determinate bonds follow in 5–8.

5–8 B is released from this *bond*, 'for' this is a deed of *gift* and not a bill of
sale, and the implication is that the giver can determine the conditions of
his gift, 'For how do I *hold* thee but by thy *granting* ...?' S does not deserve
'that *riches*', seemingly a striking clash of plural and singular, explained in
OED with reference to the French *richesse*, and citing 'England's Richess
depends absolutely on her Foreign Trade' (1687).

The dramatic tone of the poem continues in the rhetorical question of
line 5. It is as though S is talking to the beloved on the day he realised their
love had to end. The core of the argument is the gulf between the high value
of B and the worthlessness of S. It would therefore support this argument
if line 5 were read to bring out at least the first three iambic stresses, 'For
hów do Í *hold* thée but by thy *gránting* ...?' S does not deserve 'this fair
gift', meaning both this handsome gift and this gift of B's beauty. In line 8

S's *patent*, his title deed, reverts to the giver, 'back again is swerving'. A *patent* is a document conferring a right, as in *MND* 1.1.79–81:

> So will I grow, so live, so die, my lord,
> Ere I will yield my virgin patent up
> Unto his lordship.

In this context 'swerving' might be expected to be a legal term, but there appears to be no example of the word used in that sense.

9–12 S now produces a 'legal' argument to support the case against himself, opening in lines 9–10 with a parody of legal repetitiousness. B's decision to grant arose from a misunderstanding, *misprision* being a legal term with technical meanings (*OED* 1a and b), and this legal flavour survives here as in *1H4* 1.3.26–7, 'Who either through envy or misprision | Was guilty of this fault.' The last legal touch comes in line 12, where B's gift comes home to him again, as a result of his improved *judgement*, or as Kerrigan (1986) writes, 'on (your) having second (and better) thoughts'.

13–14 S now drops the metaphor of love as a financial contract, and says plainly how he once saw it, and what it now is. The understated eloquence, as in line 2, is spoken in a colloquial tone. He had been a king. Kings have flatterers, and flatterers desert their kings. His flatterer was a dream, but now he is awake, 'In sleep a king, in waking no such matter.' The last three throwaway words sum up an elaborate image, and say more than any talk of grief or desolation could. The last three words of Sonnet 75, for example, are similar.

Sonnet 87, like Sonnet 30, is a description of a phase of love by means of a multiple metaphor from the world of financial law. In the first dozen lines of this poem there are perhaps twenty terms relating to financial value (if the count includes the quadruple giving in 7–11). Some readers may find that the rhetorical play of wit and fancy is too clever to succeed as poetry, or that love is cheapened if it is viewed as a commercial transaction. Not so. First, it is not a theme with twenty variations, but a progressive argument. Lines 1–4 lay out the disparity of terms between the parties to the contract, and assert the freedom of one of the parties. Lines 5–8 give the reason for this freedom, that the contract was a deed of gift. In 9–12 it is argued that the gift can be reclaimed because it was based upon a misprision. Second, the monotonous repetitions of the first and second personal pronouns (22 instances in the 13 lines between 'thou' and 'my' in line 1, and 'I' and 'thee' in line 13) mimic the jargon of the law, and also convey the obsession of the lover. Third, this is a metaphor, not an equation. S is looking at resemblances between his love and another area of life, and finding some details which move because they are accurate, and some which move because they are not. Legal contracts are vital for the protection and welfare of the parties involved, but they are not lovers' pledges, and their language is glaringly not the language of love. Love's commerce is conducted by other means. The legal technicalities in the poem as much as say, 'Love's not like this. You did not love me because I deserved it, but I love you so much that, even if it were a legal contract, I would release you from it.'

In the beginning of this love, when S realised in Sonnet 20 that he loved a man, he expressed his amazement in 14 lines, each of which had an extra syllable and therefore ended with a feminine rhyme. In Sonnet 87, when he says farewell to that love, every line ends with a feminine rhyme except lines 2 and 4, and the rhyme these two make is a vile concatenation of legal terms, 'estimate' with 'determinate'. This lumbering sound may also be helping to mock the polysyllabic Latinate pomposities of the law (see 46.9 and 11). The love story ends as it began, with feminine rhymes. Since there is only a sprinkling of these in the intervening sonnets, this is no coincidence. At the end of love he looks back at its beginning.

This is one of the anthology sonnets, and read by itself it is the heartbroken utterance of a man who is ending a love because of the pain it costs him. But when it is read as part of the plot of the Sonnets, it is seen as an ending to the group 76–87 in which S has tried to cope with the threat imposed by a rival poet or poets who are also rivals in love, as is implied in every poem except 77 and 81, whose relevance to the group is discussed at the end of the notes on 77, 79 and 80. S has conducted a cautious and skilful campaign with two principal weapons. The first is praise of B and assurances of his love. The second is a stealthy two-pronged attack upon his rival(s), praising 'the proud full sail of his great verse' and insisting upon the inferiority of his own 'saucy bark', a sick and tongue-tied Muse. He is too shrewd to overdo direct abuse of competitors but undermines his praise by overstating it in terms so glowing that the sarcasm is unmistakable. Nevertheless the truth slips out at 83.12, 84.14 and 86.1–12. He has used his own humility as a strategy in other sonnets, notably in 72.13–14, and part of the tactic has been to urge that the beloved is so far above him that he owes nothing and is totally free to do what he wants (see 57 and 58). In this context 87.1–12 could be read as a formal legal definition of their relationship which is so absurd in legal terms that even B would be tempted to protest against it. Sonnet 87 could then be a false farewell, a stratagem not unknown in love's exchanges.

Two arguments support this theory. The first is the edifice of legal technicalities highlighted by the simple statement of misery in 13–14. The flimsiness of S's case is disguised by the legal flummery particularly in lines 9–10. The notion that a gift may be declared invalid if the donor realises that he is in some way better than he thought, or that the recipient is worse, could not be contemplated in any imaginable legal system. This is the picture of a man trying to win favour by self-abasement.

The second argument in favour of seeing the sonnet in its dramatic context is that this poignant final farewell is followed immediately by a group of sonnets in which S admits that he himself has been at fault, and in Sonnet 93 and thereafter reveals that the beloved has been unfaithful to him. The gloves have been on in Sonnets 76–87. They are about to come off.

∞ 88 ≪

When thou shalt be disposed to set me light
And place my merit in the eye of scorn,
Upon thy side against myself I'll fight,
And prove thee virtuous, though thou art forsworn.   4

With mine own weakness being best acquainted,
Upon thy part I can set down a story
Of faults concealed wherein I am attainted,
That thou, in losing me, shall win much glory,   8
And I by this will be a gainer too.

For, bending all my loving thoughts on thee,
The injuries that to myself I do,
Doing thee vantage, double vantage me.   12
    Such is my love, to thee I so belong,
    That for thy right, myself will bear all wrong.

When you decide to despise me, I'll fight for you against myself,
    and prove you virtuous, though you are false.
I can tell a tale that will prove my guilt, do you credit,
    and I too will gain from it.
Concentrating my thoughts on you, the injustices I do to myself
    will advantage me twice—
I love you so much that I shall put myself in the wrong
    to put you in the right.

1–4 The first line has a gentle sting in it, 'When you take it into your head
to make light of me', hinting that S is the victim of the beloved's whim,
and the word 'merit' in line 2 does not weaken the sting. It is not virtuous
to hold anyone's merit up to ridicule. The fight S promises is a legal battle,
as analysed in the previous sonnet, and continued here by 'prove' and
'forsworn' and 'upon thy side', this last as in 138.8 and in *LC* 113, 'But
quickly on this side the verdict went.' S will fight on the beloved's side,

274

arguing the case against himself. This same resolve was presented in even more dramatic terms at 49.11–12, 'And this my hand against my self uprear | To guard the lawful reasons on thy part.' Here he leaves little room for doubt. He will prove the beloved virtuous, 'though thou art forsworn'. Perhaps this is a diplomatic ambiguity. It either states or hints that the poets of 76–86 were rivals in love, and that they had successes.

5–8   The legal metaphor continues. 'Upon thy part' is a variant of 'Upon thy side' in line 3, and is also used in legal contexts, as in 49.12 just quoted. 'Set down' in the sense of 'put on record' may also contribute. The jailer's daughter whose captive has escaped in *TNK* 3.2.17–18 will 'set it down | He's torn to pieces.' S knows his own weaknesses better than anyone, and therefore 'can set down a story | Of faults concealed'. He will not confine himself to truth; this is a *story* of faults of which he is 'attainted', and in this context 'attainted' will carry some of its legal associations, 'accused' or 'convicted' (see 82.2). He is stopping short of a confession. This story will win the beloved some credit, but there is a sting. The beloved will win some credit but will scarcely deserve to 'win much glory' from such a story.

9–12   S himself will be a gainer too, gaining double vantage, and this is the main difficulty in the sonnet. One vantage is that he is a gainer by having to concentrate his thoughts on the beloved (10). The second advantage is not clearly stated, though it lies behind 13–14, where he almost says that he so belongs to the beloved that he has become the beloved (see 36.2 and 62.13), in which case an advantage to the beloved is also a second advantage to himself.

At first reading this poem seems like an expression of total love, of altruism, even self-sacrifice, a declaration that the interests of the beloved are all S cares about. But we hear the advocate behind the lover, and observe that he implies throughout that the faults are the beloved's: the hint in the first line that he is treating S unjustly, his contempt for S's merit in 2, S's self-abnegation in 3, the beloved's falseness and therefore the false verdict that he is virtuous in 4, S's honesty in 5, the story told by S to defend the beloved in 6 and discredit himself in 7, the great [but hollow] glory of a dubious verdict in the beloved's favour in 8, and in the last line S's acceptance of all the guilt in order to put the beloved in the right. This is attack masquerading as defence.

Say that thou didst forsake me for some fault,
And I will comment upon that offence.
Speak of my lameness, and I straight will halt,
Against thy reasons making no defence.   4

Thou canst not, love, disgrace me half so ill,
To set a form upon desirèd change,
As I'll myself disgrace, knowing thy will.

I will acquaintance strangle and look strange,   8
Be absent from thy walks, and in my tongue
Thy sweet beloved name no more shall dwell,
Lest I, too much profane, should do it wrong
And haply of our old acquaintance tell.   12

    For thee against myself I'll vow debate,
    For I must ne'er love him whom thou dost hate.

If you say you left me because of some fault of mine,
   I'll give lectures on the subject. Say I'm lame and I'll start limping.
You cannot discredit me any more than I shall discredit myself,
   once I know your wishes.
I will not acknowledge you, walk where you walk, or mention your name,
   in case I blaspheme by revealing that we once knew each other.
I'll promise to argue against myself. I must never love one whom you hate.

1–4 It would be ordinary English to say 'if you were ... I would ...' Use
the command and the ordinary becomes dramatic. So, in line 3, 'Say I'm
lame, and instantly I'll limp' conjures up a comic scene. The drama is
heightened by the inversion of the iambic rhythm in the first two syllables
of each command, 'Sáy that thou dídst' and 'Spéak of my lámeness'. This
sonnet develops the argument of 88.3, 'Upon thy side against myself I'll
fight', corresponding to 89.13, 'For thee against myself I'll vow debate'.

Here S will 'comment upon' the charge against him, expound it at length. For 'comment' in that sense see 85.2. Once again love has become a legal issue with 'offence' and 'defence'. He will admit his guilt and offer no defence.

5–7 'To set a form upon desirèd change' suggests that the beloved might wish to devise a framework to justify the change he desires to make, perhaps a change of lover, 'in order to give an appearance of decorous normality to the separation for which you wish' (Burrow 2002). In his criticisms the beloved would 'disgrace' S, dishonour him, and also make him out to be less than gracious, disfigure him, as in 33.8. No matter how severe the criticisms, they would be less than half of what S would have to say against himself, if once he knew what the beloved wanted.

In line 7 some editors start a new sentence after 'disgrace', influenced by the fact that the Quarto has commas after 'disgrace' and 'will' – 'As I'll my self disgrace. Knowing thy will | I will acquaintance strangle …' Ingram and Redpath (1978) argue against this punctuation. They see the phrase 'knowing thy will' as strongly attached to 'desirèd' in the previous line, and to break the movement at 'disgrace' seems to them 'excessively untypical of the *Sonnets*'.

8–12 Shakespeare loved puns, and critics vary in their perception of them. Vendler (1997) makes much of her discovery of a pun in 'mistaking, making, a king, waking', at the end of 87, and 'strangle' and 'strange' are in some relationship in 89.8. A little safer than these are 'thy will. | I will' in 89.7–8, because there are multiple plays on the word 'will' in Sonnets 135 and 136. Here the latent sense would be that he is best qualified to disgrace this William because, as at 88.5, he knows all about himself.

'Strangle' in line 8 is an astonishing word, all the more for 'strange' at the end of the line. S will see the beloved, and be about to call out to him, but will choke back, stifle, the words of greeting, But his language is more violent – he will strangle the words (as though they were kittens). A similar metaphor is used in *AC* 2.6.120–2, 'the band that seems to tie their friendship together will be the very strangler of their amity.' S will look strange, meaning that he will look, or not look, at the beloved as a stranger would. In 49.5 S was afraid that the beloved 'would strangely pass'. When S says he will 'be absent from thy walks', he is sadly remembering how they used to engineer their meetings. Darcy employed a similar stratagem to meet Elizabeth at the beginning of chapter 35 of *Pride and Prejudice*.

'I shall never mention your name' would be a simple promise, but in

9–10 it comes loaded with love. It is 'thy sweet beloved name' ('sweet' is the ruling epithet in these poems, once in every three sonnets), and that name shall no longer dwell on his tongue, a phrase much more intimate than 'shall no longer be on my lips'. He is resolved not to be profane in harming the beloved's name. The mention of profanity implies that he is revering the beloved as though he were a god. And what does this blasphemy amount to? Forgetting himself and revealing their old acquaintance. Old acquaintance should never be forgot, but S will force himself to forget it. 'Haply' is the key word. The orator/lover is apologising for a fault which is scarcely a fault, a possible slip of the tongue which would be caused by his irrepressible love.

13–14   The earliest meanings of 'debate' are (1) strife, quarrelling, and (2) fight, conflict. Although I do not find these elsewhere in Shakespeare, 88.3 and 'hate' in line 14 suggest that they may be active here. Monosyllables add edge to 'For I must ne'er love him whom thou dost hate.' Is this self-denial, or an appeal for a denial by the beloved?

On the face of it this poem is a pledge of love undeterred, an undertaking never to embarrass or criticise the beloved, never even to defend himself, but rather to support any accusations the beloved may make against him. But in previous sonnets S has been unscrupulous and adroit in plucking at the heart strings. Here in line 2 tactful silence would have been the courteous response of a rejected lover, not detailed arguments supporting the case against himself. In line 3, if accused of a deformity, he will immediately mime it. In line 7, if the beloved disgraces him, he will join in and disgrace himself. He makes it clear that the truth does not matter. All he wants is love. And these fulsome responses move from words to actions in lines 9–12. This is not loyalty, chivalry or altruism, but self-abasement tooled by an orator to win pity. The last words of the poem are a statement begging for the answer, 'Of course I don't hate you.'

G. K. Hunter (1953) in Jones (1977), 122
Sonnet 89 is presented as a 'still' from a love drama, a picture in which the gestures not only make up a present harmony, but hint (with subtle economy of means, which reveals the dramatist) at a psychological background, so that a powerful reaction is built up, as if to a history of love.

ఴ 90 ಞ

Then hate me when thou wilt, if ever, now,
Now, while the world is bent my deeds to cross,
Join with the spite of fortune, make me bow,
And do not drop in for an after-loss.   4
Ah, do not, when my heart hath 'scaped this sorrow,
Come in the rearward of a conquered woe.
Give not a windy night a rainy morrow
To linger out a purposed overthrow.   8

If thou wilt leave me, do not leave me last,
When other petty griefs have done their spite,
But in the onset come, so shall I taste
At first the very worst of fortune's might,   12
   And other strains of woe, which now seem woe,
   Compared with loss of thee will not seem so.

If you are going to hate me, hate me now when I am suffering.
Do not be the last enemy. Let the first be worst, and nothing that happens
   after that will seem bad.

From Sonnet 76 onwards S has been haunted by the possibility that he is about to lose the beloved, a possibility which he presented as a farewell in 87, a willingness to accept all the blame in 88, and in 89 a promise that if the beloved left him he would not enter his life in any way. Here, S begs that if the blow must fall it should fall immediately. Despite the tone of resignation, S insists in each of these sonnets that he still loves, and pleads for pity and a return to love, at the same time implying that the beloved is responsible for the breach.

1–4 He ended Sonnet 89 by talking as though the beloved hated him. Immediately Sonnet 90 begins by asking the beloved to hate him, if ever, now. This is manipulative, 'You hate me. So hate me when you want, if ever [you want, and if you do, do it] now.' 'If ever, now' sounds like

279

natural speech rising out of misery, and the monosyllables are part of that effect. This is clearly an appeal to the beloved, 'Surely it hasn't come to this?'

To support the appeal for pity S now invokes his present misfortunes (which are unknown to readers of the poems). 'The world is bent my deeds to cross' is almost a live metaphor of the world veering from its own course in order to block his. And spiteful fortune is heaping burdens on him to make him stoop under their weight. In line 4, 'do not drop in' has not been explained. Editors cite *AC* 3.13.163–4, where Cleopatra asks for heaven to send poison hail if her heart is ever cold towards Antony, and let 'the first stone drop in my neck', where 'stone' is a hailstone and therefore not relevant. The phrase may be dignified, 'Do not fall into my life', but it is more likely to be the precursor of our informal 'Do drop in for a glass of wine', a colloquialism not recorded before Pepys (1667), 'Mr. Pierce, the surgeon, dropped in' (*OED* 27). This interpretation has been condemned as bathetic, but bathos would be eloquent if it suggested that the beloved's behaviour was likely to be casual and heartless. 'After-loss' sounds like a brilliant coinage. Although *OED* cites dozens of compounds of 'after' from afterbirth and after-clap to after-wit, neither commentaries nor dictionaries offer other instances.

5–8 These four lines say the same as 1–4, using a military metaphor. He wants the beloved's rejection not to come after he has *'scaped* a sorrow, as the *rearward* of defeated enemies, where 'rearward' is our rearguard, as in 'the soldiers of our rearward' in Philemon Holland (1609). In its application he asks the beloved not to wait till he has *conquered* other woes and then leave him; if his purpose is to *overthrow* him, let him not drag out the campaign, not 'linger out a purposed overthrow.' The military metaphor extends to *onset* in 11, the first wave of an attack, and to *might* in 12, as in 139.7.

The power of the spoken language registers in the repetition of 'now' in the first two lines (it is as though we are listening to a man trying to explain himself); in line 5 with 'Ah, do not' coming after 'And do not' in 4; and 'Give not a windy night a rainy morrow' is like the proverbial weather saw 'Small rain allays great winds' quoted by Burrow (2002) on *Luc* 1788.

9–14 Plain language continues with repetition and plain monosyllables in the appeal, 'If thou wilt leave me, do not leave me last'; in 11–12 with the hiss of 'last … spite … onset … taste … first … worst'; and at the end, where the lameness of the last four words of 13 and 14 could be read as though the speaker was not quite persuading himself, and the verse almost breaks down at the strange rhyme, 'seem woe' with 'seem so'.

'Strains' in Shakespeare often refers to breeds or lineages, but here simply to kinds. The first 12 lines of the sonnet form a setting for the final couplet, a brave epigram but not convincing. Its value is that it makes yet another compliment to the beloved, and yet another declaration of love, no matter that his wish that the beloved's hatred would come before other ills will be contradicted in Sonnet 92, where hate would cause his instant death.

The logic is signposted: two commands in lines 1 and 3, negative commands in 4, 5, 7 and 9, rounded off with a return to the positive in 11, 'But in the onset come'. This edition divides after line 8 to mark the beginning of the reason for this implausible request. The loss of the beloved would cause him such grief that nothing else he could ever suffer would seem like grief, a glowing compliment and a reiteration of love.

Vendler (1997)
The true organiser of 90 is the word *woe*. Its essential graphic components, in both true and reversed order (*wo, ow*), are sprinkled eleven times through the poem: now, now, world, bow, sorrow, woe, morrow, overthrow, worst, woe, woe. Seven of the eleven instances appear in the rhyme position, in both phonemic possibilities, 'oh' and 'wo', and the usage is thereby conspicuously foregrounded.

ஒ 91 ଐ

Some glory in their birth, some in their skill,
Some in their wealth, some in their bodies' force,
Some in their garments though new-fangled ill,
Some in their hawks and hounds, some in their horse,   4
And every humour hath his adjunct pleasure
Wherein it finds a joy above the rest.

But these particulars are not my measure.
All these I better in one general best.   8
Thy love is better than high birth to me,
Richer than wealth, prouder than garments' cost,
Of more delight than hawks or horses be,
And having thee, of all men's pride I boast,   12

    Wretched in this alone, that thou mayst take
    All this away, and me most wretched make.

Different people take pride and pleasure in different things,
but my delight is general, better than all these particulars.
    Through your love I boast of everything that men take pride in,
wretched only because, if I lose you, I become the most wretched of men.

1–6 Different people glory in different activities, and find pleasure in
them. Seven groups are mentioned, and only one, in line 3, is explicitly
criticised. What is 'new-fangled' is the fashion of the moment, and it is
showy. What is 'new-fangled ill' is also badly made, therefore not only
showy but also shoddy. Although the other six activities are listed without
comment, there does seem to be the ghost of a smile at those who 'glory in
their birth', then in the near-rhyme between 'birth' and 'wealth', and in
the country sports in line 4, where hunting with hawks and hounds and
horse are carefully distinguished, but all three described in terms of the
animals involved, and all beginning with the same letter. If S is expressing
some amusement at these activities, the alliteration in 'humour hath his' in

282

the following line may continue it. To accompany the plural 'hawks and hounds', 'horse' could be taken to be a plural as commonly used, for example in *TS* 3.3.78–9, where Petruccio calls for his horse, and his servant replies, 'Ay, sir, they be ready.'

In ancient and medieval physiology, the temperament is formed by the mixture, *temperamentum*, of the four chief fluids or 'humours' in the body – blood, phlegm, choler and black bile (in Greek *melancholia*). In line 5 it is the blend of these fluids that makes a man take up some activity – hunting, say, or prettifying himself – and each activity gives to its practitioner the pleasure connected with it, 'its adjunct pleasure', in which he takes far more delight than he takes in anything else.

7–12   In 7–8, S declares that the measure of these particular joys is not the measure he uses in assessing his own. His joy is not particular but general, and is better than all these others. What is this general best? 'Thy love' is the answer, and S supports the claim by slighting half of the list of the other pleasures, and the tone is humorous. His love is 'bétter than high bírth', where the force comes in the alliteration and in the stress which is almost demanded on 'hígh'. It is also 'rícher than wéalth', a striking paradox, and 'prouder than garment's cost', mildly mocking, since 'cost' is ostentatious display of wealth, as in 'the rich proud cost of outworn buried age' in 64.2. 'Pride' too has a satirical edge when applied to ostentatious dress, as in *H8* 1.1.23–5, 'The *mesdames*, too, | Not used to toil, did almost sweat to bear | The pride upon them.' The horse has become horses, and the hounds have disappeared. It is as though these pursuits are trivial and of no consequence, 'All these I better in one general best.'

This is a risky argument. To say that some glory in X and some in Y, but I glory more in Z, is reasonable. To say that X and Y are particulars, but that Z is general, would be difficult to maintain. He tries to conceal this difficulty in line 12, where he boasts 'of all men's pride', meaning presumably that his pride in his love is equal to the whole sum of pride taken by all other men in all their different pursuits. But that still does not make his delight general rather than particular. He is straining language and logic to reach towards the peerless quality of this love of his.

13–14   The conclusion is a play of opposites. He *boasts all* men's pride, but he is *wretched* in *this* respect *alone*, namely that the beloved could take *all this* away, and make him *most* wretched [of *all* men]. After the boasting in 1–12, the tone suddenly changes and the truth emerges. He *is* wretched and he knows that he could be the *most* wretched of men if he lost his love. Sonnets 87–90 have shown that this is a real fear.

Classical Background

> Some say that an army of horsemen
> is the most beautiful thing upon the black earth,
> others an army of foot-soldiers or a fleet of ships,
> but for me it is whatever one loves.

So wrote Sappho in the seventh century BC, and this structure is often found in Greek and Roman literature, in Pindar, for example, at the beginning of the first *Olympian* and Xenophon in *Memorabilia* 1.6.14. Shakespeare will have heard it in Psalm 20: 7, 'Some trust in chariots, and some in horses: but we will remember the name of the LORD our God.' The most famous example is the first of Horace's *Odes*, where he pokes gentle fun at those who enjoy chariot racing, politics, money-making, farming, seafaring to pursue the import trade, drinking, war and hunting. Then:

> As for me, it is ivy, the reward of learned brows,
> that puts me among the gods above. As for me,
> the cold grove and light-footed choruses of nymphs
> and satyrs set me apart from the people,
> if Euterpe lets me play her pipes and Polyhymnia
> does not refuse me her Lesbian lyre.
> But if you enrol me among the lyric poets,
> my soaring head will touch the stars.

Like Shakespeare, Horace makes fun of other people's pleasures. The competitor in the Olympian Games rises to the gods when he collects dust on his chariot and scorches the wheels as he grazes the turning post. The huntsman stays out under a cold sky, forgetting his young wife; Horace too is out in the cold woods but with Greek nymphs and randy males. Horace's soaring head will touch the stars, but not too seriously. S does not make fun of himself, and ends with an epigram that darkens the delight of 11–12 with wretchedness. Horace does not go in for being wretched.

The point of all this is not to establish that Shakespeare is writing in the form of a priamel (as studied by Race (1982)), nor to point to similarities (they are not important), but to focus on differences. Horace mentions

284

eight different ways of life, and describes his own as though it is *similar* to two of them. S mentions seven delights and says that his way is *better* than all of them. Horace is serious about his writing but talks lightly about it, while S makes a bold claim and a dubious boast – that his love is general whereas others are particular. This comparison brings out the more cerebral quality of the sonnet. It presents an intellectual argument, and like all the sonnets it is an exploration of love. Horace's poem has a broader human interest, and a greater variety of tone. In the ode there is more humour than wit, whereas the sonnet has more wit than humour.

What is surprising about this declaration of love is that it follows so soon upon the grand farewell to love in Sonnet 87. This could be an argument against the suggestion in these notes that the Sonnets are a continuous love drama. On this interpretation they might appear rather to be a collection of separate poems. But these notes argue that this is a dramatic series of words by a lover to his beloved. In Sonnets 78–86, S conducted a campaign against rival poets/lovers, culminating in what has been argued to be the 'false farewell' gambit in 87, followed by four more poems contemplating the end of this love. His appeals have failed, so the lover once again reverts to his familiar line, 'You and love are still my argument', as he said in 76.10, but the plot is moving on. Sonnet 87 was S's farewell to the beloved; Sonnet 91.13–14 reveals that the real danger is that the beloved will say farewell to S. Sonnet 92.1 confirms this development and Sonnets 93 and 94 accept, with anguish, that the beloved has already done so.

Burrow (2002), on 'humour' in line 5
OED's first instance of the word in this sense is from Healey's translation of St Augustine's *City of God* (1610), a work which was being set in Eld's print-shop at roughly the same time as the Sonnets.

But do thy worst to steal thyself away,
For term of life thou art assurèd mine,
And life no longer than thy love will stay,
For it depends upon that love of thine.   4
Then need I not to fear the worst of wrongs,
When in the least of them my life hath end.

I see a better state to me belongs
Than that which on thy humour doth depend—   8
Thou canst not vex me with inconstant mind,
Since that my life on thy revolt doth lie.
O what a happy title do I find,
Happy to have thy love, happy to die!   12

    But what's so blessèd fair that fears no blot?
    Thou mayst be false, and yet I know it not.

You may slink away from me, but you will be mine as long as I live,
   because I will die the moment you leave me. That is the worst
   that could happen. I do not fear it, because I shall be dead.
I do not depend on your mood, because my life ends when you leave me.
   I am happy to live and happy to die.
But nothing is perfect. What if you are false and I don't know?

1–6 Sonnet 91 ended with the thought that the beloved might leave S and
make him wretched. 'But', opens Sonnet 92, 'leave me if you like. It will
not hurt me.' Like the other two sonnets which begin with 'But' (16 and
74), this poem carries on the argument where its predecessor stopped.
    Sonnet 89 started with two commands which were read as conditions,
'Say X, and I will comment', meaning '*If* you say X, I will comment.' This
sonnet too opens with a command, and could be read in the same way, '*If*
you do your worst to sneak away from me, you are securely mine for as
long as I live. I do not need to be afraid of your leaving me [the worst thing

that could happen to me], because then I would be dead, and death is the least of my fears.' The link between love and life is forged in lines 2–6 with 'life ... life ... love ... love ... life' and renewed in lines 10 and 12, 'life ... love'. He sang a different tune in Sonnet 89. There if the beloved left him S would take the blame and walk away.

It is human nature for lovers who suspect that they are about to be abandoned to think the beloved is planning to 'steal away' without being noticed. In Virgil's *Aeneid* 4.305 Dido accuses Aeneas of exactly this. He denies it a dozen lines later, and at 4.587 she wakes up one morning to see his ships leaving port in full sail. In 'for term of life' there is a legal flavour, as in *LLL* 1.1.16–18, where three men 'Have sworn for three years' term to live with me | My fellow scholars, and to keep those statutes | That are recorded in this schedule here.' The legal flavour continues in 'assured', formally assigned, which sometimes means 'betrothed', as in *CE* 3.2.145–6, when a kitchen wench laid claim to Dromio, 'called me Dromio, swore I was assured to her'.

Again and again this poetry has the dramatic immediacy of the spoken language. In line 4, for instance, before two lines of solid monosyllables, 'it depends upon your love' would be a pious platitude, but when S says, 'it depends upon that love of thine', he is somehow pointing to the beloved as he speaks. The present tense of 'hath end' is also immediate. Flat-footed grammar might prefer 'would end', but S's death is there before his eyes.

7–12 'This is much better for me than having to depend on your humour', where 'humour' could refer to temperament (91.5), but the word often suggests mood or caprice, as in *MW* 2.3.70, 'See what humour he is in.' 'Thou canst not vex me with inconstant mind' might mean that the beloved's general changeability cannot vex him, but in this erotic context inconstancy points to another fear, made explicit in 'my life on your revolt doth lie', meaning, 'I will die if you are unfaithful to me.' 'Revolt' in Shakespeare is sometimes used of inconstancy in a lover. Othello, for instance, at 3.3.192–3 said of Desdemona that he would never have 'The smallest fear or doubt of her revolt, | For she had eyes and chose me.' 'Title' in line 11 is a title deed, certifying right of possession, and therefore reactivating the legal flavour of line 2. In 11–12 each time the word 'happy' occurs it may include the notion of good fortune.

13–14 This happy title deed is 'blessèd fair', but what has such heaven-sent beauty that there is no blot on it? He asks the question and the answer is ambiguous. 'Thou mayst [at some future time] be false, and yet I know it not.' But 'mayst' could be a present tense, and that makes a much more dramatic ending. He suddenly realises that the man he loves may already be false and he does not know it. His love may already be ended and he is still alive. As in the previous sonnet, his whole brave argument dramatically collapses in the final couplet.

At 'Thou mayst' S has stopped just short of accusing the beloved of infidelity. This diplomatic ambiguity has already been part of S's strategy in this sequence of sonnets, for example in 88. If challenged, he has always been in a position to reply that he has been misunderstood.

Ovid was tortured by a similar anxiety in *Amores* 1.4.69–70, but dealt with it differently, 'But whatever happens tonight, tell me tomorrow you said no – and stick to your story', these last words translating '*constanti voce*', in Guy Lee's delicious 1968 translation.

So shall I live, supposing thou art true,
Like a deceivèd husband. So love's face
May still seem love to me, though altered new,
Thy looks with me, thy heart in other place.   4
For there can live no hatred in thine eye,
Therefore in that I cannot know thy change.

In many's looks the false heart's history
Is writ in moods and frowns and wrinkles strange,   8
But Heav'n in thy creation did decree
That in thy face sweet love should ever dwell;
Whate'er thy thoughts or thy heart's workings be,
Thy looks should nothing thence but sweetness tell.   12

How like Eve's apple doth thy beauty grow
If thy sweet virtue answer not thy show.

So I shall be like a deceived husband, assuming you are true.
   So love may seem still to be love although you love someone else.
   Since hate cannot live in your eye, I cannot know you have changed.
Many faces show their falseness; yours shows only sweet love.
Your beauty is like Eve's apple if your virtue be not as sweet as it looks.

1–6 Sonnet 90 began with 'Then' to link it with 89; Sonnet 92 began with 'But' to link it to 91; Sonnet 93 begins with 'So' to link it with 92.14, 'Thou mayst be false, and yet I know it not.' He continues: 'In that case [So], I will behave like a deceived husband and assume that you are true.' The pattern is repeated in lines 2–4. 'In that case [So again] love's appearance may still seem true to me' although it is altered. But the text reads not 'appearance' but 'face'. 'Love's face' is indeed the appearance of love, but it is also the face of S's beloved, important in this poem, with 'looks ... eye ... looks ... frowns ... wrinkles ... face ... looks ... show' all bitterly contrasted with 'heart' in 4, 7 and 11.

S knows that he is being betrayed, and is manoeuvring. The best possible result would be that the beloved would refute the charge, but S does not dare make it directly, in case refutation is not forthcoming. Next best is that the beloved would confess, apologise, and swear to be true in the future. For that eventuality S must tread softly, speak lovingly, and avoid direct accusations, but there is no doubt about his bitterness. Gloomy suspicion lurks in every line from 1 to 6 (except 4), and from 11-14 (except 12). 'Thy heart in other place' is a way of saying, 'thy heart with another lover', and the bitterness is smeared with honey in lines 5, 9–10 and 12. S knows he cannot argue with a face which reveals nothing, and for the sake of the future he sweetens his suspicions with compliments.

'For' in 5 is equal to 'because' and is picked up by 'Therefore'. '*Because* there can live no hatred in thine eye, *for that reason* in that [eye] I cannot know thy change.'

7–12 Many have the history of their false hearts written on their faces in the form of passing moods and frowns, and the strange wrinkles which record them, but the beloved is different. Heaven has decreed that sweet love should always live in his face, whatever is in his heart. The double edge cuts. S praises his sweetness, but realises that it reveals nothing. No matter what he is thinking or feeling, 'thence', from his face, his looks always register sweetness.

13–14 The compliments stop, and S looks below the surface. In Genesis 3: 6, 'When the woman saw that the tree was good for food, and that it was pleasant to the eyes, and a tree to be desired to make one wise, she took of the fruit thereof, and did eat, and gave also to her husband with her; and he did eat.' But there is many 'A goodly apple rotten at the heart. | O, what a goodly outside falsehood hath!' (*MV* 1.3.100–1). Sweetness may have a rotten core, '*If* thy sweet virtue answer not thy show.' As at the end of 91 and 92, S stops just short of accusing the beloved of infidelity.

The Garden of Eden is the setting for lines 13–14. Heaven decreed the creation of the beloved in line 9, and Adam 'is of course the original *deceived husband*' (Burrow 2002).

They that have power to hurt and will do none,
That do not do the thing they most do show,
Who moving others are themselves as stone,
Unmovèd, cold, and to temptation slow,   4

They rightly do inherit Heaven's graces
And husband nature's riches from expense.
They are the lords and owners of their faces,
Others but stewards of their excellence.   8

The summer's flower is to the summer sweet,
Though to itself it only live and die,
But if that flower with base infection meet,
The basest weed outbraves his dignity.   12
    For sweetest things turn sourest by their deeds:
    Lilies that fester smell far worse than weeds.

Those who can hurt and do none, who do not do what they do look capable
    of, who move others but themselves feel no emotion—
they husband what Heaven has given them and control their faces,
    unlike those who do not have full mastery over their gifts.
The summer flower is sweet though it lives only for itself;
    lilies that fester smell far worse than weeds.

'This elusive poem is perhaps the most discussed in the collection' (Kerrigan 1986). The crucial difficulty lies in lines 3–4 describing those 'Who moving others are themselves as stone, | Unmovèd, cold'. These are harsh words expressing a negative judgement, but they are set in eight lines full of terms of approval and praise from the first line through 'rightly', 'Heaven's graces', 'nature's riches', 'lords and owners'. Flattery to cushion scolding has just been seen in 93.5, 9–10 and 12.

In Sonnets 87–94, S suspects that the beloved is going to leave him, or may already have done so. In 87 he takes leave of the beloved, 'Farewell, thou art too dear for my possessing', and there is no word of complaint or jealousy, only an admission of his own unworthiness (he feels it has all been a dream and he is now awake). In 88 if the beloved does leave him he will publicly declare that the beloved is in the right (although there are suggestions, notably in lines 4 and 14, that this is not the truth). In 89 he is willing to admit to any offence the beloved may accuse him of and to accept the end of love without complaining (but line 14 reveals what it will cost him). Sonnet 90 begs the beloved to leave now if he is going to leave (but lines 13–14 reveal that this is the cruellest blow that could ever fall on him). In 91 his love makes him the happiest man alive (but lines 13–14 admit that he is wretched). In 92 he again is happy, now because he cannot live to lose his love, but would die if his love was false to him (but lines 13–14 destroy that position – what if the beloved were false and he does not know it?). If he were betrayed, argues Sonnet 93, he would not know it because the beloved's face always shows only love ('How like Eve's apple ...). In 90, 92 and 93 each first word picks up the last words of the poem that goes before, binding these sonnets into a coherent sequence. 'Show' is the last word in 93.1 and in 94.2; 93 ends with a rotten apple and 94 with festering lilies; 93 and 94 both brood over the inscrutability of the beloved's features, fearing they are false, and fearing to say so.

Throughout this sequence he never says outright that the beloved has been unfaithful, but carefully words his fears with such terms as 'mayst' and 'if'. And each sonnet has a similar general shape – a complimentary opening and a sting in the tail. They are scorpion sonnets:

In sleep a king, but waking no such matter.	87.14
That for thy right, myself will bear all wrong.	88.14
For I must ne'er love him whom thou dost hate.	89.14
And other strains of woe, which now seem woe,	
Compared with loss of thee will not seem so.	90.13–14
Wretched in this alone, that thou mayst take	
All this away, and me most wretched make.	91.13–14
Thou mayst be false, and yet I know it not.	92.14
How like Eve's apple doth thy beauty grow	
If thy sweet virtue answer not thy show.	93.13–14
For sweetest things turn sourest by their deeds:	
Lilies that fester smell far worse than weeds.	94.13–14
Take heed, dear heart, of this large privilege:	
The hardest knife ill-used doth lose his edge.	95.13–14

1–4   In 87–93 the complimentary preambles have been substantial, some-times filling the first 12 lines. All these sonnets practise a standard tech-nique of ancient oratory, *conciliatio benevolentiae*, winning the approval of the audience, in this case the beloved. Here in Sonnet 94 *conciliatio* is curtailed. Only lines 1 and 5–8 are favourable, or seem to be.

In Sonnet 93 Heaven decreed that in the beloved's face 'sweet love should ever dwell', and now in 94 lines 1–2 and 5–8 also seem to make a virtue of that unchanging face, but this apparent praise is interrupted and undermined by the bitterness of lines 3–4. 'To temptation slow' might seem to be a compliment, but, although it might be praise on the lips of a priest, it is anything but on the lips of a lover, particularly after the condemnation in 'as stone, | Unmovèd, cold'. The virtuous Angelo who is corrupted by power in *MM* is 'a man whose blood | Is very snow broth; one who never feels | The wanton stings and motions of the sense' (1.4.56–8). Here 'the effect is of a desperate search for terms of praise with which to describe someone who has caused ... pain' (Burrow 2002). The explanation of the elusiveness of this poem is that it is a continuation of 93. It repeats the calculated gambit of 93.6, 'no hatred in thine eye ... I cannot know thy change', and of 93.10–11, 'in thy face sweet love should ever dwell, | Whate'er thy thoughts', the same flattery and the same bitterness, just falling short of outright accusation. S is doing everything in his power to take a charitable view of the behaviour of the beloved, and to tread softly. 'Rightly' in line 5 has to be read as an attempt to sweeten criticism by making it sound like praise, but bitterness prevails. The summer's flower is sweet, but he knows that 'sweetest things turn sourest by their deeds: | Lilies that fester smell far worse than weeds.'

The striking effect in the first two lines is the sound, as stripped down in the paraphrase given above, and intensified by the monosyllables. Rollins (1944) calls this an 'unpleasant repetition', but the plainness of the utterance, with its four occurrences of 'do', carries a portentous solemnity, perhaps aided by a distant recollection of the despairing words of the General Confession in the Book of Common Prayer, with its four occurrences of '(un)done', 'We have left undone those things which we ought to have done; And we have done those things which we ought not to have done; And there is no health in us.' The same device is used in a different situation in *AYL* 2.3.35–6, 'This I must do, or know not what to do. | Yet this I will not do, do how I can.'

5–8   In 5–8 these unfeeling people are the stony-hearted who inherit and hoard their riches, spending nothing, and they are frequently denounced in the Sonnets (2.5–9, 4.1–14 and 9.9–12). Behind them, here as in Sonnet

4, looms the parable of the talents in Matthew 25. Three servants each received talents from their lord (the word occurs in 94.7 and eight times in six verses in the parable). Two of the servants traded and accumulated and were rewarded ('Well done, thou good and faithful servant'), but the third husbanded his talent by burying it in the earth, and was in consequence cast 'into outer darkness'. Elizabethan readers might have noticed that the hoarder is praised in 94.5–6, but condemned in the parable.

9–14 The beloved was the wicked and slothful servant, and now his beauty becomes a summer flower, living and dying only to itself. It does add to the sweetness of the season, but its fragrance will turn to stench if it becomes diseased. The beloved is associated with 'beauty's rose' as early as the second line of the first sonnet. Now 'The basest weed outbraves his dignity', and the ambiguous personal pronoun, 'his', refers first to the flower but, being standard for 'its', also sharpens the allusion to the man.

As in 93.9–14, sweetness carries the argument from praise to warning in 94.9–14, but here the tone is more bitter, with base infection setting in and reducing sweetness and dignity to rottenness. The target is clearly the beloved, but still there is no direct accusation of infidelity, only the hazards to the summer flower in lines 9–14, 'if that flower with base infection meet'. It does not actually say that the beloved is infected, but there is no doubt that he is.

The next development in the plot of the Sonnets will come in the direct accusation of shame and sin and sport and ill report and vices and blot in Sonnet 95. Lines 9–14 of Sonnet 94 are a turning point in the drama, and all the more powerful because the poem is impersonal. 'For the first and almost the last time ... Shakespeare writes impersonally, neither addressing the friend, nor describing him explicitly as he, and scrupulously avoiding *I* and *me* and *my*' (Kerrigan 1986). But 95 will tell it plain, 'O in what sweets dost thou thy sins enclose!'

How sweet and lovely dost thou make the shame
Which like a canker in the fragrant rose
Doth spot the beauty of thy budding name!
O in what sweets dost thou thy sins enclose!   4

The tongue that tells the story of thy days,
Making lascivious comments on thy sport,
Cannot dispraise but in a kind of praise—
Naming thy name blesses an ill report.   8

O what a mansion have those vices got
Which for their habitation chose out thee,
Where beauty's veil doth cover every blot,
And all things turns to fair that eyes can see.   12

Take heed, dear heart, of this large privilege:
The hardest knife ill used doth lose his edge.

You are lovely but shameful, a rose with a canker just spotting the bud.
Gossip does not hurt you, because your name blesses what is said.
Your vices have a lovely home, which beautifies all the blemishes.
Be careful with the privilege. The hardest knife ill used loses its edge.

1–4   After eight poems hinting that the beloved is false, S now speaks the plain truth. This poem is clearly one of the sequence. Like most of the others it begins where its predecessor ended. Sonnet 93 ended with Eve's apple. Sonnet 94 ended with 'Lilies that fester' and Sonnet 95 begins with 'a canker in the fragrant rose'. Sweetness links three sonnets, ending 93 three times, and 94 twice, where 'sweetest things turn sourest'. Now it begins 95 twice, where shame is made sweet, and sweets enclose sins.

   The canker is the vice that loves the sweetest buds in 70.7 and the beloved was free of it. Here it is just beginning to show as a spot on the outside of the bud, and the beloved's sins are just beginning to destroy his good name before he reaches maturity. What starts as simile, 'like a canker', becomes more powerful by gliding into metaphor as shame, 'Doth spot the beauty of thy budding name'. S is not content to say that the beloved is like a diseased rose, but presses on to see his name as a bud with a spot on it. This same glide occurs famously in 29.12, where 'my state, | Like to the lark' is a simile which glides into metaphor when that state 'sings hymns at heaven's gate'.

5–8 The 'tongue' in line 5 is the collective tongue of gossip. Comments are elaborate explanations, more commentaries than comments (see 89.2), and sport is often amorous in Shakespeare, as it clearly is in 96.2. S does not say what the beloved's sins are, but gossip does. S is accusing the beloved, but softening the blow by suggesting that the accusation is not from him, but from common talk. He goes on to tone this down even further, by saying that not even lewd talk can amount to criticism, because the very mention of the beloved's name turns dispraise into praise. Again, as often in the last dozen sonnets, S is using praise to soften criticism. Three times he refers to the beloved's good name, in lines 3 and 8, in an attempt to persuade him to preserve it.

9–12 He drops the pose that gossip speaks and not himself, as yet another metaphor begins, when the beloved's vices are tenants in a lovely house. If the metaphor were sustained they would have sought out this lovely house so that they could practise their sins behind the curtains, but no. In line 11 it is not curtains but a *veil* that 'covers every *blot*' (two new metaphors in one line) and turns everything into beauty.

13–14 After indictment, endearment, 'Take heed, dear heart'. The last line sounds like a proverb but is not cited anywhere before Shakespeare. Hamlet is full of clichés, and Shakespeare is our greatest composer of proverbs.

Salacious commentators find a phallic suggestion. 'You are keen, my lord, you are keen,' says Ophelia to Hamlet (*Ham* 3.2.236–7), and there is no mistaking the sexual implication of his answer, 'It would cost you a groaning to take off mine edge.' But here the sonnet is arguing that a young man with a good reputation can ruin it by bad behaviour, and it is absurd to find the notion that 'ill-judged promiscuity threatens the young man's potency' (Duncan-Jones 1997). Although 'swords and penises are commonly associated in the period' (Burrow 2002), this thought does not fit the argument, or the tone. S is threatening the young man with disgrace, not with impotence.

Some say thy fault is youth, some wantonness,
Some say thy grace is youth and gentle sport.
Both grace and faults are loved of more and less.
Thou mak'st faults graces that to thee resort.   4

As on the finger of a thronèd queen
The basest jewel will be well esteemed,
So are those errors that in thee are seen
To truths translated, and for true things deemed.   8

How many lambs might the stern wolf betray
If like a lamb he could his looks translate?
How many gazers mightst thou lead away
If thou wouldst use the strength of all thy state?   12

But do not so; I love thee in such sort
As thou being mine, mine is thy good report.

*Some say your fault is your youth, some say it is sexual indulgence,
    some say your charm is your youth and high spirits.
Just as a cheap jewel on a queen's finger is much admired,
    so your errors are thought to be admirable.
A wolf might deceive many a lamb if he could look like one.
    If you wished, you might lead away many an admirer.
Don't do that. You are mine. So your good name is mine.*

1–4 The first two lines present three opinions of the beloved's behaviour:
that his fault is his youth; more sternly, that it is his wantonness (lines 11–12,
not to mention the thrust of the last ten sonnets, make it clear that this charge
relates to his sexual conduct); more indulgently, that these are not faults but
graces, attractive features natural to his youth – not wantonness but the
high spirits expected in a young gentleman. Polonius warned Ophelia that
young Hamlet could 'walk with a larger tether' (*Ham* 1.3.125–6).

Surprisingly, his actions, whether said to be faults or graces, are loved 'of more and less' which means 'by high and low' (see *Mac* 5.4.12 and *2H4* 1.1.208). This makes good sense after 'gentle' in the second line (see 81.9). The nobility, the 'more', love to see such liveliness in a young gentleman, and so do the lower classes, the 'less'. The reason follows. [Such is his charm that] he makes the faults that gather round him seem like graces. His faults have become his retinue. 'The image is of a great lord whose suitors arrive as *faults*, but are immediately elevated to *graces*' (Duncan-Jones 1997).

Chiasmus, the ABBA structure, is frequent in these poems. Here, the arrangement is varied, 'fault … grace … grace … faults … faults … graces'.

5–8　The simile compares a cheap jewel, admired when worn by a queen, to the beloved's errors judged true because he committed them. The telling words are 'true' and 'true things'. They apply to the jewel in the simile, which is false but praised as though it were genuine, and to the young man's faults of inconstancy. They are faults, but are 'translated', transformed into truth. The most famous translation in this sense is in *MND* 3.1.113, 'Bless thee, Bottom, bless thee. Thou art translated.'

9–12　What follows is no simile – there is no 'just as the stern wolf … so'. It is not a metaphor – S does not say that the beloved is a wolf. Call it rather an analogy – suddenly the topic is wolves and lambs, and readers have to wait for the relevance. 'How many lambs might the cruel wolf deceive if he had the power to translate his looks [to make himself] like a lamb?' Now the relevance: 'How many admirers might the beloved lead away if he exploited the strength of all his state, presumably the power derived from his high rank, wealth and beauty?' Line 12 reactivates the thought of his aristocratic status which was touched upon in lines 2 and 3.

It is standard practice to fit the terms of an image tally with terms in the literal, as 'translate(d)' in line 8 links the literal to the analogy in line 10, and as 'gazers' and 'lead away' do here. Just as a wolf disguised as a lamb might betray lambs by leading them away from the flock, so the beloved could lead away gazers who adored his beauty, and 'gazers' may suggest grazers, in this context sheep. It is an instinct of lambs to follow. 'Grazer' occurs only here in Shakespeare, but the same fanciful connection was to catch Shakespeare's imagination in *WT* 4.4.108–9, where Camillo sees the shepherdess Perdita and says, 'I should leave grazing were I of your flock, | And only live by gazing.'

13–14　'Do not do this. I love you in such a way that you are mine, and therefore your good name is mine, and I do not want it destroyed.' This couplet occurs also in 36.13–14, as Kerrigan (1995) observes (see his comment below). In Sonnet 36 S did not want the beloved to ruin his reputation by consorting with a worthless person like himself. Here in Sonnet 96 he does not want the beloved's promiscuity to destroy his own reputation.

Kerrigan (1986), on lines 13–14

Shakespearean indolence or uncertainty is not impossible ... If, however, one takes the couplet as consciously deployed, it is immediately striking that 36 and 96 end the first and last groups of sonnets critical of the youth (35–6, 92–6). The common couplet makes the two groups rhyme, as it were, pointing up their relationship with a duplication entirely consistent with the intricate, echoing, repetitive mode of these late sonnets, reconsidering early concerns.

ꙮ 97 ꙮ

How like a winter hath my absence been
From thee, the pleasure of the fleeting year!
What freezings have I felt, what dark days seen,
What old December's bareness everywhere! 4

And yet this time removed was Summer's time,
The teeming Autumn big with rich increase,
Bearing the wanton burden of the Prime
Like widowed wombs after their lord's decease. 8

Yet this abundant issue seemed to me
But hope of orphans, and unfathered fruit,
For Summer and his pleasures wait on thee,
And thou away, the very birds are mute, 12
    Or if they sing, 'tis with so dull a cheer
    That leaves look pale, dreading the winter's near.

My absence has been like a winter,
and yet it has been summer and autumn, bearing the fruits of spring.
But for me it was barren and joyless. Without you birds do not sing and
*   leaves grow pale.*

1–4 The bare bones of the argument are simple, but 'This splendid sonnet does not too readily reveal all its secrets' (Ingram and Redpath 1978). It starts with a simile. The beloved's absence during summer and autumn, the pleasant parts of the year, has been like a winter. Sleepy as ever, the Quarto gives capital initials to Winter, Autumn and Summer in lines 1, 6, 11 and 14, but not to summer and prime in 5 and 7. The above version capitalises the seasons from 5 onwards to bring out the personification.

    The winter of absence has dragged on with echoing alliterations and assonance in 'What fréezings ... félt, what dárk dáys séen'. 'Freezings' is a noun only here in Shakespeare, and 'dáys' begs for emphasis against the expected iambic beat. Days should not be dark. December is an old tramp, shivering in the cold, without a coat on his back.

5–8   In 'this time removed' it is not time which has been removed but the beloved, 'this time of your absence'. Such transferred adjectives are not uncommon (see 2.11). The period of absence was summer and early autumn, before harvest (6). Autumn is personified as a pregnant woman, teeming, as in 'this teeming womb of royal kings' in the great praise of England in *R2* 2.1.51. The metaphor continues in '*big* with *rich* increase, | Bearing the *wanton* burden of the Prime ... abundant issue'. In line 8 the rich harvests of autumn are like the *wombs* of pregnant widows. Spring, their lascivious father, is no more. These four italicised terms come together in *MND* 2.1.128–31, when Titania sits upon the yellow sands with her votaress,

> When we have laughed to see the sails conceive
> And grow *big*-bellied with the *wanton* wind ...
> ... her *womb* then *rich* with my young squire.

9–14   Autumn was abundant, 'yet' her children had no father. Orphans, here as often, is used of children who have lost one parent. 'This abundant issue' is the fruit on the tree, and when it comes to fullness it is *fatherless*, as literal merges with metaphorical.

Summer is master of revels, personified by 'his', and his attendant pleasures wait upon the beloved. But there is no singing because the beloved is absent and the birds are moping. The observation is sound, but the explanation is absurd. Birds quieten down in the summer (102.7–8), but not out of sympathy with human suffering.

In line 13 the argument corrects the metaphor, 'Or if they sing, they sing so dolefully that the very leaves on the trees change colour, growing pale [and no doubt shivering with fright], thinking that winter is on the way.'

The absence of S from the beloved may be a literal absence, but, in view of the placing of this sonnet after the bitter quarrels from Sonnet 87 onwards and the apologies that follow in 100–3, the plot of the Sonnets makes it likely that this absence is a euphemism for estrangement. S has been absent from the beloved's heart, as at 41.2 an eloquent metaphor on the lips of this great metaphorist, given weight here by the ring composition. The poem begins and ends with winter, all the more severe if it implies a breach in their love. If so, this sonnet is a shrewd opening gambit in his campaign for reconciliation, which will follow in 99–109.

From you have I been absent in the spring,
When proud-pied April, dressed in all his trim,
Hath put a sp'rit of youth in every thing,
That heavy Saturn laught and leapt with him.   4

Yet not the lays of birds, nor the sweet smell
Of different flowers in odour and in hue,
Could make me any summer's story tell,
Or from their proud lap pluck them where they grew.   8
Nor did I wonder at the lily's white
Nor praise the deep vermilion in the rose.

They were but sweet, but figures of delight
Drawn after you, you pattern of all those.   12
    Yet seemed it winter still, and, you away,
    As with your shadow I with these did play.

I have been absent during all the joys of spring,
but neither bird nor flower gave me pleasure.
They were only imitations of you. For me it was winter and I was playing
*   with your shadow.*

1–4 In Sonnet 97 December was an old tramp, Autumn a pregnant
widow, Spring a wanton lover, Summer a master of revels. In Sonnet 98
April is a sprightly young man, a sharp dresser in his clown's outfit, 'the
pied coate off a foole' (*OED* 1575). 'Proud-pied' is gorgeously variegated
in colour. There is now such 'a sp'rit of youth in every thing' that even the
old god Saturn gets up to dance, though heavy with years (and in astrology
the planet associated with melancholy). His high spirits seem to be well
served by the spelling in the Quarto, not 'laughed' but 'laught' coming
after 'sp'rit'. The weight of the verse is at the beginning with 'héavy Sáturn'
and it races away at the end with 'láught and léapt with him'. The last two
words are best spoken lightly, with no emphasis on 'him'.

5–10 'Lays' is poetic diction (see 100.7), and gently sardonic. No matter how sublime the songs, S will find no cheer in them. Line 6 is another example of the freedom of Shakespeare's word order. He means 'Of flowers different in odour and in hue'. In *WT* 2.1.27 'A sad tale's best for winter', so in line 7 'summer's story' is cheerful. The lap in line 8 is the lap of mother earth, and it is proud because it is richly coloured with spring flowers.

Sometimes a line of poetry is ravishing and no explanation is necessary or possible. So it is with lines 9–10. Kermode (2002, 151) cites, without a reference, a remark by T. S. Eliot about 'the bewildering minute, the moment of dazzling recognition, from which one draws back and, having regained composure, tries to think of something to say about an experience too disconcerting to be thought of as simply pleasant.' Lines 9–10 may cause one of these bewildering moments.

Line 10 is sometimes misremembered, 'Nor praise the deep vermilion of the rose'. The mistake explains what Shakespeare wrote. The colour of rose petals lightens towards their outer edges. The deep vermilion of a red rose is seen at its deepest '*in* the rose', down at the base of the petals.

13–14 The beauties of spring are pleasant enough, but to S not real delight, only representations of it, modelled on the beloved. He is the pattern which they try to replicate. Therefore spring does not seem to be spring, but winter. The beloved being absent, S played with flowers, meaning that he enjoyed them, but only as shadows of the beloved. 'Shadow' has its usual meaning, but after 'drawn' and 'pattern' it also suggests that summer's flowers are pen or pencil drawings of the one he loved (53.10). S dotes upon the beloved, and his obsession is conveyed by the repetitions of 'you(r)' in 12–14. The beloved fills up his lines (86.13).

The commentary on 97 ended with an attempt to decide whether 'absence' referred to physical separation or emotional estrangement. From Sonnet 87 onwards there have been quarrels leading to estrangement, and the physical separation which goes with it. S is now searching for arguments which will help him to achieve reconciliation, and in speaking of absence he may be alluding tactfully to the past.

Vendler (1997)
What we do know is that *p-lay* is a compound by which the *lay* of a bird has been prefaced by the consonant (*p*) associated throughout the sonnet with the young man and the season, and visible in *proud-pied, April, spirit, leapt, proud, lap, pluck, praise, deep, pattern,* and *play*. (This erotic use of *-p-* will reach its *p*hallic apogee in 151, where it mutates into cynicism.)

ಜಿ 99 ಲ

The forward violet thus did I chide,
'Sweet thief, whence didst thou steal thy sweet that smells
If not from my love's breath? The purple pride
Which on thy soft cheek for complexion dwells
In my love's veins thou hast too grossly dyed.'   5

The lily I condemnèd for thy hand,
And buds of marjoram had stol'n thy hair.

The roses fearfully on thorns did stand,
One blushing shame, another white despair,
A third, nor red nor white, had stol'n of both,   10
And to his robb'ry had annéxed thy breath,
But for his theft, in pride of all his growth
A vengeful canker eat him up to death.

More flowers I noted, yet I none could see
But sweet or colour it had stol'n from thee.   15

I scolded the violet, 'You stole my love's fragrance,
and crudely misused the colour of his cheeks.'
Lilies were drab beside your hand and marjoram had stolen your hair.
One rose blushed, one paled with fear, a pink one stole your fragrance
but was cankered.
Every flower had stolen your sweetness or your colour.

1–5 S is addressing the beloved. He tells him that he had been in a garden
and had scolded the violet for his crimes. He details offences by the lily, the
marjoram and three different roses. The charge sheet includes 'thief ... steal
... condemnèd ... stol'n ... stol'n ... robbery ... annexed ... theft [with the
death penalty] ... stol'n'.

The blatant injustice begins with the adjective 'forward', meaning that
the violet is early, which is true, but also suggesting that it is presumptuous

and pushy, which is not true, because it is a low, shade-loving plant, proverbially shrinking. Yet in line 3 the modest violet will be accused of pride for assuming the imperial purple.

The flowers are clearly innocent as charged. This is not a serious poem, but play on a conceit. Commentators find the second line 'weakly plodding, and tautological' (Evans 1996), 'among the least metrically refined in the Sonnets' (Burrow 2002), but perhaps a good reader could do something with it to bring out the tone of mock severity. The indictment is expressed with long -e- four times, sharp sibilants in -s- and -c-, seven in ten words, subtly supported by aspirates in -th-, -f-, -wh-, -th-, -th- and -th- (the last three on alternate syllables) and the whole intoned in monosyllables. The effect of that last sentence might be suggested by bold print, **'Sweet thief, whénce didst thou stéal thy swéet that smélls ...?'** After this the key changes for the fragrance of 'If nót from my lóve's bréath'.

The violet is personified by being given a complexion. He wears the purple 'for', instead of, complexion, and he did not simply steal it. This is robbery with violence. He slit the victim's veins and steeped his petals in the current of his blood. The result is that the violet's colour is not the exquisite blue of the beloved's veins but a gross purple pride.

6–7 S has been quoting what he said in charging the violet. He now reports his other charges in indirect speech. He tells the beloved that he condemned the lily 'for', by comparison with, the beloved's hand, and says that marjoram had stolen his hair. There are many different forms of marjoram, but lines 2–3, 11 and 14 may point to sweet marjoram, which John Gerard's *Herbal* (1597) says has 'a marvellous sweet smell'. Its tiny white or purplish florets appear in dense clusters at the top of the stem. Line 7 therefore seems to be describing a head of tightly packed curls.

8–13 'The roses fearfully on thorns did stand', but roses grow on stems, not on thorns. There is a proverb, 'to stand on thorns', meaning to be anxious, to be on tenterhooks. 'The thorns we stand upon' in *WT* 4.4.585 are dangers. The red rose is stressed, conscious of his guilt and blushing with shame. The white rose is pale with fear and anxiety, and the distress of both is represented by the strain on the language. The red is blushing shame and the white is [blushing] white (!) despair, both in despair on the stand as they wait to be sentenced.

The word 'pink' is not used to denote a colour until 1720, but line 10 wittily describes it. Another rose had stolen the beloved's red and white, and mixed them (see 130.5), and had 'annexed' to that crime, added to that theft, the fragrance of the beloved's breath. 'Annex' is often used in legal contexts. For this double theft, vengeance was severe. 'Loathsome canker lives in sweetest bud' (35.4), but it does not show until the flower begins to bloom. Into this bud had crept the invisible worm, which waited till the bloom was full, 'in pride of all his growth', and then 'eat him up to death'. 'Eat' is the Elizabethan past tense. Canker does not nibble round the edges, but devours the whole bloom, eats it up from the centre.

14–15 This is not a great poem. Three points tell against it. It is the only sonnet in the collection which has 15 lines. Second, it is the only sonnet which is a reworking of someone else's poem. 'Though numerous Sonnets in the Quarto glancingly echo works by Shakespeare's contemporaries, none relies directly on a source – except 99': see Kerrigan (1986), quoted below. Third, unlike most of the other sonnets, it does not deal with a specific situation or phase of this love affair, and does not have a developing argument or dramatic movement or implied interchange between the lovers. It is rather a string of witty conceits, the sort of praise which any lover might have written at any time to his beloved.

But not every lover would have been as eloquent. One possible explanation of all this is that Shakespeare was goaded by a sonnet in Henry Constable's 1592–4 volume *Diana* (see Kerrigan 1986), and saw that the conceit had possibilities. He wrote about 40 plays in 20 years, not to mention his poetry, and this sonnet could have poured out from his teeming imagination. He may have noticed that it had 15 lines and thought that he would revise it later. Eventually it could have been put unrevised into this place in the copy which found its way to the printer. Shakespeare seems not to have read the proofs (see note on 33.14).

This subjective judge finds it has wit, fancy and music in the characterisation of the flowers. Those who doubt this should read the Constable sonnet. Shakespeare's catalogue is a comic sketch with a doting lover going round a garden and haranguing the flowers in an amusing stream of lover's flattery, exaggerated and obviously false, a joke which the recipient would see and enjoy. The prosecution opens with an indignant rhetorical question addressed to the violet, with an eloquent overspill into line 3. This is followed by a monstrous accusation of assault with violence by a violet. Line 5 has a whiff of the mysterious beauty of 98.9–10. The worst criminals are the three roses in 9–13, and they are not addressed, but stand there at the bar of justice awaiting sentence, with their guilt written on their faces as one of them is condemned on the spot to a horrible death. The final couplet, powerful because of the change of tone, drops the conceit, and finds yet another way of uttering the eternal truth, that at times for the lover there is nothing in the world so beautiful as the beloved.

The function of literary critics is to point to what's there and explain it if necessary, not to put their personal evaluations between text and reader. This note has breached this law, provoked by judgements which seem too solemn.

J. M. Robertson (1926) in Rollins (1944)
... certainly a poor production, abounding in cheap diction ... Many, probably, will agree Shakespeare never wrote such feeble stuff.

Tucker Brooke (1936) in Rollins (1944)
This sonnet is poetically the poorest in the entire collection.

Kerrigan (1986)
... the poet so insistently expounds the notion that the world is the young man's likeness that we hear the unusual but unmistakable tones of Shakespeare writing without complete conviction:

> My lady's presence makes the roses red
> Because to see her lips they blush for shame.
> The lily's leaves, for envy, pale become,
> And her white hands in them this envy bred.
> The marigold the leaves abroad doth spread,
> Because the sun's and her power is the same.
> The violet in purple colour came,
> Dyed in the blood she made my heart to shed.
> In brief, all flowers from her their virtue take;
> From her sweet breath their sweet smells do proceed ...
> From Sonnet 1.9 in Henry Constable *Diana* (1592–4)

It is surely most significant that here, where reversed semblancing has become unambiguously hyperbolic, and the world of things been reduced to a set of conventional types (the violet, the lily, the damasked roses) – it is surely striking that here, uniquely in the volume, Shakespeare has written directly through a source ... and even so produced something formally irregular: an odd fifteen lines. 'Unfinished', say the editors; 'unrevised'. But one wonders whether the author of *A Lover's Complaint*, the scourge of bloated praise and 'proud compare', could, even in seeking to make his friend an Adonis, have wished to bring such a poem as this quite round.

Evans (1996)
... [perhaps] a first or early draft which he failed to revise. Some evidence for this may perhaps be seen in the weakly plodding and tautological second line and the syntactical confusion in the relation of lines 6 and 7.

Duncan-Jones (1997)
The extra-long sonnet is slack rather than rich.

ॐ 100 ॐ

Where art thou Muse, that thou forget'st so long
To speak of that which gives thee all thy might?
Spend'st thou thy fury on some worthless song,
Dark'ning thy power to lend base subjects light?   4

Return, forgetful Muse, and straight redeem
In gentle numbers time so idly spent.
Sing to the ear that doth thy lays esteem,
And gives thy pen both skill and argument.   8

Rise, resty Muse, my love's sweet face survey,
If Time have any wrinkle graven there.
If any, be a satire to decay,
And make Time's spoils despisèd everywhere.   12

     Give my love fame faster than Time wastes life.
     So thou prevent'st his scythe and crooked knife.

Where are you, Muse, ignoring what gives you your power?
     Are you wasting your poetic passion on rubbish?
Come back and atone for your idleness. Sing to my beloved,
     who values you and gives you your skill and your subject.
Awake, look at his face. Has it any wrinkles? If so, jeer at them.
Give fame to my love faster than Time diminishes life,
     and so prevent his scythe.

1–4 Sonnets 97 and 98 brood on absence. Now the Muse has been absent,
forgetting to inspire poems in praise of the beloved, the giver of her
strength. The rhetorical question in the first two lines is barbed with
monosyllables. 'Fury' is the 'poet's rage' of 17.11. Has she been squandering this gift, 'Dárk'ning thy pówer to lend báse súbjects líght'? According
to the Conjectural Chronology in Grazia and Wells (2001), xix–xx, Shakespeare wrote the Sonnets between 1593 and 1603, and during that period

he wrote the poems and more than 20 plays, and none of them is 'a worthless song'.

5–8 The tone is severe. The Muse has to redeem the time she has wasted and do it 'straight', immediately. The word has an amusing tinge to it here and at 45.14 and 89.3. The tautness of the writing in these poems often comes in the interaction of opposites, *spending* on what is *worthless*, *darkening* in order to give *light*, *base* opposed to *gentle*, *redeeming* in numbers what is *spent*. Perhaps 'numbers' continues the financial picture as the coinage for this transaction, buying back in numbers. Line 8 says what has been said before (38.2–3), that the beloved provides the inspiration, and the subject matter.

9–12 The Muse is *resty*, an old word for 'indolent', confirming the idleness of line 6, as in 'Weariness | Can snore upon the flint when resty sloth | finds the down pillow hard' (*Cym* 3.6.33–5). The Muse, who has been asked to sing to the beloved's ear, is now told to look at his face [to see] if any wrinkles have been engraved on it during her long absence. If this is even a possibility it means that it has not been a short separation that has led to this break in the stream of poems of love. If the Muse sees any wrinkles she must become 'a satire to decay', make a mockery of it. Decay is the work of time, 'Time's spoils'. S bids his Muse bring them into contempt everywhere.

13–14 She is to perform this task by giving fame to the beloved faster than Time can cause decay and waste of life. 'Prevent' has its literal Latin sense of 'come before', as in George Herbert's 'Self-Condemnation' (*The Temple*, 1633), where he argues that by our sins we anticipate our punishments at the Last Judgement: 'Thus we prevent the last great day, | And judge ourselves.' 'Give my love fame,' says S, 'and by doing so you move faster than Time. You give immortal life before his "scythe and crooked knife" can do their work.' 'Scythe and crooked knife' is sometimes condemned as an empty hendiadys (the Greek for 'one by means of two'), padding to fill out the metre, but a 'crooked knife' is a sickle and that is not the same as a scythe. The poem ends by calling up the standard picture of old man Time at work swishing his scythe in grain crops and long grass in the fields of life, but he also prunes shrubs and hedges with a sickle.

Taken in context, after the bitter farewell poems of 87–96, Sonnets 97 and 98 can be read as S's opening gambits towards a reconciliation, by describing his suffering during the separation; and now Sonnets 100–3 are working towards the same objective. After the cheerful fancy of 99 these four poems support his case not with reference to inconstancy, but by witty excuses for the break in the flow of poems of love. Evans's headnote points the way, describing it as 'an obvious self-excusing ploy by which he attributes his silence to his "forgetful" and wandering Muse'. She is a truant in 101.1.

The syntax is a clue to the tone – two accusing rhetorical questions followed by a stream of seven commands in lines 5, 7, 9, 11, 12 and 13. She has fallen down on her duty through forgetfulness and laziness, and he is letting her know exactly what she must now do to redeem herself. Sonnet 99 was an indictment of flowers, obviously unjust and unrealistic, a *jeu d'esprit*. In 100 S admits that his flood of love poems has dried up, and he has found someone to blame. The fault is not his, but the Muse's, and he is giving her a good talking to.

This cannot be serious. S and the beloved and any reader at any time after the writing of this poem would know that the failure of the Muse is the failure of the poet, and that his silence is caused by the break in their love recorded in 87–98. This is yet another humorous insight into the slipperiness of this lover, in lines 2 and 8 admitting the importance of the beloved and hinting at his own gratitude, condemning the worthlessness of his other writings in 3–6, praising the beloved's taste in 7, his beauty in 9, and promising him immortality, all this in a high-spirited assault on a culprit whom they both knew was entirely innocent. It is negotiation with a smile, an olive branch offering and asking for a renewal of love. Line 7 is part of the stratagem, 'You like what I used to write.' Evans (1996) does not see humour here, 'Many critics feel that 100–103 lack any sense of conviction or emotional involvement.'

Vendler (1997), on Sonnets 100, 101, 103
All of these sonnets represent the displacement of the poet's anxiety of performance onto his surrogate the Muse.

� 101 ✂

O truant Muse, what shall be thy amends
For thy neglect of truth in beauty dyed?
Both truth and beauty on my love depends;
So dost thou too, and therein dignified. 4

Make answer Muse. Wilt thou not haply say,
'Truth needs no colour with his colour fixed,
Beauty no pencil, beauty's truth to lay,
But best is best if never intermixed?' 8

Because he needs no praise, wilt thou be dumb?
Excuse not silence so, for't lies in thee
To make him much outlive a gilded tomb,
And to be praised of ages yet to be. 12
        Then do thy office, Muse. I teach thee how
        To make him seem long hence as he shows now.

You have played truant, Muse, and neglected my beloved's truth and beauty.
Perhaps you will say that truth and beauty need no paint.
Just because he needs no praise, that does not mean that you can be silent.
    You have it in your power to make him immortal. Do your duty.
    I'm teaching you how to preserve his beauty for posterity.

1–4 Shakespeare, being a dramatist, has invented a scene in which S is a
teacher and his Muse, who was an idler in Sonnet 100, is now a naughty
pupil. She has played truant, and teacher is asking her, as teachers do, what
shall be a suitable punishment for her neglect. Truth and beauty depends
on the beloved (Elizabethan English happily gives a singular verb to a plural
subject, as at 41.3–4). They could not exist without him, nor could the Muse.

5–8 The schoolmaster speaks severely to his idle pupil. 'Answer me, girl.
You will perhaps say that truth and beauty need no poetic colouring from
you, that truth, whose colour is fixed, cannot be improved by poetic paint.'

In line 7 'pencil' is an artist's brush, etymologically a diminutive of the Latin *penis*, a tail, and 'to lay' is 'to put on in layers' (*OED* 41a, citing from 1570, 'to laie colour on a picture'), as in Milton's tirade against the 'Gods ridiculous' of the Greeks, with 'their swelling Epithetes thick laid | As varnish on a Harlot's cheek' (*Paradise Regained* 4.343–4). So truth and beauty need no paint.

This clever and impertinent pupil dresses up her answer in systematic repetitions of truth, colour, beauty and best, as though it were a philosophical argument, as she dares to mimic and cap her master's repetitions of lines 2–3. But this imagined rascal is even cleverer than that. She even has the wit to correct her teacher. Lines 2–3 imply that the beloved is truth *dyed* in beauty. Now the pupil cheekily argues back, saying that truth 'with his colour fixed', does not need colour.

9–14 Having invented arguments for his pupil, this schoolmaster now demolishes them. 'Of course, we all know he needs no praise, but that does not mean you can be silent. You have it in your power to win him immortal fame. I'm here to teach you how. Off you go, do your duty, and make him live for ages yet to come.'

Commentators do not hear the voices of teacher and pupil in this sonnet, but the interpretation is signalled by 'I teach thee how' in line 13, which rounds off the truancy with which the poem begins. Between, the teacher probably puts a schoolmasterly edge on the first line by giving 'shall' its iambic stress, 'what sháll be thy aménds ...?' The didactic tone continues in the rhetorical question in 1–2, the scolding blended with flattery in 4, the brusque command in 5, and the sarcasm in putting downright impertinence into the mouth of the pupil in 6–8. Another rhetorical question follows in 9, and another command as he tells her to stop making excuses. The final instruction follows in 13 with teacher standing over pupil, reminding her of her duty and telling her what she should be doing, prodding her with monosyllables. The stern tone is helped by the two curt sentences in lines 5 and 13 if full stops are accepted as in the text above. Strong punctuation in mid-line is rare, and usually effective, as in 13.6 and 14, and 104.3.

Shakespeare has clearly observed the ways of schoolmasters. This is a humorous treatment. The travesty of a Latin lesson in *MW* 4.1.9–49 is farce, but both scenes are well observed. He may even have had a short spell as a schoolmaster, if Aubrey is right, 'He understood Latine very well, for he had been in his younger yeares a schoolmaster in the countrey.' Aubrey was told this by William Beeston, whose father had been a member of Shakespeare's theatre company, and Honan (2005, 60 and 71) finds this not particularly surprising or unlikely but 'one of the best authenticated reports we have of him'. Being a professional actor and a master of language and narrative with a prodigious wit and sense of humour, if he was a teacher he must have been a good one.

This sonnet is an ingenious ploy in S's reconciliation strategy. In the first eight lines he admits that he has been negligent, but saves face by blaming his Muse and showering extravagant praise on the beloved. In the rest of the poem he promises to make him immortal – the same graph of argument as in Sonnet 100, but expressed in this amusing classroom vignette. There is nothing surprising in a lover praising the beauty of his beloved, but there is one astounding thing in this sonnet. From 88–93 there are many allusions to the untruth of the beloved, from 'forsworn' in 88, through 'inconstant' and 'false' in 92, to massive indictments of shame, vices and festering infection in 93, 95 and 96. Now, when S has endured separation and wants to return to love, he tries to wipe out the past by a quadruple assertion of the truth of one who has been false. Throughout these poems the rhetorical lover has explored with consummate ingenuity every possible argument to plead his case. Now, after the breach, he forgives without mentioning the offence, apologises without apologising, and issues a retraction without recalling the accusations he is retracting.

Vendler (1997)
Though the actual presence of the beloved in the world may be entirely sufficient for the moment, the world needs art to keep his appearance alive in the future, after his death. The Muse errs, says the speaker-poet, by forgetting her future usefulness. There is, however, no need for her in the present, according to this poem. Eternizing becomes here the *sole* function of art.

❧ 102 ❦

My love is strengthened, though more weak in seeming.
I love not less, though less the show appear.
That love is merchandised, whose rich esteeming
The owner's tongue doth publish everywhere.   4

Our love was new, and then but in the spring,
When I was wont to greet it with my lays,
As Philomel in summer's front doth sing,
And stops his pipe in growth of riper days;   8
Not that the summer is less pleasant now
Than when her mournful hymns did hush the night,
But that wild music burdens every bough,
And sweets grown common lose their dear delight.   12
    Therefore, like her, I sometime hold my tongue,
    Because I would not dull you with my song.

I write less in your praise now, but not because I love you less. A lover who
*   over-praises is a salesman.*
I sang when our love was new, as the nightingale sings in the spring then
*   stops, not because summer is less pleasant, but because other birds are*
*   singing and familiarity cloys.*
I too at times am silent, because I do not wish to bore you with my song.

The notes on Sonnets 100 and 101 argue that S is trying to heal the breach
so emphatically declared in Sonnet 87 and described in those intervening
sonnets which accuse the beloved of infidelity. During this estrangement
there has been a break in the flood of love poems, and Sonnets 100–3
express regret for this neglect. This is a new defence. 'I was once the only
poet praising you, but now there are many, and I do not want to bore you.'
This argument gives him an opportunity to show scorn for his rivals, an
opportunity he seizes in lines 3, 4, 11, 12 and 14.

1–4 The argument of lines 3–4 was even more pungently expressed in

21.14, 'I will not praise, that purpose not to sell.' Scorn continues the commercial metaphor in 'whose rich esteeming', and in the picture of a salesman, *owning* wares and touting them everywhere.

5–14 The second word in four of the first five lines is 'love'. S wishes the estrangement to be over, and keeps harking back to their former love. 'Our love was new', would be a literal statement. 'Our love was then but in the spring' is a metaphor which ties in with the nightingale simile. He used to *greet* their love with his *lays* (gently sardonic as at 98.5), and these two words used of the poet also connect the literal to the nightingale simile. In Milton, *Paradise Regained* 2.280, the lark soars 'to descry | The morn's approach and *greet* her with his song', and 'lays' is commonly used of birdsong, as in Shakespeare's *PP* 14.18, 'And wish her *lays* were tunèd like the lark'.

In lines 5–6, S has spoken of human actions in terms which fit birdsong, in order to marry the simile to what it illustrates. In 7–8, when Philomel 'stops his pipe', birdsong is described in human terms as in *TN* 1.4.32–3, 'thy small pipe | Is as the maiden's organ, shrill and sound.' To stop a pipe would normally mean to block the holes with the fingers in order to play different notes. Here, mischievously, it refers to the tiny throat of the bird, not altered for pitch, but simply blocked and silenced. Like other birds the nightingale ceases to sing in June, in 'summer's front', and stops his pipe 'in growth of riper days'. Just so, S no longer writes in praise of the beloved.

To say that the nightingale stops singing because all the other birds are singing in high summer is wrong. All English birds sing in the spring, the time of nest-building and mating, and quieten down in July. Besides, the nightingale sings at night and does not suffer from competition. The reason he stops his pipe in summer has nothing to do with the song of other birds. Shakespeare knew this perfectly well, but put forward this invention in order to support S's argument in defence of his own silence. Some would say that this untruth mars the poetry; others, that it does not matter; others note that S has a grievance against rival poets and derides 'that wild music' in order to excuse his own silence. In that case the error enriches the poetry as revealing yet another ingenious argument by this unscrupulous lover.

Line 11 suggests that the music of summer birdsong is so heavy that it weighs down the branches of the trees. Birds sometimes weigh down branches, but to suggest that their music could do so is to reduce birdsong to absurdity and mock the meaningless chirruping of his rivals. 'I sometime hold my tongue' implies that other poets never do. Another play adds to the derision. In music 'burden' is the bass line, as Shakespeare understood, contrasting it with 'descant' in *Luc* 1132–4, 'For burden-wise I'll hum on

Tarquin still.' The song of other birds (and poets) is a dead weight and also a drone.

There is a problem about the nightingale: Philomel 'stops *his* pipe' in line 8 and sings '*her* mournful hymns' in line 10. Line 8 is correct. It is the cock that sings and not the hen. Duncan-Jones (1997) cites Sir Philip Sidney in the *Old Arcadia* 66.13–14, 'As for the nightingale, wood-music's king, | It August was, he deigned not then to sing.' Lines 10 and 13 preserve the poetic convention, based upon the story of Philomela, always feminine in classical mythology. In Ovid's *Metamorphoses* 6.412–674 the Thracian king Tereus married Procne, ravished her sister Philomela, and silenced her by cutting out her tongue. Philomela wove the story on her loom ('Great is the ingenuity of grief', in Donald Hill's translation of '*grande doloris ingenium est*'), and Procne's revenge upon her husband was to murder their son Itys, and feed the flesh to his father. When Tereus pursued the sisters, he was changed into a hoopoe, Procne into a swallow, and Philomela into a nightingale. Hence 'her mournful hymns' in line 10; yet why should the nightingale be masculine in line 8, but feminine in 10 and 13 and in a dozen other passages in Shakespeare? An easy solution is to change 'his' in line 8 to 'her', as do many editors. If the Quarto reading 'his' is retained, Shakespeare has followed the truth of nature by making the cock sing, and has also avoided the embarrassment of comparing S to a female. But the discrepancy might not be such a shock to Elizabethan ears. 'His' is frequently used where we would write 'its' (see 73.10 and 74.7). 'Its' never occurs in Shakespeare's poems and only ten times in the plays. To the Elizabethan ear, therefore, 'stops his pipe' would be what 'stops its pipe' is to us, and the inconsistency when the bird is personified as a female in 10 and 13 is less conspicuous than it would be in modern English.

Grey (1927), 62
The nightingale sings abundantly in the day-time but … it falls silent and takes no part in the sunset chorus. It cannot be that it fears, but perhaps it disdains, the competition with other birds. Then an hour or so after the last thrush has descended from its song perch and the last robin has ceased to sing, the nightingales will begin to fill the night with sound.

Grey (1927), 80
Yet early in June, before summer has fairly come, we note that song is beginning to fail. The nightingale, absorbed in the labour of feeding its young, ceases to sing. After the first week in June, the falling-off in song is very rapid.

℘ 103 ℛ

Alack, what poverty my Muse brings forth,
That, having such a scope to show her pride,
The argument all bare is of more worth
Than when it hath my added praise beside!   4

O blame me not if I no more can write!
Look in your glass and there appears a face
That overgoes my blunt invention quite,
Dulling my lines and doing me disgrace.   8

Were it not sinful then, striving to mend,
To mar the subject that before was well?
For to no other pass my verses tend
Than of your graces and your gifts to tell.   12
　　And more, much more, than in my verse can sit
　　Your own glass tells you when you look in it.

What poor poetry I write! My subject is better by itself than when I praise it.
Don't blame me. Look in the mirror
　　and you see a face that shames my verse.
Would it not be a sin to spoil what I want to improve? My only wish
　　is to tell of your graces, and they show far better in your mirror.

1–4　This poem provides yet another invention to support the excuses in
Sonnets 99–102. Such is the beloved's beauty that praise from S demeans
it. The Muse brings forth verse in other sonnets (see 38.11), but in line 3
the beloved, who is the argument, the subject, of the verse, becomes a baby,
worth more naked than when clad in S's poetic finery .

5–8　'Alack' begins line 1. 'O' begins the first command in line 5. This is
poetry of the spoken voice, and the dramatic tone is supported by the
monosyllables. In line 6 routine syntax would read, 'If you look in your
glass, there will appear ...', but instead of 'If', there is a command, and

instead of the future, 'will appear', there is a vivid present. There appears a face that soars above S's blunt invention, *dulls* his lines (there is a glimpse of an unsharpened blade), and puts him to shame. 'Invention' in line 7 is a backward glance at 'argument' in line 3. In rhetoric, invention is the finding of arguments (see 38.3).

9–14   After the exclamations and commands in 1–6, line 9 begins a rhetorical question in which S justifies his failure to write poems of praise by arguing that to write them would be a sin. The eloquence comes in the edge which alliteration gives to the language, 'striving to mend, | To mar ... your graces and your gifts'. 'Mend your speech a little', says Lear to Cordelia, 'lest you may *mar* your fortunes' (*KL* 1.1.93–4).

In the final couplet the beloved's beauty reduces S to self-correction in a rush of monosyllables, 'And more, much more'. 'Sit' is a surprising word. Can anything sit in verse? No, but one can sit for a portrait, and the beloved's mirror is a kind of portrait. The poem ends so flatly as to convey the collapse of eloquence, 'when you look in it'.

C. C. Stopes (1904) in Rollins (1944)
Perhaps the poorest of all Shakespeare's sonnet-endings. [Rollins comments: 'Perhaps she is distressed by the piling up of nothing but monosyllables in the couplet (see the notes to 43.13 f.). But such couplets end 2, 18, 26, 43, 115, 134, 147, 149, and perhaps 64, 129, and 136.']

❦ 104 ❧

To me, fair friend, you never can be old,
For as you were when first your eye I eyed,
Such seems your beauty still. Three winters cold
Have from the forests shook three summers' pride,   4
Three beauteous springs to yellow autumn turned
In process of the seasons have I seen,
Three April perfumes in three hot Junes burned,
Since first I saw you fresh which yet are green.   8

Ah yet doth beauty, like a dial hand,
Steal from his figure, and no pace perceived.
So your sweet hue, which methinks still doth stand,
Hath motion, and mine eye may be deceived.   12

For fear of which, hear this, thou age unbred,
Ere you were born was beauty's summer dead.

To me you are still as beautiful as when my eyes first looked into yours.
Three years have passed and you have not changed.
But beauty passes imperceptibly, even yours, though I may not see it.
Hear this, ages yet to come, beauty's summer was dead before you were born.

1–8 'Eye' and 'eyed' make a polyptoton, the same word used in two different forms. Put 'I' between them and this makes a monster, a pseudo-polyptoton, a play between one word and a completely different one which has the same sound (see 30.3). Evans (1996) makes a stern comment, 'An Elizabethan reader would doubtless have found the "witty" result more pleasing than we do.' This astounding play may be explained as a reference to that astounding moment in S's life when his eyes first met the eyes of the beloved. Shakespeare knew about this. When Miranda and Ferdinand first met, 'At the first sight | They have changed eyes' (*Tem* 1.2.443–4). Eyes play a vital part in love in the Sonnets, for example in Sonnet 5, 'The lovely gaze where every eye doth dwell', and in Sonnets 14,

17, 20, 23, 24 (a sonnet with five mentions of eyes), 78 and 132. In *LLL* 4.3.310, 'A lover's eyes will gaze an eagle blind', and eyes are mentioned more than 50 times in that comedy of love.

The drama of line 3 may be heightened by the full stop after the sense break. Heavy punctuation with a sharp change in tone in mid-line is not common in these poems, and when it occurs it tends to be expressive, as at 101.5 and 13, 108.5 and 110.6.

The glowing compliment of the opening is followed by 'Three winters cold', the beginning of a sombre description of the procession of the seasons, with the word 'three' five times in five lines, musically spaced and phrased. The repeated spoiling of beauty is weirdly worded in line 6, 'In prócess of the *séa*sons have I *séen*'. Evans (1996) comments, 'seen: witnessed'.

9–12   Lines 1–8 assert that the beloved seems to have defied the decay of time. 'Ah yet' now begins a dramatic self-correction. Sober reflection has reminded S that beauty steals imperceptibly from its figure, that is from the form of the beautiful person. It is like the hand of a clock which moves stealthily from hour to hour round the numbers on the dial, 'and no pace perceived'. According to Burrow (2002), watches had only one hand, the hour hand, until about 1675.

So the beloved's 'sweet hue', beauty of form (see 20.7), which he sees as standing still, has motion [like a dial hand], and his eye *may be* deceived. In 9–10 he acknowledged that beauty does change, so he *has been* deceived but it would not help his case to write the glorious compliment in the first eight lines, and then say it was wrong, 'Mine eye *has been* deceived ... You are looking a little older.' 'Methinks' in line 11 plays its part in this contortion. In the Sonnets it always accompanies a false statement (see 14.2). 'Methinks' occurs some 160 times in Shakespeare and only here would the metrical stress fall on the first syllable, 'méthinks', suggesting 'Of course, I may be wrong.' S hunts with the hounds and runs with the hare, trying to preserve both compliment and truth.

13–14   'For fear of which', is part of the deception – as though there were any possibility that the beloved's beauty might somehow be immune from decay.

The sonnet is rich in its changes of tone. The beloved is addressed in glowing terms in the first three lines. The next five are a gloomy generalisation on the transience of the seasons. In 9–10 comes a true and sad general observation on beauty, and that is followed by the precarious suggestion that the beloved might escape the universal law, all setting the scene for the grand proclamation in the final couplet as S raises his voice and speaks to generations yet unborn, 'hear this, thou age unbred', 'thou' being the singular collective, which gives way to the plural 'you', as he turns to the individuals who will be alive, as though they already were there listening. 'Ere you were born' addresses a vast audience, and Ingram and Redpath (1978) cite T. G. Tucker, who, at the word 'hear', caught the 'oyez' of the herald making a public proclamation.

'Beauty' and 'beauteous' bind the argument together in four places. The eye began the love and in line 12 the eye may be deceived. And colour runs through the whole poem – winters dash down the summers' pride, [proud-pied] spring [with its drifts of daffodils] turns to yellow autumn, but the beloved, unlike the woods of line 4, is still fresh and green, as he is at the end of Sonnet 68. His 'sweet hue' adds another touch of colour, the perfumes come from April flowers, and a last glimpse of summer comes in the last words of the poem.

Vendler (1997)
Booth, commenting on 128, calls 104's repetition *eye I eyed* a 'self-conscious rhetorical gimcrack.' But in Laurence Olivier's recitation of this poem to Katharine Hepburn (in the movie *Love Among the Ruins*), these (apparently) awkward repetitions in line 2 were revealed as the stammering of a lovestruck boy, astonished at his first glimpse of the potential intercourse of love.

ঙ 105 ଔ

Let not my love be called idolatry,
Nor my beloved as an idol show,
Since all alike my songs and praises be
To one, of one, still such, and ever so.   4

Kind is my love today, tomorrow kind,
Still constant in a wondrous excellence.
Therefore my verse, to constancy confined,
One thing expressing, leaves out difference.   8

'Fair, kind, and true' is all my argument,
'Fair, kind, and true' varying to other words,
And in this change is my invention spent,
Three themes in one, which wondrous scope affords.   12
   Fair, kind, and true have often lived alone,
   Which three, till now, never kept seat in one.

My love is not idolatry nor is my beloved an idol. I worship only one.
My love is ever kind and constant. So my verse is always the same.
Fair, kind, and true is my theme, and it gives wondrous scope.
   No one till now has ever been all three.

1–4 Some critics, perhaps misled by lines 7–11, find this poem dull. It
combines three propositions, all expressed in the language of Christian
worship: first, that S adores the beloved, and only the beloved; second, that
the beloved is kind, beautiful and true, a trinity like 'faith, hope and
charity' in 1 Corinthians 13: 13; third, that the beloved is always the same,
'Jesus Christ the same yesterday, and to day, and for ever' (Hebrews 13: 8).
   '*Let not* those that seek thee be confounded' (Psalm 69: 6). The language
of the Bible begins this poem, as it begins Sonnet 116, and idols and idolatry
are condemned a hundred times in the Bible, starting with the first
Commandment.' The phrase 'songs and praises' in line 3 also carries a note
of piety. Praise of God fills the Psalms (well over a hundred citations in

Alexander Cruden's *Concordance*). The plural 'praises' adds a score of mentions, as in Psalm 9: 11, 'Sing praises to the Lord.'

S protests that he is no idolater, because he worships one god – not a sound argument. Worship of a human being is idolatry. 'Although all polytheism is idolatrous, it does not follow that all monotheisms are orthodox' (Booth 1977).

At Morning Prayer a dozen times in the year, on the great feast days, the Creed of St Athanasius was said or sung. In 26 of the clauses of its definition of the 'Catholick Faith', it minutely ponders the mystery of 'God in Trinity, and Trinity in Unity', beginning with 'There is *one* person of the Father, another of the Son: and another of the Holy Ghost. But the Godhead of the Father, of the Son, and of the Holy Ghost, is all *one*: the Glory equal, the Majesty *co-eternal. Such* as the Father is, *such* is the Son: *and such* is the Holy Ghost' (my italics). In half a dozen of the similar clauses which follow, 'such' gives way to 'so', and that variation is reproduced in line 4 of this sonnet, 'still such, and ever so.' Lines 4 and 5 recall also the *Gloria Patri*, 'As it was in the beginning, is now, and ever shall be: world without end. Amen.' These words must have been engraved on Shakespeare's brain in the days of his childhood.

5–8 'Kind ... today, tomorrow kind' harks back to 'yesterday, today and ever' in the Gloria Patri. 'My kindness shall not depart from thee ... saith the LORD' in Isaiah 54: 10, and the Psalmist cries, 'How excellent is thy lovingkindness, O God!' (Psalm 36: 7). In the Authorised Version, where God's kindness and lovingkindness are mentioned more than 70 times, the 'wondrous' works of God are praised a dozen times, and his excellency nearly 30 times.

The beloved is kind, and he is also 'Still constant in a wondrous excellence'. The sexual fidelity of the beloved was a burning issue in Sonnets 86–98, so that praise of the beloved's constancy comes near to being an apology for past accusations of inconstancy, just as oblique praise of the beloved's truth in Sonnet 101 follows tirades against his falsity, notably in 95–6. This 'apology' paves the way for the triple assertion of his truth in lines 9, 10 and 13.

Another reason for the inclusion of constancy is that it sets up the argument of 7–11. Because the beloved is unchanging, S must 'write all one, ever the same | And keep invention in a noted weed' (76.5–6), 'leaving out difference', avoiding anything different.

9–14 He praises the beloved as though he were a trinity. Three times (and that is part of the wit) he is 'fair, kind, and true'. Just as the Athanasian Creed explores the mystery of the Trinity in repetitive language, so here S explores with ostentatious repetitions the threefold qualities of the beloved, ending with the mystery of the Three Persons in One, 'co-eternal together', as in the Creed. The three adjectives are seen as three persons lodging together in some state, keeping their seat in one mansion (13), and even here there may be a glimpse of the divine. 'I am a God, I sit in the seat of God, in the midst of the seas' (Ezekiel 28: 2 and see Job 23: 3).

Complaints about tautology are unsympathetic. This poem borrows the character of ritual, to suggest that for S the beloved is as a god, as he will say explicitly in 110.12. Ritual enshrines great truths, and the same words can be uttered a hundred times a day, and still have power. Here the incantations are cunningly modulated. In lines 1–2 'love' speaks to 'beloved' as 'idolatry' speaks to 'idol'. Line 4 comes in four blocks of which the last is the longest, 'To *one*, of *one*, still *such*, and ever *so*.' 'Kind ... today, tomorrow kind' forms a chiasmus. '*Still cón*stant ... to *cón*stancy *cón*fined' sounds what it says. In line 11 S's powers of invention are exhausted. Or so he says, but then comes the master stroke. In stressing 'one' in 4, 8, 12 and 14, he insists upon his monotony, but in 12 the pun flaunts his ingenuity, 'Three themes in *óne*, which *wón*drous scope affords.' In these 14 lines only one syllable that does not carry the metrical stress demands emphasis, and it is at the end, 'Which three, till now, néver kept seat in one.' He means it.

The Holy Trinity of Father, Son and Holy Ghost, Three in One, lies behind lines 8–12, but now in 13–14, in the beloved, there is a union of beauty, kindness and truth which has never existed before. This poem has been held to be sacrilegious, but lovers need some latitude. It would take a churlish priest to condemn them for seeing the divine in the one they love, to frown when Juliet says at 2.1.155–6, 'Swear by thy gracious self, | Which is the god of my idolatry.' This sonnet is not making any point about religion, nor about any philosophy. It is a love poem, and love allows wit.

Vendler (1997)
The strategies of this Sonnet – its reprise of the cultural oppositions between Christianity and an aesthetic Platonism, between the Good and the Beautiful; its clever invention of an erotic religion structurally and ritually indistinguishable from Trinitarian Christianity; its enacting of Trinitarian relations in its triune segmentation of octave, Q3, and couplet; and its playful insertion of the key word 'one' in groups of two show us what Shakespearean invention is.

ಖ 106 ಚ

When in the chronicle of wasted time,
I see descriptions of the fairest wights,
And beauty making beautiful old rhyme
In praise of ladies dead and lovely knights,   4
Then, in the blazon of sweet beauty's best
Of hand, of foot, of lip, of eye, of brow,
I see their antique pen would have expressed
Ev'n such a beauty as you master now.   8

So all their praises are but prophecies
Of this our time, all you prefiguring,
And for they looked but with divining eyes,
They had not skill enough your worth to sing.   12
  For we which now behold these present days
  Have eyes to wonder, but lack tongues to praise.

When I read descriptions of long-dead beauties,
  I see that the writers were trying to describe beauty such as yours.
Their praises are prophecies, falling short because they never saw you,
  [and no wonder] for we who see you also fail.

1–8 The 'chronicle of wasted time' is past history, and 'wasted' takes a
gloomy view of it. In this old chronicle S has seen descriptions of
beautiful people now dead. That is simple but what follows is not. He
has also seen that their beauty makes beautiful the poetry written about
them. In 'ladies dead and lovely knights', the adjectives float. The
knights were not only lovely but they are dead; and more eloquently,
the dead ladies were lovely. Rollins (1944) notes that Hazlitt (in his 1852
Supplementary Works edition, 452) records that this passage 'was a peculiar
favourite of Charles Lamb'. It uses a Latin trick, as in Horace, *Odes* 3.13,
where the kid to be sacrificed will stain the cold water of the spring with
his red blood, and we sense the clarity of the water and the heat of the
blood.

In line 5 a blazon is a coat of arms, and then a public record of excellence, a proclamation. So in this proclamation S sees that the ancients wished to express just such beauty as the beauty which the beloved now masters, that is possesses, as in *MV* 5.1.173–4, 'the wealth | That the world masters'. But the word may carry a little more weight, something like 'rules', as in 63.6, 'And all these beauties of which now he's king'. In Elizabethan English 'will' and 'would' often convey desire, as in *AYL* 1.2.242, 'I'll ask him what he would.' Here, then, 'would have expressed' means 'wished to express'.

Shakespeare knew the importance of highlighting syntax. The structure of the first half of this eight-line sentence is 'Whén in the chrónicle ... I see', and its second half is built round 'Thén in the blázon ... I see', and the link is marked by the sound of lines 1 and 5, the only lines in the poem in which the initial iambic beat is reversed.

9–14 'The old poets failed in their attempts to express superlative beauty, and for (= because) they never saw beauty like yours, and they could not do you justice, *for* (= because) we who see you also fail.'

Throughout this sonnet there runs a vein of gentle humour at the expense of old poets: a chronicle is a fusty document (in *2H4* 4.3.126 'the old folk' are 'time's doting chronicles'); the past is wasted time; *wights* are human beings but it is a hoary word which 'would have carried the tone of self-consciously affected archaism that made it a favourite with Spenser' (Booth 1977); it would have been at home in 'old rhyme'; 'ladies dead and lovely knights' has a strangeness to it; 'blazon' belongs to the ancient disciplines of heraldry; 'of hand, of foot, of lip, of eye, of brow' is making fun of the anatomical catalogues satirised in Sonnet 130. There is no other line like it in the Sonnets, but a similar trick conveys infinite scorn in *AC* 3.2.16–18:

> Hoo! Hearts, tongues, figures, bards, scribes, poets cannot
> Think, speak, cast, write, sing, number – hoo! –
> His love to Antony.

All this is caught up in 'their antique pen', a patronising phrase, as in 17.12 and *MND* 5.1.2–3, where Theseus says, 'I never may believe | These antique fables, nor these fairy toys.'

Duncan-Jones (1997), on line 5
The exclusion of 'hair' and 'breasts' from this wittily compiled *blazon* of bodily beauties continues the subtle accentuation of masculine attributes.

Not mine own fears, nor the prophetic soul
Of the wide world dreaming on things to come,
Can yet the lease of my true love control,
Supposed as forfeit to a cónfined doom.   4

The mortal moon hath her eclipse endured
And the sad augurs mock their own preságe.
Incertainties now crown themselves assured
And peace proclaims olives of endless age.   8

Now with the drops of this most balmy time
My love looks fresh, and Death to me subscribes,
Since spite of him I'll live in this poor rhyme,
While he insults o'er dull and speechless tribes,   12
    And thou in this shalt find thy monument,
    When tyrants' crests and tombs of brass are spent.

Neither my own fears nor any gloomy prophecies can end my love,
   as though it were subject to a closing date.
The moon has suffered eclipse, prophets of doom are disappointed,
   uncertainties are resolved, and endless peace is guaranteed.
This balmy rain has freshened my love, and death submits to me.
   While he exults over the dumb, I shall live in my poor poetry,
   your monument, when memorials of tyrants have passed away.

1–4 S has no fear that his love will end, not if all the prophetic powers of
the world were united, 'the prophetic soul | Of the wide world'. The
notion of a world soul goes back to Pythagoras, Plato and the Stoics, the
anima mundi, the amalgam of god, spirit, reason and *aither* (the purest
form of fire), a dynamic continuum which surrounds and governs our
world, and to which all life returns at the moment of death. According to
Kerrigan (1986), 'dreaming on' may be a little irreverent. Caesar dismisses
the soothsayer as a dreamer at *JC* 1.2.26, and Hotspur mocks 'the dreamer

Merlin and his prophecies' at *1H4* 3.1.146. 'Yet' in line 3 means something like 'despite all that'. Lines 3 and 4 are heavy with legal language. 'Summer's lease hath all too short a date' in 18.4, but S's lease of love is unconfined. 'Control' has a legal tinge in 125.14. 'Confined' can appear in legal contexts (*OED* cites from H. Parker, *Jus Pop.* 37 (1644), 'A lord may have a more confined power over his slave than he has over himself'). 'Doom' can be used of a judgement or sentence at law, as in *2H6* 4.8.12, 'your highness' doom of life or death'. S holds a lease on love which neither fears nor prophecies can control, as though it were subject to forfeiture by a court that could impose a time limit, 'a cónfined doom'.

5–8 'The prophetic soul of the wide world' got it wrong. There has been an eclipse of the moon, and it brought a fever of gloomy predictions. Lear's Gloucester would have expected this. 'These late eclipses in the sun and moon portend no good to us ... nature finds herself scourged by the sequent effects. Love cools, friendship falls off, brothers divide; in cities mutinies; in countries, discord' (*KL* 1.2.101–6), and sure enough line 8 suggests that this particular eclipse inspired prophecies of war. But all these gloomy forecasts have been disproved, uncertainties are crowned as certainties, and the forecasters of doom mock themselves (and surely each other). Prophecy is confounded and there is no likelihood of war.

Olive trees grow slowly and live long. When Greek cities were at war, they tended to destroy each other's olive groves, so olives became associated with peace. For us too, the olive branch proclaims peace, but in line 8 'peace proclaims olives of endless age', and Ingram and Redpath (1978) suggest that 'the line, like so many in Shakespeare, is potently magical rather than cogently logical.' In prose, peace proclaims an endless age in which olives will be allowed to grow unharmed.

9–14 With 'Now' in line 9, the poem moves from politics to S's love now freed from fear of premonitions and prophecies. S's love is freshened, like a plant in the spring rain, and balmy with the April perfumes of 104.7. Death, in effect, signs a document submitting to the poet, allowing him to live on in his own feeble rhyme, and the modest disclaimer softens the boast. In line 10 'love' refers not to the beloved, but to the emotion, as it does in line 3. Death acknowledges S as his superior, but tramples upon 'dull and speechless tribes', meaning, presumably, all these people who do not write deathless poetry. Not only will the poet live on in this verse, but it will also be a monument to the beloved, a monument which will not decay like the brass tombs of tyrants with their heraldic crests. The argument has come full circle. 'I have no fear [that my love will end] ... I, and my beloved, shall survive in this poetry.' The first four lines and the last six refer to the freshening of S's love, and 5–8 relate that to affairs of state.

This simple interpretation places this poem in the plot of the Sonnets. After the breakdown of love, S has sought reconciliation, excused his failure to write poems in praise of the beloved, denied any weakening of his love (102.1), and has again showered praise on the beloved in Sonnets 104–6. Now in Sonnet 107 his love is renewed, his fears are over, predictions have proved false, and he glories in his love, claiming that it can never end.

But this is to ignore problems which have caused this poem to be buried under a mountain of scholarship. The central problem is the dating of the eclipse mentioned in line 5. Rollins (1944, 263–9) refers to the arguments of about 40 scholars who have dated it to a dozen different years between 1579 and 1609. It does not ease the difficulty if George Wyndham (1898) in Rollins (1944) is right in observing that there were 21 eclipses of the moon, total or partial, visible at Greenwich during the years 1592–1609.

Recent commentators have been swayed by Kerrigan's masterly treatment (1986), which connects the sonnet with the death of Queen Elizabeth and the accession of James VI of Scotland in 1603. Kerrigan lists many details which fit this suggestion: 'A considerable outburst of anxious astrology and prediction preceded the Queen's death ... Much was at stake, Elizabeth had announced no successor, and both Catholics and Protestants feared the accession of a ruler less sympathetic to their religious liberty than the late Queen had been.' As she lay dying, there were more than a dozen possible successors, including James VI of Scotland and the Infanta of Spain. There was therefore reason to fear strife at home and invasion from abroad.

Line 5 could refer to the Queen, who had been praised for half a century as Diana, the chaste goddess of the moon. The moon goes and comes again, but Elizabeth was 'the mortal moon', and she suffered permanent eclipse when she died. But the gloomy predictions were not fulfilled, and the gloomy prophets who made them now ridiculed their own prophecies. They had feared uncertainties, but, now James is crowned, their anxious uncertainties are themselves crowned as assured benefits, and there is none of the civil strife which had been expected. The mood of that time is caught in John Donne's sermon of 1617, quoted at length by Kerrigan (1986): 'showers of rain all night, of weeping for our sovereign. And we would not be comforted, because she was not ... And yet Almighty God shed down his spirit of unity, and recollecting, and reposedness, and acquiescence upon you all ... that a King, born and bred in a warlike nation ... should yet have the spirit of peace so abundantly in him, as that by his counsels, and his authority, he should sheathe all the swords of Christendom again.' England had been at war with Catholic Spain since 1583, and James saw himself as the peacemaker king, *rex pacificus*, claiming in his first address to Parliament that his arrival in London in 1603 brought peace and amity 'where war was before'; that he also brought peace within, an end to civil strife; that it was his hope that 'it would please God to prosper and continue for many years this union, and all the other blessings of inward and outward peace which I have brought with me.' Ward (1934) in Rollins (1944) cites Gervase Markham, *Honour in his Perfection* (1624), saying that in 1603 James I 'enters not with an Olive Branch in his hand but with an whole Forrest of *Olives* round about him; for he brought not peace to this Kingdom alone, but almost to all the Christian Kingdomes in Europe.' Line 8 of the sonnet, 'And peace proclaims olives of endless age' fits these claims exactly.

In line 9 'the drops of this most balmy time' have freshened the flower of S's love, but, if this sonnet is attached to the coronation of 1604, the image has another application. Balm was a fragrant unguent, and drops of it anointed the head of the monarch in the coronation ceremony. 'Let all the tears that should bedew my hearse | Be drops of balm to sanctify thy head,' says the dying king to his son at *2H4* 4.3.242–3.

In line 12 to insult is to triumph over, an extension of its literal Latin meaning 'to leap upon', seen in *TA* 3.2.71, 'Give me thy knife. I will insult on him.'

The last line seems to tell against Kerrigan's interpretation (1986). James is praised, and so too is Elizabeth, and yet the poem ends with a disparaging statement about 'tyrants' crests'. If Shakespeare was speaking of the two monarchs as tyrants, he would be in trouble. But he surely left the contemporary political scene at line 8, and is now looking to his love and to its future. 'Tyrants will erect brass tombs with heraldic crests, but your monument will stand when they have crumbled.' By this time S is not thinking of Elizabeth and James, but is saying again what he has already said so often, notably in Sonnet 65.

೫ 108 ೫

What's in the brain that ink may character
Which hath not figured to thee my true spirit?
What's new to speak, what now to register
That may express my love, or thy dear merit? 4

Nothing, sweet boy; but yet, like prayers divine,
I must each day say o'er the very same,
Counting no old thing old – 'thou mine, I thine',
Ev'n as when first I hallowed thy fair name, 8

So that eternal love, in love's fresh case,
Weighs not the dust and injury of age,
Nor gives to necessary wrinkles place,
But makes antiquity for aye his page, 12
    Finding the first conceit of love there bred,
    Where time and outward form would show it dead.

What have I written that has not explained my true self to you?
   What's new to say or write about my love or your qualities?
Nothing, sweet boy; but I must always say the same
   and, as in daily prayers, not find the old words old,
so that love pays no attention to time, but makes age its page,
   finding love as it was when it was born.

1–4 If S had written 'What's in *my* brain', he would have been claiming
only that he had done his best. 'What's in *the* brain' is bolder. He has
written all that could be written, he has done all that could be done by the
brain of man. 'Character' is in play with 'figure'. 'What is there that could
be written down in letters, 'characters', which has not drawn a picture, a
'figure', of my true spirit? 'My true spirit' is a coup. It could mean 'myself
as I really am', which would be simple, but it could also suggest 'my true
and faithful spirit', a claim he dare not make outright in view of his
confessions of guilt which open the next three sonnets. The philanderer

talks as though he is a faithful lover, implying what he dare not say unambiguously because it is not true.

In line 3, 'What's new' is varied to 'what now'. There is nothing new to say in general, and nothing to record at this moment as he sits writing this sonnet. Some editors emend 'now' to 'new' producing an obvious balance, but losing immediacy, subtlety and variety, or, as Ingram and Redpath (1978) say, 'the vowel change is both pleasing in itself and also calls more attention to these words than mere repetition would to the word "new".'

5–8 S asks his rhetorical questions in four polished lines and answers them crisply, 'Nothing, sweet boy'. The one-word answer and the tender endearment (only here in the Sonnets) dramatically change the tone. As in Sonnet 105 he now compares his repeated declarations of love to the set prayers recited daily, and sometimes several times daily, in Elizabethan churches and households. For the believer, repetition does not weaken the power of ritual, and S must repeat his simple declaration again and again, and not think of the old words as being old as he does so. 'Say o'er' is defined in *OED* 13e as 'repeat from memory', citing 'Let the poorer sorte oftymes saye over theyr *Pater Noster*' (1564). Lines 6–8 mimic the formula of worship by assonance, repetition and monosyllables, 'I must each *day say* o'er the very *same*, | Counting no *old* thing *old* – "thou *mine*, I *thine*".' These last four words resemble the Song of Solomon 2: 16, 'My beloved is mine, and I am his.' 'Ev'n as when first I hallowed thy fair name', is a clear reference to the Lord's Prayer, the *Pater Noster*, 'Hallowed be Thy name'. S thinks of the beloved as a god. This is not blasphemy, lowering the divine to the human, but raising the human to the divine.

In this context 'thy fair name' may be another echo of the Song of Solomon (2: 10), 'Arise, my love, my fair one, and come away.' 'Fair' occurs 11 times in the seven short chapters of that book. The religious flavour lingers into the beginning of line 9. The eternal is a matter for God, not man, as shown by all the passages cited in *OED*.

9–14 Lines 9–14 can be taken in two ways. The first possibility is that S is pondering a general mystery – in short, that when love is old it is as fresh as when it was new. In line 9 love is eternal, and in every new instance it pays no heed to the damage that age inflicts, but finds young love in an aged lover, where outward appearance would suggest that love is dead. But this is a love poem addressed to the 'sweet boy', and this general reflection must have some bearing on the declaration of the first eight lines. In 63.4, 77.5 and 100.10, S has already spoken darkly about the time when wrinkles will assail the beloved. Here then, he could in lofty general terms be saying that he would still love the young man when his beauty faded. Every time S sees him would be like the first. Much need of such an assurance in view of the accusations that have gone before, and the confessions that follow in 109–11. These views could easily be combined. It can be useful to propound a general principle and leave the listener to apply it.

In lines 9–10 love is eternal and every new case of it pays no attention to age. Love does not weigh the dust and injury of age, but old people are not always dusty. The wit lies in the suggestion that nobody in their right mind weighs dust, and nobody in their right mind ceases to love when age damages the one they love.

In line 11 love accepts that wrinkles must come, but accords no importance to them, but this is expressed with a picture of some formal occasion. At a dinner or in a procession one would give place to one who deserved respect, but eternal love gives no place to wrinkles. From this formal scene the brain of the poet suddenly, and mischievously, leaps to visualise old age, 'antiquity' as love's pageboy, 'for aye his page'. The boy, Cupid, has an aged attendant. These metaphors play round the simple statement in 104.1, 'To me, fair friend, you never can be old.'

Finally, in yet another play of contrasts, love would for ever find that the idea of love would be *conceived* and *bred* in this aged page, just there where appearances would show it as *dead* [and long past breeding]. This suggestion finds conception in 'conceit' and a glimpse of 'born' in 'bred'(104.13–14).

There is another possible understanding of these last six lines, starting from the word 'page' and calling in the other references to writing in lines 1–4, and perhaps in the dust of 10 which suggests books rather than men. 'As I understand it,' writes Vendler (1997), 'the word *page* here means not "a serving boy," but rather the page one reads; and "to make antiquity one's page" is to choose to read love poems by early authors ... Eternal love, when it arises in a new instantiation, does not take into account age and wrinkles, but instead sees how analogous the eternal youthfulness of personal feeling is to the paradoxical freshness of feeling encoded in old books by and about people long dead.' I do not believe this. It is not the way of love 'to choose to read love poems by early authors' or ponder the 'freshness of feeling encoded in old books'. Old love poetry is mocked in Sonnets 17.12 and 106. The message is rather, 'I love you now as I did in the beginning. My love never grows old, is always young.'

O never say that I was false of heart,
Though absence seemed my flame to qualify.
As easy might I from my self depart
As from my soul, which in thy breast doth lie.   4

That is my home of love. If I have ranged,
Like him that travels I return again,
Just to the time, not with the time exchanged,
So that my self bring water for my stain.   8

Never believe, though in my nature reigned
All frailties that besiege all kinds of blood,
That it could so preposterously be stained
To leave for nothing all thy sum of good,   12
    For nothing this wide universe I call
    Save thou, my rose. In it thou art my all.

Never say that I was false of heart, although my absence suggested
    that my love was cooling. My soul lives in your breast.
That is my home, and I come back to it, punctual and unchanged,
    bringing water for my stain.
Despite the weakness of my flesh, I could never leave you for nothing.
    The world holds nothing for me except you, my rose, my all.

1–4 Is the absence literal, or is it an emotional rift? Lines 8–11, with
'stain', 'frailties', 'all kinds of blood' and 'stained', leave no doubt. Whether
or not S has been absent, he has certainly been unfaithful. This poem is an
elaborate and hypocritical apology, buttressed by assurances of undying
love. The most cunning evasion is in the first line. 'O never say that I was
false *of heart*' is almost an admission that he has been false with his body.

In lines 3–4 the two departures are made to sound equally impossible by
the similarity between 'selfe' and 'soule'. The rhetoric is more easily heard
in the common Elizabethan spelling in the Quarto, 'As easie might I from

334

my *selfe* depart | As from my *soule*', a play on words blurred by the comma commonly printed after 'depart'. The same device is at work in line 8, 'So that my *selfe* bring water for my *staine*.' The thought of line 4 has already appeared in 22.7, where his heart lives in the beloved's breast.

5–8   In Sonnets 50–1 his travels were literal journeys, but the tone of the language here is quite different. The absence, departure, ranging and travels include sexual infidelities. S is not a traveller (or not only a traveller), he is a philanderer. Booth (1977) sees 'the grossness of the speaker's fraud ... in solemnly making a logical-sounding equation between two non-comparable things: the journeys of a traveller and the promiscuous sexual relations of a lover'. 'If I have ranged' has the beautiful 'if' of a confessed sinner granting that it is just possible that he may have done wrong.

In line 7 S boasts of the punctuality of his return, as though it excused his infidelities during his absence, and as though the charge of falsity is refuted by the claim to be just, 'just to the time', meaning time of return, 'not with the time exchanged', suggesting that he has not changed, never wavered, he has been just, meaning 'faithful' (see 138.11) all the time that he has been unfaithful. 'Exchanged' meaning changed seems to occur only here in English. The extra syllable conveniently carries the metre along.

In line 8 the traveller returns so that he may bring water for his stain, and again Booth (1977) sees what is going on: 'The essential idea of this line is the implied argument that since the speaker's crime was his departure, his return cancels it.' This effrontery is inflated with an air of piety in a hint of holy water, and in tears of remorse – all this from a man who knows that 'Th' offender's sorrow lends but brief relief | To him that bears the strong offence's cross' (see 34.11–12).

9–14   The tactics now move from self-defence to praise of the beloved and to the self-righteousness which began the first line. 'O néver say' is picked up in the earnest appeal of the ninth, 'Néver believe'. He asks the beloved never to say and never to think, but he does not deny the charge.

'Preposterously' in line 11, 'before-after-ously', is used with a keen sense of its literal meaning, as in *OED*, citing Nashe (1589), 'those that are called Agrippae being preposterously borne with their feete forward'. In *TS* 3.1.9–12, the suitor pretending to be a Latin teacher calls the suitor pretending to be a music teacher a 'preposterous ass' for not knowing 'the cause why music was ordained! | Was it not to refresh the mind of man | *After* his studies?' S is trying to ingratiate himself by saying that it would be preposterous to believe that his nature could be stained by putting any rival *before* the beloved, but he goes further. The lovers with whom he has been consorting are 'nothing', as against the vast sum of the qualities of the beloved. The whole universe is nothing. 'For nothing this wide universe I call | Save thou, my rose. In it thou art my all' – an eloquently broken line. After the fulsome praise come the passionate endearment and declaration of total devotion, masquerading as simple truth in its dress of monosyllables.

The beloved is having none of it, and says so, as can be deduced when 109.1, 'O never say that I was false of heart' is followed by 110.1, 'Alas 'tis true! I have gone here and there.' The beloved never speaks in these dramatic poems but it is sometimes easy to know what he has said.

To be quite clear, this poem is no sort of evidence for any episode in the life of William Shakespeare. This is no guilty lover pouring out weak excuses, but a dramatist fashioning the character of a dishonest lover.

Duncan-Jones (1997)
wide universe expands on the *wide world* of 107.2, perhaps partly to accommodate the sound *you*, the second person plural, alluding to 'everyone else in the world except thou'.

℘ 110 ℘

Alas 'tis true! I have gone here and there,
And made myself a motley to the view,
Gored mine own thoughts, sold cheap what is most dear,
Made old offences of affections new.   4

Most true it is that I have looked on truth
Askance and strangely. But by all above,
These blenches gave my heart another youth,
And worse essays proved thee my best of love.   8

Now all is done, have what shall have no end.
Mine appetite I never more will grind
On newer proof, to try an older friend,
A god in love to whom I am confined.   12

　Then give me welcome, next my heav'n the best,
　Ev'n to thy pure and most most loving breast.

It's true. I have ranged widely, made myself a fool, squandered my treasure,
　　and hurt my old lover by taking a new.
I have truly given truth a sideways glance, but I swear
　　this brought youth back to my heart. Experiment proved
　　that you are the best that love can offer.
It is ended. Take what will not end. Never again will I whet my appetite
　　on new loves to test the old, my one and only god of love.
You are next to my heaven. Take me back to your pure and loving breast.

1–4 He begins Sonnet 109 with 'O never say that I was false ...' and adds
in line 9, 'Never believe ...' But the beloved clearly did believe, and did say,
and now S owns up, 'Alas 'tis true I have', and again in line 5, 'Most true it
is that I have'. The very structure of 110.1–5 echoes the structure of
109.1–9. It is part of the same conversation.

　In 109 travel was repeatedly a metaphor for sexual infidelity, and in

110.1 'I have gone here and there' continues that metaphor. 'Motley' is the parti-coloured dress of the fool, and here it means the fool himself, as in *AYL* 3.3.71, 'Will you be married, motley?' S has made himself a fool. This does not mean simply that S has been on tour. The appalling lines 8 and 10–11 make it clear that this play-acting was sexual. See the end of the commentary on 111.

In line 3 'gored' is often taken to mean wounded, but it is difficult to imagine S goring his thoughts in that sense. A gore is a gusset, a triangular piece of material serving to produce difference in width, in a skirt for example, and the verb also occurs as in *OED*, which cites 'sails gored with a sweep' in 1794. This sense would fit the picture presented by 'motley', and sharpen it by suggesting that the characteristic parti-coloured costume of the fool was made by stitching triangles of cloth of different colours into his baggy breeches. Ingram and Redpath (1978) add another possibility. In heraldry, a gore was an area bounded by two curving lines, and a gore sinister was a mark of cadency or abatement of honour, a badge of disgrace. This would go with what comes after. This patch that he has stitched into his [loving] thoughts has disgraced them. It would be best to keep each of these last two interpretations in mind.

He has cheapened love by spending it too extravagantly. He has *sold* what was most *precious* in his life, his love for the young man. Out of these new affections he has 'made old offences', committed offences against his former lover. This loose use of an adjective is not uncommon in these poems. In 2.11 'make my old excuse' means 'make my excuse when I am old'. Compare 55.9 and 74.11.

5–8 S has been false in love. He has not looked straight at truth, but sideways, as though it were a stranger passing in the street (see 89.8). He now swears an oath by heaven, and the break before it in the middle of line 6 gives intensity, as in 104.3 and 109.14.

'To blench' is to deceive, to cheat, and blenches were deceitful tricks – a fair allusion to his recent behaviour, but the latest citation of that meaning in *OED* is from 1340. *OED* also offers the meaning 'side-glances'. This would fit quite well after 'askance', but the only citation in that sense is this line of the sonnet. In Shakespeare the verb is used five other times and in three of these it means 'to swerve, to turn aside' – in *MM* 4.5.5, 'sometimes you do blench from this to that', in *WT* 1.2.335 and in *TC* 2.2.67. This sense fits perfectly with 'I have gone here and there' in line 1.

'Another youth' is often taken to mean 'a different boy'. The triviality of this interpretation makes it unlikely. Besides, the tenor of the confessions dragged out of him in recent sonnets is that he has played the field, 'ranged', 'gone here and there', indulged in 'new affections', 'worse essays'. There is no talk of a single lover. It is effrontery to argue that his infidelities have rejuvenated him, but even more boorish is his monstrous excuse in 8 that he has taken other lovers to test them against the beloved. This is an ingenious invention, but could any lover say this and hope to scape whipping?

9–14 Now comes his undertaking for the future, rendered all the more solemn by monosyllables, 'Now all is done, have what shall have no end.' The paradox carries a promise, 'My infidelities are now ended, accept what will never end, [my love].'

The guarantee comes with a startling metaphor. Even in the first third of the twentieth century the knife grinder would push his cart round the streets, and at his cry housewives would bring down their knives to be ground on his wheel. Here the knife is S's sexual appetite, and the 'newer proof' is new lovers. He had been sharpening his libido by sexual experiments. Booth (1977) cites Cotgrove's *Dictionary of the French and English Tongues* (1611) under 'pierres', 'Mettre toutes pierres en oeuvre, put all the stones to work ... applying to a wench that suffers any man's stones to *grind* at her mill.'

At the mention of his older friend, here again, as in Sonnet 109, he moves from admissions, excuses, promises and subterfuge to flattery. The beloved is 'A god in love' and from now on his only lover, in his eyes second only to heaven itself. Into this praise S weaves an appeal to be taken back, reinforced by the most false and calculating of flatteries, 'Ev'n to thy pure and most most loving breast.' In Sonnets 95 and 96 the beloved was anything but pure.

The opening words of 110 connected it to the beginning of 109. The 'most most loving breast' connects it to 109.4–6, where his soul lay in the beloved's breast, the home to which he was returning.

Booth (1977), on line 13
[He comments on 'Then give me welcome':] Note the summary effect inherent in the non-signifying antithetical complements that inoperative potential senses of the components of this phrase provide for elements prominent at the beginning of the poem and in the new beginning at line 9.

O for my sake do you with Fortune chide,
The guilty goddess of my harmful deeds,
That did not better for my life provide
Than public means, which public manners breeds.   4

Thence comes it that my name receives a brand,
And almost thence my nature is subdued
To what it works in, like the dyer's hand.

Pity me then, and wish I were renewed,   8
Whilst like a willing patient I will drink
Potions of eisel 'gainst my strong infection –
No bitterness that I will bitter think,
Nor double penance to correct correction.   12

　　Pity me then, dear friend, and I assure ye
　　Ev'n that your pity is enough to cure me.

Scold Fortune for me, the goddess guilty of my misdeeds.
　　She made me take up a public career that produces public manners.
As a result my name is branded and my nature is almost suppressed.
Pity me then, and I will take my medicine and not find vinegar bitter,
　　nor think a double dose a double penance.
Pity me, dear friend, and that will cure me.

1–4 Why does S ask the beloved to remonstrate with Fortune on his
behalf? It is a rhetorical device. To say, 'It's not my fault, but Fortune's',
would be feeble. To ask the beloved to take the matter up with Fortune is
to insinuate that the beloved is on his side and might be willing to act on
his behalf.

The 'harmful deeds' are his acts of sexual infidelity. He tried to deny
them in Sonnet 109, and in Sonnet 110 he protested that they were all over.
Now he blames the goddess Fortune for them. It's all her fault for not

providing him with an adequate income, so that he had to make his living as an actor, a profession conducted in the public eye, and therefore bound to lead its practitioners into 'public manners', coarse and raffish behaviour. A statute of 1572 cited by Burrow (2002) is directed against 'rogues, vagabonds and sturdy beggars'. It included actors in its remit, and 'linked the theatre with vagrants, tinkers, and bearwards'.

Nowadays we do not chide *with* Fortune, but chide her. Yet the construction is noted in *OED* 4b, and occurs occasionally in Shakespeare. For example at *Cym* 5.5.126 Sicilius begs Jupiter to fall out with Mars and 'with Juno chide'. In line 2 'The guilty goddess of my harmful deeds' is written instead of 'The goddess guilty of my harmful deeds', perhaps to lend emphasis by the jolt. Here, as in line 6, Shakespeare's word order is more free than ours. In line 4 'means' is a singular noun, as in *WT* 4.4.620, 'by this means'. So his public career breeds public manners. Actors live by public favour, and therefore learn to court it. As Kerrigan (1986) says, it is a career 'which encourages vulgar display and unfeelingly superficial charm'.

5–7 'Thence', because of his profession as an actor, his name is branded and thence too his [virtuous] nature is almost subdued. In Shakespeare's England criminals could be branded (see comment on 112.2), on the breast with V for vagabond, on the forehead with P for perjury, on the thumb with M for murder. Ben Jonson's thumb was so marked for killing an actor in a duel in 1598. S's claim that the damage to his good name is the result of his profession is an excuse, and what follows goes further. His nature is not 'subdued to', not overwhelmed by, the low company he has to keep while at work, but it *almost* is. By implication, then, despite his confession in Sonnet 110, he is not really guilty.

Burrow (2002) notes that English dyes of this period were woad-based and indelible, and Shakespeare would have known about dye-stained hands because his father was a glover.

8–12 Now S appeals for pity, promising to be a good patient and take his medicine. 'Eisel', vinegar, was used, sometimes blended with honey to make oxymel, as a preventive and remedy for the bubonic plague, which raged intermittently in London from 1592 until 1609, when these poems were printed. The word 'eisel' may have survived as the trade name of 'Izal', used in the twentieth century as a disinfectant and mouthwash (later, for toilet paper). S is now dressing up his sexual misdemeanours as though they were an illness. This continues until the last words of the poem. So genuine is his repentance that he will not think vinegar bitter; nor will he think bitter a 'double penance to correct correction'. This suggests that if one draught of vinegar is not enough to cure his infection he will accept a second to correct the first.

13–14   Sonnet 109 is punctuated at lines 1 and 9 by imperatives, Sonnet 110 by repeats at lines 1 and 5. Here in Sonnet 111 the appeal for pity in line 8 is poignantly repeated in line 13, 'Pity me then, dear friend'. After hinting that he was the innocent victim of circumstance and slander in 1–7, he now admits his strong infection in 10, and appeals for pity. He is of course willing to drink vinegar, but, if only the beloved would pity him, that would not be necessary – 'Pity me then while I drink vinegar, pity me and I won't need to.' This also saves him from the danger of having to commit himself to a literal undertaking, and shuffles responsibility for the future on to the shoulders of the beloved, exactly the device he used in the first line of the poem.

It might seem that Shakespeare is a scheming hypocrite, wriggling to conceal and play down his guilt in order to worm his way back into the affections of the beloved he has betrayed. Not so. That would be to read the Sonnets as an account of what happened, a collection of poems based upon Shakespeare's own behaviour. The conviction behind this commentary is that the Sonnets are an invented drama in the form of poetic utterances spoken by an imaginary lover to his beloved. They are not evidence for Shakespeare's life. S in these notes is not Shakespeare but a character created by a dramatist for this love drama.

   Sonnets 110 and 111 seem to torpedo that theory. Since both poems appear to be spoken by an actor and Shakespeare was an actor, the poems could be taken to be autobiographical. This is a false conclusion. A dramatist is bound to use his own experience of life in his fictions. What more natural than that he should on occasion invent arguments that spring from his own experience? That does not mean that the Sonnets record a phase in his life.

From *Street Jewellery* 66 (November 2003)
Izal advertising jingle current in the 1920s and 1930s (for line 10, 'eisel'):
> Georgie Porgie, pudding and pie,
> Kissed the girls and made them cry;
> Izal gargling changed all this,
> Now they cry to get a kiss.

112

Your love and pity doth th'impression fill
Which vulgar scandal stamped upon my brow,
For what care I who calls me well or ill
So you o'er-green my bad, my good allow? 4

You are my all the world, and I must strive
To know my shames and praises from your tongue,
None else to me, nor I to none alive,
That my steeled sense or changes right or wrong. 8
In so profound abysm I throw all care
Of others' voices, that my adder's sense
To critic and to flatt'rer stoppèd are.

Mark how with my neglect I do dispense— 12
 You are so strongly in my purpose bred
 That all the world besides, methinks they're dead.

Your love and pity heal the brand on my brow. I don't care what others say,
 if you let my virtues cover up my vices.
You are my world, so that I listen only to you, deaf to all else.
The reason for my indifference is that for me the rest of the world is dead.

Sonnet 111 ended with an appeal for pity. Between sonnets, S's beloved has
pitied him, and his love and pity fill the impression 'which vulgar scandal
stamped upon my brow'. T. G. Tucker's commentary in his 1924 edition
of the Sonnets describes efforts made by criminals to fill in the indentations
made by branding. Now all S asks is that his friend should cover his defects
with green (as a creeper covers a ruin or an unsightly wall?) and should
grant there is good in him. In 111 he admitted guilt. He is now the innocent
victim of vulgar scandal.

5–11 'To me you are all the world and I must strive to know your opinion
of my behaviour, whether it is praise or blame.' 'Well or ill', 'my bad, my

good', 'shames and praises', 'right or wrong', 'To critic and to flatt'rer' – S is making it clear that he fully accepts the beloved's right to judge him.

Line 7 is loosely attached to its sentence, 'None else [being alive] to me, nor I [being] alive to any'. Grammarians used to call this an absolute construction, 'The enemy having been defeated, Caesar returned to camp.' It occurs also in 149.3 and 151.5. The sentiment of line 7 has appealed to several poets, to Horace in *Epistles* 1.9, for example '*oblitusque meorum, obliviscendus et illis*', and to Alexander Pope in *Eloisa to Abelard* 1.208, 'The world forgetting, by the world forgot'. In line 8, S is alive to no one else , [so] that he rejects the right of all voices except the beloved's to change his sense of either right or wrong. This sense, this judgement, is to be of steel, and therefore unbending, not deviating from the beloved's jurisdiction, impenetrable to all else. Burrow (2002) judges lines 7–8 to be among the most obscure in the sequence. Here again, as in 111.2 and 6, the word order is surprising. There is nothing unusual about 'or … or' for 'either … or', but the placing of the first 'or' is strange. The obvious order would be 'my steeled sense changes or right or wrong.' But it is Shakespearean, as in *Luc* 875, 'But ill-annexed Opportunity | Or kills his life, or else his quality', not '… kills or his life or else his quality'.

'Into such a bottomless chasm do I throw all respect for opinions voiced by others, that, like the deaf adder, I stop my ears to critics and to flatterers.' 'The deaf adder that stoppeth her ear' (Psalm 58: 4) is not deaf physiologically, but rather decides not to hear, and achieves this 'by fixing one orifice to the ground and stopping the other with his tail'. Ingram and Redpath (1978) were given this information by Mr Lucas, who found it in the thirteenth-century encyclopedia by Bartholomeus Anglicus.

12–14   A dispensation is a licence to do what is forbidden, so line 12 means that he condones his own neglect [of other voices], as in *MM* 3.1.136–7, 'Nature dispenses with the deed so far that it becomes a virtue.' The last two lines give his reason for this indifference, 'you are … so *bred* in my purpose', as much a part of my nature, as though you had been *born* as part of me, so much so that as far as I am concerned there is nothing alive in the world but you, 'all the world besides, methinks they're dead'. This suggests the live tones of colloquial speech. Every time 'methinks' occurs in the Sonnets (see 14.2, 62.5 and 104.11), it gives warning of an exaggeration. The last line is sometimes criticised on the grounds that it repeats line 7. Not so. It is a fitting climax, far more shocking.

The Quarto reads, 'That all the world besides me thinkes y'are dead.' 'You are dead' makes no satisfactory sense. Line 7 points to the conclusion that it is the rest of the world that is dead, not the beloved.

Since I left you, mine eye is in my mind,
And that which governs me to go about
Doth part his function, and is partly blind,
Seems seeing, but effectually is out.   4

For it no form delivers to the heart
Of bird, or flow'r, or shape which it doth latch.
Of his quick objects hath the mind no part,
Nor his own vision holds which it doth catch.   8

For if it see the rud'st or gentlest sight,
The most sweet-favoured or deformèd'st creature,
The mountain or the sea, the day or night,
The crow or dove, it shapes them to your feature.   12

   Incapable of more, replete with you,
   My most true mind thus makes mine eye untrue.

Since I left you my eye is in my mind. It only seems to see.
For it gives nothing to my mind, and does not itself hold what it sees.
For it changes everything into your shape.
Being full of you, my most true mind has no room for anything else.
   It is making my eye untrue.

1–4 'Eye' stands for 'eyes' throughout. The poetic singular raises the
tone, and works dramatically, personifying the act of seeing as a co-opera-
tion between two agents, eye and heart/mind. The personification is reinforced by 'his' referring to 'eye' in 3, 7 and 8.

   For 'part' = 'partly' in line 3, compare *Oth* 5.2.302, 'This wretch hath
part confessed his villainy.' 'Effectually' is four syllables, 'effectu'lly'.
'Seems seeing' is like a familiar Latin turn of phrase. *Video* means I see,
videor means I seem, and Latin writers occasionally play one off against the
other, as does Ovid in *Ex Ponto* 2.4.7–8, '*ante oculos nostros posita est tua*

semper imago | et videor vultus mente videre tuos, 'Before my eyes there is always your image | and in my mind I seem to see your features.' This could be a coincidence, but Ovid was staple fare in Elizabethan grammar schools.

5–8 What governs S to go about [and do his daily business] is indeed 'eye', but that is only part of eye's work. What is meant by saying that the eye 'effectually is out'? The explanation is introduced by 'For'. For whatever eye latches [upon], it should deliver an image of it to heart, but it fails to do so. Nor does mind have any part in, does not grasp, the quick objects seen by eye. Quick objects, like bird or flower, are alive, as in 'the quick and the dead'. The bird is also quick in the sense of swift, and the monosyllables of line 6 go with the speed of flight and sight. In short, neither heart nor mind receives what eye catches, and eye itself cannot hold it.

9–12 What does that mean? The explanation is introduced by 'For'. For whatever eye catches changes into something else. Everything it sees becomes the beloved. A list is now given consisting of five contrasting pairs, the last three, in 11–12, normally printed with six commas as in the Quarto. If this scatter is reduced to three as above in order to articulate the pairs, that not only helps the reader but also brings out the sweep of thought in all five pairs. The phenomenon is unconfined. It covers the whole range of visible things from one extreme to another. Crows, for instance, may be carrion, and doves are emblems of peace and love.

In lines 9–10 'rud'st' and 'deformèd'st' even sound rude and deformed, and the ugliness is intensified when this 'deformed'st creature' rhymes and contrasts with the beauty of the beloved's 'feature' in 12. The music of the verse depends upon the shaping of the five pairs to a great swell in line 10, and part of that music is the variation of stress on the word 'or'. It occurs five times in four lines, and would carry the iambic beat twice, in 'The most sweet-favoured ór deformed'st creature, | The mountain ór the sea', accelerating to the monosyllables of 'the dáy or níght, | The crów or dóve'.

13–14 'My mind is full of you.' 'Incapable' means 'not having room for' and therefore is in play with 'replete'. Othello's revenge has room to, has the capacity to, swallow his bloody thoughts in *Oth* 3.3.460–3:

> Ev'n so my bloody thoughts with violent pace
> Shall ne'er look back, ne'er ebb to humble love,
> Till that a capable and wide revenge
> Swallow them up.

S's mind has no room for anything else because it is replete with the beloved.

In the last line logic would be served if it overrode the iambic expectation, if 'true' were emphasised to contrast with 'untrue', 'My móst trúe mínd thus mákes mine éye úntrue', where the weight of the paradox is increased by quintuple alliteration of -m-. In the Quarto the last line reads, 'My most true minde thus maketh mine vntrue.' This would make sense if 'untrue' were a noun, 'makes, causes, my error', but 'untrue' is never a noun in Shakespeare. Some editors try to heal the line by bringing in some mention of eyes in the plural, for example, 'maketh m'eyne untrue', but the simplest solution is what is printed above. It also rounds off the logic. The first line puts his eye in his mind, and mind makes eye untrue.

The opening riddle has been manipulated to slip in another justification for S's infidelity, and this chicanery comes with the usual accompaniments, praise of the beloved's beauty as implied in 9–12, and a declaration of passionate love, 'My mind is so full of you, that whatever I look at, it is you I see.' As usual, this is not the introspection of a stricken heart, but a drama exploring the character of a licentious lover attempting to argue his way back into the affections of the person he has betrayed. If so, the opening 'Since I left you' (weasel words for infidelity) is yet another dab of hypocrisy.

❧ 114 ❧

Or whether doth my mind, being crown'd with you,
Drink up the monarch's plague, this flattery?
Or whether shall I say mine eye saith true,
And that your love taught it this alchemy,   4
To make of monsters and things indigest
Such cherubines as your sweet self resemble,
Creating every bad a perfect best
As fast as objects to his beams assemble?   8

O! 'tis the first, 'tis flatt'ry in my seeing,
And my great mind most kingly drinks it up.
Mine eye well knows what with his gust is greeing,
And to his palate doth prepare the cup.   12

If it be poisoned, 'tis the lesser sin
That mine eye loves it and doth first begin.

Does King Mind drink up this flattery [from Eye] or was he taught this
alchemy by love?
It is the first. Eye is responsible, serving what he knows his king likes.
If it be poison, his offence is the less severe because he loves it and drinks it
first himself.

1–8 S's vision is affected, so that everything he sees is now the beloved or
like him (see 113.12 and 114.6). Who is responsible? Mind or Eye? Mind
has become a king (1, 2, 10), and Eye, perhaps a flatterer, is his cupbearer
(2, 9–14). Is the optical illusion Eye's responsibility for serving this flattering cup? Or is Eye truthful, not a flatterer, and this illusion the effect of
love, and therefore the responsibility of Mind? In Sonnet 113 S concluded
that Mind is the guilty party, making Eye untrue. Sonnet 114 revisits the
problem, and this time the answer is different and Eye is the culprit. S now
describes the illusion, supplementing the 10 examples of 113.9–12, and
calling it alchemy, whereby men tried to turn base metals into gold.

'Things indigest' in line 5 goes back to the famous opening of Ovid's
Metamorphoses, where, before sea and earth and air and sky separated out,
Nature had one face, which men in later days called Chaos, a crude, indigest
mass in which no shape remained constant, '*rudis indigestaque moles …
nulli sua forma manebat*'. From *KJ* 5.7.25–7, 'you are born | To set a *form*
upon that *indigest* | Which he hath left so shapeless and so *rude*', and from
3KH6 5.6.51, where the humpback Richard is called 'an *indigested* and
de*form*èd lump', it seems that Shakespeare knew this passage in the Latin.
The monsters and formless lumps of line 6 are now transformed into the
glories of the Christian heaven, as Eye sees them as cherubim, the highest
rank of angels after seraphim. 'Every bad a perfect best' sums up the
change. Lines 5–7 are a daring combination of pagan and Christian.

The description of the process of vision in line 8 appears also in *VA* 487,
and in 1052–3, where Venus saw Adonis injured and her eyes 'threw
unwilling light | Upon the wide wound that the boar had trenched | In his
soft flank.' The common theory was that in the act of seeing the eye shot
out beams of light towards the object (see 20.6), but in this sonnet there is
a difference. The objects viewed in line 8 actually assemble to receive the
beams in the royal court of King Mind, and they assemble quickly, as
quickly as courtiers to the radiance of the royal presence, as quickly as the
906 knights created by James I in four months in 1603 (Honan 1999, 298).

9–12   In line 9 exclamation and repetition indicate in a lively conversational tone that S has suddenly come to a conclusion. In lines 1–8 he asked
a question, 'Is Eye responsible for these optical illusions, or was it Mind,
influenced by love?' He now suddenly realises that Eye is the guilty party,
corrupting Mind by flattery.

In ancient Rome a grandee might have a slave to act as a *praegustator*, a
pre-taster, to check his food and wine before he consumed it. Shakespeare
knew the practice, 'Who did taste to him?' 'A monk, I tell you … whose
bowels suddenly burst out' (*KJ* 5.6.30–1). Eye is *praegustator* to King Mind,
and naturally he well knows what his master likes, what (a)grees with his
taste, 'his gust' (Latin *gustus*). Eye then prepares the wine. Great King Mind
not only drinks it, he drinks it up 'most kingly', with a royal swagger as in
line 2. S is making fun of his own mind as a gullible king deluded by
flattery. Mind and Eye are seen as vivid persons, particularly in 10–14.

13–14   If a poisonous wine is approved for consumption, the taster is
guilty, but Eye is less culpable than might appear, because he did not act
out of treachery or carelessness. The wine-taster's defence is that he loved

the wine himself, and that he was the first to drink it. A malicious poisoner would not have loved the potion, and would have tried hard not to swallow it. This vivid conceit is yet another way of expressing a message familiar to the beloved, that he is supremely beautiful, 'a perfect best' resembling the cherubim (6), that S loved him at first sight (see 104.2), and that this love transforms the whole world for him (lines 4–8). In Sonnet 113 his love was a love of mind. In 114 it is a love of eye. All in all, it is a love of heart (46.14), of mind and of eye.

๑ 115 ๙

Those lines that I before have writ do lie,
Ev'n those that said I could not love you dearer.
Yet then my judgement knew no reason why
My most full flame should afterwards burn clearer. 4

But reck'ning Time (whose millioned accidents
Creep in 'twixt vows and change decrees of kings,
Tan sacred beauty, blunt the sharp'st intents)
Diverts strong minds to th'course of alt'ring things. 8

Alas, why, fearing of Time's tyranny,
Might I not then say, 'Now I love you best',
When I was certain o'er incertainty,
Crowning the present, doubting of the rest? 12

Love is a babe: then might I not say so
To give full growth to that which still doth grow?

*I lied when I said I couldn't love you more. I did not then know how my
love could increase.
But time brings many changes.
Why shouldn't I have said, 'I will never be able to love you more', glorying
in the present, and not knowing about the future?
Love is a baby. Why should I not have said that, allowing for its future
growth – and it's still growing.*

1–4 A shock opening. A lover admits he lied. And this is a man who has
gone on about 'true' and 'truth' nearly a score of times in the last dozen
poems. It is of course a feint. To confess to a lie is to claim a form of
honesty, and this particular confession is even more cunning. In Sonnets
109–11 S admitted that he had been false. The beloved is being led for a
moment to expect another admission of guilt, and instead S now confesses
a lie he told in the past, when their love was young, when he said that he

could never love more dearly than he did at that moment. In those days he had no reason to believe that there could be greater wonders in store. But the metaphor in line 4 is more eloquent. When love was new it was a huge flame, and he thought that the fire could not be greater, but of course the red heart of an established fire gives more heat than the roaring flames of a fire just lit. So the pseudo-confessional beginning sets up the compliment in 3–4 and the assurance of continued devotion in 14.

5–8 Time reckons up the accounts. In Sonnet 65 time's changes are relevant to the visible world, 'neither brass nor stone nor earth nor boundless sea … but time decays'. Here they are relevant to the particular human situation. They creep in between persons making vows and prise them apart (as S and the beloved have been estranged); they change royal decrees (how could S hope to be exempt?); they blunt the keenest intentions (S's intentions were keener than anyone's); Time diverts the course of strong minds and makes them alter things (and S is no weakling but a man of his word).

These four points are heavily weighted with self-justification. The tanning of sacred beauty seems not to fit into the list. Why in line 7 has S taken the risk of implying that the skin of the beloved, into whose good graces he is trying to creep, may be beaten and chopped by tanning (see 62.10)? Perhaps this apparent gaffe is another calculated strategy. In 104.9–12 and perhaps in 108.8–12, he cautiously hinted that the beloved's beauty would not last for ever. He may be doing the same here, equally gently. This is to assure the beloved that, if his complexion should ever be impaired, S's love would still go on growing, and growing from a base line where it had been immense. 'Gather ye rosebuds while ye may' is also lurking in the background.

When 'diverts' occurs near 'course', a strong mind is a mighty river which diverts its course. It was flowing in one direction, and changes to flow in another, 'altering things', instead of keeping them constant. The change is no evidence for weakness in a river (or in S).

In 109–10 he admitted his infidelities. In 111 he made excuses and begged for pity. In 112 he undertook to obey the beloved, who in 113 was all the world to him. In 114 there is a devious statement of his total devotion. He is now suggesting that his infidelities were not his fault, but the fault of 'this bloody tyrant Time' (16.2).

9–12 'I lied about my love, yet I could not have known how it was to grow.' The key words are 'might I not then say'. Having admitted his error, he now claims that at the time it was understandable and forgivable, 'Could I not in those days [reasonably] have said, "Now I love you best"?' He was 'certain o'er uncertainty', certain about the future, because the present was so wonderful that he was certain the future could not equal it. This is repeated in the next line. He was 'crowning the present', glorying in it, and not knowing what was to come. For him it was the best imaginable time. Might it not then, in these early days, have been reasonable to say, 'Now I love you best'? On this explanation these lines are hammering home the argument of lines 3–4.

13–14   Lines 13–14 repeat it with a metaphor. After all, Love is a babe, so when S said Love could never be better he was allowing that full growth would follow, 'To give full growth to that which still doth grow.' Babies grow, and sure enough his love grew and is still growing. It is just possible that S is trying to joke his way out of trouble. The statement 'Love is a babe' could hardly be uttered without pointing towards Cupid, but Cupid does not seriously help the case. It was well known that he did not grow, 'For he hath been five thousand year a boy' in *LLL* 5.2.11.

In line 10 'then' refers to time, 'Might Í not thén say …?' In line 13 it does not carry the metrical stress 'Lóve is a bábe: then míght I nót say só …?' It may also have a different meaning, 'therefore', 'Love is a babe: might Í therefore nót say, "Now I love you best"?' After all, exaggeration is permitted in praising babies. From Sonnet 18 onwards, love was perfection, but it is a paradoxical perfection because it is still improving. The little lie he confessed in the first line is turned into an extravagant compliment.

Lines 10–14 have been intensely discussed. This note has taken 'might I not' in 10 and 13 as introducing questions by which S defends himself against the charge of lying in the past, the subject of the sonnet as announced in the first line. Most commentators take line 13 as a statement in which S confesses a present error, 'But now I know that love is a baby which continues to grow. Therefore I should not say "Now I love you best" ' (Burrow (2002)). This note suggests that 'Might I not say …?' in lines 13 and 10 are both questions, referring to past time, to the mistake he made when his love was young, the lie that he before hath writ.

✂ 116 ✃

Let me not to the marriage of true minds
Admit impediments. Love is not love,
Which alters when it alteration finds,
Or bends with the remover to remove.   4

O no, it is an ever fixèd mark
That looks on tempests and is never shaken.
It is the star to every wand'ring bark,
Whose worth's unknown, although his heighth be taken.   8

Love's not Time's fool, though rosy lips and cheeks
Within his bending sickle's compass come.
Love alters not with his brief hours and weeks
But bears it out ev'n to the edge of doom.   12

   If this be error and upon me proved,
   I never writ, nor no man ever loved.

When there is a marriage of true minds, let nothing come between them,
*   even if one of them changes or is absent.*
Love is a beacon immovable in the storm, the Pole Star to every ship.
Love's not Time's slave. Time cuts down beauty,
*   but love lasts till Judgement Day.*
If I am proved wrong in this, I never wrote and no man ever loved.

1–4 'Those whom God hath joined together, let not man put asunder.'
'Let not' has a religious flavour, as, for example, in Psalm 31: 17, '*Let me*
not be ashamed, O LORD: for I have called upon thee.' Two other sonnets
begin on the same religious note, 36 with 'Let me *confess*', 105 with 'Let
not my love be called *idolatry*'. This is not simply an overtone. The first
11 words of this poem are a play on the language of the marriage ceremony
in the Book of Common Prayer. 'Therefore if any man can shew any just
cause, why they may not lawfully be joined together, *let* him now speak

... I require and charge you both, as ye will answer at the dreadful day of *judgement* when the secrets of all hearts shall be disclosed, that if either of you know any *impediment* why ye may not be lawfully joined together in Matrimony, ye do now *confess* it.' 'Confess' is italicised here because it is close to 'admit' in the sonnet, and 'judgement' is italicised because it is alluded to in line 12, by 'doom', the Last Judgement (see note on line 12 below). If *impediments* were raised at the banns or the wedding ceremony, 'the solemnization must be deferred, until such time as the truth be tried' (BCP 313). The Church had its procedures. For instance, 'If there be any of you who knoweth any *Impediment*, or notable Crime, in any of these persons presented to be ordered Deacons, for the which he ought not to be *admitted* to that Office, let him come forth in the Name of God, and shew what the Crime or *Impediment* is' (BCP 575–6). In effect, S is speaking as the bishop who has to assess an impediment. If he does so and finds it invalid, he will not *admit* it.

This is the grave and authoritative language of ecclesiastical law applied to a loving relationship between a beautiful youth and a middle-aged man who sees his face as 'beated and chopped with tanned antiquity' (62.10). Marriage between two men was unthinkable. To keep well away from such blasphemy, this is a marriage of *minds*. The break in the middle of line 2, here as elsewhere, lends weight (see 117.1, and comment on 104.3).

Burrow (2002) has a perceptive note on lines 3–4: 'Disturbingly, the *polyptoton* (the repetition of a word in a different form) is used to insist on constancy: *remover ... remove* and *alters ... alteration*.' It is as though love is love and does not change, but remover changes to removes, and alters to alteration. The remover in this context could be either the partner who goes on a journey, or the partner whose affections have strayed. S has travelled in 110.1 and 113.1, but literal travel sometimes merges into sexual aberrations, as in 109.5–8, 110.2–4 and 117.5–8. The true lover does not deviate, change course, to abandon the partner who departs. The message is that the beloved ought not to alter just because S has been unfaithful.

The metre is part of the power of these lines. The first four lines in the two neighbouring sonnets read quite smoothly as iambics, except perhaps for 'My móst fúll fláme' in 115.4. By contrast, 116.1–4 has much syncopation between iambic expectation and the emphases of natural speech. Some syllables demand emphasis although they would not carry the metrical stress, as in 'Let me nót to the marriage of trúe minds | Admit impediments. Lóve is not love ...' In addition, half a dozen syllables which would be expected to carry the metrical stress demand to be read without emphasis, for example, 'the' and 'to' in line 4.

5–8 'O no' represents the speaking voice, almost a stage direction for a shake of the head. A mark never moving in storms must be a sea-mark, a beacon or lighthouse. Coriolanus tells his young son to be 'like a great sea-mark … saving those that eye thee' (*Cor* 5.3.74–5). But in here it is not sailors heaving in a storm who eye the mark, but the mark, vividly personified, that looks unmoved on tempests. The nautical image continues with love as a fixed star. According to Dava Sobel in *Longitude* (1996, 4), 'any sailor worth his salt could gauge his latitude well enough by the length of the day, or by the height of the sun or known guide stars above the horizon', the angle of elevation of the Pole Star increasing as the ship sails northwards in the northern hemisphere. The 'ever fixèd mark' must be the Pole Star. Its worth has been explained as its inestimable value to mariners. In context this is feeble. Every sailor knew the value of the Pole Star, and it would be laughable to suggest that its worth was unknown in this context. The worth of a planet, astrologically, is its effect upon life on this earth. The Pole Star has no known astrological 'worth', but the notion that a star might have influence is part of popular astrology, as in *Tem* 1.2.183, 'A most auspicious star whose influence | If now I court not …'

In this line the Quarto reads 'higth', and for once this edition shows some respect for Q's spelling, accepting Munro's emendation 'heighth'. It seems to give force to the line if 'héighth' speaks to 'wórth'. A similar effect may occur at 91.1–2.

9–12 The Shakespearean fool is subservient to his king, but love is not subservient to 'this bloody tyrant Time' (16.2), nor does it come within the compass of his sickle. Time swings his curved sickle, but here it is not curved but 'bending', and this may play upon its effect on aged bodies, like the unkindness in *R2* 2.1.134–5, which would resemble 'crooked age, | To crop at once a too-long withered flower'.

After Time's work with the sickle 'the edge of doom' suggests death. But, being so near the play on the ceremony of marriage at the beginning of the poem, it also glances at sense 6 in *OED*, 'the day of judgement' (see 145.7). If 'doom' is so taken, love lasts beyond death, to the second before sentence is passed on that dreadful day.

Part of the eloquence of this great poem comes from the earnest insistence of its tone, and that is built on the rigour of its structure. A powerful reading of it would lay gentle weight on 'Love is not love', 'O no it is', 'Love's not', 'Love alters not', 'nor no man ever loved.'

'Shakespeare's best sonnet' (Wordsworth) has traditionally been read as the noblest expression of the constancy and strength of human love. But this has been challenged. Kerrigan (1986), for instance, the shrewdest of modern commentators, finds it boastful and sentimental: 'The convoluted negatives of the last line ... show the poet protesting too much, losing confidence in his protestations, or at least inviting disagreement with them ... Indeed, the strenuousness subverts itself grammatically' (1986, 53), because of the Elizabethan notion that 'two negatives affirm'. This is going too far. Double negatives are not uncommon in an emphatic negative sense in Shakespeare. No natural reading of this line could have failed or could now fail to sense the massive negative force of 'nor no man ever loved' (see 5.12 and 19.10). But Kerrigan has just cause for unease. To say that true love does not change is simply false. Some love lasts a lifetime, but even if it does it alters, and many true minds that have joined have parted.

This is the 116th sonnet in a collection devoted to the love between the poet and a young man. Sonnets 109–21 form a group in which S admits his infidelities and asks to be forgiven. He flatters his beloved, pleads for pity, and multiplies outrageous excuses and far-fetched arguments in an attempt to win his way back into favour. An extreme example is 117.13–14, where he begs the young man not to hate him because his sexual indulgences were attempts to prove 'The constancy and virtue of your love'.

So then in Sonnet 116 S has embedded this praise of unalterable love in a mountain of excuses and admissions of infidelity. Read in context, the noble expression of the constancy and strength of human love is a diplomatic manoeuvre, calculated praise of the constancy and virtue of love to a man whose inconstancy S has often railed against. In the light of this, 'Let me not to the marriage of true *minds*' carries a message, 'Our bodies have not been true' (see 109.1, 'O never say that I was false of *heart*'), 'but we do truly love each other, and that love can never alter.' This eulogy of love is implicitly his appeal to the beloved to honour it, and also a promise to do the same himself from now on.

To repeat yet again, these poems are not best read as accounts of events in Shakespeare's life, but as a drama of love, an invention of incidents that might arise in love, and of arguments that a lover might possibly deploy in them. In writing them the playwright has written a play in 152 scenes (153 and 154 are outside the drama). There are gaps, surprises and inconsistencies in the plot, but so there are in love. The speaker of these poems would not be the first or last lover to appeal as here to the unalterability of love when his love has altered.

Accuse me thus: that I have scanted all
Wherein I should your great deserts repay,
Forgot upon your dearest love to call,
Whereto all bonds do tie me day by day;   4
That I have frequent been with unknown minds
And giv'n to time your own dear-purchased right;
That I have hoisted sail to all the winds
Which should transport me farthest from your sight.   8
Book both my wilfulness and errors down,
And on just proof, surmise accumulate,

Bring me within the level of your frown,
But shoot not at me in your wakened hate,   12
   Since my appeal says I did strive to prove
   The constancy and virtue of your love.

Accuse me of sins of omission (1–4) and of commission (5–8),
*   proven crimes and crimes of which I am suspected.*
Frown, but do not hate me.
I was testing your love.

1–10 In Sonnet 87 there were nearly a score of legal terms. Here 'accuse', 'wherein' and 'whereto' are legal jargon, the third echoing the second as the charges are read out, each at the beginning of its line. The charge sheet continues with 'that' in lines 1, 5 and 7. The legal flavour is maintained by 'repay', 'dearest' (compare 87.1), 'bonds do tie', 'dear-purchased right', 'Book … down', 'just proof', 'surmise accumulate', 'appeal', 'prove'.

   The first eight lines contain five accusations: that S has 'scanted', skimped, his duties of repaying the beloved for all he has done for him; that he has forgotten to call upon the beloved, to whom he is every day in debt; that he has been 'frequent … with unknown minds', consorted with nonentities, every Tom, Dick and Harry; that he has 'giv'n to time your own dear-purchased right', meaning that he has given to hours of the day attention which rightfully belonged to the beloved in view of the love he had given S; that he has happily sailed off, choosing all the winds 'Which should transport me farthest from thy sight.' 'Transport' fits this nautical metaphor, though transportation as a form of legal punishment is not recorded till the middle of the seventeenth century. Travel is a euphemism for sexual infidelity in Sonnets 109–21 and in 116.3–4. The hoisting of sail and the wind selection suggest how eagerly S ranged, and 'transport' admits how far he roved. And in lines 2–6 this stream of confessions is sweetened by praise of the beloved, his great deserts and dearest love, his own daily debt and the value of what he has received.

Lines 9–10 complete the charge sheet with two general character flaws, and the beloved is urged to record not only what is proved, but also to add crimes S may be assumed to have committed. By admitting that some charges against him have been proved, he has contrived to end his humble confession by implying that he has at other times been the victim of injustice.

The lofty opening of Sonnet 116 was in a weighty, dislocated rhythm. Here in 117, when there are so many items on the charge sheet, the rhythm is mechanical, with no breach of the basic iambic rhythm except the inversion of the first words of 9 and 11, 'Bóok both my wílfulnéss' and 'Bríng me withín'. The inversion is common in this metre, but even so, as spaced in the poem, it makes an effective climax for the case against the accused.

11–14 Now comes the sentence. In 'Bríng me withín the level of your frown' the frown is a gun or a bow. Level it to aim, but not to fire, 'But shoot not at me in your wakened hate'. This could imply that the beloved's hate is already aroused, 'your hate is already wakened, but do not shoot at me'. But 'wakened' is more likely to be part of his appeal, 'do not feel hatred and shoot me'.

In the final couplet S makes an appeal in extenuation of his offences, and it is so inept, so grotesque, that a man with Shakespeare's understanding of human nature could never have made it on his own behalf: 'I've been away and neglected you and had lots of love affairs, but I was doing it to make a strenuous attempt to test you.' Any man who spoke like this to a lover would be taking his life in his hands. This outrageous conclusion to the sonnet, added to similar shameless arguments in other sonnets in this group (notably 109.5–8 and 110.6–11), confirms the interpretation advanced at the end of 116. In these poems 109–21, at this phase in the plot of the Sonnets, the dramatist is developing the character of the offending lover and ingenious apologist. The qualifications for being a dramatist include this ability to represent the thinking and feeling of fictitious characters. Words given in a play do not reveal the views of the playwright, and they are not evidence for his life. S is not a portrait of the author, but a fiction using some parts of his experience of life and of literature, and moulding them into works of his imagination.

An advantage of this approach is that it brings this sonnet into harmony with those around it, including even 116. In all the poems of this group he accepts his guilt, and they are all manoeuvres to win back the beloved.

Dover Wilson (1966)
It would be difficult to find a greater contrast, contradiction one might say, in the Quarto text than this and the preceding sonnet. We pass without any connection from a sublime declaration of perfect concord to a confession of neglecting the Friend for the company of persons of no importance. Some displacement here cannot be denied.

ဆ 118 ��

Like as, to make our appetites more keen,
With eager compounds we our palate urge;
As, to prevent our maladies unseen,
We sicken to shun sickness when we purge— 4

Ev'n so, being full of your ne'er cloying sweetness,
To bitter sauces did I frame my feeding;
And, sick of welfare, found a kind of meetness
To be diseased ere that there was true needing. 8

Thus policy in love, t'anticipate
The ills that were not, grew to faults assured,
And brought to medicine a healthful state
Which, rank of goodness, would by ill be cured. 12

But thence I learn, and find the lesson true,
Drugs poison him that so fell sick of you.

Just as we stimulate appetite with sharp tastes,
and make ourselves ill by purges,
even so, being full of your sweetness,
I took bitter sauces and chose to be ill.
So in love, anticipating ills led to faults,
as I tried to cure health with sickness.
This taught me that the drug [of infidelity] poisoned the man
whose sickness was love for you.

S has been unfaithful, and has produced a stream of denials, evasions, excuses and grovelling appeals. Now he finds two explanations as ingenious and far-fetched as anything that has gone before. This poem consists of two similes, one from diet in lines 1–2 expounded in 5–6, the other from medicine in lines 3–4 and 7–14.

A simile is a comparison of one thing with another of a different kind.

361

Sonnet 95, for instance, begins with a simile which compares a shameful act by a reputable person to a canker in a rose. This, logically, might run, 'the shame, like a canker in the rose, spoils the beauty of your name.' But 95 reads 'the shame | Which, like a canker in the fragrant rose, | Doth *spot* the beauty of thy *budding* name.' Shame does not spot and names do not bud. 'Spot' and 'budding' are applied to the literal shame, although they are terms which belong to the comparison, the rose. By such crossing of the divide, speaking of A as though it were B, similes are made more vivid and more persuasive. This common pattern has been called transfusion of terms.

So, in lines 5–6, instead of giving a literal account, S describes his emotions in terms of diet, 'full', 'cloying sweetness', 'bitter sauces' and 'feeding'. In the rest of the sonnet he describes his emotions in medical terms, 'maladies', 'sicken', 'purge', 'sick', 'diseased', 'medicine', 'healthful', 'ill(s)', 'cured', 'drugs', 'poison', 'fell sick'.

1–2, 5–6 In line 2 'eager' is bitter (French *égar*) as in vinegar, and in Horatio's words on a cold night on the battlements of Elsinore, 'It is a nipping and an eager air' (*Ham* 1.4.2). 'Compounds' is gliding towards the medical metaphor which follows. For 'compounds' in a medical sense, see 76.4.

One frames pictures by putting frames round them. So in line 6 S framed his feeding by putting bitter sauces on his food, perhaps round the plate. He did so 'being full of your ne'er cloying sweetness'. This is dangerous ground. It is not tactful for a man to say that he had affairs because he was tired of his lover's sweetness. S hopes to avoid this danger by a compliment assuring the beloved that although he is full of his sweetness, it never cloys. The Quarto's reading 'nere cloying' has encouraged some editors to print 'near cloying'. This is a disaster – 'I had affairs because you were nearly too sweet.' Happily, Burrow (2002) points out that 'Q follows a consistent pattern ... that "nere" is the contracted form of "never" and "neere" is the equivalent of "near".'

3–4, 7–8 The rest of the poem develops the medical simile, based upon the common practice of taking laxative purges as preventives against illness. These preventative purges often induced vomiting and other forms of sickness, 'We sicken to shun sickness when we purge.' 'Maladies unseen' are illnesses which have no symptoms.

9–12 In love this policy of anticipating non-existent ills has led to ills which really do exist. 'Ills' is a term with medical overtones, and 'faults' abandons medicine to admit that he behaved badly. After cloaking his misbehaviour in a medical disguise, S has owned up to the crime, but unobtrusively, in one word.

13–14 On 'him that so fell sick of you' Booth (1977) writes of 'the unflattering harshness of the suggestion', and Duncan-Jones (1997) thinks that S grew weary of the company of the beloved. This is to misunderstand the wit. This poem begins with the absurdity of preventing maladies of which there are no symptoms, of making ourselves sick in order to avoid sickness, of being full of a taste that never cloys, of being sick with well-being, of finding it somehow appropriate to be diseased when there is no need for it, of anticipating non-existent ills, of applying medicine to health, of an excess of goodness. How could any reader fail to see that this is a catalogue of absurdities? S is admitting the lunacy of his recourse to the drug of sexual promiscuity when he had no sickness, no symptoms. The beloved is health. He never cloys. He is welfare and goodness. 'Sick of you' is not 'unflattering harshness' but the climactic absurdity in this abject apology. The last thing S would wish to do at this moment would be to insult the beloved. After this madding fever his wish is to return to his content, to his old love, which is now fairer, stronger and greater (119. 12–14). The beloved would have understood the wit.

� 119 ❧

What potions have I drunk of Siren tears
Distilled from lymbecks foul as hell within,
Applying fears to hopes and hopes to fears,
Still losing when I saw myself to win!   4

What wretched errors hath my heart committed,
Whilst it hath thought itself so blessed never!
How have mine eyes out of their spheres been fitted
In the distraction of this madding fever!   8

O benefit of ill! Now I find true
That better is by evil still made better,
And ruined love when it is built anew
Grows fairer than at first, more strong, far greater.   12

  So I return rebuked to my content,
  And gain by ills thrice more than I have spent.

What grief have I suffered, losing when I thought I was winning!
What blunders has my heart made when it thought itself blest!
*   How were my eyes deceived!*
The advantage is that my old love is now made still better.
So I return rebuked to a love much greater than what I left behind.

1–4   These lines combine two images. The Sirens are females who lured
mariners on to the rocks by their songs. So S has been lured to destruction
by the tears of a new lover, perhaps female. But Sirens did not weep. One
explanation of these tears might be that this new lover used tears instead of
songs to lure her victim, and S succumbed. But the tears also form a glide
to the second image.

  'Lymbecks' are alembics, apparatus for distilling. In this process a flask
of liquid is heated and steam is trapped in a tube, the beak, which rises a
little and then slopes downwards. This tube is kept cool, steam condenses

in it, and liquid drips into a receptacle, the receiver. Since the boiling point of alcohol is lower than that of water, this liquid is a spirit. So these 'lymbecks foul as hell within' are flasks of liquid from which the potions are distilled, and drip like tears into the receiver. This lymbeck is the new lover, foul as hell within, and S has drunk her tears with dire effect.

In distillation *heat* is applied to *cold* liquid in a flask, and running water is applied to the outside of the tube to cool it and condense the *hot* steam. So S has been 'Applying fears to hopes and hopes to fears', cold fear of losing the old love, warm hope of winning the new. The word 'applying' strengthens the notion that the process of distillation is involved in these lines, as it is even more technically in *Mac* 1.7.65–9.

5–8 In Sonnets 113 and 114 S pondered whether it was his eyes or his heart that was deceived, and arrived at two different answers. Here he solves the problem by blaming both. His heart committed wretched errors while thinking itself supremely blessed. His eyes have been fitted out of their spheres. 'Spheres' are usually said to be sockets. But this may be too simple. Eye sockets are not spherical, and 'fitted' is the opposite of the required sense. A solution might start from *Ham* 1.5.17, 'Make thy two eyes like stars start from their spheres.' According to ancient astronomers, spheres were transparent hollow globes which revolved round the earth carrying the separate heavenly bodies (*OED* 2). In *AC* 3.13.147–9, 'my good stars that were my former guides, | Have empty left their orbs, and shot their fires | Into the abyss of hell.' So too in *AW* 1.1.85–8. If in the sonnet Shakespeare is thinking of the eyes as being like stars, the two have leapt out of their spherical containers in different directions and been fitted out of these spheres into places where they did not belong, in the abyss of madness, 'In the distraction of this madding fever.' They might also have been distracted in a literal sense. If eyes are distracted, it suggests that they are disfocused, forced apart, as in *AW* 5.3.35–6, 'to the brightest beams | Distracted clouds give way.'

9–12 In Sonnet 118 he tried in vain to heal what was good by applying what was evil. Here he has done the same again, but this time the treatment is successful. Ill has its benefit – 'better is by evil still made better', made even better. Love may be ruined, but when it is rebuilt it becomes more beautiful, stronger and greater. In this detail Sonnet 119 contradicts 118. Similarly 113 blames Mind, and 114 blames Eye, whereas now 119.5–8 blames both. Such differences demonstrate the powers of invention of a poet who understands that lovers can put the same material to many different uses.

The requirements of sound building, according to Vitruvius' famous definition (*De architectura* 1.3.2), are strength, utility and beauty, *firmitas, utilitas, venustas*. Vitruvius was translated from Latin into Italian by Palladio and was known in England in Shakespeare's day through the work of Inigo Jones. Love rebuilt (11) therefore comes near to fulfilling this law of three, and the rebuilding flags the architectural metaphor. The triad is wittily adapted by changing utility, which has little to do with love, into magnitude, 'far greater', which is not part of any definition of sound building. Building requires strength, utility and beauty. Ruined Love rebuilt is more beautiful, stronger and far greater.

13–14 So S has been rebuked by experience, and surely also by his old lover to whom he has now returned, and with whom he has found contentment. He has thus gained much more, three times more, than he has spent. This could not possibly refer in any way to the ejaculation of semen, but Burrow (2002) thinks it could. Rather, after his lapses S has discovered that the beloved is three times more precious than anything he has bought in his recent experiences, 'than I have spent'. The settling of this account in the only monosyllabic line of the sonnet gives to the closing compliment the strength of simplicity.

ꙮ 120 ꙮ

That you were once unkind befriends me now,
And for that sorrow which I then did feel,
Needs must I under my transgression bow
Unless my nerves were brass or hammered steel.   4
For if you were by my unkindness shaken
As I by yours, you've passed a hell of time,
And I, a tyrant, have no leisure taken
To weigh how once I suffered in your crime.   8

O that our night of woe might have rememb'red
My deepest sense how hard true sorrow hits,
And soon to you, as you to me then, tend'red
The humble salve which wounded bosoms fits—   12

But that your trespass now becomes a fee.
Mine ransoms yours, and yours must ransom me.

The fact that you once wronged me stands me in good stead now, and
  my misery then weighs on me now to think how you must be suffering.
If only that dreadful night had reminded me how hard sorrow hits
  and I had humbled myself to comfort you—
except that your old sin is a fee I paid. Now you must pay for mine.

S's transgression in line 3, unkindness in line 5 and trespass in line 13 are
his infidelity, which has been the main subject since Sonnet 109. But the
beloved too was guilty of 'sensual fault' (35.9), and more than once, as
recorded in 33–5, 40–2, 57–8 and 92–6. The sonnet explains how that
befriends S now. The simple and obvious argument would be that S forgave
the beloved in the past, and therefore the beloved ought to forgive S now.
But the argument is more complex.

   First of all, forgiveness by the victim is not the point, but swift and
convincing contrition and repentance by the offender. When the beloved
was the guilty party, S suffered acutely, and the offender soon offered 'The

humble salve which wounded bosoms fits' (11–12). Now, when S is the offender, he has forgotten how much he himself then suffered, and has failed to provide that same humble salve. The salve is not here defined, but 34.14 gives some indication. It is not enough for the erring lover to come back, nor are shame, repentance and sorrow enough to cure the grief. It is the offender's tears which 'ransom all ill deeds'. Now that S is the offender he has not immediately shown that degree of remorse, not applied that salve of humility to the wounds he has inflicted on the beloved.

1–8 In line 3, where S must bow under his transgression, the tone is biblical. In Isaiah 24: 20 'the transgression thereof shall be heavy upon the earth', and in Lamentations 1: 14 Jeremiah bears the yoke of his transgressions on his neck. So too would S have to bow under the weight of his transgression, unless his nerves were of brass or hammered steel. The metaphor demands that the nerves, as usual in Shakespeare, are the sinews, the physical strength that bears the weight, but the word may also register in the technical sense of the fibres which carry sensation and emotion, never so used in Shakespeare, but Francis Bacon in 1626 writes about an eye, 'thryst forth, so as it hanged a pretty distance from the Visuall Nerve' (*OED* 2.8). It would be more than bold, but typical of Shakespeare to conceive of such fine nerves as 'brass or hammered steel'.

In line 5 S is now the betrayer, and realises that, if the beloved has suffered as he himself once suffered, he has passed through 'a hell of time'. The phrase is not our weary cliché, 'a hell of a time', but a continuation of the religious allusion in line 3. The beloved has suffered as though in the place of eternal torture, and S now realises it when he remembers his own suffering, and realises also that he has not bothered to consider this. His behaviour has been tyrannical (7).

9–12 'Remember' means 'remind', as in *Tem* 1.2.244, 'Let me remember thee what thou hast promised.' Now comes a passionate exclamation, 'If only our night of woe could have reminded my heart, my deepest consciousness, how hard true sorrow strikes.' 'Our night of woe' could be metaphorical, a period of estrangement, a dark night of the soul, but it makes a more vivid narrative if 'night' is taken to mean what it says. They have spent one painful night of recriminations and quarrelling. This interpretation has some slight support in 'soon' in line 11. 'If only I had then been humble at the beginning of that miserable night', by offering the humble salve in line 12. Instead it is fair to guess that there was denial, evasion, recrimination. 'Our night of woe' referring to his tyrannical behaviour is then a face-saving apology, typical of S in Sonnets 109–12 and 118–19. So too he does not frankly confess that he forgot, but in lines 9–10 he blames that night for not reminding him. Such a character would not have stopped short of counter-accusations. It would have been a long night.

13–14 'I wish I had behaved differently – *except that* you hurt me and I forgave, so now I hurt you and you must forgive.' The connection, 'But that', is loose, yet not difficult to grasp. The first dozen lines are an intense expression of regret. In the final couplet, he leaps from apology to effront-ery. At 'But that', he suddenly realises a strength in his position, and contradicts what has gone before. He has no need to apologise, no need for the remorseful exclamation of 9–12. He suddenly realises that the previous infidelity of the beloved now becomes a fee. S paid it in the past as ransom in the form of pardon for his infidelity (34.14). Now S has erred, and the beloved has to pay him back. The tone changes in line 13 from passionate sorrow to mischievous cynicism, 'I wish I had been more humble – except that it is not required. My ransom was prepaid.'

Commentators have found it difficult to make 'But that' meaning 'except that' connect with what goes before, and offer a less vivid explana-tion: 'But that your trespass' stands for 'However, that trespass of yours', like 'that thy spirit' standing for 'that spirit of yours' in *AC* 2.3.18.

After the religious tone of 'transgression' and 'hell' in lines 3 and 6, 'trespass' and 'ransom' in lines 13–14 heighten the effrontery. 'Trespass' is conspicuous in the Lord's Prayer, and 'ransom' is mentioned a dozen times in the Bible, 'the Son of man came ... to give his life a ransom for many.' (Mark 10: 45). The language of Christianity is applied to sexual licence.

In many of these poems the end looks back at the beginning, as in Sonnets 53, 86 and 101. If the first line were to be read by itself, it would go well with line 14, 'I forgave you once. That befriends me now because you must forgive me.' But between the two statements of this hard-headed *quid pro quo* argument, S offers sympathy for the beloved in 5–6, a confession of his own failure in 7–8, and praise of the beloved in 11–12.

'Tis better to be vile than vile esteemed,
When not to be receives reproach of being
And the just pleasure lost, which is so deemed
Not by our feeling but by others' seeing.   4

For why should others' false adulterate eyes
Give salutation to my sportive blood?
Or on my frailties why are frailer spies,
Which in their wills count bad what I think good?   8

No, I am that I am, and they that level
At my abuses reckon up their own.
I may be straight though they themselves be bevel.
By their rank thoughts my deeds must not be shown,   12
   Unless this general evil they maintain—
   All men are bad and in their badness reign.

It is better to be vile than thought vile without having the joy of it.
   Others see our behaviour as vile, but we don't feel it is.
Why do adulterers greet me as one of them? Why are my frailties spied on
   by those frailer than myself, who decide to think evil what I think good?
I am what I am, and those who target my misdeeds are listing their own.
   I may be straight though they be crooked. My actions should not
   be judged by their foul minds, unless they hold that all men are evil.

1–4 To have a bad reputation when you don't deserve it means you are
criticised for pleasures you don't have, 'when not to be [vile] receives
reproach of being [vile] and the rightful pleasure [is] lost'. Our conduct is
deemed vile by critics who *see* it as such, although we do not *feel* it to be
vile. After 120 sonnets devoted to the subject, this pleasure refers to the
love he has enjoyed with the young man.

5–8 The eyes of these critics are 'adulterate'. The word occurs seven times in Shakespeare, and 'adulterous' only twice. All nine occurrences refer to adultery. So those who judge him to be vile are adulterers, and hypocrites. He admits his 'sportive blood', his lively, sparky behaviour, but does not wish to be hailed in the street and claimed as a crony by hypocritical adulterers. But 'Give salutation' is subtler than that. If 'false adulterate eyes | Give salutation', it would be a sideways, conniving glance, with a raising of the eyebrow or a knowing wink. No wonder he is angry. He knows he has frailties, but theirs are greater. 'Which' in line 8 stands where we would say 'who', as in 106.13 and 124.14. Monosyllables punch their weight in 8.

9–14 And monosyllables continue in God's words to Moses in Exodus 3: 14, 'I am that I am.' The tones of total authority express S's defiance. 'No' is an indignant protest. This monosyllabic eloquence is not weakened in lines 11 and 12. The extra eleventh syllable in 'level' and 'bevel' may even sharpen the contempt. 'Level' means aim in gunnery or archery, as in 117.11–12, and 'bevel', only here in Shakespeare, means oblique, and therefore out of the true, a surprising word, no doubt arrived at for the rhyme, but no less effective for that.

The final couplet is a baffling argument. He says he does not want his actions to be judged by prudish hypocrites, unless they argue that all men are wicked and thrive by wickedness. But what would be the drift of that argument? It could be a vigorous way of reducing the proposition to an absurdity – 'unless we are all villains, and of course we're not'. Or it could be a disarming modesty – 'I know all men are sinners, myself included, and, if that's what they mean, I cannot deny it, but they are pretending that there is something especially vile about my conduct. And there isn't.' Neither of these interpretations provides the expected sting in the tail. It may be worth asking whether 'their badness' must be all men's badness. If it refers rather to the gossipers' vice of hypocrisy, this would provide a sting in the tail, 'unless they maintain that everybody, including myself, is as hypocritical as they are'.

Thy gift, thy tables, are within my brain
Full charactered with lasting memory,
Which shall above that idle rank remain
Beyond all date, ev'n to eternity,   4
Or at the least, so long as brain and heart
Have faculty by nature to subsist.

Till each to razed oblivion yield his part
Of thee, thy record never can be missed.   8
That poor retention could not so much hold,
Nor need I tallies thy dear love to score.

Therefore to give them from me was I bold,
To trust those tables that receive thee more.   12
    To keep an adjunct to remember thee
    Were to import forgetfulness in me.

The notebook you gave me is written letter by letter on my brain,
    and will last for ever, or as long as brain and heart survive.
While they exist that record will not perish. A notebook could not hold it.
That's why I gave it away. I trusted the tables of my mind.
    To keep a written record would be to suggest that I could forget.

1–6 The tables are notebooks, counsel-keepers (*2H4* 2.4.269), commonplace books in which Elizabethans recorded thoughts, observations, whatever they wanted to remember, like the book S gave to the beloved in
Sonnet 77. The beloved has given his tables to S, and S has committed the
unpardonable offence of giving them to someone else – even more unpardonable if the recipient is a new lover. Is this a shadowy early appearance
of the Black Lady? S now attempts to defend the indefensible. Every letter,
every character, is unforgettably inscribed on the tables of his brain, where
they will last much longer than will 'that idle rank' of characters, those
lines of lifeless letters in the notebook, 'ev'n to eternity', he says, and

corrects himself immediately. He will not remember till the end of time, but only while his faculties permit. The beloved is lodged in his brain and heart, but there will come a time when his brain and heart will not exist.

7–10   To raze is to destroy, to level with the ground, but it could also, as here, mean the same as to erase (*OED* 3, last citation, 1709). See 25.11. While S's powers survive, the 'record', the memory, of the beloved will never be erased. A poor little notebook could never retain as much as that vast archive, 'That poor retention could not so much hold'.

To belittle even further the notebook he has given away, he compares it to a tally, an innkeeper's slate. 'There shall be no money,' cries the rebel Cade in *2H6* 4.2.74–5, 'All shall eat and drink on my score', and in *1H4* 2.5.26–7 Hal quotes an underskinker, 'Anon, anon, sir! Score a pint of bastard in the Half-moon!' (a skinker is a tapster, and bastard is a sweet Spanish wine). For every customer there would be a stick, his tally, and every debt would be recorded by a notch or score.

11–14   Such records in low-class inns and on tables like those in the first line are unworthy of this precious subject matter, so S gave the notebooks away, and trusted *tables* that would carry more of the beloved. 'Remember me,' said the Ghost, and Hamlet replied in 1.5.97–9, 'Remember thee? | Yea, from the *table* of my memory | I'll wipe away all trivial fond records.' To keep an *aide-mémoire* to remind him of the beloved would be to imply that S could forget him, but again the language is tooled to present an eloquent balance and to sharpen the final epigram. 'An adjunct to remember thee' would balance 'to import forgetfulness in me'.

This sonnet posits unpardonable behaviour on the part of S. No prudent lover would have passed an intimate document on to a third party, or would have dared to produce such an outrageous defence if he had. But there is no need to believe. These poems are inventions of events and situations which could be imagined to occur in love, and inventions of what could be said if they did. They are explorations of love, including some of its furthest reaches. The effrontery of the defence that S erects in this sonnet, as in 120, is an invention of reasoning for an invented situation, and in particular it is an example of the outrageous ingenuity which is a leading characteristic of S, the hero of this drama. They are not arguments deployed by William Shakespeare in order to extricate himself from a social blunder.

No, Time, thou shalt not boast that I do change.
Thy pyramids, built up with newer might,
To me are nothing novel, nothing strange—
They are but dressings of a former sight.⁣ 4

Our dates are brief, and therefore we admire
What thou dost foist upon us that is old,
And rather make them born to our desire
Than think that we before have heard them told.⁣ 8

Thy registers and thee I both defy,
Not wondering at the present nor the past,
For thy recórds and what we see doth lie,
Made more or less by thy continual haste.⁣ 12

   This I do vow, and this shall ever be—
   I will be true despite thy scythe and thee.

No, Time, I shall not change. Your new pyramids are not new,
   simply old ones dressed up.
We admire what is old, pretending it is born for our pleasure
   rather than remembering we have heard it all before.
I defy you, Time, you and your past records and what we see now.
   You make things seem greater or smaller as you rush along.
I vow to be true for ever despite you.

1–4 Time is addressed throughout, and not only addressed but ha-
rangued. He is a boaster, an incompetent innovator whose 'newer might'
produces 'nothing novel', a decorator not a creator, a fraudster hawking
old goods (6), a liar, always in a hurry (11–12). The dramatist sees Time as
a character who needs a good talking to. The first accusation suggests that
pyramids are one of Time's achievements, and proceeds to belittle them.
This could refer to the Egyptian pyramids built in the fourth millennium

BC. S would be sneering at them on the grounds that Time showed no originality in constructing them. This supposes that there were pyramids before Khufu (died 3666 BC). These buildings are all rehashes of earlier models.

But contemporary readers could scarcely have failed to read this as a sneer at the extravagance of the coronation of James I of England in 1604, when 3000 carpenters erected 'pyramids, built up with newer might', to line the route of the procession (Harbage (1950), 62–3; and Honan (1999), 303). Perhaps Shakespeare himself played a part in the parade (see 125.1–2). Such a sneer would be surprising in an actor-writer whose company had just received the patronage of the new king in May 1603, and had changed its name from the Chamberlain's Men to the King's Men. This is at the least an impertinent remark likely to damage Shakespeare's career and pocket, but there are similar tones in 114.8 and 125.1–2. An explanation may lie in the history of the Quarto. It is not certain that Shakespeare intended this collection of poems for publication (see on 33.14).

5–8 Because our lives are short, we admire what is long-lived. But Time is a card-sharper, cheating us by palming, fisting, his cards (see *OED* foist). We imagine he has produced these erections to please us personally, and we do not reflect that we have already heard all about them.

9–12 Old buildings are 'registers' and 'records' of past time, and the focus now moves to documents, inscriptions, histories. In 10–12 there are four contrasting pairs: registers and Time (9); present and past; records and present sights; more or less. Each of the last three seems to preserve the present–past contrast. In line 12 then, the past looms large, seems more, whereas present moments pass in such 'continual haste' that they seem less. We do not apprehend their importance.

13–14 Time's past achievements offer nothing novel, present moments hurry by, and now the poem reaches its destination, the future. My love will not change, but will last for ever. This is the point, and it is hammered home in characteristic ring composition by the crucial three lines 1 and 13–14, 26 monosyllables in 28 words. They might all be read slowly, and end with some hissing. The poetry is splendid for the vitality in the voice, the unscrupulous ingenuity of the lover/pleader, and the impudence of a man defying what he knew to be inevitable – all to find yet another new way of making a claim he has just undermined in 122.4–6, and to give a promise he had already so often given and so often broken.

ဆ 124 ဗ

If my dear love were but the child of State,
It might for Fortune's bastard be unfathered,
As subject to Time's love or to Time's hate,
Weeds among weeds, or flow'rs with flowers gathered.　　4

No. It was builded far from accident;
It suffers not in smiling pomp, nor falls
Under the blow of thrallèd discontent,
Whereto th'inviting Time our fashion calls.　　8

It fears not Policy, that heretic
Which works on leases of short-numbered hours,
But all alone stands hugely politic,
That it nor grows with heat nor drowns with show'rs.　　12

　　To this I witness call the fools of Time,
　　Which die for goodness, who have lived for crime.

If my love depended on worldly success, it would be subject to Fortune.
　Time could gather it like a flower or [tear it out like] a weed.
It is immune from accident. It does not suffer in prosperity,
　nor is it a slave to discontentment, which today's fashions invite.
It does not fear political power with its short-term accounting,
　but stands alone, a massive polity, unaffected by drought or rain.
I call to witness Time's fools, who have lived for crime, and die for goodness.

1–4 This is easy to summarise: 'If my deep affection were dependent on
the state, or were the product of worldly circumstances, it would be subject
to time and fortune.' But the poetry here depends on the metaphors, and
the first metaphor is a dramatic scene with four characters, his deep love (a
child); the State (the father, perhaps); Fortune (an adulterer, who might
have been the natural father); Time (a character who could expose the child
as a bastard, 'unfather him', if he disliked him, or who might keep the

secret if he loved him). But this is a false scenario – his love is not the child of State, not the product of worldly circumstances, and not at the mercy of Time or Fortune. If Time the gardener loves what he sees, he gathers it as flowers. If he dislikes it, he gathers it as weeds. Nothing escapes.

'Flow'rs is monosyllabic in its first occurrence in line 4 (and in line 12), but bisyllabic at the end of 4. This metrical variation is not an expedient the poet has been driven to, but an effect he enjoys (see 86.5).

5–8 S's love is above (mis)fortune, built (note, it is much stronger than a flower) far from accident. Those who are enjoying the full pomp of worldly success can suddenly be afflicted in the middle of it, but S's love 'suffers not in smiling pomp' because it doesn't have any. Nor can it be struck down by 'thrallèd discontent', the grumbling which people are slaves to these days.

9–12 'Policy' in 9 is to be connected with 'State' in the first line. This suggests the machinations of the powerful, not only in politics but also in the law (it works on leases), in accountancy (it numbers hours) and in religion (it is a heretic). Policy of politicians, solicitors, accountants and priests is not truly politic, and will not last. It is S's love which stands alone, a true republic, immensely prudent, 'hugely politic', and suddenly the metaphor of line 4 revives. This love is not [a flower] dependent on heat, or vulnerable to flooding. This praise of S's love ends, as it began, with a monosyllabic line.

13–14 To support his case against worldly ambition and success, S now summons witnesses, not to speak, for they are dead, but as silent demonstrations of the result of their own misguided lives. The fools of Time are idiots. They are also Shakespearean fools, jesters performing to amuse their master, Time. The run of the argument would lead to those who live for worldly success, but it leads instead to those 'Which die for goodness, who have lived for crime.'

Many explanations have been put forward. The interpretation that best supports the point that worldly success is illusory is that many who have lived a life of crime enjoy deathbed conversions.

Another interpretation leans on 'heretic' in line 9, to suggest that those who die for goodness are martyrs (hundreds of Protestants under Queen Mary, hundreds of Catholics under Elizabeth), but this fails because not many martyrs lived for crime.

Were't aught to me I bore the canopy,
With my extern the outward honouring,
Or laid great bases for eternity,
Which proves more short than waste or ruining?   4

Have I not seen dwellers on form and favour
Lose all and more by paying too much rent,
For compounds sweet forgoing simple savour,
Pitiful thrivers in their gazing spent?   8

No! Let me be obsequious in thy heart,
And take thou my oblation, poor but free,
Which is not mixed with seconds, knows no art
But mutual render, only me for thee.   12

Hence, thou suborn'd informer! a true soul
When most impeached, stands least in thy control.

It meant nothing to me that I carried the canopy,
    or tried to build an eternity. That soon crumbles.
I have seen courtiers lose all by overspending, successful and sad, wasting
    away as they admire the great, and sacrificing the simple for the complex.
Let me be obsequious in your heart. Accept my humble offering,
    free and simple, me in exchange for you, and you for me.
Away with you, bribed informer. A true soul is least at risk when most
    accused.

1–4   The bare bones of the argument are 'Could it mean anything to me
that I carried the canopy, or tried to lay foundations for immortality? Have
I not seen ambition leading to a fall? All I ask is to be allowed to love you
and be loved, and nothing can harm me.' This crude simplification is
necessary because the first line is often paraphrased as 'Would it mean
anything to me if I *were to* carry the canopy?' This is possible, but it seems

better to take 'bore' and 'laid', as referring to the past, like 'Have I not seen' (5). The opening question would then be about something that has already happened, not about a possibility. It seems he actually 'bore the canopy', 'hangings suspended over a throne or held over a person walking in procession' (*OED*, citing 'they beare the foure staves of the canapie at the time of his coronation', 1576). When King James VI of Scotland came to London to reign as James I, within a few weeks he conferred his patronage on Shakespeare's acting company, who then became liveried servants of the crown. The Chamberlain's Men became the King's Men. When James entered the city in a grand procession on 15 March 1604, 'Shakespeare and eight of his fellows were each given four and a half yards of cheap red cloth for gowns since the troupe was a royal organisation; from the Crown that was a routine gift' (Honan (1999), 303). Shakespeare was made a Groom of the Chamber in 1604, and may well have carried the king's canopy on some such occasion. (Much of this information is gleaned from Grazia and Wells (2001), 106, 123 and 124.)

S is unimpressed by pomp. In 'With my extern the outward honouring', 'the outward' is not a respectful term for a royal display, and 'extern' is used in only one other place by Shakespeare, where Iago is saying that when his actions reveal his heart 'in compliment extern' he might as well wear it on his sleeve 'for daws to peck at' (*Oth* 1.1.63–5). There 'extern' is an adjective. It is not recorded as a noun in *OED* except in this sonnet. Here, as in *Othello*, it could be spoken with a sneer.

When S asks if it could mean anything to him that he 'laid great bases for eternity', the eternity he aspired to build was the immortality of the beloved in these poems. He now senses that he is nearing the bitter end of love, and seems to be admitting failure. Such eternity 'proves more short than waste or ruining'. This is expressed in a building metaphor. Instead of laying down great foundations or creating great plinths for honorific statues, he finds that his [poetic] building is short-lived. The failure of these 'great bases for eternity' contradicts the claims advanced, for example, in 81.3–9, 'Your name from hence immortal life shall have' and 'Your monument shall be my gentle verse'. But there are traces of disillusionment in 122.5–6, 123 and 124. Now he knows his edifice will soon be a ruin.

5–8 The building metaphor shifts to 'dwellers on form and favour' who are 'paying too much rent', hoping to win favour by following the norms of fashionable society. The costs are high and they lose all. Courtiers fall into this category of 'dwellers on form and favour', and S has made it clear in lines 1, 2 and 9 that he is no courtier.

One of the consequences of such high living is that exotic cuisine is required, including complex dishes, with the result that the palate loses the delight of wholesome natural ingredients simply cooked. Horace preached to this text in *Satires* 2.2.70–7, praising simple fare, '*simplex esca*', as opposed to mixtures such as boiled and roast, or shellfish and thrushes, making a dubious dinner, '*cena dubia*', sweet compounds that will turn to bile, '*dulcia se in bilem vertent*'. Those who enjoy such a diet may thrive, but they are to be pitied, wasting their lives gawping at the rich, and ruined by their admiration for the great. In lines 7–8 compound is contrasted with simple, and sweet with savour, in each case to the advantage of the latter.

9–12 S is happy to be obsequious, to bow the knee like a courtier, but not to a king, only to the beloved, and not in any external show of obedience, but privately within the beloved's heart. An oblation is an offering to a god (*LC* 223–4), as already hinted in line 7, which recalls Leviticus 1: 13, 'an offering made by fire, of a sweet savour unto the LORD'. Here, for 'offering', the Bishops' Bible has 'oblation'. Oblation with its simple savour is freely given, and, as Horace argues in *Odes* 3.23, gods welcome simple offerings from a pure heart – no 'seconds', no additives, no second-rate ingredients (*OED* B.1.5). Burrow (2002) notes from *OED* 3 that 'second pressings of oil, and second crops of honey and wheat, are inferior to the first.' S's offering knows no art except the art of mutual giving. S's gift of himself to the beloved is clearly stated in 9–12, but the beloved's gift of himself to S is quietly implied in the word 'mutual'. To say it outright would have been to invite refutation.

On line 9, as reported by Rollins (1944), 'Max Deutschbein calls attention to the frequent use ... of the brusk negatives, *O, O no, O none* (as in 61.9, 65.13, 116.5 121.9, 124.5). These expressions, as well as *O, Alas, Lo*, give to the sonnets "the impression of dramatic monologs in which a partner in conversation is challenged". '

13–14 The true soul is S himself. Impeachment is prosecution for treason or other high crime, usually against the state. Who is the bribed informer? According to Duncan-Jones (1997), this could 'refer cryptically to some "actual" individual', but she thinks it most probable that it is Time, 'the explicit addressee of Sonnets 123–5'. But Time is not addressed in 124 or 125. S may be alluding to talebearers who have relayed gossip about him (121), but perhaps there never was an informer, and S is speaking at large, 'Let anyone come and give evidence against me for lack of respect towards crown or state. My wealth is the love of my beloved, and nothing can deprive me of that. A true soul stands least in the control of informer, any informer, because his wealth is not of this world.' Again Horace sounds behind this sentiment. In *Odes* 3.3, nothing shakes the firm-set mind of the just man who holds to his purpose, *'iustum et tenacem propositi virum'*.

There is a possible objection to this interpretation of 125.5–9 and 11–12. This commentary has constantly attempted to avoid the autobiographical fallacy. The Sonnets are not an account of Shakespeare's love affairs, but a drama with a plot and three main characters – S, the beloved youth and the Black Lady. Now suddenly it argues that Sonnet 125 carries glimpses of William Shakespeare's attitude to courtiers and the court, and in particular to the accession of James I. This could be supported by other such glimpses, notably 123.2 and 124.5–11.

This is not an outbreak of the autobiographical fallacy. Glimpses of the politics of the day occur in the plays, in *Macbeth*, *Measure for Measure* and *The Tempest*, to mention only those cited by Anne Barton in Grazia and Wells (2001), 124. Any dramatist is free to refer to contemporary life and use particulars of his own experience, but his play is not his life story. See the end of the note on Sonnet 111.

It is easy to believe that Shakespeare would not have been impressed by James as the successor of Queen Elizabeth. Unlike the Queen, according to Dudley Carleton, one of his courtiers, James 'took no extraordinary pleasure' in the public theatres. He did not even speak English. Although he was welcomed to England by throngs of suppliants and floods of poems, there is no reason to suppose that any of the poems was written by Shakespeare. It would not be surprising if Shakespeare felt little warmth for James, and 'it is improbable that James ever had more than the slightest idea who Shakespeare was' (Barton, in Grazia and Wells (2001), 124–5; and see Honan (1999), 299).

O thou, my lovely boy, who in thy power
Dost hold Time's fickle glass, his sickle hour,
Who hast by waning grown, and therein show'st
Thy lovers with'ring as thy sweet self grow'st.   4

If Nature, sovereign mistress over wrack,
As thou goest onwards still will pluck thee back,
She keeps thee to this purpose, that her skill
May Time disgrace and wretched minutes kill.   8

Yet fear her, O thou minion of her pleasure,
She may detain, but not still keep her treasure.
Her audit, though delayed, answered must be,
And her quietus is to render thee.   12
        (   )
        (   )

O my lovely boy, you rule over Time. As you grow your lovers wither.
Nature is preserving you to humiliate Time and murder his minutes.
You are her treasure, but she will not keep you for ever.
  She will pay her dues and her payment will be you.

1–4   This is the last sonnet devoted to the young man whom S has loved.
It is the only sonnet which rhymes by couplets, rather than by alternate
lines, and it is the only sonnet in 12 lines. The brackets at the end are as
printed in the Quarto of 1609.

Only here and at 108.5, 'sweet boy', is the word 'boy' used of the
beloved. 'O thou, my lovely boy' is the most passionate endearment he has
ever addressed to the young man he has loved, and the last, but, as ever with
this poet, emotion comes with logic. The first four lines are about the
beloved's boyish loveliness. It is not only unimpaired, but grows as time
passes. Time is in his power. This is expressed in two metaphors. The first
appears in the fickle glass of Time that grows by waning. A glass that grows

by waning is an hourglass, as the sand trickles down to fill the bottom half. In *WT* 4.1.16–17 Time 'slides o'er sixteen years', saying, 'I turn my glass and give my scene such growing | As you had slept between.' Just so: as the beloved's sweet self grows, his lovers wither with age, and not only S. The plural has a bitter taste. The second metaphor is Time's 'sickle hour'. Time's scythe was at work in 116.10, cutting away at beauty, and here Time's 'sickle hour' is his pruning time. The beauty of the beloved is a sweet crop growing while his lovers wither. 'Time's fickle glass, his sickle hour' has a strange effect, like the play between 'minutes' and 'minion' in lines 8–9, and between 'fairing' and 'foul', and 'face' and 'false', in 127.6. For this effect see Introduction, p. 6, under 'Similation'.

Horace in *Odes* 2.15 has a similar thought, as he advises his friend not to hurry the young girl, 'Time runs on and has no mercy. It will credit her with years it takes from you.' Shakespeare does not spatter his work with classical references, but this makes half a dozen in four successive sonnets, in 123.2 (in *Odes* 3.30 Horace claims that his poems will outlast the pyramids), in 124.12 (in that same ode Horace claims that his poetry will not be destroyed by rain or wind) and in 125.7–14 (in *Satires* 2.2 Horace extols simple recipes and condemns compounds, and in *Odes* 3.3 he extols the true soul, and commends the simple offerings of the poor).

5–8 'Wrack' is ruin, the work of Time, and Nature is Queen over it. In a vivid picture she is tugging back the beloved as he goes forward, keeping him young as he ages, and she is doing it for her own purpose. She is striving to humiliate her enemy Time, and kill his wretched minutes, the rank and file of his infantry.

9–12 But, though the beloved is Nature's minion, her treasure, he must still be afraid. 'Minion', like the French *mignon*, is sometimes used of children, according to *OED*, citing 'I cannot abide the folly of some fathers who make some one of their children their darling and minion' (1596). In a typical wordplay, Time has his minutes, Nature has her minion. She can keep him, but not for ever. Even Nature has to pay her accounts, to *answer* them, as the 'proud king, who studies day and night | To *answer* all the debt he owes to you' in *1H4* 1.3.182–4. The proud king will answer his account with a 'bloody payment', but, when Nature pays her account to Time, the quietus (= payment) she will render will be the beloved. 'Render', referring to payment, occurs also in 125.12, and 'quietus' is an accounting term. Burrow (2002) quotes John Webster, *The Duchess of Malfi*, 3.2.186–7, 'You had the trick in audit-time to be sick, | Till I had signed your *quietus*.' The word quietus, from medieval Latin, was added to paid accounts, being short for *quietus est*, 'he is quit'. From this usage it came to be used when a man paid his debt to Nature and died, as in *Ham* 3.1.77–8, 'When he himself might his quietus make | With a bare bodkin.' Suicide would settle his account.

Debate has raged about the end of this poem. Shakespeare seems not to have read the proofs of the Quarto, and it may be that the printer is responsible for the omission of two concluding lines. But Shakespeare is responsible for the other oddity, that this is the only sonnet that rhymes in couplets. Being responsible for that, he may also be responsible for the oddity of a 12-line sonnet. If that were so it would have to be interpreted. This sonnet marks the end of love, and the end comes in a broken utterance. Hamlet died in mid-sentence at 5.2.310 and there is another broken utterance in *1H4* 5.4.82–6:

> O, I could prophesy,
> But that the earthy and cold hand of death
> Lies on my tongue. No, Percy, thou art dust,
> And food for—

Percy dies, and Harry completes the sentence, 'For worms, brave Percy.'

Love is finished. Nature will hand the beloved over to Time, and at this moment the mould of the Sonnets breaks.

D. A. Traversi (1938) in Rollins (1944)
It seems worth noting that the word *time* is used seventy-eight times in 1–126 and not once in the remaining sonnets. Rearrangers have not always observed this fact.

In the old age black was not counted fair,
Or if it were, it bore not beauty's name;
But now is black beauty's successive heir,
And beauty slandered with a bastard shame.   4

For since each hand hath put on Nature's power,
Fairing the foul with art's false borrowed face,
Sweet beauty hath no name, no holy bower,
But is profaned, if not, lives in disgrace.   8

Therefore my mistress' eyes are raven black,
Her eyes so suited, and they mourners seem
At such who not born fair no beauty lack,
Sland'ring creation with a false esteem.   12

Yet so they mourn becoming of their woe,
That every tongue says beauty should look so.

In the past black was not thought fair, or not said to be, but now black is
true beauty, and false paint has made beauty the mother of a bastard.
For now that everyone does Nature's work and makes the ugly fair,
beauty's good name is lost, and her sanctuary disgraced.
That is why my mistress' eyes are black, grieving
that ugliness slanders creation by being made to look beautiful.
But her grief is so becoming that everybody says this is what beauty should be.

In terms of the plot of the Sonnets, the beloved youth has faded from view,
and a mistress, traditionally known as the Dark Lady, has come on the
scene. As Booth (1977) observes, 'Not all of the last twenty-eight sonnets
explicitly concern the dark lady, (e.g. 128, 129), but, as the company of
sonnets to a young man invites a reader to think of sonnets 1–126 as
addressed to (or written about) a man and to assume that the beloved in
those 126 is the same man throughout, so all unparticularized references to

a beloved in the last twenty-eight sonnets invite a reader to assume the same female beloved referred to here.'

There is no reason to call this character the Dark Lady. She is black in 127.1 and 3 and in 131.12; her eyes are black in 127.9, in 130.4 and throughout 132; her hair is black at 130.4; and her character is black in 131.13 and 147.14. She is dark only once, and that with reference to her morals, in 147.14, 'Who art as black as hell, as dark as night.' Perhaps 132.13–14 may imply that her complexion too is black but whether it is a sallow, olive complexion or whether she is a negress, is not revealed ('blackamoors' were to be seen in Elizabethan London (Picard 2003, 110–11)). The mock-insult of 130.3, 'her breasts are dun', does not solve the problem. Scholars debate her identity. A judicious survey is in Bate (1997, 54–8).

1–4   The poem begins with a shock, 'In the old age black was not counted fair'. If 'fair' refers to blond hair and fair skin, black could never in any age have been thought fair. This drives the reader to give 'fair' its other common sense, 'beautiful'. Traditionally beauty is fair not dark, but poets have contradicted tradition, as in 27.12 and Sir Philip Sidney's *Astrophil and Stella* 7.10–11, where Stella has black eyes, and nature 'even in black doth make all beauties flow'. This complex poem is built upon these two different meanings of the word 'fair'.

The basic sense is simple, 'Once only fair people were thought beautiful, but cosmetics have now made everyone blond and my mistress shows that the only true beauty nowadays is black.' This clear proposition is given poetic resonance by the lurking metaphor of a family imbroglio. Beauty is the mother of two children, call them Fair and Black. Fair has long been thought to be the one that took after its parent, but recently it has been exposed as false, painted by cosmetics (5–6). It has therefore forfeited the family name, and Beauty is slandered and reputed to have a bastard child. The point is made again in line 12.

The Sonnets raise argument to the level of poetry, and argument demands repetition of terms. Here the repetition is shaped to be eloquent. 'Beauty' occurs in three successive lines, but in lines 2 and 4 the metrical beat falls on the first syllable as in normal speech, while in line 3 sense demands that the iambic beat is interrupted, 'But nów is bláck béauty's succéssive héir.' The variation highlights the logic and gives tone of voice to the verse.

5–8   How is beauty slandered? '*For* ever since everyone usurped the function of Nature and beautified the ugly by cosmetics .... beauty has lost her sanctity.' The falsity of cosmetics is conveyed with a fourfold alliteration in 'Fairing the foul with art's false borrowed face.' Commentators either do not hear this effect or think it unimportant, but Shakespeare heard it, and thought it important enough to shape the language for it. He uses the word 'fair' as adjective, adverb or noun about 900 times, but I find it only here as a verb (but time unfairs beauty in 5.4). In the similation noted in 126.2, 'fickle' and 'sickle' are similar and sound similar. Here in line 6 the contrasts between 'foul', 'false' and 'fairing' add venom to the charge.

'Name' in line 7 implies good name, and also looks back at line 2. Bastards are likely to lose the family name. If Beauty can be profaned, the suggestion is that she is a goddess. But now the goddess is profaned, treated irreverently, or lives not in her holy bower but in disgrace, and is unrespected, or worse, being produced by paint or dye.

9–12 This is why the eyes of the Black Lady are black. They have put on mourning at the sight of those who have no native beauty but command the whole appearance of it, being made to look beautiful by cosmetics. Such 'beauties' slander creation, 'with a false esteem', by giving a false impression of it.

Line 10 has an eloquent conversational adjustment. To build a bridge between the black eyes and the notion that they are mourning, S checks and repeats himself, 'her eyes are raven black, her eyes are wearing suits of mourning black', as in 132.3. Some editors spoil this by changing the second 'eyes' to 'brows', and take 'brows' as eyebrows, citing in support *LLL* 4.3.256, 'O, if in black my lady's brows be decked'. But there 'brows' refers not to eyebrows but to a forehead fringed with head hair. A simpler solution might be to alter 'and' to 'that' in line 10.

13–14 Manipulating the metaphor to end with a compliment to his mistress, S reports the general view that her eyes are models of beauty. Mourning garb so becomes them, they are so beautiful in it, that everyone says that this is what beauty ought to look like.

This is the first scene of the last act of the drama of the Sonnets. Earlier scenes are linked by shared words and concepts. For example, 'the child of State' in 124.1 is dealt with throughout 125, and fashion and favour, pomp and ceremony, are topics in both poems. The illusion of eternity in 125.4 is refuted again in 126.2 and 10, and the flowers of 124.4 and 12 reappear in 126.4. Similarly, this last act is not a separate playlet, not an afterthought, but is meshed into what has gone before, notably with the striking and rare metaphor of the disinherited bastard in 124.2 and 127.4.

How oft when thou, my music, music play'st
Upon that blessed wood whose motion sounds
With thy sweet fingers, when thou gently sway'st
The wiry concord that mine ear confounds,　　　　4
Do I envy those jacks that nimble leap
To kiss the tender inward of thy hand,
Whilst my poor lips, which should that harvest reap,
At the wood's boldness by thee blushing stand.　　　8

To be so tickled they would change their state
And situation with those dancing chips,
O'er whom thy fingers walk with gentle gait,
Making dead wood more blest than living lips.　　　12

　　Since saucy jacks so happy are in this,
　　Give them thy fingers, me thy lips to kiss.

When you play the virginals, I envy the jacks that leap to kiss the palm
　　of your hands, and my poor lips blush at their boldness,
longing to change places with the keys your fingers skim over.
They are happy with that, so give them your fingers to kiss,
　　and give me your lips.

1–8　The first eight lines are one sentence, 'When you play, when you sway the harmony, I envy the jacks.' When the young man listened to music in 8.1, he was called music, 'Music to hear, why hear'st thou music sadly?' Now in Sonnet 128 the Black Lady plays at the keyboard and she too is addressed as music. The wood of lines 2 and 12 is the wood of the keys, whose movements sound [in time] with her fingers. Lines 3–4 describe the same scene more vividly, when she confounds his ear and eye by swaying the concord of the wires, the strings. It is as though the harmony were visible, swaying in the air. The Quarto has a comma after 'sway'st', making his mistress sway as the motion of the keys sounds the concord, and so referring to those keyboard players whose heads and torsos sway as they mime the music, but this mannerism would be extremely unlikely at the virginals. Some scholars even see the hands of players oscillating as they hold down the keys to extract vibrato from the strings, from their 'wiry concord'. A clavichord player does just this with fingers and wrist to produce vibrato, but the mechanism of the clavichord is quite different from what is described in line 5.

The mechanism suggests that the Black Lady is playing the virginals, in which the inside end of each key has a jack, a piece of wood to which was attached the quill which rose to pluck the string when the key was depressed. (The larger harpsichord was not yet being made in England. It was 'a new-invented instrument of music' in Evelyn's Diary, 5 October 1664.) In quick music, if the lid of the instrument is open, the rising jacks might seem to be dancing. A difficulty arises in line 6 because the jacks, being at the inside end of the keys, could not possibly touch the inside of the player's hand. Nor does it help to suggest that 'jacks' are correctly visualised in line 5, but that in line 6 the eye switches to keys rising to touch the pads of the fingers after the note is played. The pads of the fingers are not the inward of the hand. Scholars are severe on this misuse of the term 'jacks', but there is a more tolerant interpretation.

Lovers in the literary tradition sometimes wish they could be trans-formed into some object or creature used by the beloved. Touchstone kissed the cow dugs which Jane Smile's pretty chapped hands had milked in *AYL* 2.4.46–7; Booth (1977) cites Romeo, who longed to be a glove on Juliet's hand (2.1.66); Fastidious in Ben Jonson's *Every Man Out of His Humour* wished a thousand times to be a viola da gamba as he saw Saviolina tickling it (the viola da gamba is held between the legs); Robert Tofte envied a lapdog in *Laura* 2.25; and Barnabe Barnes in *Parthenophil and Parthenope* wished he were his beloved's urine. This sonnet is saved if the reader does not take it seriously, but as a *jeu d'esprit* in this tradition. Part of the fun is that the facts have to be stretched to destruction in order to demonstrate the extravagance of the adoration. 'Jacks' is needed for the personification. In *TS* 2.1.157–8 'she did call me rascal, fiddler, | And twangling jack', where a jack is an impudent upstart. Portia knows she can put on man's dress and imitate the swagger of 'these bragging Jacks' in *MV* 3.4.77. In this character sketch in the sonnet there are nimble-leaping jacks, bold wood, dancing chips and saucy jacks. These are the predatory gallants who are S's rivals for the affection of the Black Lady, and he is making fun of them. He cares little about the mechanism of the instrument.

Neither keys nor jacks 'kiss the tender inward' of the performer's hand, but no matter. He sees the saucy jacks dancing during a fast passagio, a swift division, and casts them as rivals in love. But he also knows that lute players anchor the little finger while the other fingers pluck the strings towards the palm of the hand, as though the strings were eager to tickle them. In *TA* 2.4.44–6, 'lily hands | Tremble like aspen leaves upon a lute | And make the silken strings delight to kiss them.' The palms of the hands were touched in love play, as in *Oth* 2.1.253–4, 'Didst thou not see her paddle with the palm of his hand?', and in *WT* 1.2.127 Leontes imagines his wife is 'virginalling' on his friend's palm. Shakespeare has here combined two different hand positions in two different instruments in order to exploit two different images. He knew that jacks do not touch the hand of a virginals player, but he made them 'nimble leap' to do so in order to set up the final pun and climax on 'saucy jacks'.

Lines 7–8 leap to a new picture and a new conceit. S's lips are personified. These poor jealous lips are not only standing by the instrument [devotedly turning the pages for their beloved?], but are blushing at the shameless cavorting of jacks as they leap to kiss the inside of her hand. Lips do not blush. Lest this be taken seriously, he now throws in an outrageous metaphor. These kisses are a harvest, and his lips should be reaping it.

'Envy' in line 5 is probably to be read with the accent on the second syllable, as in *TS* 2.1.18, 'Is it for him you do envý me so?' The only other metrical surprise in the poem is in the line that rounds off the great sentence in 1–8, 'At the wóod's bóldness bý thee blúshing stánd', where the unexpected stress on 'wood's' against the iambic expectation emphasises its boldness, and the iambic stress on 'by' clarifies the sense.

9–14 To be tickled by his mistress's fingers, his lips would like to change state with the dancing chips, becoming wood instead of flesh, and with the keys 'O'er whom thy fingers walk with gentle gait'. This might suggest undignified subjection, but her fingers would not be trampling on his lips but walking gently over them, and her 'gentle gait' is a double tribute to her beauty, and to the nimble lightness of her touch. S's poor lips have held the stage in 7–12, standing there blushing, to set the scene for the last line. S's wish is that they could enjoy something more than the music. The jacks are perfectly happy with the underside of her fingers. So he tells her to let the saucy fellows have them. He'll settle for her lips and kiss them with his own.

(My friend Layton Ring has advised me on the musical technicalities.)

✂ 129 ✄

Th'expense of spirit in a waste of shame
Is lust in action, and till action lust
Is perjured, murderous, bloody, full of blame,
Savage, extreme, rude, cruel, not to trust;   4
Enjoyed no sooner, but despisèd straight;
Past reason hunted, and no sooner had,
Past reason hated, as a swallowed bait
On purpose laid to make the taker mad;   8
Mad in pursuit, and in possession so;
Had, having, and in quest to have, extreme;
A bliss in proof, and proved a very woe;
Before a joy proposed, behind a dream.   12

　　All this the world well knows, yet none knows well
　　To shun the heav'n that leads men to this hell.

Lust in action is a waste of spirit, and before action it is totally vicious;
　　despised as soon as enjoyed;
　　hunted beyond reason and, after taken, hated;
　　mad in pursuit and in possession;
　　extreme after, during and before;
　　bliss in the act, misery in what follows;
　　promised joy, in retrospect a dream.
Nobody knows to avoid this heaven that leads to hell.

1–4　Duncan-Jones (1997) gives a paraphrase: 'Sexual intercourse (*lust in action*) is the (ultimate) means of squandering energy and becoming morally compromised.' This is dangerously wrong. Sonnet 129 is not about sexual intercourse, but about sexual intercourse undertaken in lust.

　　The last act of the drama of the Sonnets started with a rich conceit in praise of the Black Lady in 127, continued with a flirtatious fantasy about her in 128, and now proceeds to this condemnation of the hell of lust. There is none of this in the first 126 sonnets, nothing like it in the account of S's love for the young man. The word 'lust' occurs 30 times in *VA* and *Luc*, but only here in the Sonnets. It enters with the Black Lady. This is a different country (see comment on 133.5). Similarly she is said to be cruel (see comment on 149.2), and proud (see 140, 141 and 144), but these words are never used of the young man.

A moral diatribe against lust saying approximately the same thing seven times in 12 lines could be a bore, but not with this poet. One thing that prevents it is the logic which pervades the lyricism, flagged instantly in the second line with 'lust in action, and till action lust', where the very order of the words reverses the order of the experience.

Lines 3 and 4 give nine descriptions of lust, but this is no dead inventory. At 'perjured' lust has ceased to be an abstraction and is a person, therefore more vivid. The catalogue has also its own music. Every one of the nine descriptive terms is a single word except the fourth and ninth, each at the end of its line, 'full of blame' echoed by 'not to trust'. 'Bloody, full of blame' is sharpened by the alliteration of 'bl-'. 'Rude' would be expected not to bear the metrical accent, but the line cannot be spoken without giving it a stress – not jingling along – 'extréme, rude, crúel' – but 'extréme, rúde, crúel', and the jolt is all the crueller for the assonance of 'rude' and 'cruel'. The list begins with perjury and ends with deceit, 'not to trust'. Truth and untruth battle it out in Sonnets 1–126; in the Black Lady sonnets untruth prevails.

The poem opens with an unforgettable line, and part of its power may be the pivot of meaning on the word 'waste'. When expense of spirit is a waste, that is a brief touch of the commercial metaphor so common in these poems. A waste might be a waste of money. When it is 'a waste of shame', it becomes a vast desert.

5–12   Lines 1–4 dealt with lust during the act and before it, line 5 with lust during and after, and lines 6–8 complete the trio with lust before, during and after, where the curt analyses are broken as the tone swells in the centre of the poem into the simile of poisoned bait in 7–8, linked to line 9 by madness. Hunting is the metaphor in 6–8. A lustful human being is like an animal taking a bait. In this case the woman laid it, the man took it, and it drove him mad. Claudio describes lechery as a poison bait in *MM* 1.2.120–2, 'Our natures do pursue, | Like rats that raven down their proper bane, | A thirsty evil; and when we drink, we die.' The strict time divisions of before, during and after are the logical underpinning which has given variety and lucidity to the poetry in lines 1–8. The analyses continue, but the shapes keep changing. After the swelling simile in the centre of the poem, in line 10 past, present and future come together in one climactic line, with the polyptoton of 'Had, having, and in quest to have', but there is a twist, as 'after, during, before' reverses chronology.

In 11–12 he prepares for the cruel climax of the final couplet by restating the times of possible pleasure. In 11 present is set against past, 'bliss in proof' is during the experience, and when proved it is true misery; in 12 future is set against past, a joy in prospect, and afterwards a dream. Bliss and joy are foretastes of the heaven of 14; a very woe and a dream are foretastes of hell. In this context a dream must be a nightmare. But that may not be all. In *Luc* 211–12 the ravisher Tarquin asks himself, 'What win I if I gain the thing I seek? | A dream, a breath, a froth of fleeting joy.'

After the opening statement in lines 1–4, the order of events may illuminate the inexhaustible variety at Shakespeare's command. Call the three times of lust in action before, during and after, and they could be shown as b, d and a, as follows: in 5 da | 6–8 bda | 9 bd | 10 adb | 11 da |12 ba. In this poem, as so often, the mighty intelligence of the poet is quietly at work, and the strength of his logic is the foundation of his poetry.

13–14 The climax is sharpened by its monosyllables, and the colloquial irony of 'well knows ... knows well'. It's not a matter of not knowing how to avoid lust. The difficult thing is to know to avoid it. In view of the tendency for the end of a sonnet to hark back to its beginning, in 'well knows ... knows well', there may be some effect in the repetition of the ABBA structure of line 2. Such chiasmus appears in 2, 9, 11 and 13, meshing with antithesis, ABAB, in 1, 5, 6–7, and 12.

To despise sexual pleasure and hate it after enjoying it is a pattern familiar in medieval Christianity. After intercourse every animal is gloomy, '*post coitum omne animal triste.*' These sonnets do on occasion exploit religious terminology, usually in extended metaphors. But serious religious reflection occurs only in Sonnet 146.

Obscenity

Most modern commentators find this poem full of sexual innuendos. For example, in the first two lines, some cite Paroles' description of the stay-at-home in *AW* 2.3.276–8, 'He wears his honour in a box unseen, | That hugs his kicky-wicky here at home, | Spending his manly marrow in her arms', and use that passage to suggest that 'th'expense of spirit' could suggest the ejaculation of semen into a shameful waist. This absurd approach continues throughout the poem to the very end. In lines 13–14, noting that the male organ is often called an 'all', commentators find passages in which the female organ is a 'well', 'heav'n' refers to woman, and 'hell' is 'slang for the vagina'.

This is unforgivable. Many words in English have a wide range of meanings. Readers or listeners plot their route through thickets of association by the simple method of seizing on meanings relevant to the context. The above interpretations are like the jokes based on what the actress said to the bishop, except that those are sometimes amusing.

It is a disease of contemporary literary criticism to import possible meanings of words into passages where they do not register. This poem is a fierce analysis of the pain of lust without love, and to load it with these obscene innuendos is to demean it. (For further examples of scholastic lewdness, see the extracts printed at the end of the notes on 54, 64, 95, 131, 133, 134, 137 and 141).

ဆ 130 ର

My mistress' eyes are nothing like the sun;
Coral is far more red than her lips' red;
If snow be white, why then, her breasts are dun;
If hairs be wires, black wires grow on her head;   4

I have seen roses damasked, red, and white,
But no such roses see I in her cheeks;
And in some perfumes there is more delight
Than in the breath that from my mistress reeks;   8

I love to hear her speak, yet well I know
That music hath a far more pleasing sound;
I grant I never saw a goddess go—
My mistress when she walks treads on the ground.   12

    And yet by heav'n I think my love as rare
    As any she belied with false compare.

My mistress's eyes, lips, breasts, hair are not like sun, coral, snow, wire.
I have seen roses and smelt perfumes and my mistress does not compete.
I love her voice, but music is lovelier. I don't know about goddesses, but she
   walks on the ground.
And yet I think her as rare as any woman praised by false comparisons.

1–4 This poem is a list of trite comparisons used by poets to praise their
mistresses. Against these exaggerations, S poses as the plain blunt man
telling the truth about the woman he loves. By admitting that she does not
have these impossible virtues, he hopes to be believed when he comes to
praise her in the final couplet.

    As in the lists of Sonnets 66 and 129, some of the art is in the variety.
The structure of the second line differs from the structure of the first, her
eyes are nothing like the sun, coral is redder than her lips. Lines 3 and 4
have the rhetoric of anaphora in the repetition of 'if'. In the first line he

refuses his mistress a compliment which could not be true, and is therefore no great deprivation. Nobody has eyes like the sun. In line 2 he denies a comparison that could be true, but is not very damning (not all of us know the colour of coral). He then tightens the screw. Instead of denying praise to his mistress, he now insults her, in terms as false as the compliments he has been making fun of. If the Black Lady is a white woman, this is satirising the cliché that a mistress's breast is as white as snow; if she is a black woman, Duncan-Jones (1997) would be right to say that in this sonnet 'the speaker boasts defiantly of his mistress's dark colouring and lack of the conventional attributes of female beauty', but she goes on: 'This may suggest that the traditional forms of beauty celebrated in love poetry are unnecessary to provoke desire: all that is necessary is that the object of desire is female and available.' It will not suggest that to many people.

Nor could anyone believe that hair could be wire. This last insult is based upon the practice of binding hair into elaborate constructions by means of extremely fine wire. This gives free rein for love poets to enthuse. Edmund Spenser is an honourable example in *Epithalamion* 154, 'Her long, loose, yellow locks lyke golden wire', or in his *Amoretti* 37.1–4, 'What guile is this, that those her golden tresses | She doth attire under a net of gold: | And with sly skill so cunningly them dresses, | That which is gold or heare may scarse be told?' In view of all this, black wires are an insult which is no insult.

5–8 The articulation changes. Not four comparisons each in its own line, but two comparisons each filling a couplet. The Quarto puts a comma after 'damaskt', and this leads some readers to take the whole phrase to refer to one rose, a damask rose which would be part red, part white. This is not an attractive comparison. A cheek part red and part white would be either painted or unhealthy, streaked like a *Rosa mundi* or blotched. *OED* rules that the original damask rose was pink, *Rosa gallica damascena*, and in Pierre-Joseph Redouté's painting *Rosa damascena italica* is a delicate pink, *d'un rose tendre*, without a trace of red or white. This accords with *AYL* 3.5.121–4, where 'There was a pretty redness in his lip, | A little riper and more lusty-red | Than that mixed in his cheek. 'Twas just the difference | Betwixt the constant red and mingled damask.' Rosalind, disguised as a boy, has a lip a little redder than her cheek, and her cheek is not red and white but a blend, pink in fact, a word not found referring to colour until 1720 (see *OED* B.1). Besides, if S says he has seen roses of three different colours, pink, red and white, but none of them on his mistress's cheek, this is more persuasive than saying that he has seen roses striped red and white. The more roses the better.

The technique of insincere insult reaches its peak in line 8. The word 'reek' is always unpleasant in Shakespeare, sometimes extremely so, as in 'the reek of a lime-kiln' in *MW* 3.3.73–4 and 'reek o'th' rotten fens' in *Cor* 3.3.125.

9–12 Anaphora gave eloquence in lines 3–4. Now it comes in lines 9 and 11, with 'I love' and 'I grant' harking back to 'I have' in line 5, and forward to 'I think' in line 13.

You can tell a goddess by her gait. When Venus appeared in disguise to her son Aeneas, he did not recognise her till she was leaving him. Then he knew by her walk she was truly a goddess, '*vera incessu patuit dea*'. Perhaps Virgil's *Aeneid* 1.402–6 is behind 'I grant I never saw a goddess go'.

13–14 Unlike the mistresses of other poets, S's mistress 'treads on the ground'. It should not be necessary to say that the mockery in this poem is directed against poets, not in any degree against S's mistress. That is now made explicit, and an oath, 'by heav'n', embedded in other monosyllables, gives the cutting edge of natural speech to his praise of beauty, so much more credible than the flim-flam mocked in lines 1–12. His mistress is 'as rare' (keeping up the pretence of modest truth, he does not say she is rarer) 'As any she belied with false compare', where he continues the monosyllables of truth to expose the lies in 'belied' and 'compare'.

This note has concentrated on the variety of the syntax from item to item of this list, but the vigour and humour of the poem depend even more on the conversational tone of voice. In the first line 'nothing like' has a racy sound, and line 2 is all the livelier if it is read with its metrical accent on 'her', 'Córal is fár more réd than hér lips' réd' (unlike the miraculous red lips of the mistresses of sentimental love poets). Line 3 has the inexpressible 'why thén', something like 'I would not dream of attempting to deny it'. A comma is supplied above after 'then' to suggest that this line might best be read accenting 'then' with the metrical beat. The roses are introduced in a new, but also conversational way, 'Í have seen róses'. Haven't we all? But we do not all have the music of 'damasked, red, and white', and 'sée I' in the next line is also live speech with a lovely variation in stress after the unaccented 'seen'. 'Reeks' is a shock and a smile. Of course his mistress's breath does not reek. In lines 7–8, again plain speech is deployed, this time with the power of monosyllables in the lovely words, 'I love to hear her speak', which in this context are not at all weakened by the praise of music that follows. 'Far more' after line 2 sounds like a conversational phrase. In 9 'yet well I know' has the tone of voice of a man who is under no delusions. In 13 'I grant' is an ostentatious confession that he has never done something that no man has ever done, while insinuating the notion that he is entirely honest. Then, in the claim which is the climax, S throws in a colloquial oath to guarantee his integrity. This is language as it is spoken, here written by a master, and conveying character and satirical tone of voice.

The music of the verse is another part of the poetry and the satire. Where S states the harsh truth about his mistress, he tends to violate the smooth coincidence of word stress and iambic rhythm. The end of the second line is a jolt, however read. In line 4 'black' does not carry the metrical beat, but is naturally read with greater emphasis than the syllables of 'wires' on either side of it, something like 'If háirs be wíres, *bláck* wires grów on her héad'. In line 12 'tréads on the gróund' is an aggressive assertion of plain fact, before the serene smooth-sailing confidence of the last two lines:

And yet by heav'n I think my love as rare
As any she belied with false compare.

The only other line which ends at the run like line 12 is line 4, 'grów on her héad', another rough commonsense statement.

To assess Sonnet 130, editors transcribe a dire poem by Thomas Watson from his *Hekatompathia or Passionate Centurie of Love*, published in 1581. The numbers at the end of its lines refer to the relevant lines in Sonnet 130:

Harke you who list to heare what sainte I serve:	
Her yellow lockes exceede the beaten goulde;	4
Her sparkeling eies a place in heav'n deserve;	1
Her forehead high and fair of comely moulde;	
Her wordes of musick all of silver sounde;	9, 10
Her wit so sharpe as like can scarce be founde;	
Each eybrowe hangs like Iris in the skies;	
Her eagles nose is straight of stately frame;	
On either cheeke a rose and lillie lies;	5, 6
Her breathe is sweet perfume or hollie flame;	7, 8
Her lips more red than any corall stone;	2
Her necke more white than any swans that mone;	3
Her brest transparent is, like any chrystall rocke;	3

Her fingers long, fit for Apolloes lute;
Her slipper such as Momus dare not mocke;
Her vertues all so great as make me mute:
　What other partes she hath I neede not say,
　Whose face alone is cause of my decaye.

Every line of the first 10 of Shakespeare's sonnet is a riposte to such fulsome flatteries by Watson. The differences are the differences between poetry and doggerel. Of Watson's 18 lines, 13 begin with 'her', but the important feature is not Shakespeare's variety but the effects of the variations. His easy and expressive conversational tone of voice beggars Watson's dismal inventory of beauties. A measure of the gulf is the contrast between the ends of the two lists. Watson falls back on a feeble recollection of the end of Ovid's description of love in the afternoon at *Amores* 1.5:

Who does not know the rest? Exhausted then slept we.
May many many afternoons turn out so well for me.

　In Shakespeare there is a strong undercurrent of association between the items. The first four lines go from sun to snow, and red, white, black, pink, red, dun, white and gold run through the first six. These are ruled by sight, smell takes over in 7–8, sound in 9–10, motion in 11–12. The damask rose in 5 has a delicious perfume and it is still wafting in lines 7–8.
　According to Kerrigan (1986), 'Ironically some of the metaphors satirised in Sonnet 130 are used of the young man in earlier poems.' Unjust. When S compares the young man, for example to sun or stars in Sonnet 7 or 14, the comparison leads to creative exploration of the correspondences or differences, to vivid and original calculations and conceits, not to the perfunctory associations satirised in this sonnet.

ஜ 131 ෲ

Thou art as tyrannous, so as thou art,
As those whose beauties proudly make them cruel,
For well thou know'st to my dear doting heart
Thou art the fairest and most precious jewel. 4

Yet in good faith some say that thee behold
Thy face hath not the power to make love groan.
To say they err I dare not be so bold,
Although I swear it to myself alone. 8

And to be sure that is not false I swear,
A thousand groans but thinking on thy face
One on another's neck do witness bear
Thy black is fairest in my judgement's place. 12

In nothing art thou black save in thy deeds,
And thence this slander as I think proceeds.

You are as cruel as proud beauties because you know I dote on you.
Some say you could never make a lover groan. I swear, privately, you can,
and confirm my oath with a thousand groans, proving that in my eyes
 black is most fair.
Your only blackness is in your actions. Hence the slander.

1–4 In Sonnet 127, the first appearance of the Black Lady, it is established
that black is fair, and this paradox lies behind the whole of Sonnet 131.
'You are as tyrannical, being what you are, as if you were like those made
proud and cruel by their beauty.' 'So as thou art', just paraphrased as 'being
what you are', is elusive. What is she? The beginning of the sonnet is
explained at the end. The point is that this woman is black, despised for it
in lines 5–6, and yet she is as tyrannical as cruel beauties are. In 'whose
beauties proudly make them cruel' the word order is surprising. A
smoother version would be 'whose beauties make them proudly cruel'.

The advantage of what Shakespeare wrote is that 'proudly make' visualises the beauties as living agents who strut proudly around making people cruel. These poems are full of fleeting personifications, of dramatic characters, like the groans of line 10.

Lines 3–4 explain why she behaves in this way. The reason is that ('For') she is well aware that S's fond heart adores her. She is so precious to him that she can rule him like a tyrant. 'Well thou know'st' means that she is well aware (and exploits it). The same rueful tone of voice was heard in 87.1, 'And like enough thou know'st thy estimate.' That hint is confirmed in 'my dear doting heart', 'dear' meaning loving, fond, as in Sonnet 31.6 and *TGV* 4.3.14–15, 'what dear good will | I bear to Valentine.' Here it joins 'doting' to emphasise the intensity of his love.

5–8 'Others do not share this admiration, saying in good faith' (it is a sincere judgement, not a gratuitous insult) 'that your face could not make anyone groan with love. I dare not be so bold as to say publicly that they are wrong, but I swear it privately to myself.' At the end of line 6 there is a hint of a smile. It is not that the Black Lady's face is unable to make a lover groan, but that it is unable to make love itself groan. The humour of lovers' groans will reappear in a court of law in 9–12.

9–12 'To confirm that what I swear is true, I groan a thousand times just thinking of your face.' Again the dramatist personifies. As Kerrigan (1986) notes, 'It seems inconceivable that the groans might be *thinking*, until each sigh is given a *neck* in line 11.' The groans are characters in a little courtroom scene, a thousand witnesses crowding in to testify that in S's judgement black is fairest, and sudden light is thrown back on 5–8, on 'in good faith' (they are honest witnesses), on S's humility in line 7 (he hesitates to pronounce on a matter which is *sub judice*) and on 'I swear'. The legal scene has taken shape, and the three monosyllabic lines in 6, 7 and 9 may convey some of the severity of legal language. 'One on another's neck' means that the groans are rushing along, one close behind the other. The phrase is proverbial and occurs in 1594 in Thomas Nashe's *Unfortunate Traveller* 2.262, 'Passion upon passion would throng one on anothers necke.' The rush is into the witness box in the lawcourt, the place of judgement, mentioned explicitly in line 12. It is a case of slander (14). S's groans are a thousand witnesses all attesting that the black of his mistress has the power to make a lover groan. Her black is fairest in his judgement.

13–14   How then is the slander of lines 5–6 to be explained? Why do people say that nobody could love her? The only answer S can think of is that she is black, evil, in her actions. This again throws light backward. The critics did speak in good faith, they had a serious point to make. Now we know why he could not refute them outright in line 7 and say they erred. He knows they were, in a sense, right.

The Sonnets have dealt with disappointments, suspicions and betrayals, but S has never before said that he loves someone who is black at heart. But now Sonnet 131 explains 129. This is lust, not love. The bitterness and the drama lie largely in the elaborate defence of the Black Lady against slander, an imposing defence which leads to a deadly indictment. This whole ingenious fortification has been erected as a platform for a fierce attack.

In novels and plays the end of one chapter or scene often whets the appetite for the next. The impetus of the plot of the Sonnets leaves us here with a problem. What are her black deeds? Only tyrannical treatment of her lover? Sonnet 132 will heighten the suspense in a poem that praises her beauty, and begs for her heart's love. Sonnet 133 will then explain the black deeds in 131.13.

Duncan-Jones (1997), on line 10
… because *groans* are ambivalent, being more frequently associated with 'pain or distress' (*OED* groan 1a) than erotic delight, the hyperbole of *A thousand groans* activates a suspicion that the speaker's response to his lady is not wholly adoring, and may even hint at the possibility that he has been venereally infected by her.

❧ 132 ☙

Thine eyes I love, and they, as pitying me,
Knowing thy heart torments me with disdain,
Have put on black and loving mourners be,
Looking with pretty ruth upon my pain.   4

And truly not the morning sun of heaven
Better becomes the gray cheeks of the east,
Nor that full star that ushers in the even
Doth half that glory to the sober west,   8
As those two mourning eyes become thy face.

O let it then as well beseem thy heart
To mourn for me, since mourning doth thee grace,
And suit thy pity like in every part.   12
    Then will I swear beauty herself is black
    And all they foul that thy complexion lack.

Your eyes pity me, and have put on black,
    knowing that your heart despises me.
The morning sun does not so beautify the eastern sky,
    nor does the evening star so glorify the twilit west.
Since mourning becomes you, let your heart too put on mourning.
    Then will I swear beauty is black, and all not black are foul.

1–4 The Black Lady's heart despises him, but there is pity in her eyes, and
he loves them. They are black, so he fancies they have put on mourning,
and 'ruth', pity, makes them beautiful.

5–9 Indeed, they are so beautiful that they become her face more than the
morning sun or the evening star becomes the sky. As usual the similes gain
purchase from their links to the context. Such links are sometimes purely
verbal, sometimes even puns, as here, where the simile of the *morning* star
illustrates the lovely *mourners* of line 3 and triple *mourning* in lines 9 and

403

11. In line 9 indeed the Quarto absent-mindedly prints 'morning eyes'. There are also links between 'become' and 'beseem', and between 'Doth half that glory' and 'doth thee grace'. But the correspondences also carry cunning compliments. The Black Lady corresponds to the *gray* eastern sky before sunrise, but her eyes are 'the morning sun of heaven'. She is also like the *sober* west, but her eyes are 'that full star that ushers in the even'. In *RJ* 3.2.10–11 night is addressed as 'Thou sober-suited matron all in black'. If the evening sky is seen as sober-suited in 8, this tallies with 3, where the Black Lady's eyes 'have put on black', and also with 12, where he begs her heart to suit her pity, to clothe it in a suit of mourning black. S is exalting the beauty of her eyes by comparing them to the heavenly bodies at their most beautiful, the rising sun and the evening star glowing against the dull background of twilit sky.

Why is the evening star 'full'? Venus deserves the name as the brightest of the stars, but its brightness is part of the rhetoric here because the *full* star does not give *half* the glory to the west as the *two* mourning eyes give to the Black Lady's face, making a number game like 38.9–10.

10–14 Her face is beautified by her black eyes, and S wishes that her heart were beautified by mourning for him, clothing her pity for him in that same black suit as her eyes wear in line 3. To deduce from a woman's black eyes that she is pitying her lover's suffering may seem to be a feeble conceit, but there is a meaning to it. He is susceptible to eyes (104.2) and reads sadness and pity in their blackness. If only her heart, like her eyes, would put on black for him, her heart and her whole body and soul 'in every part' would then show pity for him. The poem is yet another way of declaring his love and pleading for hers. Like so many of the Sonnets, it carries a cargo of praise of the lover's beauty, here in more than half the lines.

℘ 133 ∝

Beshrew that heart that makes my heart to groan
For that deep wound it gives my friend and me.
Is't not enough to torture me alone,
But slave to slav'ry my sweet'st friend must be?   4

Me from myself thy cruel eye hath taken,
And my next self thou harder hast engrossed.
Of him, myself, and thee I am forsaken—
A torment thrice, threefold thus to be crossed.   8

Prison my heart in thy steel bosom's ward,
But then my friend's heart let my poor heart bail.
Whoe'er keeps me, let my heart be his guard.
Thou canst not then use rigour in my jail.   12

And yet thou wilt, for I, being pent in thee,
Perforce am thine, and all that is in me.

Cursed be your heart, for making mine groan by wounding
my friend and myself. Is it not enough to torture me alone?
You took me from myself and him from me. I have lost
him, myself and you – triple torment, thwarted three times.
Imprison my heart in your breast, but let my friend out on bail.
Let my heart go surety for him, then you can't ill-treat him.
But you will. You are my prison, and you have power over me and mine.

1–4 'Beshrew' can be used in a mild or affectionate tone, 'Beshrew my
heart, | I think you are happy,' says Juliet's nurse at 3.5.221–2. But here it
is serious, as borne out by a cruel word in every one of the first eight lines.

There is a narrative thread. S began Sonnet 131 with his own 'dear
doting *heart*', and ended with the Black Lady's black deeds, but did not go
into detail. In Sonnet 132 her *heart* was tormenting him and he begged for
pity. He received none, and now in Sonnet 133 he at last reveals what her

heart has done, causing a wound which makes his own *heart groan*. She has taken the young man he loves to be her lover. The key word 'heart' occurs four times in 9–11, and in 12–14 he realises that her heart is his prison and knows no pity.

Line 4 is challenging. The young man may be a slave to S's mistress, but how can he be a slave to slavery? Commentators explain it as 'a slave to domination', implying vaguely that he is doubly a slave, but that is not an impressive sense. Every slave is a slave to slavery. Shakespeare makes great use of polyptoton, juxtaposition of the same word in different forms. Other examples occur in this same sonnet, in lines 5, 8, 11 and 13. Perhaps in 'slave to slavery' he has stumbled into an established pattern of thought, and fallen short of his usual intense accuracy.

5–8   The Black Lady's eye has stolen him from himself. He seems to have already had a similar experience in happier days, when first he looked the young man in the eye (104.2). He never uses the word 'cruel' of him, but it is met throughout the Black Lady sonnets, here and in 131, 140 and 149. This is a different kind of love (see comment on 129.2).

'To engross' is a commercial term, meaning to buy up the whole (or as much as possible) of a commodity in order to sell it on at a profit. The bitterness of the metaphor is enforced by 'harder', perhaps an adverb, as in our phrase 'to work harder'. This acquisition is even more ruthless, more mercenary. She has taken S from himself, and now she has engrossed his second self, 'that other mine' (134.3), and deprived him of herself – a triple loss, crisply recorded in line 7. Line 8 is normally written, following the Quarto, without a comma, but 'thrice threefold' would mean that S has suffered nine losses, which would make bad arithmetic for the sake of a rhetorical flourish. The comma after 'thrice' cures this. It is thrice a torment, so to be thwarted three times.

9–12   As he begs the Black Lady to release the young man, in every line to the end of the poem there is at least one allusion to imprisonment, 'prison', 'ward', 'bail', 'keeps', 'guard', 'rigour', 'jail', 'pent', 'perforce'. A ward, as in our hospitals, is a place of confinement, and in this context her 'steel bosom' in line 9 suggests steel bars and door fittings in a prison cell. S asks her to free the young man's heart to be guarded by his own. His hope is that if the beloved's heart were released on bail, and guarded by his own, the Black Lady's rigour could not harm it.

Most commentators take a simpler view of lines 10–11. Understanding 'bail' as meaning 'imprison', and 'guard' as meaning guardpost or jail, they see a different argument, 'Let my heart imprison the beloved's heart and become his jail.' This is simpler but not so interesting, not so loving, and there are other difficulties. 'To bail' means to liberate, not to imprison, and 'guard' never refers to a building, only to those who guard. It is better to give both words their normal meaning.

So then his heart is offering to stand bail for the young man's, and act as its guarantor. In line 11, 'let my heart be his guard', he is not thinking of his heart as a strict jailer, but as a loving guardian who would show none of the Black Lady's rigour. It is not until line 12 that he arrives at the notion of his own heart being a jail within a jail, to prepare for the final epigram which will destroy the case he is trying to argue.

13–14   He knew, even as he proposed the arrangement, that it would fail. 'Who'er keeps me' is the tell-tale phrase. He had spoken as though he had control over his own heart. Realism now prevails. S's heart is a prisoner in the Black Lady's breast, and she can therefore do as she wishes. 'I, being pent in thee, | Perforce am thine, and all that is in me.' This jail within a jail is an ingenious conceit, it is also another way of attempting to express an intense emotion. She would never release the young man, and never allow S to love him. With this confession of helplessness comes a declaration of total submission. Being her prisoner, S grants that the power lies with her to do as she wishes with the young man and with himself.

Burrow (2002), on line 2
deep wound grave injury; a wound inflicted by Cupid's arrow (with a pun on the 'wound' of the vagina).

So now I have confessed that he is thine
And I myself am mortgaged to thy will,
Myself I'll forfeit so that other mine
Thou wilt restore to be my comfort still.   4
But thou wilt not, nor he will not be free,
For thou art covetous, and he is kind.

He learned but surety-like to write for me
Under that bond that him as fast doth bind.   8
The statute of thy beauty thou wilt take,
Thou usurer that put'st forth all to use,
And sue a friend came debtor for my sake.
So him I lose through my unkind abuse.   12

Him have I lost. Thou hast both him and me.
He pays the whole, and yet am I not free.

Now he is yours and I'm mortgaged to you, I'll forfeit myself to free him,
  but you are too greedy to agree, and he is too kind [to ask].
All he did was to underwrite my bond. You are a moneylender
  demanding payment from one who went surety for a friend.
I have lost him. You have us both. He pays my debt, but I am not free.

1–6 'So' gathers up the gist of Sonnet 133, where S tried to negotiate terms
of release for the young man, to no avail. He now admits that he has lost
his beloved and toys with an arrangement whereby he could free the young
man by giving himself to the Black Lady.

The sonnet carries a financial metaphor from 'mortgaged' in line 2 to
'pays' and 'free' in 14. The first two lines say the beloved is the property
of the Black Lady, and that S himself is mortgaged to her, temporarily in
her possession, until he has paid his debt to her. In line 3 he proposes to
cancel that arrangement by giving himself outright to the Black Lady on
condition that she releases the beloved, who is 'that other mine', 'my next

self' (133.6). But here in line 5 he realises that the solution will not work, and that realisation comes in monosyllables here in 134.13 as in 133.13. She will not accept it because she is greedy and jealous, and the beloved will not ask to leave her because he is kind, too kind to be cruel and tell her that he wishes to be free of her. The future run of the plot suggests another explanation of this kindness. He is staying with her because he does not want to leave her, a possibility S is not yet able to contemplate.

7–12 But the beloved was kind in another way. He had agreed *only* to act as guarantor for S, *only* to underwrite his contract, '*but* surety-like to write for me', and she will hold him to it. 'I'll have my bond,' cried Shylock in *MV* 3.3.4, 5, 12, 13 and 17, and the Black Lady insists that she will have her statute. This bond that binds both men to the lady is the statute of her beauty, a contract whereby she grants the use of it, and in exchange takes possession of the user. She now sues the young man, though he came into debt purely for the sake of his friend.

What does that mean? How did the young man, acting as surety, underwrite S's contract with the lady? How can that underwriting have put him in her power? One possible explanation is that S was still loving the young man after he had taken the Black Lady as his mistress. In this fraught situation the young man might have appealed to the lady, at S's request (11–12), to allow his friendship with S to continue, to be a comfort to him (4). But, whatever support he offered to S, he fell under the same statute of her beauty, 'that bond that him as fast doth bind' (8). The recipient of the message loved the messenger, as Orsino loved Cesario in *Twelfth Night*. The Black Lady lay with him, and he became hers. S's bitterness is sharpened by the sexual insult in 'usurer', 'use' and 'abuse' in 10–12, sneers by polyptoton, perhaps intensified by 'sue' in 11 and 'lose' in 12. Polyptoton (see comment on 133.4) is common in Shakespeare. Here, for example, it sounds to strong effect in lines 3, 5 and 8.

If some such background is posited for the sonnet, how the beloved argued S's case with the Black Lady is unimaginable, but during the discussions the deed was done. This explains the strange word 'learned' in line 7. The young man did not need to learn to write, or even to under-write. What he learned to do was to love this woman. In 11 S had exposed the beloved to danger by allowing him to plead on his behalf, to 'come as debtor', meaning to become a debtor, like Lady Percy, who 'came a widow' in *2H4* 2.3.57. S now sees that it was an abuse of love, 'my unkind abuse', to expose his beloved to such danger.

13–14 The dire result is summarised in monosyllables, reinforced by polyptoton in 'Him *have I* lost. Thou *hast* both him and *m e*.' The young man is now paying her, and paying in full. But there is no justice. S is still not free because she will not release him.

This speculation is only one way of making sense of this poem. A poet who had consummate skill in making complex arguments clear has failed to do so here. Perhaps the explanation is that the narrative expounded above is so banal that Shakespeare knew better than to spell it out. The poem works as a brilliant surface display which suggests some such intense amorous transaction, leaving readers to peer into the mist to see it. This, as stated so often, is not an account of anything that happened to William Shakespeare, but the latest episode in the plot of these poems, exploiting this new character arriving so late upon the stage.

T. G. Tucker (1924) in Rollins (1944)
The woman has compelled both men to render carnal service to her beauty. She insists on having in that relation the friend as well as the poet, whose service does not satisfy her claim. He playfully pleads that his friend has merely acted for him (cf. 40.5–6), and that he is willing to take the whole burden upon himself, if she will give up the friend. But neither she nor the friend is so inclined.

Burrow (2002), on line 14
The pun on *w hole* (an alternative spelling for 'hole' in this period) might suggest that the friend is paying for sex with the mistress.

❧ 135 ☙

Whoever hath her wish, thou hast thy will,
And Will to boot, and Will in overplus –
More than enough am I that vex thee still,
To thy sweet will making addition thus.   4

Wilt thou, whose will is large and spacious,
Not once vouchsafe to hide my will in thine?
Shall will in others seem right gracious,
And in my will no fair acceptance shine?   8

The sea, all water, yet receives rain still,
And in abundance addeth to his store,
So thou, being rich in will, add to thy will
One will, of mine, to make thy large will more.   12

      Let no unkind, no fair beseechers kill.
      Think all but one, and me, in that, one Will.

You have a strong will, and have me, Will, more than enough of me.
Will you not accommodate me as generously as you do others?
The sea is all water and accepts rain. You are all willing desire,
      why not accept me?
Let no unkind or handsome [lovers] defeat my plea.
      Think of all your lovers as one, and me as part of that one.

This sonnet is bewildering because it contains the word 'will' 14 times in six different senses. The first 'will' refers primarily to decision, determination (abbreviated below as D). In line 2 'Will' is mainly William, the speaker, 'Will in overplus – | More than enough am I' (abbreviated as W). In line 4 the salient reference is to the Black Lady's sexual charm and sexual desires, lust, libido (abbreviated as L). In line 5 the auxiliary verb (A) 'wilt thou vouchsafe' is drawn into the game, and 'will' is among other things the Black Lady's sexual appetite (L above). But line 6 forces a revision. The 'will' is now the penis (P), and therefore, in retrospect, it is the penis in 2 and the vagina in 4 and 5 (V).

The poem would be difficult to interpret if 'will' meant one thing in each of its occurrences, but line 6 has just shown that the game is not so simple. In any passage the word may carry several different meanings. Certainty is not possible. Shakespeare himself would be hard put to it to define his own puns, or even to paraphrase the poem, but it may help new readers through the jungle to have some sort of chart, and it may also be useful to compare the text in the Quarto of 1609, as printed below. Capital letters in the margin point to the salient senses of each occurrence of the word 'will'. Lower case suggests some lurking sub-senses.

Who euer hath her wish, thou hast thy *Will*,	Dl
And *Will* too boote, and *Will* in ouer-plus,	W, Wp
More then enough am I that vexe thee still,	
To thy sweet will making addition thus.	LV 4
Wilt thou, whose will is large and spatious,	A, DLV
Not once vouchsafe to hide my will in thine,	PV (thine)
Shall will in others seeme right gracious,	LP
And in my will no faire acceptance shine:	LP 8
The sea all water, yet receiues raine still,	
And in aboundance addeth to his store,	
So thou beeing rich in *Will* adde to thy *Will*,	Lp, LV
One will of mine to make thy large *Will* more.	Pd, LV 12
Let no vnkinde, no faire beseechers kill,	
Thinke all but one, and me in that one *Will*.	LPW

This Quarto text distributes italics and initial capitals for no discernible reason. '*Will*' is unhelpfully given italics and an initial capital seven times, in lines 1–2, 11–12 and 14. It also puts commas at the end of lines except at the end of quatrains, 4, 8 and 12, apparently as a matter of habit rather than sense. My own printing above offers a capital initial only where the personal name seems to be salient, in lines 2 and 14.

1–4 In the first line 'will' must be different from 'wish', but something like it. Women have wishes but the Black Lady is an unusually determined character. The rest of the poem suggests that she has also a keen sexual appetite, as marked above by L and V. 'Will to boot' could hint at that. Will is also a cameo appearance for William Shakespeare in the plot, as discussed at the end of the note on Sonnet 136. 'Will in overplus' then suggests a lusty Will, a Will who still vexes her even after she has had too much of him (2 and 6), in both places offering a glimpse of the penis, as suggested above.

In line 3, S keeps on vexing her with his demands, thus making an addition to her sweet will. This cannot imply that he is making love to her, because lines 6–8 make it clear that she is refusing him. Line 4 perhaps suggests that his advances are adding to her sexual life the burden of refusing him, a burden which taxes the sweetness of her nature. Into this concentration of obscene puns he has squeezed a droplet of praise.

5–8 The auxiliary verb 'wilt' in play with 'will' is a polyptoton. When her 'will is large and spacious' it must mean that her libido is generous as well as large, and 'spacious' implies that her vagina is accommodating. The lady is promiscuous, as is hinted in 134.10, and made brutally explicit in 137.6 and 10. When S wants to hide his will in hers, he clearly wants to hide his penis in her vagina, and he is not allowed to, 'in [the case of] his will no fair acceptance shines', appears. 'Spacious' and 'gracious' are trisyllabic, with the second syllable touched very lightly, more like 'spa-ci-ous' than our 'spash-ous'.

9–12 Lines 9–12 are a simile. The heavy hints of her promiscuity in lines 5–8 are strengthened by comparing her store of libido and its replenishment to sea and rain. '[Just as] the sea, all water, receives rain and adds abundantly to its store, so you, being rich in will, add one other will to your vast will.' When the sea 'addeth to his store', 'his' almost personifies him as a hoarder. After line 6, the second 'will' in 11 must refer to her vagina, and the first in 12 to his penis. Lines 11, 12 and 14 of the sonnet are all entirely monosyllabic.

13–14 The sense of line 13 as punctuated above could be 'Let no unkind [suppliants], no fair suppliants kill [this request].' This seems to be the least unlikely interpretation of the line. Its advantages are that the contrast between 'unkind' and 'fair' is characteristic, and that it preserves the Quarto's comma after 'unkinde'. Its disadvantages are that words have to be supplied before that meaning can be divined, and that even so the verb 'kill' is strange on this interpretation. On the other hand 'kill' is sometimes used with impersonal objects ('all pure effects', 'this blessed league', 'thine honour', 'his quality' in *Luc* 250, 383, 516, 875). Most scholars solve the problem by printing 'no' in inverted commas to make it the subject of 'kill' and beseechers its object, 'Let "no" unkind no fair beseechers kill', which could be explained as 'Let a churlish negative not kill any handsome suitors.' But S would probably not object if it did. A third possibility is to take 'unkind' as a noun, and so 'Let no unkindness kill lovely suitors', but 'unkind' is never used as a noun.

The last line as punctuated in this edition is lewd and insulting. 'Think all but one, and me, in that, one Will', where 'one Will' suggests one lover, one penis, one William. All he is asking is to be one of many, as at 136.6. It could also be printed, 'Think all but one, and me in that one, Will.' But that weakens the insult, and isolates Will, making him ask to be special, when the most he dare hope is to be one of the crowd. Duncan-Jones's solution keeps the punctuation of the Quarto, 'Think all but one, and me in that one Will', and comments, 'Regard all your ... lovers as a single one, and treat me as your only object of desire/man called William/occupant of your sexual space' (Duncan-Jones 1997). This dilutes the insult, and also makes him ask for what he knows is not on offer. He has long given up hope of being her only lover (5–8). But perhaps the Quarto here preserves Shakespeare's punctuation, leaving readers free to juggle possibilities. After all, the poem is a maze of puzzles. This plodding exposition is offered as one guide through it.

Partridge (1968), 218–19
[All three references in the first two lines] are to *Will* Shakespeare himself and to lust and to the sexual organs; compare the punning in the last four lines of the sonnet. In these four lines, the word-play becomes so intricate that one may easily lose the thread – unless one remembers that Shakespeare delights in investing a single word not merely with two meanings but often with three and perhaps even, as in the final *Will*, with four.

❧ 136 ❧

If thy soul check thee that I come so near,
Swear to thy blind soul that I was thy *Will*,
And will, thy soul knows, is admitted there.

Thus far for love my love-suit, sweet, fulfil.   4
Will will fulfil the treasure of thy love,
Ay, fill it full with wills, and my will one.

In things of great receipt with ease we prove
Among a number one is reckoned none.   8
Then in a number let me pass untold.

Though in thy store's account I one must be,
For nothing hold me, so it please thee hold
That nothing, me, a something sweet to thee.   12

Make but my name thy love, and love that still,
And then thou lov'st me, for my name is *Will*.

If your soul objects that I come so near, swear that I used to be your will.
[The] will has entry to the soul.
Do so, and Will will satisfy you, yes, fill you with wills,
and my will one of them.
One is not a number, so in that vast number let me pass uncounted.
Though I must be one in your stocktaking, think of me as nothing,
if only that nothing is something sweet to you.
If you make will your love, then you love me, for my name is Will.

1–3 In Sonnet 135 'will' occurred 14 times in 14 lines in six different senses, and 'Will' (= William) appeared in the second line and the last. In Sonnet 136 'will' occurs seven times in six senses, and 'Will' again appears in the second line and the last. This is no doubt a coincidence, but it is no coincidence that each poem ends on the same climax with the word 'will'/'Will', punning on the name and the penis. In 135 the Quarto prints 'will' sometimes italicised and with a capital, with no consistency or reason. In 136 it appears as above and this time it makes sense. Here '*Will*', with an initial capital and italicised, is among other things William.

'Check' is a lovely word. Scottish parents still check their children when they are naughty. They reprimand the child and stop the nuisance. So in *AW* 1.1.64–5, 'be checked for silence, | But never taxed for speech', and in *2H4* 1.2.196–7, where Falstaff explains what a good influence he has on the young prince, 'I have checked him for it and the young lion repents.' Here, then, the Black Lady's soul is speaking sternly to her, and S is planning to hoodwink him – not a difficult task, since he is blind. Soul is likely to check the Black Lady for allowing this man to come too close. S advises her to tell Soul the truth, 'that I was thy *Will*, your lover Will, but, being blind, Soul does not see capital letters or italics and assumes that all is well, since, as Cruden says in his *Concordance*, 'Will is that faculty of the soul whereby we freely choose or refuse things.' It resides in the soul and is therefore entitled to be admitted to its own home. 'As thy soul knows' is a sly parenthesis.

4–6 'Sweet' is in play with 'suit' and introduces a string of puns, as printed in the Quarto:

> Thus farre for loue, my loue-sute sweet fullfill.
> *Will*, will fulfill the treasure of thy loue,
> I fill it full with wils, and my will one.

Kerrigan (1986) has an imaginative note: 'fulfil … fulfil … fill … full (lecherously unfolding the word as though undressing it, exposing with seductive tardiness its sexual potential).' Add the Quarto spelling, the spatterings of 'love' and 'will', all peaking in the monosyllables of line 6 and 'one' in alliteration with 'wills' and 'will', and the effect is even greater.

Some editors follow Q in taking 'love-suit sweet' together, whereas this edition takes 'sweet' as an address to the Black Lady. A sweet love-suit is difficult to imagine, but 'sweet' is many times applied to the object of S's love, and often stands by itself as a term of endearment in the plays, as in 'Trust me, sweet,' in *MND* 5.1.99. It is as though 'suit' reminds him of how sweet his mistress is, just as in 128.1 he thinks of her as music when he hears music played.

At one level, lines 5–6 mean that, if she allows S to come near her, he will fulfil her desire for love. But after 135.5–8 the treasure of a woman's love is her vagina, as in *TA* 2.1.131–2, where Aaron urges on his 'brave boys' to gang rape and violence in the woods, 'There serve your lust, shadowed from heaven's eye, | And revel in Lavinia's treasury.' '*Will*' in line 5, is William, libido and the penis. In line 6 he will enlist all three to fulfil the treasure of her love, yes, to fill her vagina full of penises, one of them being his own. This accords with 135.14 and is a snarling allusion to her sordid promiscuity.

The Quarto has a comma at the beginning of line 5, '*Will*, will' as though to give the reader pause to work out the full implications of '*Will*', and also to separate it from the auxiliary verb 'will' that immediately follows (compare 135.5). In line 6 the Quarto reads 'I'. This breaks the flow. 'Ay' or 'aye' meaning 'yes' was often spelt as 'I' in the sixteenth and eighteenth centuries, and the change of 'I' to 'Ay' gives the line a conversational vigour, 'I'll fulfil it, | Yes, I'll fill it full', so providing double filling and double fullness. Ruminative 'Ay' is familiar from *Ham* 3.1.67, 'To sleep, perchance to dream. Ay, there's the rub.'

7–9 'Things of great receipt' are capacious receptacles. A proof that one is not a number is given in Macrobius, *Somnium Scipionis* 2.2. Just as in geometry a point is not a body, but produces bodies from itself, '*corpus non est, sed ex se facit corpora*', so one is not said to be a number but is the source of numbers, '*monas numerus esse non dicitur, sed origo numerorum*'. This nonsense is exploited by Elizabethan poets, as noted at 8.14. S uses it here as an insult – you have so many coins in your treasure that one more will not be worth counting, you receive so many lovers in your vagina, one more won't make any difference. Now comes a commercial metaphor with four elements, 'reckoned', 'untold' meaning uncounted, 'store's account', and perhaps 'hold' twice in 11. 'Store' here refers to what is *held* in stock, possessions. According to *OED* it does not mean shop until 1740, and until 1875 it occurs in that sense only in the United States. In 7–11 she is selling her love.

10–12 Now 'hold' comes to mean consider, 'Hold that nothing, me, to be sweet.' 'A something sweet' twists back to 'my love-suit, sweet, fulfil' in line 4. There she was addressed as 'sweet', but here he wants her to think of himself as being sweet.

13–14 In 13 he begs her to love his name. 'Love that still, | And then thou lov'st me, for my name is Will.' This makes an argument and an epigram if 'my name' differs in some way from 'Will'. 'Love X because I am X' is feeble. The mischief lies in the difference between will and Will. 'Love my name (that is, sexual pleasure and the penis), and I shall be delighted because my name is Will [you will be loving me].' This is the last twist in the tangle of puns which have twined through Sonnets 135 and 136.

In Sonnets 135 and 136 the speaker reveals that his name is Will. An obvious inference would be that these are words spoken by William Shakespeare to a mistress, and further that the whole collection is a record of an episode in Shakespeare's experience of love. This commentary takes a different view – that the Sonnets are a skilfully crafted fictitious drama with three main characters, only one of whom speaks. Of course the dramatist calls upon his experience of life (for example in 23, 111, 123 and 125), and here he has not resisted the temptation to use his own first name as a contribution to an orgy of punning. In these two poems he is speaking as himself for the sake of the puns, but the collection remains a structured fiction, a plot, not an episode in an autobiography.

Thou blind fool Love, what dost thou to mine eyes,
That they behold and see not what they see?
They know what beauty is, see where it lies,
Yet what the best is, take the worst to be.   4

If eyes, corrupt by over-partial looks,
Be anchored in the bay where all men ride,
Why of eyes' falsehood hast thou forgèd hooks
Whereto the judgement of my heart is tied?   8

Why should my heart think that a several plot
Which my heart knows the wide world's common place?
Or mine eyes, seeing this, say this is not,
To put fair truth upon so foul a face?   12

In things right true my heart and eyes have erred,
And to this false plague are they now transferred.

You blind fool Love, what are you doing to my eyes?
  They know beauty and see where it is, but take the best to be the worst.
If eyes are corrupted by doting on this promiscuous woman,
  why, Love, have you tied heart into the same mistake?
Why should it think common land is private property?
  Eyes see this. Why deny it and put a pretty veil on an ugly face?
Heart and eyes are wrong, both given over to this false plague.

1–4 The logician poet moves from eyes to heart in line 8, and his questions in lines 9–12 move from heart to eyes. He then sums up for both in 13–14. In line 1 Love is addressed as the god of love. Hence the capital letter.

The dramatist poet personifies Love, eyes and heart. Love is blind, and has ruined S's eyes (1–6 and 11–12). He is a fool, and has seized the judgement of the heart and attached it to the blind eyes in 7–10. Eyes behold and see what they don't see and know and see again and take and are corrupted and become ships riding at anchor and provide falsehoods which Love uses to forge hooks. In 11–13 they see yet again and say and put a lovely veil of truth on an ugly face. Heart too thinks and knows, and both eyes and heart have erred.

Line 4 is a shock. The argument of the poem is that his eyes have persuaded him that the Black Lady, the worst, is the best, but now 'what the best is' they 'take the worst to be'. There would be no problem if the line read, 'Yet what the worst is take the best to be.' A possible explanation might start from the remark in Vendler (1997) that 'the desperate confusions of 137 are made visible not only by its frantic questions and hypothesis and alternative proposals …' The line would then be an optical illusion demonstrating, enacting, the blindness of love and the corruption and error of S's eyes – 'they see not what they see' – but that is not convincing. I cannot understand this line.

5–8 The obscenities of 134–6 culminate here in two savage metaphors. If his eyes, corrupted by over-partiality in looking at the Black Lady too favourably, are now 'anchored in the bay where all men ride', why have they enslaved the judgement of his heart? Ships ride (see 80.10), and the Black Lady is a bay in which every ship and all men ride at anchor, ships rising and falling with the waves. Riding is a vulgar term for sexual intercourse, as in *OED* 3, and as when Orléans teases Bourbon for calling his horse his mistress in *H5* 3.7.51–2, 'you rode like a kern of Ireland, your French hose off', where a kern is an Irish foot-soldier. But the nautical metaphor does not end at line 6. Not only are eyes 'anchored in the bay where all men ride', but out of their falsehoods Love has forged hooks to grapple the heart to ships which are the deluded eyes. In Elizabethan times hooked grappling irons were in regular use in peacetime to moor one boat alongside another, in wartime to board enemy vessels. So here Love has forged the claws of the grapnels which bind the judgement of the heart to the eyes whose falsehood has provided the metal. Grappling is referred to half a dozen times in the plays, for example in *Mac* 3.1.107, where a favour 'grapples you to the heart and love of us', and in *Ham* 1.3.63, 'Grapple them unto thy soul with hoops of steel', as commonly printed. Here Pope did not see how he could grapple with hoops, and emended to 'hooks' in his edition. It is not fair to reject that emendation as 'a piece of 18th-century literalism', as Harold Jenkins does in the Arden Shakespeare commentary (1982). Nobody grapples with hoops.

9–12 From the nautical to the agricultural, 'Why should heart believe common land to be private fields?' *OED* (several 7a) cites from 1583, 'The commons ... are inclosed, made several.' 'The wide world's common place' carries even more savagery than 69.14, 'thou dost common grow.' 'Common houses' are brothels in *MM* 2.1.43. A similar connection of images occurs in *LLL* when at 2.1.218 Boyet says, 'I was as willing to grapple as he was to board', and five lines later the badinage between Boyet and Katherine moves on to country matters. When he asks her to grant him pasture, she replies 'Not so, gentle beast, | My lips are no *common*, though *several* they be.' In 9–10 there is an eloquent variation between 'Why shóuld mý héart ...' and 'Which mý heart knóws ...' For other examples, see 138.9–10. In lines 11–12 eyes see that the Black Lady is promiscuous but say she is not, and the metaphor changes again, when eyes put a veil of truth over an ugly face.

13–14 Love has blinded S's eyes and deceived the judgement of his heart in a matter of right and truth. In Sonnet 113 mind/heart was blamed. In Sonnet 114 the trouble started with eye. In 141 heart will be responsible, in 148 eye is false, but here eyes and heart are both at fault, both led into error by Love. Lines 3 and 4 seemed to recall the superiority of his former beloved, and that interpretation is confirmed by line 14. Eyes and heart are now transferred from the best to the worst, from true to false, and to a deadly plague, the Black Lady. Lines 3–4 and 12–14 contrasted her with the beloved youth, an exercise more powerfully conducted in Sonnet 144.

Vendler (1997)
The word *plague* seems chosen as the last term in the alliterating sequence *plot*, *place*, – ; and also, in its ending –*ue*, to act as an antonym of *true* in the preceding line; the word *ague*, visually (though not phonetically) incorporated in *pla**gue*** may also have pleased Shakespeare, given that 'My love is as a fever' (147); he would have been aware of the derivation of *ague* from *fièvre aigue*, or 'sharp fever'. The word *plague* itself, by its derivation from *plaga* ('wound'), may have seemed apposite to an effect of Cupid's arrow (cf. 139, '*Wound* me not with thine eyes .../*wound* with cunning'). Or *plaga*/wound may suggest the vulva.

ℰ 138 ℛ

When my love swears that she is made of truth,
I do believe her though I know she lies,
That she might think me some untutored youth,
Unlearnèd in the world's false subtleties.   4

Thus vainly thinking that she thinks me young,
Although she knows my days are past the best,
Simply I credit her false-speaking tongue.
On both sides thus is simple truth suppressed.   8

But wherefore says she not she is unjust?
And wherefore say not I that I am old?
O, love's best habit is in seeming trust,
And age in love loves not to have years told.   12

    Therefore I lie with her and she with me,
    And in our faults by lies we flattered be.

She says she is true and, though I know she lies,
  I believe her to make her think me a young innocent.
Thinking she thinks me young although she knows I'm not,
  I believe her lies. Each of us is suppressing the truth.
Why not admit it? She knows the best dress for love is pretence of loyalty,
  and I want to conceal my age.
So we lie together flattering each other by our lies.

1–4 No one swears they are true unless doubts have been raised. The
Black Lady goes further. She swears 'that she is made of truth', implying
that she has never been unfaithful, although in Sonnets 134–7 S has raged
about her infidelities. He knows she is lying, but in an act of deliberate
self-deception he decides to believe, hoping to persuade her he is young and
inexperienced. The older man (in 1609 he was 45) is touchy about his age.
'Untutored youth' and 'unlearnèd' are the language of education.

5–8   He keeps up this calculated self-deception, although he knows it does not deceive his mistress, and the folly of all this is audible in 'believe ... know ... think ... thinking ... thinks ... knows ... credit', a great false-work of ABCCCBA. He believes her although he knows she lies, vainly thinking she thinks, although she knows. Similar but glibber tangles appear *AW* 2.1.157, 'But [I] know I think and think I know most sure', and in Thom Gunn's poem 'Carnal Knowledge', 'You know I know you know I know you know.'

Deception continues in line 7, where 'simply' suggests naïvety (he is not naïve but scheming), and in line 8, where 'simple truth' is plain truth. Polyptoton is the repetition of a word in a different form. Here it is repetition in a different form *and* a different meaning, polyptoton with a twist demonstrating the treachery in the subject matter. 'Simple' has yet a third common meaning. What is simple is single, not composite or complex, and in 8 Shakespeare, the arch-contraster, opposes 'simple' to 'both'.

Each is lying, she in pretending to be faithful, he in pretending to be young. This is a demonstration of lies at the heart of love. But there are lies and lies. Her lie is an act of betrayal, his is a harmless attempt to pose as a gullible youngster. He sees through her lie but subscribes to it as a tactic of continuance – a willed suspension of disbelief.

9–12   'Why does she not admit she is unjust?' She is unjust to him in the sense that she is untrue, picking up the argument from the first line. The same word is used again of truth in love, and again it rhymes with 'trust', in *PP* 18.19–22:

> Serve always with assurèd trust,
> And in thy suit be humble true
> Unless thy lady prove unjust
> Press never thou to find a new.

'Why does she not admit she lies?' in 9; 'Why do I not admit that I do the same?' in 10. The answer to 9 comes in 11 and the answer to 10 comes in 12. No ageing lover likes to have his age 'told', which may carry two meanings of the word, 'revealed' and 'counted' (see 30.1). But what is the answer to line 9? Why does she not admit that she is false? If trust means confidence, reliance, line 11 is no answer. She is not lying because she wishes to seem to trust her lover. The explanation is that 'trust' could be used to mean fidelity, honesty, as in *RJ* 3.2.86, 'There's no trust, no faith, no honesty in men.' The best habit love can wear is a habit, a dress, of apparent honesty. She knows she looks her best if she pretends to be faithful.

The language of natural speech gave drama to lines 2–6. A similar technique represents the idiom of lovers' recriminations in 9–10, when 'whérefore sáys she nót' is followed not by 'whérefore sáy I nót', but by 'whérefore sáy not Í', an effect like the minute variation in 54.12, 58.12, 115.10 and 13, and 124.4. Again S weighs the balance against his mistress. He does not want her to know his age. She does not want to admit she has a troop of lovers.

13–14 After the balanced lines 9–12, the interplay of persons becomes denser, with 'I ... her ... she ... me' in 13, before the two join in 'our' and 'we' in line 14. The last three sonnets have carried a cataract of obscenities and risqué puns, which make it impossible to read this final couplet as though it refers only to falsehood. They flatter each other with their *lies* as they *lie* together making love, the wit and the picture sharpened by an early sense of the word 'flatter', to touch or stroke lightly and caressingly (see 33.2). The wit carries a supercargo of bitterness.

This sonnet and 144 were printed as the first poem in *The Passionate Pilgrim* (1599), ten years before the Quarto. This is either an early version by Shakespeare himself or a misremembered effort by some person unknown. In either case it offers an insight into Shakespeare's poetic techniques. The text below is taken from Burrow (2002), 341:

> When my love swears that she is made of truth,
> I do believe her (though I know she lies),
> That she might think me some untutored youth,
> Unskilful in the world's false forgeries. 4
> Thus vainly thinking that she thinks me young,
> Although I know my years be past the best,
> I, smiling, credit her false-speaking tongue,
> Outfacing faults in love with love's ill rest. 8
> But wherefore says my love that she is young?
> And wherefore say not I that I am old?
> O, love's best habit is a soothing tongue,
> And age (in love) loves not to have years told. 12
> Therefore I'll lie with love, and love with me,
> Since that our faults in love thus smothered be.

The first verbal difference is in line 4, 'Unskilful in the world's false forgeries.' In the Quarto 'unlearnèd' joins 'untutored' to continue the educational metaphor, but 'false forgeries' is a weak phrase. All forgeries are false, calculated deceptions undertaken for financial gain, whereas the subtleties of lovers may have other objectives.

In line 6 the 1599 version offers 'Although I know my years be past the best' for the Quarto's 'Although she knows my days are past the best'. The earlier version barely makes sense in the tight argument of the poem. Of course he knows his own age. The point is that she knows it. Besides, 'years' lacks the cruelty of 'days'. A man of 45 is older every day. 'Years' is in its place in line 12.

In line 7, 'I, smiling, credit her false-speaking tongue' is a vivid picture of the self-deceiving lover bravely pretending to believe what he knows to be false, but the Quarto version offers the bitter polyptoton of 'simply' and 'simple' in 7 and 8 and the typical rhetorical contrast between 'simple' and 'both'. It is as though the writer of this version has shied away from the repetition in 'simple' and 'simply' because he thought the repetitions weak.

'Outfacing faults in Love' by means of lying is again a vigorous picture, but 'with love's ill rest' is obscure, and therefore a failure. It is not clear how faults in love could be subdued with unhappy restlessness (sleepless nights?) of love. Perhaps 'with' is meant just to connect 'faults' and 'ill rest', 'I believe her, and put a bold face on faults along with interruptions to our love.' But no defence gives this the lapidary force of 7–8 in the Quarto.

The startling finding is in line 9. This is a totally different poem. It now becomes clear that in this poem the mistress's false oath in the first line is a forgivable lie about her age, like S's. It is a slight and superficial poem about two lovers lying to each other about their ages. In the context of the Black Lady poems in the Quarto, she is swearing that she is faithful to S when it has been established that she is not, and that he is suffering. Sonnet 138 is neither slight nor superficial.

In 11 the 'soothing tongue' as love's best habit raises a smile, but is oceans away from 'seeming trust', the cynical acceptance of the need for hypocrisy in love. And tongues do not don habits.

In the earlier version 13 does not have the later sonnet's eloquent interweaving of pronouns, and in 13–14 their faults are smothered by love in triplicate – a vivid picture, but a shallow comedy of manners. The lovers kiss and make up. In the Quarto they flatter each other, living and loving in untruth.

It is not easy to believe that Shakespeare could have written anything so weak as what appears in *The Passionate Pilgrim*. It is therefore likely to be a poorly remembered version, simplified and trivialised, by some person unknown.

O call me not to justify the wrong
That thy unkindness lays upon my heart.
Wound me not with thine eye, but with thy tongue.
Use power with power, and slay me not by art.   4
Tell me thou lov'st elsewhere, but in my sight,
Dear heart, forbear to glance thine eye aside.
What need'st thou wound with cunning when thy might
Is more than my o'erpressed defence can bide?   8

Let me excuse thee: 'Ah, my love well knows
Her pretty looks have been mine enemies,
And therefore from my face she turns my foes
That they elsewhere might dart their injuries.'   12

Yet do not so, but since I am near slain,
Kill me outright with looks, and rid my pain.

Do not ask me to justify your unkind treatment of me.
   Wound me with your tongue, not your eye. Say you don't love me,
   but don't eye others when you're with me.
Let me excuse you: 'She knows the damage her eyes have done me,
   so she is sparing me and turning them on my enemies.'
Don't do that. I'm nearly dead. Look at me and put me out of my pain.

1–8   The Black Lady is making him suffer and he can think of no way of
excusing her. It is her eye that wounds in lines 3, 6, 10 and 14, and he is
sensitive to the language of eyes (see 104.2). She is a woman and her eye is
'false in rolling' (see 20.5). Let her destroy him by the power that comes
from her power of speech, but not by the arts of her eye.

  She has moved on to another lover, 'Tell me thou lov'st elsewhere', and
'elsewhere' carries the same weight as in 61.13–14. She has let him see her
darting side glances at another man, just as in *KL* 4.4.25–6 Regan says she

observed Goneril giving 'strange oeillades and most speaking looks | To noble Edmond'.

This scene is pieced together from 'elsewhere' and 'aside' in 5–6 and 12. He is suffering so acutely that it is not a matter of asking her not to stare at this other man; even a glance is wounding. This is part of her cunning art (4 and 7). She has wrongfooted him. It would surely be impossible for any reasonable person to object to a glance.

9–12   In line 1 he refused to justify her, but now, after brooding about her eyes, he suddenly thinks of a possible excuse, 'Ah, it's because she knows her eyes have hurt me that she's turning them on others.' The sonnet is addressed to the Black Lady, but here in lines 9–12 he is suddenly speaking to himself. She ceases to be 'thou', and becomes 'my love'. It is as though the excuse is so far-fetched that he dare not say it to her for fear of being ridiculed. It is simply a desperate idea he is trying out. This is dramatic writing. 'Ah!' begins it as the idea strikes him, but he gives up the idea as soon as he has put it into words, 'Yet do not so'.

The suffering lover senses that he is whistling to keep his courage up. He knows the excuse is as self-deluding as earlier excuses he invented for the young man in Sonnets 42 and 61. In line 10 'her pretty looks' might be a compliment, but lines 13–14 show that this is as pained as 41.1, 'Those pretty wrongs that liberty commits'.

13–14   When he realises the folly of this, he finds a way of turning it into an appeal for pity. 'Do not look at others. I'm almost slain, so turn your eyes on me and kill me outright.' 'Slain' refers to death by violence, often therefore in battle, and the sonnet is full of battle terms, 'Wound ... power ... power ... slay ... wound ... might ... o'erpressed ... defence ... bide ... enemies ... foes ... dart ... injuries ... slain ... Kill ... outright ... rid', making 17 occurrences on a generous count. 'Bide' in line 8 is enlisted as a military term as in *3H6* 2.2.83, 'bide the mortal fortune of the field', and in *RJ* 1.1.209–10, 'She will not stay the siege of loving terms, | Nor bide th'encounter of assailing eyes.' On 'rid', Booth (1977) cites *R2* 5.4.11, 'I am the King's friend, and will rid his foe.'

On line 14 Kerrigan (1986) notes, 'Though the likely source for this is Sidney *Astrophil and Stella* 48 ... "A kind of grace it is to slay with speed", it evokes a host of Elizabethan love poems in which the mistress's eye is like Medusa's or the basilisk's.' This is true, but Shakespeare wields the cliché with a difference. Sidney's point is that a swift death is more merciful than a slow. S is arguing that it is a courtesy of war to kill a mortally wounded enemy.

Be wise as thou art cruel. Do not press
My tongue-tied patience with too much disdain,
Lest sorrow lend me words, and words express
The manner of my pity-wanting pain.   4

If I might teach thee wit, better it were,
Though not to love, yet, love, to tell me so,
As testy sick men when their deaths be near
No news but health from their physicians know.   8

For if I should despair, I should go mad,
And in my madness might speak ill of thee.
Now this ill-wresting world is grown so bad,
Mad sland'rers by mad ears believèd be.   12

That I may not be so, nor thou belied,
Bear thine eyes straight, though thy proud heart go wide.

Be as wise as you are cruel. Do not try me too high
* or I shall find words to describe my suffering.*
It would be better to say you love me, even although you don't.
* Dying men hear nothing but good news from doctors.*
If I despaired, I would go mad and might criticise you,
* and madmen are believed by mad listeners.*
Since I do not want to go mad, nor you to be slandered,
* keep your eyes straight, though your heart wander.*

1–4 'I am patient and silent, but have the wisdom not to press me too
hard, or I may find words to tell how you have made me suffer.' In 'The
manner of my pity-wanting pain', 'pity-wanting' is unpitied, just as in
TGV 2.6.12 the man who wants wit is without it.

Burrow (2002) cites a valuable passage from William Harrison, *The
Description of England* (1587), 'Such felons as stand mute and speak not at

their arraignment are *pressed* to death by huge weights laid upon a board that *lieth* over their breast and a sharp stone under their backs' (Harrison 1994, 191). This is a reference to *peine forte et dure*, 'pressing to death' (*OED* peine). There are allusions to this in Shakespeare, notably in *R2* 3.4.73, 'O, I am *pressed* to death for want of speaking', and in *TC* 3.2.203–7, where Pandarus makes a lewd joke of it. Here S asks her not to *press* his patience. He is mute, 'tongue-tied', but his sorrow may lend him words, and the words may squeeze out, '*express*', his pain.

5–8 The poem starts with advice to the Black Lady to be wise. Now S offers to teach her wit, a worldly wisdom, to teach a woman to lie to a man, to tell him she loves him although it is not true. The misery in this is that he is begging to be lied to, and knows it. This is a return to the self-deception of Sonnet 138 and the failed attempt at it in 139.9–12.

He finds a comparison. She ought to be kind and lie to him. After all, when a man is dying and being difficult, his doctor does not tell him the truth, but talks only of prospects of health. The comparison is bleak. The doctor's words are lies, and the patient is near death. So was S at the end of 139.

9–12 Pleading his case with his usual ingenuity, he now argues that it would be in her own interest if she pretended to love him. He advances his argument in four steps: first, 'if I should despair, I should go mad' (note the compliment – to lose her would be to lose his sanity); second, 'in my madness [I] might speak ill of thee' (note another compliment – speaking ill of her would be madness); third, the world twists the words of mad slanderers to make bad worse (note that he is concerned for her welfare); fourth, the mad slander will be believed (note the blackmail – 'Do what I ask, or you will suffer'). In the last half-dozen sonnets he has subjected her to abuse, often obscene. Remarkably, he now implies that she is blameless. Readers of recent sonnets know what she is and they will appreciate the manoeuvre. There was another strategic withdrawal in Sonnet 88.

13–14 In 139 he begged her to tell him if she loved someone else, but not to glance at other men when she was in his company, and that modest request came with an appeal for pity in the final couplet. In 140.1–8 he keeps asking for pity, but he is now asking for something else. He wants her to tell him that she loves him although it is not true. This is followed by an apparent assumption of her innocence, 'nor thou belied', and an expression of concern for her reputation in the eyes of the world. The last line does not repeat his request in lines 1–8 that she should say she loves him, but retreats to the more modest position of 139.6. He begs her not to glance aside at other men when she is with him. 'Though thy proud heart go wide' allows her heart free range. He has given up. He has no hope of preventing her from having other lovers.

The sonnet has departed from the abusive mode, and S has spoken accommodatingly, as an advocate making an appeal. A suppliant does not abuse. But his true feelings glimmer through the epigram of the last line. The opposite of straight is crooked, 'bevel' in 121.11–12. 'Bear thine eyes straight' harks back to 139.6, where he asks her not to glance aside, but the language is ambiguous in 'though thy proud heart go wide'. Is this saying that it might go wide, or that it already does? Sonnet 88.4 can also be taken in two ways. This last line visualises her eyes looking straight forward on a narrow front, although her heart may wander, 'go wide'. S is abject in his appeals, and as an advocate is treading a minefield, but truth will out. 'Straight' sounds like 'strait' meaning narrow, the opposite of 'wide', and Shakespeare loves opposites. The hint is that her broad way leads to destruction. 'Wide is the gate, and broad is the way, that leadeth to destruction ... strait is the gate, and narrow is the way, which leadeth unto life' appears in the Sermon on the Mount in Matthew 7: 13–14.

✂ 141 ✄

In faith, I do not love thee with mine eyes,
For they in thee a thousand errors note,
But 'tis my heart, that loves what they despise,
Who in despite of view is pleased to dote.   4

Nor are mine ears with thy tongue's tune delighted,
Nor tender feeling to base touches prone,
Nor taste, nor smell desire to be invited
To any sensual feast with thee alone.   8

But my five wits nor my five senses can
Dissuade one foolish heart from serving thee,
Who leaves unswayed the likeness of a man,
Thy proud heart's slave and vassal wretch to be.   12

Only my plague thus far I count my gain,
That she who makes me sin awards me pain.

My eyes see your blemishes. My heart dotes on what they despise.
Neither ears, touch, taste, nor smell, have any wish to feast alone with you.
But my five wits and five senses cannot dissuade my heart from leaving me,
*   to become your heart's slave.*
My only profit is that she who makes me sin awards me pain.

1–4 The poem starts with a blunt statement in monosyllables, and personification heightens the drama. Eyes are persons in 2, and in 3 heart dotes on the
Black Lady *despite* the fact in 3–4 that eyes *despise* her. Heart is a doting fool.

5–8 Then four new characters take the stage – hearing, touch, taste and
smell. Ears take no pleasure from the music of her speaking voice, mimed
in the jangle 'thy tongue's tune delighted'. Line 6 offers a cameo of an erotic
scene. The Black Lady applies base touches but feeling is not 'tender', not
sensitive to them. She failed, as Venus failed when she tried to charm

431

Adonis in *PP* 4.7–8, 'To win his heart she touched him here and there: | Touches so soft still conquer chastity.' Taste and smell are not averse to feasts but neither of them would wish to be invited to go to a banquet of the senses *tête-à-tête* with her. The last word, 'alone', says it all. This is a comic vignette in eight lines with a dozen characters. Personification is flagged in line 4 by heart, *Who* is pleased to dote, and *Who* in line 11 defies ten sage advisers and leaves to become a slave.

9–12 [Neither] his five wits nor his five senses can dissuade heart. The senses have been dealt with in 1–8. 'Bless thy five wits,' raves Edgar in *KL* 3.4.54. They were listed by Stephen Hawes in the *Passetyme of Pleasure* (1509), chapter 24, as common wit (which Booth (1977) explains as common sense), imagination, fantasy, estimation and memory. These five terms are also defined in *Batman in Bartholomew* (1582), cited by Burrow (2002).

In line 10 heart leaves to become the vassal slave of the Black Lady, a condition S has experienced already in Sonnet 133, and under the young man in Sonnets 57–8. What heart leaves behind is not a man, but only the likeness of a man, 'unswayed', under no sway, with no heart to govern it. After 'thy proud heart' in 140.14 the pride of her heart in 141.12 is no surprise, and her pride is confirmed in 144.8. The young man is never said to be proud (129.2).

13–14 The only advantage of this plague is that the woman who makes him sin rewards him with pain. Samuel Butler explains, 'I shall suffer less for my sin hereafter, for I receive some of the punishment coincidentally with the offence.' After the end of his great love for the young man and his infatuation with the Black Lady, S has a tendency to drift bitterly towards religion. Sin is the pivot which links 141.14 to 142.1, and 144 and 146 are based on Christian thinking.

Booth (1977) ends his note on this poem with a long study of the 'eye and heart poems', 24, 46–7, 93, 132–3, 137 and 139–41. Is this sonnet simply another exercise of invention, or is it the experience of a man totally in thrall to a woman without receiving any pleasure of the senses or of the mind, but still coming back for more?

Evans (1996) surprises by referring to the suggestion in Vendler (1997), reproduced at the end of the commentary on 137, that 'plague' is a 'a play on Latin *plaga* (= wound), from which "plague" is derived, and that "wound" may be taken as metaphor for *vulva* or the vagina. Burrow (2002) has a similar approach to 141.13, 'There is also a jaunty "who cares if I got VD? It was fun" struggling somewhere in there.'

ᔌ 142 ᔍ

Love is my sin, and thy dear virtue hate,
Hate of my sin, grounded on sinful loving.

O, but with mine compare thou thine own state,
And thou shalt find it merits not reproving,   4
Or if it do, not from those lips of thine
That have profaned their scarlet ornaments
And sealed false bonds of love as oft as mine,
Robbed others' beds' revénues of their rents.   8

Be't lawful I love thee as thou lov'st those
Whom thine eyes woo as mine impórtune thee.
Root pity in thy heart, that when it grows,
Thy pity may deserve to pitied be.   12

If thou dost seek to have what thou dost hide,
By self-example mayst thou be denied.

My sin is love, and your virtue is hatred of my sinful love.
Compare your own state and you'll see that mine does not deserve
    to be condemned by your false lips.
I should be allowed to love you as you love others. Pity for me should grow
    in your heart to earn you pity from others.
If you want what you do not give, you may be disappointed.

1–2 S's sin is love, a sin based on sinful loving. What kind of loving is that?
In Sonnet 138 it was love based on lies. In 141 it was making love to the
Black Lady contrary to his judgement and his senses. Here it is a love not
unlike hers. In lines 6–8 she is profane, false and adulterous. In 10 she uses
her eyes to ask for love, and yet her dear virtue is hatred of that sort of
loving. In view of this account of her sexual behaviour, her 'dear virtue'
can scarcely be a sincere tribute. Perhaps it goes some way towards our
sarcastic use of the word 'precious', that precious virtue of yours.

3–8   In line 3 the metrical beat would fall on 'mine' and 'thine'. If it is brought out in reading, it clarifies the logic, 'Ó, but with míne compáre thou thíne' and you will see that you have no right to condemn me. Now the condemnation becomes more vivid by switching the attack from the Black Lady to her lips. After the severe monosyllables of line 5, [being red] they are seen as priests profaning their scarlet vestments. His mind then glides from church to law, another area where corruption is not unknown. These lips [being red like sealing wax] have sealed false bonds. Lips seal contracts, as when Romeo sealed 'with a righteous kiss | A dateless bargain to engrossing death' (5.3.114–15), and poured the poison. In line 8, still in the legal mode, 'revenues' are the collective items which constitute an income (OED 4), and a rent would be one of them. So marriage beds are seen as properties which offer a varied yield, rents which might include fidelity and legal offspring. The Black Lady's lips have cheated wives and husbands out of both of these.

9–12   Having asked her in line 3 to compare her conduct with his, he now insists, 'Let it be lawful for me to love you as you love those whom your eyes invite.' 'Root pity in thy heart,' he begs, and if there were any doubt what he is begging for it would be dispelled by a cliché of contemporary love poetry by which pity was 'equated with sexual compliance', as Duncan-Jones (1997) puts it with some severity. Let her plant a root of pity in her heart, and when it grows (so far there is no sign of it), the pity she gives may earn pity for herself, 'Thy pity may deserve to pitied be.'

13–14   If she hides pity, fails to show it, a time may come when she will need it herself, and others may follow her example. 'Love me, lest you be not loved' is the lurking threat. 'Mayst thou be denied' could be either warning or wish or deliberate ambiguity, 'you may be denied' or 'may you be denied', or both.

೫ 143 ೪

Lo, as a careful housewife runs to catch
One of her feathered creatures broke away,
Sets down her babe, and makes all swift dispatch
In púrsuit of the thing she would have stay,   4
Whilst her neglected child holds her in chase,
Cries to catch her whose busy care is bent
To follow that which flies before her face,
Not prizing the poor infant's discontent—   8
So runn'st thou after that which flies from thee,
Whilst I, thy babe, chase thee afar behind.

But if thou catch thy hope, turn back to me,
And play the mother's part, kiss me, be kind.   12
   So will I pray that thou mayst have thy Will,
   If thou turn back and my loud crying still.

Just as a housewife runs after a hen, her baby chases her
   and she pays no attention to his crying, so you run after
   what flies from you, while I, your baby, chase along behind.
But if you catch what you hope for, turn back, mother me and kiss me.
I will pray you get your Will, if you turn back and silence my crying.

1–10 This is a surprising sonnet, a farmyard drama with three characters,
a mother whose job includes looking after the poultry, her baby and a fowl,
perhaps a hen, which has broken out of the coop, all making a simile for
the love triangle in this part of the plot of the Sonnets. The Black Lady is
the 'huswife' (this Quarto spelling offers a homely sound, 'hússif'), the hen
she is pursuing is the young man S loved, and S himself is the baby.

   A simile is a figure of speech by which one thing is compared to another
of a different kind. Sometimes, particularly in epic poetry, there are many
such correspondences between the simile and the literal, the simile *à queue
longue*. In the text that follows italics indicate such correspondences between the simile in 1–8 and what it illustrates in 9–14:

Lo, as a careful housewife *runs* to *catch*
One of her feathered creatures broke away,
Sets down her *babe*, and makes all swift dispatch
In *pŭrsuit* of the thing she would have stay,   4
Whilst her neglected child holds her in *chase*,
Cries to *catch* her whose busy care is bent
To follow *that which flies* before her face,
Not prizing the poor *infant's* discontent –   8

So *runn'st* thou after *that which flies* from thee,
Whilst I, thy *babe*, *chase* thee afar behind.
But if thou *catch* thy hope, turn back to me,
And play the mother's part, kiss me, be kind.   12
 So will I pray that thou mayst have thy Will,
 If thou turn back and my loud *crying* still.

There is one important point of comparison not brought out by these italics. The housewife is 'Not prizing the poor infant's discontent', exactly as the Black Lady pays no attention to S's unhappiness, S being 'her neglected child', 'the poor infant', 'I, thy babe'. This poem could be taken as a moving appeal for pity to reinforce the ending of 142. The Black Lady is pursuing the young man whom S loves (she caught him in 133.6), and in 135–6 S grants her freedom to love anyone she wants provided that she still gives herself to him, the conclusion of this sonnet.

On the other hand a poem comparing the Black Lady to a farmer's wife, the young man to a hen, and S to a baby, is not likely to be entirely serious. The loftiness of the language adds to the incongruity (a stock trick with the epic simile as in Fielding's *Tom Jones*). 'One of her feathered creatures ... makes all swift dispatch | In pŭrsuit' gives the game away. That is not how Shakespeare would write, unless he wanted a touch of pomposity. Even the word 'pŭrsuit' may have a mock-heroic sound. It occurs a score of times in Shakespeare, but only here with the accent on the first syllable. The Black Lady as a careful housewife also gives pause. This would be amusing if the primary reference were to caution and conscientiousness, but, in view of 'busy care' in line 6, it is more likely that 'careful' suggests rather 'full of care'. The Black Lady is overworked, harassed.

This is a frantic crisis in the farmyard, hen escaped, hussif running, baby laid down [somewhere], swift dispatch, baby crying as he crawls or totters in pursuit, hen squawking [and fluttering] as it 'flies before her face'. Such would not normally have been part of the Black Lady's daily duties.

Another calculated misfit follows when S likens himself to a 'neglected child' and his amorous despair to a 'poor infant's discontent'. The pseudo-poignancy of the baby's predicament is intensified by the 'all swift dispatch' with which the hussif pursues the hen while 'her neglected child holds her in chase'. It was a graver matter when 'spies of the Volsces | Held me in chase' in *Cor* 1.7.18–19.

11–14 He begs her to come back to him after she catches what she hopes for, and play the mother to him. Then comes the crowning joke. 'Kiss me, be kind,' pleads the lover, and only two words in 11–14 are not monosyllables. He almost lapses into baby language, but the kindness of a mistress is not quite the kindness of a mother (see 142.11–12).

This is the last of the 'will' sonnets, and as in the others its climax is on 'Will'. In 135–6 the word is heavily punned, occurring in five or six different senses. S is praying that if she catches the young man (the hen), she may receive some of the other meanings of 'will', sexual desire, sexual activity, penis, if only she undertakes to come back, kiss and comfort her baby (S). The sense of this couplet will then correspond to his appeal in 135.5–14, 136.6–9 and, less explicitly, 142.9–10, 'I pray that you may be loved by the young man, provided you come back and make love to me.'

This note takes the sonnet as a flirtatious attempt at persuasion. Shakespeare is an accomplished comedian, and his lovers regularly tease each other, Romeo and Juliet, Beatrice and Benedick in *Much Ado About Nothing*, Rosalind and Orlando in *As You Like It*, Biron and the Princess of France in *Love's Labour's Lost*. He does not lose his sense of humour when he sits down to write sonnets. Here S is relying on the sense of humour of the Black Lady, by making her part of the fun. It would also be typical of Shakespeare to set a comic scene in a tragic context, the Porter before the 'horror, horror, horror' of the discovery of Duncan's murder in *Macbeth*, and the gravedigger before the funeral of Ophelia in *Hamlet*. Similarly, the witty genre scene of Sonnet 128 is relief before the cynicism of 129, the prettiness of 145 before the gloomy religiosity of 146. If 143 is a frivolous piece, it makes Shakespearean sense before the despair, devil and hell that follow in 144.

ဆ 144 ဿ

Two loves I have, of comfort and despair,
Which like two spirits do suggest me still:
The better angel is a man right fair,
The worser sp'rit a woman coloured ill.   4

To win me soon to hell my female evil
Tempteth my better angel from my side,
And would corrupt my saint to be a devil,
Wooing his purity with her foul pride.   8

And whether that my angel be turned fiend
Suspect I may, yet not directly tell,
But being both from me, both to each friend,
I guess one angel in another's hell.   12

   Yet this shall I ne'er know, but live in doubt
   Till my bad angel fire my good one out.

I have two loves. The better angel 'is a man right fair', the worser spirit
is 'a woman coloured ill'.
To put me in hell the female has seduced my better angel to corrupt him
and make him a devil.
With what success I do not know, but they are together,
and I guess he is in her hell.
I will not know 'till my bad angel fire my good one out'.

In this, 'the most merciless passage in English literature' according to
George Bernard Shaw, cited by Rollins (1944), logic rules. The first quatrain introduces the two spirits; the second describes the activities of the evil
female and the peril of the better angel; the third wonders whether this
good angel is already a devil in hell, the home of the bad angel; in 13–14 S
will know the answer when the bad angel ejects the good.

1–4 S has two loves – the young man and the Black Lady. The identifications are confirmed in lines 3 and 4. His 'better angel is a man right fair', and 'the worser sp'rit a woman coloured ill' (how changed from the raptures of 127 and 132). The young man is an angel throughout, and a saint in 7, whereas the woman, 'the worser sp'rit', is a female evil in 5, a bad angel in 14 and, by implication, a devil in 7, a fiend in hell in 9 and 12.

These two spirits 'suggest' him, meaning that they tempt him, a rare use of the verb with a personal object (*OED* 2a, 'to prompt (a person) to evil), but occurring where Mowbray incited the enemies of the Duke of Gloucester in *R2* 1.1.101, 'did suggest his soon-believing adversaries'. In line 2 'spirits' is two syllables, but in line 4 it is one, resembling 'sprite'. Neither here nor at 86.5 – 'Was it his sp'rit, by spirits taught to write' – need there be any reason for the difference except metrical convenience, but in each case the shorter version is applied to the inferior sp'rit.

5–8 In 134.1 and 13–14, S conceded that he had lost the man he loved, but despite that he still dreads losing him. For him this would be to enter hell. To call an evil spirit 'a female evil' is strange. Part of the explanation may be the need for a rhyme for 'devil'. She is seducing the young man, but this is expressed in Christian terms. She 'Tempteth my better angel from my side'. Just so 'Jesus was led by the *Spirit* into the wilderness, being forty days *tempted* of the *devil*' (Luke 4: 1–2; my italics). Embittered by his experience of love, S is thinking more and more in religious terms (141.14, 142.1–2 and 6, and 146).

While she becomes an evil, the young man becomes a saint, and his purity is opposed to the lady's foul pride, where pride is not only arrogance but also ostentation of dress, ornament or behaviour (see 99.3). This purity does not tally with the fierce denunciations of the young man's sexual promiscuity in 93–6, for instance, but it is not impossible that S should think away the pains of his old love in the trauma of the new. The greater evil drives out the lesser. Alternatively S is showing the flag of truce to the young man, and angling to turn him against the Black Lady.

9–12 S suspects that the woman may have succeeded in changing the young man into a devil. S cannot be certain by direct observation because they are not with him but both together, each being a friend to the other. In these poems friendship often implies a sexual relationship. In 'both to each friend' the dense wording makes the syntax obscure, but the repetition of 'both' stresses their closeness and isolates S. He does not know that the young man is a fiend in hell and suffering its torments, but it is a reasonable guess, since he is with a devil, and devils live in hell. This is plausible in human terms. A rejected lover might well torture himself by imagining how his previous lovers live together, casting one as a villain corrupting and tormenting the other.

13–14 Will S ever know whether the young man is already in hell? Only if the two angels cease to love each other and the young man comes back to him. The gulf between this prosing and the final couplet is where the poetry lives. Line 13 expresses the agony of not knowing, but 14 has two revealing twists. The first is 'till'. At this moment he does not think of 'if'. She is unlikely to keep a lover for long, and the young man will come back to him.

S does not speak plainly of a break in the liaison of the two angels, but finds an astonishing image, 'Till my bad angel fire my good one out.' He assumes that she will eject him, but 'fire' is difficult to place. The first thought is that they are now living in hell and that she will soon shoot the good angel out of it in a burst of hellfire, but the line has attracted a large set of bawdy interpretations, presented in Kerrigan (1986, 60). Scholars start from seeing 'hell' as the vagina, and not only here but also in 119.2 and 129.14. The evidence for this is in the denunciation of women in *KL* 4.5.124–6, where the gods possess only that part of women's body above the waist: 'Beneath is all the fiend's. There's hell, there's darkness, there is the sulphurous pit, burning, scalding, stench, consumption. Fie, fie, fie; pah, pah!' This evidence does not make the case. The raving of a deranged old man does not establish the meaning of words. Hell does not mean the vagina in English. Here the doubt is whether the young man is by now a devil living in hell, not whether he is in the act of sexual intercourse, and there is no call to imagine him being shot from her vagina. When the liaison of the angels reaches its end, it is natural that the one will stay in her home in hell, and natural that the other will be ejected. S visualises the raging flames belching from the mouth of hell and carrying the good angel with them. The bawdiness of 135, 136 and 143.13 does not belong in this sonnet, where comfort struggles vainly against despair.

Ingram and Redpath (1978), on line 14
Evidently a gross insult to the woman, though veiled under the innocent meaning of 'casting off'. The underlying sense is that the poet will not know whether the Friend has slept with the woman until he sees whether he has contracted venereal disease. ('Fire out' was common usage for 'infect with a venereal disease'.) [No evidence of this is offered.]

Those lips that Love's own hand did make
Breathed forth the sound that said, 'I hate',
To me, that languished for her sake.
But when she saw my woeful state,   4
Straight in her heart did mercy come,
Chiding that tongue that, ever sweet,
Was used in giving gentle doom,
And taught it thus anew to greet: 8
'I hate' she altered with an end
That followed it as gentle day
Doth follow night, who like a fiend
From heav'n to hell is flown away.   12
　　'I hate' from hate away she threw
　　And saved my life, saying, 'not you.'

1–4　This poem has only eight syllables per line, and is an anecdote rather than an argument, a madrigal rather than a sonnet. 'The five-fold iteration of similar sounds in *make … hate … sake … state … Straight* in combination with short lines and a predominance of monosyllables, creates a childish, tripping movement' (Duncan-Jones 1997). She quotes the spell cast by Oberon on Titania's lips in *MND* 2.2.33–5, 'What thou see'st when thou dost wake, | Do it for thy true love take; | Love and languish for his sake.' In 20.10 it was Nature who made the first woman. It was Venus who gave life to the female statue made by Pygmalion in Ovid, *Metamorphoses* 10.243–97. Here the hand of Love, Cupid, had made the woman's lips.

5–14　'I hate' she said, but mercy came into her heart and chided her, 'Your tongue is always sweet, always passing charitable judgement.' 'Doom' is judgement in 107.4. Mercy taught her 'anew to greet', to offer a second greeting, adding 'not you'. The same adjective 'gentle' is used twice in four lines, 'gentle doom' and 'gentle day'. This is a either a sign of slapdash writing or the repetition of a word to bind the simile to the literal, the practice seen so often and so subtly in Sonnet 143. Here the gentle doom is to the first cruel greeting as gentle day is to night.

The poem ends with another compliment, this time a simile within a simile. The second greeting is like day following night, and night is departing like a fiend flying back to hell at dawn. The ghost of Hamlet's father knew the rules (*Ham* 1.5.89–91):

> Fare thee well at once.
> The glow-worm shows the matin to be near,
> And gins to pale his uneffectual fire.
> Adieu, adieu, Hamlet. Remember me.

Many respected scholars find in 'hate away' a pun on Anne Hathaway, 'I hate from Hathaway she threw.' They therefore believe that this was a naïve early love poem addressed to her before they married in 1582. It does not seem likely that Shakespeare would have included a billet-doux written to his bride or future bride at this moment in the drama of his love for the Black Lady.

This poem is not much admired. Many have thought that it could not be by Shakespeare. Others have plausibly explained it as an early work rescued from his papers and inserted here in the Sonnets by someone else. If so, that someone had the wit to fit it quite well into the sequence, putting lines 11–12 between angels, a devil and hell in Sonnet 144 and death and the afterlife in Sonnet 146.

Poor soul, the centre of my sinful earth,
Feeding these rebel powers that thee array,
Why dost thou pine within and suffer dearth,
Painting thy outward walls so costly gay?   4

Why so large cost, having so short a lease,
Dost thou upon thy fading mansion spend?
Shall worms, inheritors of this excess,
Eat up thy charge? Is this thy body's end?   8

Then, soul, live thou upon thy servant's loss,
And let that pine to aggravate thy store.
Buy terms divine in selling hours of dross.
Within be fed, without be rich no more.   12

So shalt thou feed on Death, that feeds on men,
And Death once dead, there's no more dying then.

Poor soul, why feed besiegers and starve yourself
   while painting your outside walls?
Why spend on a crumbling house with a short lease,
   for worms to inherit your extravagance?
Body is a servant. Starve it, feed yourself, and sell your rubbish time
   to buy a divine contract. Don't lavish money on your outside.
You'll feed on death, and when it's dead there'll be no more dying.

1–4 'Earth to earth, ashes to ashes' is part of the burial service in the Book of Common Prayer. 'Sinful earth' is the body, and the soul is at its centre. In line 2 it becomes a city besieged, arrayed, by a rebel army, the body. 'Arrayed' never means besieged, but armies do march from Ireland 'in proud array' in *2H6* 4.8.28, and the word is used in a military sense elsewhere in Shakespeare. The metaphor is kept alive when the defenders are feeding their besiegers and starving themselves while painting their outside walls.

Line 2 contains what C. J. Sisson (1956) describes as 'the prize crux of the Sonnets'. The Quarto reads:

> Poore soule the center of my sinfull earth,
> My sinfull earth these rebbell powres that thee array

This text produces a line of 12 syllables and has received many emendations, 100 of which are listed by Ingram and Redpath (1978, 358–9, in a 'reduced list of possible readings'). Most of them involve a past participle. Burrow (2002) mentions 'Fool'd by, Starv'd by, Gull'd by', and prints 'Spoiled by', but none of these contributes to the argument or the imagery, and the last clashes with it if lines 2 and 3 involve siege. When a city is under siege, it is not yet spoiled or despoiled. The military metaphor and the vigorous homiletic tone would be better served by an imperative like 'Resist' or 'Defy', but the most persuasive emendation is 'Feeding', conjectured by Sebastian Evans in 1753 and printed by Vendler (1997) without acknowledgement. The word nicely heightens the absurd behaviour of the besieged soul, and tunes in to the feeding and starving metaphor of lines 7–8, 10 and 12–13, and notably line 3, 'Feeding rebels, why do you starve yourself?'

5–8   Line 5 glides from the walls of a besieged city to the walls of a crumbling house held on a short lease. Why does soul squander money on it ('fading' stays with the painting metaphor in line 4) and neglect himself? Will worms inherit all this extravagance and eat up the body which is in soul's charge? There are contractual terms in every line, 'so large cost', 'so short a lease', 'spend', 'inheritors of this excess', 'thy charge'.

In Elizabethan English a mansion is often just a house. 'In my Father's house there are many mansions,' says Jesus in John 14: 2, *in domo Patris mei mansiones multae sunt*, and the *mansio* at Vindolanda is a hotel. Jesus is not promising luxury accommodation, but lodgings, living quarters. It is foolishness to indulge in costly redecoration of decaying accommodation when all this extravagance will be eaten by worms. In line 8 'Is this thy body's end?', if 'end' means finish, is a good, indignant question – 'Is this what all your body will come to?' But if 'end' means also purpose, the question is double-edged – 'Is this what the body is for, to be cosseted at great expense to feed worms?'

9–12   After the harangue in four rhetorical questions comes the command addressed to soul, not to let the servant live at his master's expense, but to allow him to pine, waste away, in order to increase his master's stock, in order to 'aggravate thy store'. 'To aggravate' is to increase, as always in Shakespeare except at *2H4* 2.4.158, where Mistress Quickly, whose command of English is precarious, is trying to calm Pistol down, and asks him to aggravate his choler. 'Pine' in 10 harks back to 'pine within and suffer dearth' in 3, and the feeding metaphor surfaces again in 1–8 and 12 and 13. In the middle of the metaphor, line 11 moves to buying and selling as soul is commanded to sell off the time it devotes to the dross, the rubbish of worldly life, in order to buy a contract with the divine, which will not be a deal for a few short hours but for eternity. Then soul within would be fed, and body no longer rich.

The end looks back to the beginning. In line 1 'perhaps "Poor soul" implied a position of detached superiority from which the user benevolently but casually condescends' (Booth 1977). But now the former poverty of the soul and wealth of the body are reversed. The body will no longer be rich, and the soul no longer poor.

13–14 'So shalt thou feed on Death' has what Vendler (1997) calls 'the future tense of religious promise', citing the words of Jesus to the malefactor on his cross on Calvary, 'To day shalt thou be with me in paradise' (Luke 23: 43). Death feeds on men, but, if the soul feeds, it feeds on death. 'Death is swallowed up in victory' (1 Corinthians 15: 54) and, as St John says in Revelation 21: 4, 'There shall be no more death.' Shakespeare says the same with the eloquence of polyptoton in 'Death … Death … dead … dying', and the force of the colloquial in 'there's no more dying then.' John Donne is more formal in *Holy Sonnets* 10, 'And death shall be no more; death, thou shalt die.' These are exultant cries. This opinion should be checked against Vendler's view quoted below.

There are signs of a drift towards religion in Sonnets 141 and 142. Sonnet 144 is concerned with angels, spirits, temptation and corruption, and uses religious terms to set up a debate on S's experience of love. Now the clash of body and soul makes 146 the only purely religious sonnet in the collection. There is no direct mention of the young man or the Black Lady, but when he commands his soul to take control over his body there can be no doubt how this fits into the plot of the Sonnets. The failure of his love for the youth, the shame of his lust for the Black Lady and his bitterness at her treatment of him (129) have driven him to religion.

The poem has a dynamic – one question in the first quatrain, three in the second, five commands in the third, and the triumphant vision in the final couplet.

The metaphors

One metaphor frequently merges into another in the Sonnets. The first four lines are particularly iridescent. In line 1 the man is the planet Earth with soul at its centre, and earth is also flesh; in 2–3 soul is a starving city feeding its besiegers and painting the outside of its walls; in 4 it is a foolish tenant painting the outside of a building leased on a short-term contract, and there may also be a glimpse of cosmetics; in 'array' in line 2 and 'costly gay' in 4–5 he is a spendthrift in gaudy, expensive clothes; in 7–8 worms are seen as heirs of the property and the feeding is literal; in 9–10 body is a servant wasting the wealth of a master who has been neglecting his possessions, his 'store' of valuables, and soul is advised to reclaim what the servant has taken; in 11 soul is a trader urged to strike a good bargain; in 12 feeding recurs and 'rich' activates the metaphor of poverty which began with the first word. In every line in the first 12, except 2 and 3, there is at least one commercial term.

Evans (1996)
… it may be argued, I think, that 146 follows 144 naturally enough and focuses the apparently external conflict between the poet's 'better angel' and 'worser spirit' in 144 on his own inner spiritual and moral conflict – that, in a sense, the poet's 'soul' and 'body' are internalised projections of 'his better angel' and 'worser spirit'. Moreover, the 'soul' and 'rebel pow'rs' of 146 may be seen as anticipating, respectively, the 'reason' and 'the uncertain, sickly appetite' of 147.5, 4.

Vendler (1997)
The gloominess of this sonnet has little of the radiance of Christian hope. *Buy terms* divine the speaker says, but (as Booth notes) the divine is infinite and has no terms (limits). The divine is quickly obscured by the Dantesque linked rapacity of the couplet. *Death once dead* is an encouraging remark rather than a prophecy. Certainly once death is dead, there's no more dying; but will feeding on death by starving the body kill him?
[On 13–14]
I find the proliferation of 'deaths' unnervingly iterative.

℘ 147 ℃

My love is as a fever, longing still
For that which longer nurseth the disease,
Feeding on that which doth preserve the ill,
Th'uncertain sickly appetite to please.   4

My reason, the Physician to my love,
Angry that his prescriptions are not kept,
Hath left me, and I, desp'rate now, approve
Desire is death, which Physic did except.   8

Past cure I am, now Reason is past care,
And frantic mad with evermore unrest.
My thoughts and my discóurse as madmen's are,
At random from the truth vainly expressed,   12

    For I have sworn thee fair, and thought thee bright,
    Who art as black as hell, as dark as night.

My love is like a fever, craving what feeds it.
I disobeyed my physician, reason, and he has abandoned me,
*   and I am now proving that desire is death.*
I am delirious, thinking and speaking like a madman,
for I thought you beautiful, and you are black as hell.

1–4 In the second ode of his second book Horace compares greed to dropsy, as an affliction which makes the sufferer crave water, and water feeds the dropsy, '*crescit indulgens sibi dirus hydrops*', 'the dreaded dropsy grows by indulging itself'. Cravings of this sort occur also with fevers, and Shakespeare selects the telling detail, the seeming eternity of suffering. In this author '*longing* still | For that which *longer* nurseth the disease' is not idle wordplay, but suggests the patient's sense that this condition is never going to end. The absurdity of the craving is conveyed twice, first in the paradox of nursing a disease, then in feeding on something that preserves an ill(ness) in order to gratify the appetite of a sick and uncertain mind.

5–8 Now comes a comic interlude. The Physician, Reason, has been called in, has prescribed, and the Physic he recommended has saved the patient's life. But, as patients do, S has not persevered with the prescription, and, as doctors sometimes do, this one has given up his patient and gone off in high dudgeon. S's Reason has left him. Abandoned and despairing, he is proving by experience that desire is death, that his disease is terminal, and that the Physic had 'excepted' desire, removed it. The nearest support for this interpretation of 'except' is in *R2* 1.1.72, 'which fear, not reverence, makes thee to except', where 'except' is glossed as 'set aside' (by Peter Ure in the 1956 Arden Shakespeare edition). 'Except against' meaning 'take exception to' occurs in *TGV* at 1.3.83 and 2.4.153.

9–12 The proverb 'past cure, past care' expresses the traditional wisdom that, if a patient is incurable, care will not help him. Shakespeare has not merely repeated this sentiment, but has inverted it to fit his argument, 'past care, [therefore] past cure'. Now that care has abandoned the patient, he cannot be cured. In 10 his sleeplessness has driven him mad, and in 12 his thoughts are 'At random from the truth, vainly expressed '. In *1H6* 5.5.41 'He talks at random; sure the man is mad.'

13–14 The commanding logic of this writing shines clear in 11–13. 'Thoughts' and 'discóurse' are caught up in order in 12 with 'truth' and 'expressed', and then in reverse order in 'sworn' and 'thought'. He has sworn her fair but she is black as hell; he has thought her bright but she is dark as night.

The poem is not pointless hypochondria. It has been leading to its dire conclusion, all the more crushing because of its monosyllables. His love for the Black Lady became a craving and a fever and has driven him mad. It will lead to his death. The madness is defined in the last two lines, and 'fair ... bright ... black ... dark' all contain moral meanings (144.3, 152.13). The darkness is not simply the absence of light. It is the presence of evil.

Ingram and Redpath (1978), on lines 3–4
If Dowden were right in believing that there is a sequential connection, particularly through these lines, with 146, then 'that which doth preserve the ill' would presumably be the bodily love of this false woman, which would be one of the 'rebel powers' of 146.2.

❧ 148 ❧

O me! What eyes hath love put in my head,
Which have no correspondence with true sight?
Or if they have, where is my judgement fled
That censures falsely what they see aright?   4

If that be fair whereon my false eyes dote,
What means the world to say it is not so?
If it be not, then love doth well denote
Love's eye is not so true as all men's. No,   8

How can it? O how can love's eye be true,
That is so vexed with watching and with tears?
No marvel then, though I mistake my view,
The sun itself sees not till heaven clears.   12
    O cunning Love, with tears thou keep'st me blind,
    Lest eyes well seeing thy foul faults should find.

My eyes do not see true, or if they do
  why does my judgement reject what they see?
If the woman I love is fair, why does the world say she is not?
  If she is not fair, my love for her proves love's eyes are false.
How could they be true with all my waking and weeping?
No wonder I see badly. The sun does not see till the sky clears.
  Cunning Love, you blind me with tears, in case I see your faults.

1–4 Love is either the emotion or the god Cupid. In the first line it is probably both. The two questions that follow raise the problem already discussed in sonnets listed at the end of the commentary on 141. 'Is it my eyes which do not see what is there, or if they see true where has [the judgement of] my heart gone?' 'Censured' can simply mean judged, without any negative sense. 'Censure me in your wisdom,' says Brutus to the mob in *JC* 3.2.16, without expecting any disapproval.

5–8 S has asked 'is it eyes that are at fault or judgement?' and it might be expected that he would consider these alternatives one after the other. 'What if the eyes see true?' (5–6), then 'What if they are at fault?' (7–8) would be proper questions, but the debate is ruined by the word 'false' in 5. He knows his eyes are false and has arrived at this conclusion before he balances the options. The poem purports to be a contribution to the running debate between eyes and heart, but that is only the scaffolding for the condemnation of eyes, by the old truism that love is blind (8 and 13).

9–14 Before line 9 he suddenly loses patience with himself, 'No, how can it be true?' This has distressed commentators because only here in the Sonnets does heavy punctuation occur before the last syllable in the line. But Shakespeare may be allowed to do something once. This is a striking innovation which makes sure that readers hear the argument as it moves in the mind of the speaker. The effect is to dramatise S's conversation with himself, by breaking the regular tread of the metre, to insist that the world is right and his eyes are wrong.

The colloquial liveliness continues, particularly if the second 'can' is heard with a slightly stronger stress than the first, 'How cán it?' followed by 'Ó how **cán** love's eye be true?' In 10 love's eye is 'vexed with watching', troubled by wakefulness (see 61.13).

11–14 'No marvel' for 'It is no marvel' is another lively, natural turn of speech, and the analogy in line 12, 'the sun's eye is dimmed by rainclouds, why not mine by tears?' sounds like folk wisdom, though it is not cited elsewhere as a proverb.

Line 13 opens as though addressed to Cupid, 'O cunning Love, with tears thou keep'st me blind', but at 'thy foul faults' Love becomes his love, the Black Lady, as foul here as in 144.8. The bitterness of the last line is intensified by the triple alliteration in the last four words, as bitter as 137.12, 'To put fair truth upon so foul a face.' It seemed at one point that the main aim in the poem was the condemnation of eyes, but in the final couplet the poem reaches its destination – condemnation of the Black Lady. It opened with a question, 'What's wrong with my eyes?' It ends with the answer, 'They are blinded by tears caused by the foul faults of the Black Lady.'

ᔥ 149 ᙖ

Canst thou, o cruel, say I love thee not,
When I against myself with thee partake?
Do I not think on thee when, I forgot,
Am of myself all tyrant for thy sake?   4

Who hateth thee that I do call my friend?
On whom frown'st thou that I do fawn upon?
Nay, if thou lour'st on me do I not spend
Revenge upon myself with present moan?   8

What merit do I in myself respect
That is so proud thy service to despise,
When all my best doth worship thy defect,
Commanded by the motion of thine eyes?   12

But, love, hate on, for now I know thy mind:
Those that can see thou lov'st, and I am blind.

Can you say I don't love you when I take your part against myself,
   and subject myself to you?
What friend of mine hates you? Whom do you frown on that I flatter?
   If you scowl at me, don't I take instant revenge – upon myself?
I have no great gifts to make me too proud to serve you.
   My best worships your faults. You just have to move your eyes.
But go on hating me. I realise you love those who see, and I am blind.

1–4 Presumably she has said, 'You don't love me', and this poem is his
response. At first sight it begins with six rhetorical questions swelling to
the last in 9–12, all demonstrating S's subservience. More careful reading
reveals a subtler shape. In response to the notion that he does not love her,
lines 2–4 define his position of total subservience. Lines 5–8 give examples
of it from his behaviour towards the tyrant who is his mistress. In 9–12 he
looks within himself, and finds respect, service, worship and obedience.

Revealingly, the poem has no declaration of love, but speaks instead the language of tyranny – 'cruelty', 'hate', 'frown', 'fawn', 'lour', 'revenge', 'service', 'obedience' and the anxious watch kept by the subject on the eye of the tyrant. In the first 126 sonnets the young man is never 'cruel'. In the 26 sonnets that follow, the Black Lady, or what she brings, is 'cruel' in 129, 131, 133, 140 and 149. The second love is not like the first (see 129.1–2).

In line 2 'partake' must mean take sides, a meaning not found elsewhere, but supported by 35.10, 'Thy adverse party is thy advocate', and by 88.6.

In lines 3–4, the commas in the text above are an attempt to suggest 'when I, myself being forgotten, am a total tyrant to myself for your sake'. 'I forgot' on this punctuation is an example of the absolute construction noted on 112.7. The Quarto has a comma only after 'myself', suggesting 'when I forgotten am by myself, [being] a total tyrant for your sake.' Commentators offer many different interpretations.

5–8   Here is tyranny in action in the behaviour of the subject. He has no friends who are not friends of the tyrant. He [flatters the tyrant, but] does not flatter anyone the tyrant frowns upon. If the tyrant lours, scowls, he reacts 'with present moan', and takes revenge, astonishingly, upon himself. 'Present' means that the moaning is immediate, as in *AW* 2.2.59, 'And urge her to a present answer back.' In 7 'lour'st' has been felt to be a flat repetition of 'frown'st' in the preceding line, but this is unfair. 'Nay' makes it rather a self-correction, as though he is thinking as he speaks, 'It's not simply that I don't fawn upon people you *frown* at. More than that, if you *frown* at me, I punish myself.' Even with 'frown' repeated, this would not be a repetition, but a strengthening of the argument. But 'frown' is not repeated; 'lour' is a stronger word. Men frown, but 'the heavens do lour' in *RJ* 4.4.121, and clouds loured in *R3* 1.1.3. The tyrant's frown is the leaden sky before the thunderbolt.

9–12   Now comes tyranny in action within the mind of the subject. Whatever qualities he may have, none of them makes him too proud to serve the tyrant. No matter how great his own gifts, a movement of the tyrant's eyes is a command (see 25.5–8), and he bows down and worships before the tyrant's 'defect', deficiency, imperfection. Macbeth apologised for his in 2.1.16–17, 'Being unprepared, | Our will became the servant to defect.'

The worship of line 11 demonstrates the extremity of his subjection. Worship is usually accorded to the divine, and in Christianity the divine is without faults, but S worships the Black Lady despite her defect.

452

13–14   She had accused him of not loving her, the formula for demanding a denial. He now sums up his answer by addressing her as 'love', and his counter is to accuse her of hating him, 'But, love, hate on', the pathos heightened by the juxtaposition of opposites. That too sounds as though it could be an appeal for a denial, but if so he immediately moves on. He has been blind to her faults, but now he understands her. She accepts lovers who see them [and are undeterred]. The difficulty about this is that it seems rather a lame ending for the bitter monosyllables which are so common in the endings of the Black Lady sonnets, like 144, 147 and 148. The poem now seems to end on a note almost of praise, at the very least a neutral analysis of her character. In the final couplet we expect the dagger. Perhaps it is hidden. Does this last line carry insinuations? How many are 'those that can see' her faults? What sort of love is this she gives them, and they her? What sort of woman is she?

℘ 150 ℘

O from what power hast thou this powerful might
With insufficiency my heart to sway,
To make me give the lie to my true sight
And swear that brightness doth not grace the day?   4

Whence hast thou this becoming of things ill,
That in the very refuse of thy deeds
There is such strength and warrantise of skill,
That in my mind thy worst all best exceeds?   8

Who taught thee how to make me love thee more
The more I hear and see just cause of hate?

O, though I love what others do abhor,
With others thou should not abhor my state.   12
   If thy unworthiness raised love in me,
   More worthy I to be beloved of thee.

Where do you get this immense power to make me by your inadequacy
   disbelieve the truth I see, and swear the day is dark?
How can you turn foul into fair and find the infallible skill
   in your shoddiest acts to make your worst excel all others' best?
Who taught you to make me love you more the more I find cause to hate?
Though I love what others abhor, you should not abhor me.
   Loving your unworthiness, I am all the more worthy of your love.

1–4 'O from what power' suggests that it derives from the supernatural.
It even makes him deny the undeniable and swear that day is not bright.
He cannot understand how this worthless woman could hold such sway over
him, and looks at the problem from three different points of view. First, in
1–4 he asks for the explanation of a bewildering paradox. From what power
does the beloved derive the mighty power to govern by inadequacy? This all
chimes with 149.11, 'all my best doth worship thy defect'.

5–8   The second question is different, 'How does the beloved's worst excel everyone else's best?' Line 5 asks 'From where do you get this gift of making foul things "becoming", attractive, to such an extent that in your worst behaviour, in the very dross of your deeds, there is such strength and such a guarantee of skill that your worst is better than all others' best?' 'This becoming of things ill' is the making of ill things beautiful. This unusual sense of the verb occurs in *AC* 2.2.244–5, 'For vilest things | Become themselves in her', they make themselves becoming.

In her behaviour there is strength, the 'powerful might' of that first line, and there is a guarantee of skill, presumably in her manipulation of lovers, a guarantee presumably established by a record of triumphs. What can be meant by her worst that exceeds all that is best? Hypocrisy? Dishonesty? Infidelity? Whatever it is, it never fails, she is adroit, and irresistible.

9–10   The third question is the climax, the one that affects S most nearly, and it is the briefest and most monosyllabic.

11–14   No more questions. Now comes the message. I love what others detest, so you should not join others in detesting me. The punch comes in the correspondences:

| If thy unworthiness | raised love | in me, |
| More worthy I | to be beloved | by thee. |

At a technical level this sonnet is a study in contrasts, power and might versus insufficiency, lie versus true, becoming versus ill, worst versus best, love versus hate, abhor versus not abhor, and then the last couplet dismembered above. But at a human level it is the cry of a rejected lover who simply cannot understand how he can love where he has every reason to hate.

Old Adam is still around. Her immorality raised love in him, no doubt as her dear love will make him rise and fall at 151.9 and 14. The end of 151 will develop what is said at the end of 150 as the beginning of 150 developed 149.11, and as the end of 149 developed the end of 148. The plot moves on.

Love is too young to know what conscience is,
Yet who knows not conscience is born of love?

Then, gentle cheater, urge not my amiss,
Lest guilty of my faults thy sweet self prove.   4
For, thou betraying me, I do betray
My nobler part to my gross body's treason.

My soul doth tell my body that he may
Triumph in love, flesh stays no farther reason,   8
But rising at thy name doth point out thee
As his triumphant prize. Proud of his pride,
He is contented thy poor drudge to be,
To stand in thy affairs, fall by thy side,   12

   No want of conscience hold it that I call
   Her 'love', for whose dear love I rise and fall.

Love does not know conscience, yet is its parent.
So do not accuse me, because the guilt might be yours,
   since, you betraying me, I betray my better self.
My soul tells body it can win, and body needs no encouragement,
   but rises to do its duty.
I do not think it a failure of conscience on my part to call you love
   as we make love.

At first sight in line 3 it seems that S is asking the Black Lady not to urge
him to make love to her, but lines 7–14 and Sonnet 152 make it clear that
he is already doing so. 'Urge' here is therefore used to mean 'to invoke'
(Kerrigan 1986), 'to adduce in argument', as in *R3* 3.5.80, 'Moreover, urge
his hateful luxury | And bestial appetite.' 'Urge not my amiss' must
therefore mean 'do not accuse me of wrongdoing'.

   This poem begins with a baffling paradox. Love does not know what conscience is, although conscience is love's own offspring. In 3–4 S begs the Black Lady not to accuse him of wrongdoing, lest she prove to be the guilty one herself. Betraying him, by persuading him to make love to her, she makes him betray his nobler self. Lines 13–14 complete the ring composition. It is no failure of his conscience but of hers, if he uses terms of endearment as he lies with her. The fault is hers. He has already deployed this argument brilliantly in 142.1–8.

Sonnet 151 is explained by 152, where S and the Black Lady are still making love, but each knows that the other is false, and false in many different ways.

1–2 How can anyone be too young to know his own offspring? One answer would be that Love at the beginning of the first line is the naughty boy Cupid, a god who has no notion of the difference between right and wrong, 'who knows not conscience'. 'All's fair in love.' On the other hand, love at the end of the second line is the emotion of love, which can produce a kindness and honesty between lovers, a form of conscience 'born of love'. So love in the second line is not the same as Love in the first, just as Love in 148.13 is Cupid and love in 148.14 is the Black Lady.

The paradox may be highlighted by the change in rhythm. The metrical stress falls on the first 'cónscience'. The second has surely to be pronounced in the same way, and this produces a metrical variation in line 2, 'Yet whó knows nót cónscience is bórn of lóve'. This stress demanded on 'cónscience' in line 2 against the iambic expectation makes it stand out, and reinforces the argument.

3–6 In 1.12 the young man was addressed as 'tender churl'; here, with a similar oxymoron, the Black Lady is addressed as 'gentle cheater'. 'Her sweet self' has cheated him, and the cheating, guilt and betrayal are part of the war between hate and lust that has been waging in 147–50. When he warns her not to blame him, the rest of the poem reveals that his 'amiss' is to make love where there is none. If she persuades him to give way to lust, the crime is hers. She is guilty of his faults, the betrayal of his 'nobler part'.

7–12 These lines describe the amiss in a military metaphor. Soul, identical with mind in 27.4, 9 and 13, points out that Body, urged on by the Black Lady, may triumph. Flesh needs no more encouragement, but rises at her name like a spirit conjured by a magic spell. The mischievous Mercutio uses a similar invocation in *RJ* 2.1.17–27, when he is asking Romeo to appear:

> I conjure thee by Rosaline's bright eyes ...
> That in thy likeness thou appear to us ...
>   My invocation
> Is fair and honest. In his mistress' name
> I conjure only but to raise up him.

Flesh rises and points at her as though he were a pointer dog or, in this military context, a raised spear, and she is the prize of his sexual triumph. By now there is no doubt that there is a multiple play going on and that flesh is visualised as the penis, rising at the Black Lady's name, pointing at her, proud of his pride, that is his erection, standing to see to her business, 'thy affairs' in 12, and then lying detumescent by her side. 'Pride' is the erect penis. Partridge (1968) cites the modern euphemism, 'morning pride', and 'as hot as monkeys | As salt as wolves in pride' in *Oth* 3.3.408–9. This is all obvious, except perhaps the obscene sense of 'point', and that is supported by *LLL* 5.2.276–7, where Maria is mocking Dumaine's addresses to her, 'Dumaine was at my service, and his sword. | "*Non point*," quoth I. My *servant* straight was mute.' That silenced him. In line 11 flesh is content to tackle the toil of war for her, to undertake the drudgery of sexual intercourse, to stand in her 'affairs', a warrior in the battle line, and then to fall and lie exhausted after coitus, like a soldier dead at his comrade's side.

13–14 And all the while he calls her 'love', although he does not truly love her. Despite lines 3–4 she is not 'sweet' or 'gentle'. This is all pretence, loveless lust. The baffling paradox of the opening lines is explained. Cupid knows no conscience, and if she makes love to him the fault is hers. It is no failure of conscience on his part if he calls her 'love' as he makes love to her.

This has been called 'the most libidinous of the sonnets', but 135 and 136 run it close. The Black Lady sonnets, as often noted above, lead S into a different world of love from the one he travelled with the young man (129.2 and 149.1). He now is continually aware that he is betraying himself by this false love, and that she is betraying him, using him while making love to others. This has driven him to religion and obscenity, sometimes consequences of ruined love not only here but also in real life and in poetry. Catullus felt this in such poems as 76, 'O gods, pity me and take this plague from me', and 11 and 58, where his abuse of Lesbia is as coarse as anything in the Sonnets. He summarises in 85, '*odi et amo*', 'I hate and love.'

Sonnet 151 moves from ethics to religion, from conscience to guilt, from his nobler part to his gross body. Then at line 9 it plunges into physical details of sexual intercourse. But commentators find 'libidinous-ness' long before line 9, hearing 'conscience' as 'cunt knowledge'; then suggesting an obscene pun on the prick of conscience and the conscience which has no prick; then 'my nobler part' as the male member; 'farther' as a possible play on father; 'reason' on rising in line 14; 'contented' as 'cuntented'. I find no example of 'conscience' meaning knowledge of cunt. This is all silliness. The first six lines of the sonnet are the despairing cries of a character who has given his life to love and is left with this. In lines 7–14 he lashes out to wound himself and the mistress he once loved and whom he is now debauching. To import obscenity into the first six lines of this sonnet is to ruin the emotional graph and reduce the bitter opening to smut. (There is more on obscenity towards the end of the commentary on Sonnet 129.)

Vendler (1997)
Detumescence is represented not only by the semantic decline from *proud* to *poor* but also from *tr-ium-ph* to *dr-u-dge*, words which, with their initial double consonants, triple final letters and common *u* in the middle, seem to be some sort of graphic cousins. Post-coital quiet comes in *con*/[*cunt*]/*tented*, followed by an analytic third-person treatment of both the mistress (*her*) and the phallus (*thy poor drudge*), a phrase completing the turn from '*my* body' to independent third-person *flesh*, thence to the possession by the other, '*thy* drudge'.

ဆ 152 ca

In loving thee, thou know'st I am forsworn,
But thou art twice forsworn to me love swearing,
In act thy bed-vow broke, and new faith torn
In vowing new hate after new love bearing.   4

But why of two oaths' breach do I accuse thee,
When I break twenty? I am perjured most,
For all my vows are oaths but to misuse thee,
And all my honest faith in thee is lost.   8
For I have sworn deep oaths of thy deep kindness,
Oaths of thy love, thy truth, thy constancy,
And to enlighten thee gave eyes to blindness,
Or made them swear against the thing they see.   12

For I have sworn thee fair. More perjured I,
To swear against the truth so foul a lie.

I lied in loving you, but you lied twice, in breaking your bed-vow [to me]
and in deceiving your new love.
But I have lied twenty times, and always in order to misuse you.
I have lost my honesty, for I have sworn you have virtues.
By that foul lie I am more perjured than you.

1–4 This is the last episode in the plot of the Sonnets (153 and 154 are not part of the drama), and it is no surprise that it is elusive rather than informative. Here the main difficulty is to divine what is meant by the first four lines, and many solutions have been proposed. The Black Lady knows that S is forsworn in loving her, and one explanation which attracts those who look for autobiography in the Sonnets might be that this alludes to Anne Hathaway, but Shakespeare married her in 1582, and she does not seem to have played an important part in his life thereafter. In view of the tight plot of the Sonnets a more likely explanation is that in making love to the Black Lady he has broken a sworn oath of fidelity to the young man.

But she is worse. She is forsworn twice. First, she has broken her bed-vow. This is commonly taken to mean that she was married and has committed adultery. Again, this looks outside the Sonnets into the matrimonial arrangements of the Black Lady. Bed-vows can be made outside marriage, and it is odd to bring into the story at this stage the husband of a woman who is still unidentified and may not even have existed. It would be a weakness to introduce a passing allusion to a new character in the very last scene of a complex and fiercely concentrated triangular drama. An explanation which stays within the plot of the Sonnets would be that her bed-vow was a promise to be faithful to S, her original lover in this triangle, a promise she soon broke.

In that case, the act which violated the bed-vow was her seduction of the young man (Sonnets 133 and 134). But now Sonnets 151 and 152 reveal that S and the Black Lady are making love to each other again, and therefore her 'new faith torn' is her loyalty to her new lover, the young man. She has torn it up as though it were a legal contract. After having acquired this new lover, this 'new love bearing', she is now vowing her hate, her revulsion for him, as she returns to S, her former lover.

In line 3 the Quarto has its usual comma at the end of the line, and no punctuation after 'broke'. 'In act thy bed-vow broke and new faith torn' would refer twice in one line to the same act of infidelity. Lines 3–4 as punctuated in the text printed here define the double breach of faith as, first, the breaking of the bed-vow to S and, second, the subsequent breaking of her new vows to the young man. 'New' three times in 3–4 revives S's sense of betrayal. Her new love with the man S loved still rankles. This interpretation posits the same 'absolute' construction as in 149.4 and 151.5, in which a participle is loosely attached to the rest of its sentence, 'you are twice forsworn, your bed-vow [being] broken and your new faith [being] torn.'

'Forsworn ... twice forsworn ... swearing' sets the theme and it resurfaces in every line that follows. S is obsessed by the thought that he has betrayed and been betrayed. Vendler (1997) plots the repetitions: 'swear' and its variants seven times; 'oaths' four times; 'vow(s)', 'love' and 'new' each three times; I/eye(s) punning, 'perjured', 'truth', 'faith' and 'deep' each twice. One miracle in this writing is the geometry of it. 'In loving thee ... I am forsworn' is answered word by word in 'thou art ... forsworn to me love swearing'. With a typical flash of wit he is 'forsworn' in the first line, and when she is twice forsworn in the second there is 'forsworn' and 'swearing'.

5–12 He corrects himself. He is forsworn not once but 20 times. He is perjured 'most', standing for more, as in *Luc* 1792, 'Then son and father weep with equal strife, | Who should weep most, for daughter, or for wife.' His 20 perjuries will be described in 8–13. In line 7 his motive was 'to misuse' the Black Lady. The only relevant sense of the word in Shakespeare is 'deceive', as in *MA* 2.2.25, 'Proof enough to misuse the prince'. Sonnet 151 makes it clear that his deception was the dishonesty employed in lustful lovemaking, and he hates himself for it. But 'to misuse thee' recalls the Black Lady's use and abuse of her body in 134.10. The word never means 'debauch' in Shakespeare, but that sense is approached in the sixteenth century (*OED*, citing 'Bicause I have myseused here, I intende to make [her] a goode woman' (with 'here' for our 'her'), around 1540). Perhaps S is reflecting that he swore oaths, not simply to deceive, but to debauch.

As a result of his perjuries, he says, 'all my honest faith in thee is lost', but no man can lose his faith in a woman by telling her lies. In fact line 8 means that in [his behaviour towards] the Black Lady, in [the case of] the Black Lady, he has lost his own honesty. For 'faith' in this sense, see *TGV* 5.4.46–52, 'Read over Julia's heart, thy first, best love, | For whose dear sake thou didst then rend thy faith … Thou hast no faith left now.' 'Faith' here is like 'trust' in 138.11.

A crucial turn has been taken. The first four lines referred to oaths broken by S and the Black Lady to their lovers. But from line 6 onwards the subject is oaths made by S in what he considers to be squalid lovemaking. His shame and self-loathing are expressed in sarcastic repetitions of 'deep' (9). Neither her kindness nor his oaths were truly deep. The tone of voice is caught as the first 'thy' comes on a syllable that would carry the metrical stress, unlike the other three, 'óaths of thý deep kíndness, | Óaths of thy lóve, thy trúth, thy cónstancy'. The change in the dynamic for the last three could make it seem that he is skimming through a meaningless list.

In a typical contrast he gave eyes to blindness in line 11, in order to 'enlighten' the Black Lady, to see her in good light, to flatter her. He was blind to her untruth and made his eyes swear she was true.

13–14 They saw her foul, but swore that she was fair, and 'fair' as opposed to 'foul' refers to character as well as appearance (see 131.13 and 147.13–14). In Sonnets 147–51 S was deceived; in 152 he reaches new depths as he becomes the deceiver. He has lost his 'honest faith'. This is the final climax of the Sonnets. The paragon of beauty, of 'fair', hymned in 127 is now seen as foul. He loathes her, but lies with her, swearing false oaths.

Line 13 ends with 'eye' in the Quarto, but this edition accepts George Sewell's emendation 'I'. 'More perjured eye' is an implausible reading. 'Eye' is presumably meant to pick up the eyes S gave to blindness in line 11. But although eye and heart have often been personified (see the comment on 141.13–14), Eye is not a character in this poem, not the principal perjurer. Besides, what could be meant by 'More perjured eye'? More perjured than what? Her eye? Or whom? Than the Black Lady? Than S himself? Feeble. 'More perjured I', on the other hand, completes the argument – 'I am forsworn. You are forsworn twice. But I am worse, being forsworn 20 times. I am perjured more' (6).

The last paragraph of the note on Sonnet 150 shows how the plot moves on from 147 to 150. It has now moved to a bleak and bitter view of S's love for the Black Lady. It is all a lie. She is at fault in 151, but in 152 he sees that he is perjured most. The oath of line 13 is the last of all the vows in these poems, the last action in the Black Lady series, and it is a lie. His great loves have ended in a tangle of untruth, self-hatred and meaningless lovemaking.

Evans (1996), headnote
Sonnet 152 may be taken as the poet's final statement of moral revulsion against a 'love' that has led to the loss of 'all my honest faith' (8) ... it concentrates and indicts 'so foul a lie' against 'truth' (14), the whole process and present status of the poet's 'love' for the Black Lady, gathering together most of the informing themes in 127–151 (love/hate, constancy/inconstancy, truth suborned, oaths/vows sworn and forsworn, blindness of soul/mind/heart, and false-seeing eyes).

Duncan-Jones (1997), on lines 3–4
New ... bearing may be read as suggesting that the woman ... is recently married, and already expressing new *hate* for her husband, in favour of love for the speaker; or that she has betrayed both her husband the speaker in favour of some third party, either, as in 133–4, the speaker's *friend*, or yet another.

Vendler (1997)
Blame of the woman has faded in view of the greater blame with which the speaker castigates himself. The self-lacerating intelligence in the later sonnets produces a voice so undeceived about reality (*the truth*) and himself (his *perjured eye*) that the reader admires the clarity of mind that can so anatomize sexual obsession while still in its grip, that can so acquiesce in humiliation while inspecting its own arousal, that can lie freely while acknowledging the truth. To represent such a voice in all its paradoxical capacity and incapacity is the victory of Shakespeare's technique in the second subsequence.

Cupid laid by his brand and fell asleep.
A maid of Dian's this advantage found,
And his love-kindling fire did quickly steep
In a cold valley-fountain of that ground,   4
Which borrowed from this holy fire of love
A dateless lively heat, still to endure,
And grew a seething bath, which yet men prove
Against strong maladies a sovereign cure.   8

But at my mistress' eye Love's brand new fired,
The boy for trial needs would touch my breast;
I, sick withal, the help of bath desired
And thither hied, a sad distempered guest.   12
    But found no cure. The bath for my help lies
    Where Cupid got new fire – my mistress' eyes.

Cupid laid down his torch and fell asleep. One of Diana's virgin attendants
    steeped it in a cold spring, which became a hot bath with curative powers.
The torch being relit at my mistress's eye, Cupid touched my breast.
    Sick with love as a result I went to the spring. But it did not heal me.
    The bath I need is where Cupid got his fire, my mistress's eyes.

1–8   This sonnet is based upon a poem in the *Palatine Anthology*, the *Antholo-gia Palatina*, as discussed at the end of the commentary on Sonnet 154. The first eight lines are an aetiological myth, a story explaining the origin of a contemporary phenomenon, here a hot spring. How did the leopard get his spots? How did this cold spring become hot? The great exemplar in Greek was Callimachus' *Aitia* (*Causes*). In Latin Ovid was a keen practitioner.

    Cupid laid down his torch and fell asleep. The goddess Diana was famously chaste, and so, presumably, were her maids. One of them saw her chance, seized the torch and dowsed it in a cold fountain.

    Line 6 stresses the aetiology. That is why to this day and for all time to come this is a hot spring. Its heat is 'dateless lively', living for all time, and '[destined] still to endure'. 'Yet' in line 7 drives the point further home. But the water did not only become hot. For some reason which the myth does not explain, it also acquired healing properties. It grew [into] a bath which men still find a sovereign cure for 'strong maladies'.

'Against strang maladies' is the reading of the Quarto, and most editors emend to 'strange'. This text follows those who change to 'strong', because 'strang' is a variant spelling in the fourteenth to the seventeenth century, as in *AC* 2.2.162, where Antony was reluctant to draw his sword against Pompey, 'For he hath laid strang courtesies and great | Of late upon me.'

9–14 In the remainder of the poem S applies the myth to himself. 'Needs would' in line 10 is a weaker form of our 'needs must'. It has a rueful tone, 'Cupid just would choose me to test his torch on.' Like 154.2, line 9 is an example of the common absolute construction, 'Love's brand [having been] newly reignited at my mistress's eye, as a trial Cupid touched my breast [with it].' Not brilliant writing. S then fell sick, and came for treatment to this hot spring, 'a sad, distempered guest' (as though a patient at a spa). The treatment failed. He was still sick. What he needed was to get help where Cupid did, at his mistress's eyes.

Here the argument breaks down. It is perfectly sensible for a man with certain afflictions to take the waters, but, if the affliction is lovesickness and he wishes to be cured, the last place to look is in his mistress' eyes. Unless, of course, the point is that the cure for love is to enjoy it. In that case he does not want his fire put out, he wants what Cupid's torch wanted – to be set ablaze. But if that is the point it is not well made, and 153 is a feeble poem with an inept ending.

Booth (1977)
The female sex organ – a valley-fountain, a cool well – which grows hot with use and, with misuse, may come to burn and burn subsequent users with the perpetual fire of venereal disease.

Duncan-Jones (1997), headnote
In both sonnets Cupid's brand is given a bawdy application, and both draw on the twofold association of hot baths with the treatment of sexually transmitted disease and with social encounters which may cause such disease.

Vendler (1997)
In 153's interpretation, phallic heat is an ever-renewable phoenix-fire whose enduring seat is the mistress' eye, rather than the phallus itself ... Sonnet 153 envisages an ultimate cure for love (the mistress' eye) without obtaining it.

ᔥ 154 ᘏ

The little love-god lying once asleep,
Laid by his side his heart-inflaming brand,
Whilst many nymphs that vowed chaste life to keep
Came tripping by. But in her maiden hand   4
The fairest votary took up that fire
Which many legions of true hearts had warmed,
And so, the general of hot desire
Was, sleeping, by a virgin hand disarmed.   8
This brand she quenchèd in a cool well by,
Which from love's fire took heat perpetual,
Growing a bath and healthful remedy
For men diseased. But I, my mistress' thrall,   12
    Came there for cure, and this by that I prove:
    Love's fire heats water, water cools not love.

When Cupid lay asleep, a virgin nymph stole his torch and quenched it
in a cold well, which became a hot bath with curative properties.
But it failed to cure me. Water does not quench the fire of love.

1–14 This is an attempt to write a sonnet based on the same Greek epigram as Sonnet 153. It seems to start clumsily by having Cupid lay down his torch *after* he had fallen asleep, but a charitable interpretation might find an absolute construction as at 153.9, 'his brand having been laid by his side, he lay asleep.' Sonnet 153 talked of a maid of Dian's; Sonnet 154 is more interesting. Many chaste maids came tripping by (being chaste, the likelihood is that they too are votaries of Diana), but the spotlight falls on the fairest of them, and it is she who picked up the torch and quenched it in the spring.

    The application of the myth filled the last six lines of 153; here it does not fill three. The anecdote itself is correspondingly longer here, and the main additions are the awkward second line and the military metaphor in 6–8. Many *legions* had been warmed by Cupid's fire, but the *general* of love's legions, Cupid himself, had been caught sleeping and *disarmed* by a virgin's hand.

The essence of the aetiological myth is that it provides a mythological explanation of a contemporary phenomenon. This is touched upon five times in 153.6–7 and here only once, as the torch from love's fire 'took heat *perpetual*'. This new hot spring attracted invalids, who came to take the waters for their health. From the middle of line 12 the poet himself, in thrall to his mistress, visited the spring to look for a cure, but there was none, thus proving that the fire of love heats water, but water does not cool love. Whoever thought it could? The epigram does not work and the poem has no point at all. It is even less impressive than the final epigram of 153 and together they make a feeble curtain-dropper for the tragic drama of the Sonnets. They have none of the wit, complexity, logic, drama, characterisation or human interest of their predecessors, only trite classicising. If Shakespeare wrote these poems, he must have done so in infancy.

They are often defended. Scholars list half a dozen sonnet collections which end at a tangent, and 153 does connect with its predecessors. The maladies of 153.8 and the cure at the end of the sonnet recall the fever of 147, 'Past cure I am'. The mistress's eye, a vital agent in 153.9, governs many of the sonnets including 152.11–142. Perhaps Shakespeare has dug these two poems out of a drawer, and, smiling a little, has put them last as a whimsical end to a long tragedy of love. A tiny point in favour may be that the last line supports an opinion in the Song of Solomon 8: 7, 'Many waters cannot *quench* love, neither can the floods drown it.' The Song of Solomon has appeared before, in 108.7–8. Appropriately enough S agrees with it here. Nothing can resist love. The Sonnets have been a long struggle with it. On this defence the last words of this collection are not irrelevant. Love is a disease for which there is no cure.

There are other poems which astonish, and seem not to fit comfortably into the plot of the Sonnets, notably Sonnets 99 and 145. There may be a clue in Sonnet 81.5. 'Your name from hence immortal life shall have,' writes Shakespeare, and pointedly does not record it. These great love poems are remarkably reticent about his lovers, remarkably elusive about the facts of this love. Sonnet 134 is a leading example. If this were Shakespeare's policy, it has been a triumph, arousing vast speculations over the centuries. It would not be beyond Shakespeare's sense of mischief to bewilder readers by rounding off his great tragic drama with a whimsy.

Seymour-Smith (1963)
Both 153 and 154 are poor sonnets, having no connection, either in quality or theme, with 1–152.

Duncan-Jones (1997), on line 9
The fair votary probably carries an innuendo on the female organ in which the
hot desire of the male is quenched.

Vendler (1997)
In both the original epigram and in 154's interpretation of it, phallic heat is
transferable but not reignitable ... The very triviality and ancientness of these
little myths – and the comic and frivolous tone with which they treat the whole
question of passion – cool down the *deep oaths* of the rhetorically fevered poems
... Comic distance is thereby gained on the realm of Eros and even on its enemy
Diana.

The model for 153 and 154

These two poems are based upon *Palatine Anthology* 9.627, an epigram by
Marianus Scholasticus, a lawyer poet of the sixth century AD in Constantinople. It was first published in 1494, and translated several times into
English and other languages. It is not known which version Shakespeare
used (J. Hutton, *Modern Philology* 38 (1953–4), 385–403). He may even
have seen the Greek at school. A close translation would be as follows:

> Here under the plane trees Eros lay in soft slumber, worn out,
>   having given his torch to nymphs.
> 'What are we waiting for?' said the nymphs to one another,
>   'If only we could quench it,
> and with it the fire in the hearts of mortals.'
>   But when the torch set even the water on fire,
> from that moment on Erotiad nymphs pour hot bath water.

The Greek has nice touches not in the Shakespeare. Shakespeare's poems
are conceits in a void, but the first word of the Greek, *taide*, 'here', sets a
scene. The poet is actually there at a hot spring, where he claims Cupid's
torch had been dowsed, and the poem is, or purports to be, an inscription
on a plaque or stone. A second nicety is that Cupid had been 'consumed in
soft slumber', and why should he not be? He is a busy boy. Then 'consumed' for *tetrumenos* is a failed attempt to do justice to the Greek, which
is an irreverent allusion to a word which rings through Homer's *Odyssey*.
There at 1.248 in Odysseus' absence the suitors '*truchousi de oikon*', consume his house. This would make a third pleasure in the poem. It is typical
of these verse writers to display their love for Homer.

The fourth light touch is in 3–5, the girlish tone in the Greek as Diana's
maidens egg each other on to do the deed, with an amusing postponement

of the verb of speaking into the fourth line, something like 'The nymphs one to another, "What shall we do? Would that we could dowse its fire," said they, "along with the fire in the hearts of mortals."' And as a fifth visit of the Muse the nymphs' pious concern for the welfare of mankind raises a smile at the word *meropôn*, mortals, another resounding Homerism. The sixth visit is a *coup de théâtre* – Cupid's torch set water on fire!

The word 'nymphs' occurs twice in lines 2 and 3. Dryads, Naiads and Oreads are nymphs of trees, springs and mountains. Here they are maids attending the chaste goddess Diana, enemies of sexual love. Having dowsed Cupid's torch in 1–5, they depart the scene, and for the only recorded time in Greek we meet *Erotiades*, nymphs of Eros, the god of love. Marianus Scholasticus is making a waggish joke, inventing for this little bonbon a new species of nymph, *Erotiades*, a parody of *Orestiades*, a Homeric name for Oreads. The duty of Erotiads, nymphs of *Eros*, is to pour hot water, for *erotic* purposes, despite the opposition of the chaste nymphs of Diana.

There is yet another scholastic pleasantry in this poem, the eighth glint of imagination. 'Under these plane trees' is a phrase that would have set the bells ringing. In a famous passage in Plato, *Phaedrus* 229–30, Socrates and his young friend who gives the dialogue its name walk out of Athens and, after a lyrical description of the scene on the banks of the river Ilissus, they sit down by a cold water spring trickling under the shade of a tall, spreading plane tree, where, to the accompaniment of a choir of cicadas, Socrates delivers his great discourse on the subject of love, *eros*. The legal and literary friends of Marianus would have caught the reference in the opening words of the Greek.

None of this creativity and none of this pleasure has survived in these two sonnets. The Greek is a cheerful confection, and the sonnets take the fun out of it.

The *Anthologia Palatina* includes three collections, the Garlands of Meleager and of Philippus, and the Cycle of Agathias Scholasticus, a poet, historian and lawyer in Constantinople. The Cycle of Agathias includes a score of epigrams by himself, one praising a bridge (641), two (619 and 631) on baths, and the bath building in the second of these survived at least till W. R. Paton's 1904 translation in the Loeb series. There are also four on latrines including three in a suburb of Zmyrna (642–4 and 662), in the last of which he records that he himself, Agathias, father of the city, upgraded the facilities.

Only five poems by Marianus Scholasticus are included, two of them on the hot Bath of Eros (626 and 627, which is translated above). Epigram 657 is written in praise of the palace on the south shore of the Bosphoros built by the Emperor Justin II for his wife Sophia. Epigrams 668 and 669 praise a suburban park in Amasia, capital of Pontus, called the Grove of Eros, with three fountains and a presiding Naiad. It had also beautiful trees, the resort of Hamadryads, indwelling tree *nymphs*. 'Here among *the plane trees*, fresh streams of water running at its will leap forth beautifully from many-mouthed fountains' (Paton's translation). It is a sporting guess that the Bath of Eros in these sonnets was a hot spring in that Grove of Eros, and there it gushed under the plane trees, as celebrated in the epigram imitated in Sonnets 153 and 154.

Agathias and Marianus were both Scholastici, lawyers, and this is the sort of thing they wrote, elegant, light-hearted verse, sometimes inscriptions for public buildings, often singing their praises by claiming that gods were involved in them. The same gods were no doubt depicted inside the baths in mosaics or paintings, and outside in statues with metrical inscriptions.

It would be foolish to rate these few surviving works too highly, but the six lines of Marianus' epigram 627 throw eight sparks of cheerful, creative verse-writing, whereas it is not easy to find anything similar in the 28 lines of Sonnets 153 and 154. On the basis of the poems we have looked at, Marianus Scholasticus was a better poet than William Shakespeare, if, that is, Shakespeare was responsible for these last two sonnets in the collection. My own guess is that they were written by his publisher.

Select Bibliography

Abbott, E. A. (1870), *A Shakespearean Grammar*, 3rd edn

Bartlett, J. (1894), *A Complete Concordance of Shakespeare* (Macmillan)

Bate, J. (1997), *The Genius of Shakespeare* (Picador)

Booth, S. (ed.) (1977), *Shakespeare's Sonnets* (Yale University Press).

Bradbrook, M. C. (1936), *The School of Night* (Cambridge University Press)

Burrow, C. (ed.) (2002), *The Complete Sonnets and Poems* (Oxford University Press)

Duncan-Jones, K. (ed.) (1997), *Shakespeare's Sonnets* (Arden)

Edmonson, P., and Wells S. (eds) (2004), *Shakespeare's Sonnets* (Oxford)

Empson, W. (1947) *Seven Types of Ambiguity*, 2nd edn (Chatto & Windus)

Evans, G. Blakemore (ed.) (1996), *Shakespeare's Sonnets* (Cambridge University Press)

Grazia, M. de, and Wells, S. (eds) (2001), *The Cambridge Companion to Shakespeare* (Cambridge University Press)

Grey, Viscount, of Fallodon (1927) *A Charm of Birds* (Hodder & Stoughton)

Harbage, A. (1950), 'Dating Shakespeare's Sonnets', *Shakespeare Quarterly*, 1, 57-63

Harrison, W. (1994), *The Description of England* (1587), ed. G. Edelen (Dover)

Honan, P. (1999), *Shakespeare A Life* (Oxford University Press)

Ingram, W. G., and Redpath, T. (1978), *Shakespeare's Sonnets* (Hodder & Stoughton)

Jones, P. (1977), *Shakespeare, the Sonnets: A Casebook* (Macmillan)

Kermode, F. (2002), *Shakespeare's Language* (Penguin)

Kerrigan, J. (1986), *The Sonnets and A Lover's Complaint* (Penguin); repr. 1995

Leishman, J. B. (1961), *Themes and Variations in Shakespeare's Sonnets* (Hutchinson)

Martin, P. (1972), *Shakespeare's Sonnets* (Cambridge University Press)

Mattingly, G. (1959), *The Defeat of the Spanish Armada* (Cape)

Nisbet, R. G. M., and Hubbard, M. (1970), *A Commentary on Horace: Odes I* (Oxford University Press)

Nowottny, W. M. T. (1977), 'Formal Elements in Shakespeare's Sonnets', *Essays in Criticism*, 2 (1952), in P. Jones, *Shakespeare The Sonnets* (Macmillan)

Partridge, E. (1968), *Shakespeare's Bawdy*, rev. edn (Routledge)

Pevsner, N., and Metcalf, P. (1985) *The Cathedrals of England* (Viking/Penguin)

Picard, L. (2003), *Elizabeth's London: Everyday Life in Elizabethan London* (Weidenfeld & Nicholson)

Quiller-Couch, A. (1896), *Adventures in Criticism* (Arnold)

Race, W. H. (1982), 'The Classical Priamel from Homer to Boethius', *Mnemosyne*, Supplement 74

Rollins, H. E. (1944), *Shakespeare's Sonnets and Interpretative History* (Lippincott)

Rowse, A. L. (1973), *Shakespeare's Sonnets: The Problem Solved* (HarperCollins)

Seymour-Smith, M. (ed.) (1963), *Shakespeare's Sonnets* (Heinemann)

Sisson, C. J. (1956), *New Readings in Shakespeare*, 2 vols (Cambridge University Press)

Sobel, D. (1996) *Longitude: The True Story of a Lone Genius Who Solved the Greatest Scientific Problem of His Time* (Penguin)

Vendler, H. (1997), *The Art of Shakespeare's Sonnets* (Harvard University Press)

Wilson, J. Dover (ed.) (1966) *Shakespeare, The Sonnets* (Cambridge University Press)

Wyndham, G. (ed.) (1898), *The Poems of Shakespeare* (1898)

Index of first lines